Fifth edition

European Union Economics

Theo Hitiris

 Prentice Hall
FINANCIAL TIMES

An imprint of Pearson Education
Harlow, England • London • New York • Boston • San Francisco • Toronto • Sydney • Singapore • Hong Kong
Tokyo • Seoul • Taipei • New Delhi • Cape Town • Madrid • Mexico City • Amsterdam • Munich • Paris • Milan

Pearson Education Limited
Edinburgh Gate
Harlow
Essex CM20 2JE
England

and Associated Companies throughout the world

Visit us on the World Wide Web at:
www.pearsoneduc.com

First published under the Harvester Wheatsheaf imprint 1988
Fourth edition published under the Prentice Hall Europe imprint 1998
Fifth edition published 2003

© Harvester Wheatsheaf 1988, 1991, 1994
© Prentice Hall Europe 1998
© Pearson Education Limited 2003

ISBN 0273 65537X

British Library Cataloguing-in-Publication Data
A catalogue record for this book is available from the British Library

Library of Congress Cataloging-in-Publication Data
Hitiris, Theodore.
    European Union economics / T. Hitris.— 5th ed.
       p. cm.
    Includes bibliographical references and index.
    ISBN 0–273–65537–X (alk. paper)
    1. Europe—Economic integration.   2. European Union.   3. European Union
countries—Economic policy.   I. Title.

    HC241 .H573 2002
    338.94—dc21

                                                                2002028258

10 9 8 7 6 5 4 3 2 1
06 05 04 03 02

Typeset in 9.5/12.5 Stone Serif by 35
Printed in Great Britain by Henry Ling Ltd., at the Dorset Press, Dorchester, Dorset

European Union Economics

We work with leading authors to develop the
strongest educational materials in economics,
bringing cutting-edge thinking and best learning
practice to a global market.

Under a range of well-known imprints, including
Financial Times Prentice Hall, we craft high quality
print and electronic publications which help
readers to understand and apply their content,
whether studying or at work.

To find out more about the complete range of our
publishing, please visit us on the World Wide Web at:
www.pearsoneduc.com

Contents

15 Europe in the twenty-first century   333

Figures

Tables

Boxes

Preface

The present edition of this book is not a simple upgrading of EU facts and figures but a radical rewriting dictated by a milestone in European evolution: completion of the single market by monetary unification in 2002. This has led to new ways of approaching the subject of European integration. Before EMU, we were discussing the ways in which Europe should reach its target of the single market and the problems it might meet during the transition period After EMU, we must analyse what Europe should do now that it is there. Therefore, in this book we are focusing on the applied economics of European integration, eschewing long discussions on far-fetched topics which may allude to elegant economic theory but are unrealistic or irrelevant for the subject of our analysis. Hence, rigorous theory is used to the extent necessary to explain the objectives, successes and failures of the policies for economic integration in the European Union. Thus all chapters have been reconstructed by compressing or cutting out sections which have been overtaken by events, and by adding or expanding sections that have become more prominent in the course of European integration after EMU. Issues which are either non-central to the exposition of a topic, or offer additional or alternative interpretations of crucial events by examples and case studies are relegated to boxes.

Like its predecessors, this fifth edition is designed primarily for students and their counterparts in business, finance and government who wish to get a reasonably comprehensive, clear and up-to-date picture of the aims, progress and effects of the European Union and its policies. In an attempt to evoke and maintain the reader's interest and make the book intelligible, accessible to non-specialists and self-contained, a conscious effort has been made to explain specialized terms and concepts in the text, and to use only the minimum of numerical data. The text is, however, interspersed with figures which clarify theoretical points or present statistical information directly and comprehensibly. For the same reason, and in order to allow the exposition to flow as much as possible without interruption, footnotes are used sparingly and only if it is necessary to illuminate a point or to direct the reader to sources and references. Each chapter is followed by a selection of questions which can be used to test the reader's understanding of essential issues expounded in the text. For those who wish to probe more deeply into the topics raised in each section, specific references to relevant publications are given under 'Further reading' and 'Web guide' at the end of each chapter.

A feature of the book is its emphasis on the economic analysis of public policy rather than on detailed descriptions of European Union institutions and their history. After the introductory sections dealing with the basic theoretical foundations of economic integration and the treaties establishing the European Community and Union, the economic policy sections of the book are integrated closely and conform to the following standard format:

1. review of the problem confronting policy-makers;
2. identification of policy alternatives and their theoretical foundations;
3. outline of EU policy;
4. assessment of EU policy's performance relative to the objectives set out in the treaties establishing the Community;
5. evaluation and conclusions.

In explaining the origin of EU policies and their effects, account is taken of the limits of power which the treaties confer on the Union and of the constraints the member states exercise on the Union policies. The presentation of issues and their analysis and interpretation is biased towards current developments in the most important areas of the Union's economic activity.

It should become clear from the following that this book is concerned mostly with the analysis of economic integration and economic policy-making in the European Union. However, the origin of European integration is not primarily economic but political, with vast economic implications. After a long history of intra-European strife and the devastations of two World Wars, the European nations realized that only 'peace and concerted action could make the dream of a strong, unified Europe come true.'[1] Thus in 1958 they set up the European Economic Community in an attempt henceforth to resolve their differences by discussion around a table rather than on the battlefield. The reader should not forget, therefore, what Walter Hallstein, the first President of the European Commission, said in 1961: 'Make no mistake about it. We are not in business; we are in politics.'[2] This was also reiterated by Wim Duisenberg,

---

[1] The Laeken Declaration, 15 December 2001.
[2] In *Time Magazine*, 6 October 1961.

the first President of the European Central Bank, in 1999: 'The aims of European integration are not only, or even primarily, economic. Indeed, this process has been driven and continues to be driven by the political conviction that an integrated Europe will be safer, more stable and more prosperous than a fragmented Europe.'[3]

Theo Hitiris

---

[3] In a speech at the National Bank of Poland, 4 May 1999; available at www.ecb.int/key/sp990504.htm

Acknowledgements

We are grateful to the Financial Times Limited for permission to reprint the following material:

Box 4.1 from 'Cost of the EU', © *Financial Times* (8 October, 1998); Box 9.1 from 'Eastern Enlargement: Plotting Europe's new geometry', © *Financial Times* (8 December, 2000), and 'Schroder in warning on jobs access', © *Financial Times* (19 December, 2000); Box 12.1 from 'Trans-European Networks', © *Financial Times* (24 November, 2000); Box 14.2 from 'Environment law infringement: Greece fined over European Court ruling', © *Financial Times* (5 July, 2000).

In some instances we have been unable to trace the owners of copyright material, and we would appreciate any information that would enable us to do so.

The information provided by the European Union directly to the author and indirectly by its invaluable publications is gratefully received.

Supplement

A web-based Instructor's Manual is available at a Supplement Download Site from www.booksites.net/Hitiris to those teachers and facilitators who have adopted this textbook.

Bibliographical note

The references to books, official publications and statistics on EU policies are changing very rapidly. For up-to-date information the Internet is an invaluable source. For a comprehensive list of all general and specific references see: *The Guide to EU Information Sources on the Internet*, Euro-confidentiel, available at www.euroconfidential.com

Some of the general sources of information are the following:

Search engine: EU on Line:	www.europa.eu.int/
European Central Bank:	www.ecb.int/
Euro server:	www.europa.eu.int/euro
European Parliament:	www.europarl.eu.int/
European law:	www.europa.eu.int/eur-lex
Europe on the Internet, UK:	www.europanaccess.co.uk
Politics and policies in EU:	www.agenceurope.com

Abbreviations

ACP	African, Caribbean and Pacific Ocean countries: signatories of the Lomé Convention
ALTENER	Alternative Energy Programme
CAP	Common Agricultural Policy
CEE	central and eastern European countries (also CEEC)
CCP	Common Commercial Policy
CCT	Common Customs Tariff (also CET)
CEEP	European Centre of Public Enterprises
CFI	Court of First Instance
CET	common external tariff (also CCT)
CFP	Common Fiscal Policy or Common Fisheries Policy
CFSP	Common Foreign and Security Policy
CJ	Court of Justice of the European Communities (also ECJ: European Court of Justice)
CJHA	Common Justice and Home Affairs
CM	Common Market
CMEA	Council of Mutual Economic Assistance, or Comecon
Coreper	Committee of Permanent Representatives
CR	Committee of the Regions
CTP	Common Trade Policy or Common Transport Policy
CU	customs union
D-G	Directorate-General (also DG)
EAEC	European Atomic Energy Community, or Euratom
EAGGF	European Agricultural Guidance and Guarantee Fund
EAP	Environment Action Programme
EBRD	European Bank for Reconstruction and Development
EC	European Community, comprising the EAEC, ECSC and EEC. By the Treaty on European Union (TEU), article C(85), the term EEC was replaced by the term EC.
EC-6	The first six members of the EEC: Belgium (B), Germany FDR (D), France (F), Italy (I), Luxembourg (L), Netherlands (NL) (from 1958)
EC-9	The first six members of the EEC *plus*: Denmark (DK), Ireland (IRL) and the United Kingdom (UK) (from 1973)

EC-10   The first nine members of the EC *plus* Greece (GR) (from 1981)

EC-12   The first ten members of the EC *plus* Spain (E) and Portugal (P) (from 1986)

EC-15   European Economic Community (EEC), European Community (EC) or European Union Fifteen member states: Austria (AT), Belgium (B), Denmark (DK), Finland (FI), Germany (D), Spain (E), France (F), Greece (GR), Ireland (IRL), Italy (I), Luxembourg (L), Netherlands (NL), Portugal (P), Sweden (SE) and the United Kingdom (UK)

ECB   European Central Bank

Ecofin   Council of Economic and Finance Ministers

ECS   European Company Statute

ECSC   European Coal and Steel Community

ECU   European currency unit (also ecu)

EDF   European Development Fund

EEA   European Economic Area, the free trade area between the EEC and the EFTA countries or European Environmental Agency

EEC   European Economic Community

EEIG   European Economic Interest Grouping

EES   European Employment Strategy

EEZ   European Exclusion Zone

EFTA   European Free Trade Area

EIB   European Investment Bank

EIF   European Investment Fund

EMCF   European Monetary Cooperation Fund

EMF   European Monetary Fund

EMI   European Monetary Institute

EMS   European Monetary System

EMU   European Monetary Union or Economic and Monetary Union

EP   European Parliament

ERDF   European Regional Development Fund

ERM   Exchange Rate Mechanism

ESC   Economic and Social Committee

ESCB   European System of Central Banks

ESF   European Social Fund

ESPRIT   European Strategic Programme for Research and Development in Information Technology

ETUC   European Trades Union Confederation

EU   economic union or European Union

EUR   euro, €

Euratom   European Atomic Energy Authority

FDI   foreign direct investment

FIFG   Financial Instrument of Fisheries Guidance

FTA   free trade area

GATT   General Agreement on Tariffs and Trade

GDP	gross domestic product
GNP	gross national product
GSP	Generalized System of Preferences
HICP	Harmonized Index of Consumer Prices
IGC	Intergovernmental conference
IMP	Integrated Mediterranean Programme
ISPA	Investment for Structural Policies for Accession
JET	Joint European Torus
LDC	less developed country
LIFE	financial instrument for the environment
MFA	Multi-Fibre Arrangement
MEP	Member of European Parliament
MFN	most-favoured-nation
MR	Mediterranean region
NAFTA	North Atlantic Free Trade Area (USA, Canada, Mexico)
NAP	national action plans
NCB(s)	National Central Bank(s)
NIC	newly industrializing countries
NTA	New Transatlantic Agenda
NUTS	Nomenclature of Territorial Units
OCA	optimum currency area
OECD	Organization for Economic Cooperation and Development
OPEC	Organization of Petroleum Exporting Countries
PHARE	Poland-Hungary Aid for Reconstruction (Economic)
PPP	purchasing power parity
REA	regional economic association
RACE	R&D in Advanced Communications Technologies for Europe
R&D	research and development
SAP	Social Action Programme
SAPARD	Special Accession Programme for Agriculture and Rural Development
SEA	Single European Act
SEM	Single European Market
SGP	Stability and Growth Pact
SME	small and medium-sized enterprises
SMP	Single Market Programme
TA	Treaty of Amsterdam
TAC	total allowable catch
TEEC	Treaty establishing the European Economic Community (Treaty of Rome)
TENs	Trans-European Networks
TEU	Treaty on European Union (Maastricht Treaty)
THERMIE	Programme for the Promotion of European Energy Technology
TN	Treaty of Nice
UNCTAD	United Nations Conference on Trade and Development

UNICE   Union of Industries of the EC
VAT   value added tax
VER   voluntary export restraint
VSFF   very short financial facility
WHO   World Health Organization
WTO   World Trade Organization
YES   Youth Exchange Scheme for Europe

Economic integration:
objectives, policies and effects

1

Countries form regional economic associations for economic and non-economic reasons which have effects on themselves and the outside world. The main economic effect of regional economic associations is market integration and enhanced competition by trade liberalization. Further economic integration also liberalizes the markets for services, capital and labour and affects the pattern and rate of the participating countries' economic growth.

1.1 Forms of economic association

Introduction

The term *regional economic association* (REA) defines collectively the various forms of economic integration among independent states. In ascending order of the degree of integration, the relevant literature distinguishes the following four broad forms of REAs:

1. *free trade area (FTA)* = free trade between the members;
2. *customs union (CU)* = FTA + common external tariffs (CET) on trade with non-members;
3. *common market (CM)* = CU + free mobility of factors of production;
4. *economic union (EU)* = CM + common economic policy.

This classification is taxonomic, and does not represent the stages and the depth of economic integration actual economic associations go through, which usually combine the characteristics of two forms or more.

Except for the free trade area (FTA), which entails only an agreement of free trade between the member states, all other forms of integration are characterized by an internal dynamic that it can drive them to further integration. Thus, a customs union (CU) may lead to more advanced forms of integration – provided, of course, that the members agree to it. The dynamics of integration arise from increasing openness and economic and political interdependence among the participating countries. These reduce the ability of each member state to follow an independent policy course or to diverge much from the performance of the group as a whole. Increasing interdependence triggers *externalities* by each member state's spillovers and feedbacks of national economic policies on each other. In an attempt to maximize the gains, or *external economies*, and to minimize the losses, or *external diseconomies*, of interdependence, the members of the economic association adopt either *cooperative* policies to *internalize the externalities*, which advance economic integration, or *non-cooperative* policies by retracing their steps back to a looser form of interdependence, such as an FTA. In the latter case the need for *policy compatibility*, further to that already existing between countries engaged in international trade, is minimal and can be handled by existing interstate channels of negotiation and consultation. In contrast, the advanced forms of economic integration impose constraints on national policies which compel the economic association to adopt rules by elaborate new agreements and to set up special supranational institutions to administer them. Consequently, in advanced forms of integration, interstate cooperation progresses from simple compatibility to full *coordination*, *harmonization* and even *unification*. These actions may also cause externalities to non-member states, which therefore may seek to internalize them by closer cooperation with the association or eventually by participation in it. This explains why economic associations expand by *enlargement*, which consists of the *accession* of new members.

The process of economic integration

The taxonomy of forms of integration shows that as integration proceeds and openness increases, the interdependence between the member states increases, and therefore the need for cooperation is intensified. Beginning with a customs union (CU), the abolition of restrictions on intra-union trade and the adoption of a common external tariff (CET) replaces the national foreign trade policies of the member states by an integrated common trade policy of the union. Similarly, the transition of the CU to a common market (CM) includes the free mobility of factors of production, which alters their supply and prices in each member state and, thus, changes the pattern, the pace and the limits of each country's production and economic growth. Therefore, in the course of economic integration the member states voluntarily choose to restrict their national objectives and policies or even to replace them completely by targets and policies undertaken in common at the level of the union. The progress towards integration depends on the willingness of the member states to transfer real power from themselves to the supranational authority. Integration is thus a process during which the sovereign power of the member states to exercise independent national economic policy is progressively diminished. At the same time, the power of the union to design and implement common policies increases. The surrender of power and the loss of sovereignty of the national authorities is often strongly resisted. Therefore, in practice and during a long period of transition, an evolving economic union may appear to sway from crisis to crisis (as, for example, the EU). However, the willingness among the members to accept compromise and to reach consensus leads to the survival of the association, but at a higher level of integration and interdependence.

The objectives of economic integration

An issue of critical importance for the success or failure of economic integration is the nature of its objective, the purpose for which previously free, independent and self-governing states might willingly sacrifice a considerable part of their national sovereignty for the sake of integration with other countries of similar inclination. Associations between states aim in general at the realization of a benefit. It is important to emphasize that, despite the use of the term *economic association*, this benefit may not be primarily economic. For example, some of the participants in the REA, or all of them, may have strictly political, nationalistic, defence or other objectives. But whatever their eventual aim, all economic associations always have positive and negative economic implications which arise from trade liberalization and enhanced competition in an enlarged market, and these economic implications should be subjected to analysis and assessment. Inevitably, this means that countries may proceed with economic integration although its expected economic effects are positive but negligible, or even negative overall. Similarly, even if the potential economic benefit for a country from the economic union with other countries might be large, its membership in the union is not necessarily certain. Many countries value their independence and national identity more than the prospect that within an economic union they might become more prosperous.

The objective of the union often cannot be reached efficiently, if at all, by any of the participating countries on their own, without the close cooperation of the other members of the union. Therefore, participation in the union and the sacrifice of national sovereignty might be justified on the grounds of attempting to achieve a collective goal. More often than not, the costs and benefits of reaching this common objective would not be shared equally between the participating countries without the introduction of appropriate allocation rules and policies, which advance further economic integration.

Economic integration between developed countries

The essential requirements for a welfare-increasing economic association between developed industrial countries, such as those comprising the EU, are that they are of:

- comparable levels of economic development;
- similar but potentially complementary structures in production and demand.

The economic union between developed countries attempts to make this potential complementarity actual. Market liberalization and enlargement by eliminating trade restrictions between the members brings about immediate general benefits: the *static effects* of the economic association. These are the effects derived from increasing trade and competition under the existing structure of production and demand. In the longer term, the *dynamic effects* of economic integration in the enlarged competitive market are expected to accelerate development and to raise welfare by:

- improvement in the allocation and utilization of resources within and between the participating countries;
- realization of economies of scale in both production and demand;
- specialization according to comparative advantage.

The full extent of these benefits cannot be attained by the efforts of one country on its own, especially if it happens to be economically 'small'. Obviously, economic integration will bring more benefits, if in addition to exploiting the potential of the large market with increasing returns to scale, the national markets before the formation of the union were oligopolistic. Integration will open up these markets to intensive competition leading to improved allocation of resources and welfare efficiency. These may in turn stimulate research and development, inducing innovation and technical change, more investment and faster economic growth.

Box 1.1 ■ Integration among developing countries

Developing countries are usually actually and potentially similar. Therefore, the rationale of integration between developing countries is not based on the prospect of static benefits from competition-induced changes in the existing pattern of trade, which necessarily reflects their existing underdeveloped pattern of production. Their integration aims at the potential dynamic effects and the expectation that closer cooperation will foster regional markets which will shape and develop a structure of production capable of generating a greater volume and range of trade. Therefore, their integration has one main objective: the acceleration of their development by:

- enlarging the market to gain from economies of scale and the potential for developing a competitive structure;
- pooling scarce resources essential for economic growth, such as capital, skilled labour, foreign exchange and entrepreneurship;
- avoiding unnecessary and uneconomic duplication in capital investment, research expenditures and the application of modern technology.

As a result, the success of integration between developing countries must be judged in the longer term, after they have established a production sector capable of responding to increases in interregional demand. Another justification for forming economic associations between developing countries might also be that regional cooperation may increase their collective bargaining power in their economic, and sometimes political, external relations.

However, with the prospect of deriving benefits after a long period of economic sacrifice, integration between developing countries contains elements of self-destruction. These economic associations consist of two or more countries, each of which aims at the same objective – acceleration in its own development at the cost of its partners. Therefore, each member state tries to raise its own stake out of the fixed resources available for collective development. This process creates tension and leads to conflicts between the union partners which are difficult to resolve and usually result in long periods of strife and inactivity. In these circumstances, the economic associations between developing countries rarely survive long enough to reap actual economic benefits. Since the late 1950s, more than 40 economic cooperation and association arrangements between developing countries have been established. But most of them soon became inactive and some disintegrated prematurely in an atmosphere of hostility and recrimination.

Example 1

Kenya, Tanzania and Uganda formed the East Africa Common Market (EACM) in 1965. Problems started early on because of imbalances in inter-member trade and the allocation of the planned investment for economic development. By 1975 the integration arrangements went into deep crisis that finally caused the dissolution of the common market.

Example 2

The Central American Common Market (CACM) started in 1960 between Costa Rica, El Salvador, Guatemala, Honduras and Nicaragua. The troubles began when they realized that their common market was mostly *trade diverting* and that free trade was mostly favouring the countries with a relatively large industrial base. Moreover, the expected export-led growth did not materialize. In 1969, a war between El Salvador and Honduras, which started because of the discriminatory treatment of migratory workers, disrupted the operations of the CACM. During the next few years political instability and civil wars in many of the participating countries led to further problems that crippled the free trade arrangements. The CACM did survive but only in suspended animation. After many years in oblivion, it has been revived again in recent years.

1.2 The theory of economic integration

Definitions

In this section, we will examine the static and dynamic effects of economic integration. The *static effects* occur in the short and medium run under the existing structure of production and demand as a result of trade liberalization immediately upon entry into the CU. Under the static short-run effects, we will distinguish between the welfare effects of *trade creation* and *trade diversion* which arise from changes in the structure of protection and trade. The *pro-competitive effects* and the *economies of scale effects* are static effects that occur in the medium run by the enhancement of competition in the enlarged market. The *dynamic effects* come about in the longer run by the impact of changes in the economic structure of the economic union (EU) on the pattern and rate of economic growth. The section will develop under the following classification:

Static effects	
Short run	1. Trade effects (CU, FTA)
Medium run	2. Pro-competitive effects
	3. Economies of scale effects
	4. Factor mobility effects (CM)
Dynamic effects	
Long run	5. Growth effects (EU)

Trade effects of customs unions

If certain conditions are met, free trade is the best policy (see Appendix A1). Customs unions (CUs) and free trade areas (FTAs) begin with the removal of trade barriers among their members. CUs also integrate their foreign trade policies by adopting a common external tariff (CET) on trade with non-members. Therefore, if we assume that countries start from a non-optimal tariff-ridden position, setting up a CU combines trade liberalization between the member states with restricted trade with the outside world: clearly a case of discriminating trade liberalization. Eliminating one distortion in the presence of others or substituting one distortion for another does not necessarily improve welfare. This is an example of the theory of *second best* which shows that, if all the conditions for optimality cannot be made to hold concurrently, attaining some of them may increase or decrease welfare. The outcome depends on the particular circumstances: no generalization is possible. In the following we study the structure and effects of CUs.

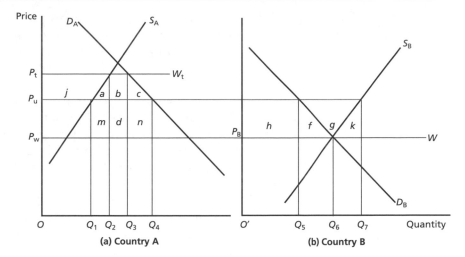

The economies of countries A and B before and after CU.

	Before CU		After CY	
	Country A	**Country B**	**Country A**	**Country B**
Price	P_t	P_w	P_u	P_u
Demand	Q_3	Q_6	Q_4	Q_5
Supply	Q_2	Q_6	Q_1	Q_7
Imports	Q_2Q_3	–	$Q_1Q_4=Q_5Q_7$	–
Import price	P_w	–	P_u	–
Tariff per unit	P_t-P_w	–	–	–
Tariff revenue	b+d	–	–	–
Exports	–	–	–	$Q_5Q_7=Q_1Q_4$
Export price	–	–	–	P_u
Trade Creation	–	–	a+c	g
Trade Diversion	–	–	d	–

Figure 1.1 **Effects of a CU between two small countries**

Trade creation and trade diversion

In general, regional economic associations cause both positive and negative trade and welfare effects on their members and the rest of the world. Whether the overall effect is positive or negative cannot be predicted accurately without a special study, case by case. We illustrate this problem with an analysis of the short-run trade and welfare effects of trade liberalization in a CU between two small, price-taking countries, A and B.

In Figure 1.1, panels (a) and (b) illustrate the markets of the two countries for a homogeneous commodity X which has no close substitutes or complements. The demand and supply curves are D_A and S_A in country A, and D_B and S_B in country B, while the perfectly elastic world supply is W. As the two countries are small, they face increasing production costs, but country B can reach self-sufficiency, with domestic demand equal to domestic supply, $S_B = D_B$, at a lower price than country A. For convenience, we assume that this equilibrium occurs at the world supply price, $P_B = P_w$, so that B's industry does not need protection from foreign competition. However, country A, facing the low-price world supply W, protects its domestic industry with a t per cent *ad valorem* tariff on imports, which shifts the world supply curve to W_t. This policy raises A's domestic price to $P_t = P_w(1 + t)$ at which the consumers buy quantity Q_3 made up by domestic supply, Q_2, and imports, Q_2Q_3, from W. Next, we assume that A and B form a CU, liberalizing trade between them and adopting a common external tariff (CET) in their trade with W. Therefore, the CU provides B's producers with a higher selling price and an expanded market where, up to a certain point, the only competition they face comes from the less efficient producers of country A. So B's producers increase production for exports to meet A's demand. But, at rising production costs and therefore prices, B's excess supply for export originates, first, from an increase in production and, second, from a decrease in domestic demand. In Figure 1.1, this process will continue until the integrated market of the CU reaches equilibrium and the combined supply of the two countries equals their combined demand, $S_A + S_B = D_A + D_B$. This also implies that B's exports equal A's imports, which occurs at price P_u. Therefore, to realize this equilibrium and keep foreign competition out, the CU has to set price P_u by adopting a CET equal to $t' = (P_wP_u/OP_w)$ per cent. As a result, in the CU A's price falls and B's price rises, affecting their supply, demand, volume and origin of their trade.

CU effects on country A

As shown in Figure 1.1, panel (a), A's consumer purchases have undergone a change of origin and an expansion, which are of particular importance. A's entire import quantity, Q_1Q_4, now comes from its CU partner, B, for two reasons:

1. import substitution:
   (a) country B for W, the quantity Q_2Q_3;
   (b) country B for A's domestic production, the quantity Q_1Q_2;
2. increase in demand following the price reduction, the quantity Q_3Q_4.

The first two components of imports, Q_2Q_3 and Q_1Q_2, make up the CU's *inter-country substitution effect*. The third component of imports, Q_3Q_4, is the CU's *inter-commodity substitution effect*, which is caused by the fall in

X's (relative) price after the tariff abolition that results in reallocation of consumer expenditure towards the cheaper good.

The increase in imports was caused by (a) replacing high-priced domestic production by partner production, Q_1Q_2, the *production effect*; and (b) increased demand for the good after its price fall, Q_3Q_4, the *consumption effect*. The import expansion associated with these two effects improves efficiency and raises welfare by the area $(a + c)$ which is termed *trade creation*.

The change in the origin of imports was caused by the discriminatory removal of tariffs which led to the displacement of the lower-cost imports from the world, Q_2Q_3, by higher-cost imports from B. This change worsens efficiency and reduces welfare by the area d which is termed *trade diversion*. Area b, which before setting up the CU was a part of A's government (tariff) revenue, and area j which was a transfer from consumers to producers, now remain with the consumers. Therefore, country A's welfare effect from setting up the CU with B is the gain from trade creation weighed against the loss from trade diversion, $(a + c - d)$. The net effect can be positive, negative or zero.

CU effects on country B

Removing tariffs within the CU affects each member country's imports as well as exports. Import effects can also be achieved by unilateral tariff cuts, but export effects require tariff reductions by others. Therefore, one

---

Box 1.2 ■ FTA vs. CU

Instead of a CU, two or more countries can form a free trade area (FTA), liberalizing trade between them and maintaining their national barriers to trade with the outside world. Since the members of the FTA maintain their own foreign trade policy and national tariffs on trade with non-members, the consumer prices of their imports differ between states. In a CU such differences disappear by market integration and competition by trade arbitrage.* In contrast, FTAs perpetuate market segmentation by adopting *rules of origin* to prevent *trade deflection*, which is defined as imports from an outside country entering the FTA through a low-tariff member country that re-exports them duty-free to high-tariff member countries. With the exception of market (non-)integration, both CUs and FTAs operate in a second-best world and, therefore, it cannot be claimed, as it often is, that FTAs are 'better' than CUs.

---

* Arbitrage is the exploitation of price differences by buying where prices are low and selling profitably where prices are high. Similarly, factors of production gain by getting employment where their rewards are higher. Arbitrage ends by trade and factor mobility which by eliminating price differences restores price equalization.

of the economic objectives of a country's participation in a CU might be to increase its exports. If the country is in full employment, then the additional demand for exports can be supplied by diverting productive resources from other activities to the export-producing sector, where they will enjoy higher rewards. So the gain from exports should be measured by the excess reward these resources now earn relative to their previous occupation. Figure 1.1, panel (b), shows the effects of the CU for the exporting country B. The increase in the price from $P_B = P_w$ to P_u enables B's producers to expand their supply to Q_7 by hiring more factors of production. However, when the price of the commodity rises, B's consumers cut down their consumption to Q_5. From these changes, B's producers gain the welfare areas $(h + f + g)$, while B's consumers lose the area $(h + f)$. Area h is a transfer within country B from consumers to producers, while area f is an outright loss for the consumers. However, B's producers expand their production by Q_6Q_7 at excess cost k above the world supply and gain the areas f and g from A's consumers as export profit. Therefore, country B's net benefit from the CU with country A is the export expansion Q_5Q_7 which causes a positive net welfare effect equal to area g.

Global effects of the CU

Country B's net welfare benefit arises from more trade – exports in this case – and therefore it can be considered as trade creation. Alternatively, and more accurately, for B's exporters this benefit is a net profit (revenue *minus* cost), a rent identical with an income transfer from country A to country B. Country A could have been better off by purchasing its total imports, Q_1Q_4, from W at price P_w than from B at price P_u. Had country A done so, its government would have also got a tariff revenue – the area $(m + d + n)$, which is now lost to B's exporters partly as profit, $(f + g)$, and partly as excess production cost, k, over W's competitive supply price. Although in this case the CU benefits only country B and makes A worse off, it may still be beneficial for both if B gains more than A loses. Nevertheless, under the assumptions we have made, *ex post* and from a global welfare perspective, the CU between A and B is trade diverting and cannot be justified on static economic considerations alone. Note also that:

■ Trade diversion harms the rest of the world, W, whose exports to A are replaced by exports from B.
■ The CU gives rise to conflicts of interest:
   (i) in A, between consumers who gain, and producers who lose from the CU;
   (ii) in B, between producers who gain, and consumers who lose, from the CU.

Box 1.3 ■ Conditions for positive welfare effects in CUs

Keeping in view Figure 1.1 (a) and the relevant concepts of trade creation and trade diversion, we observe that in general the static effects for a country removing its tariffs in a CU are larger:

(a) the higher the price elasticity of domestic demand, domestic supply and imports, and the higher the level of tariffs: both of these affect the size of trade creation $(a + c)$;
(b) the lower the initial value of imports and the lower the price difference between the union partners and the outside world: both of these affect the size of trade diversion d.

The overall welfare effect emerges in the comparison of 'before' vs. 'after' the removal of the tariff on the intra-union trade of commodity X. Since countries trade many commodities, each partner in the CU will realize trade and welfare effects from imports and exports. The net outcome of these effects can be negative for certain countries and positive for others, with net welfare effect for the CU as a whole negative or positive. These ambiguities arise from *the second-best* nature of CUs which replace one set of distortions (national universal tariffs) by another (discriminating trade liberalization with tariffs against the outside world). Obviously, a non-preferential tariff reduction leads to pure trade creation and a non-preferential tariff increase to pure trade diversion. Since CUs involve *preferential* tariff changes, their net welfare effect is ambiguous.

Pro-competitive effects

If the size of a country's market is limited and competition is imperfect, then the participation of a country in a CU establishes competition and results in welfare benefits. Figure 1.2 illustrates such a case in the market of country A, with demand curve D_A and supply curve S_A. Production in A is undertaken by a monopoly for which the country's demand is its average revenue (AR), with corresponding marginal revenue curve MR, and the supply is its marginal cost (MC). Therefore, setting profit maximization as its objective, the monopoly produces quantity Q_A which it sells at price P_A, much higher than the CU's price P_u. Depending on relative cost conditions, when country A joins the CU it may end up as exporter or importer. For simplicity, we assume that A remains competitive at the same quantity as before its accession in the CU. But A's price falls to the CU price P_u and its consumers choose to buy more of this good, the quantity Q_u, which is made up by the quantity Q_A supplied by the domestic, now competitive, producer, and imports Q_AQ_u from the rest of the CU. As a result, A's consumers benefit by the welfare area $(c + d + g + z)$ while the domestic producer loses $(c + d)$, for a net benefit for the country equal to $(g + z)$. This welfare benefit is the result of enhanced competition in country A after its accession in the CU.

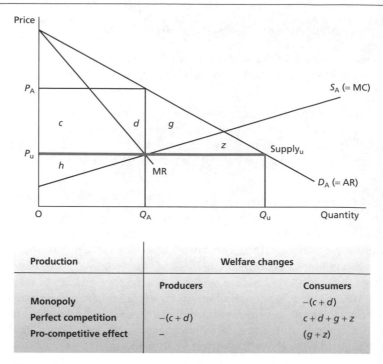

Figure 1.2 Pro-competitive effects of economic integration

Production	Welfare changes	
	Producers	Consumers
Monopoly		$-(c + d)$
Perfect competition	$-(c + d)$	$c + d + g + z$
Pro-competitive effect	–	$(g + z)$

Economies of scale effects

We have so far assumed increasing production costs in the countries forming the CU and constant production costs in the world markets. In a CU of relatively small price-taking countries with protected national markets it is possible that demand is not sufficiently large to allow production plants of the most efficient size. However, access to the enlarged market of a CU may provide the conditions for optimum size production and the opportunity for cost reductions from exploiting economies of scale.[1] In the real world, much trade occurs because of economies of scale rather than comparative advantage. This is evident from the large volume of intra-industry (or two-way) trade: the trade of similar goods between countries using similar inputs and technology (such as the EU, the USA, Japan). Gains from cost reductions arising from economies of

---

[1] *Internal economies of scale* accrue to the firm because of its own expansion, while *external economies of scale* accrue to the firm because of expansion of the industry in which it operates. The analysis here concerns internal economies of scale which can arise in every production activity.

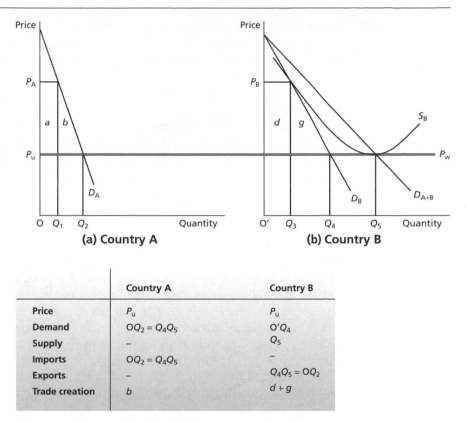

Figure 1.3 **Economies of scale in a CU**

	Country A	Country B
Price	P_u	P_u
Demand	$OQ_2 = Q_4Q_5$	$O'Q_4$
Supply	–	Q_5
Imports	$OQ_2 = Q_4Q_5$	–
Exports	–	$Q_4Q_5 = OQ_2$
Trade creation	b	$d + g$

scale may potentially account for the major benefits of free trade within the CU.

Figure 1.3, panels (a) and (b), depicts the case of a CU between countries A and B when production of a commodity X is subject to economies of scale. The demand curves of the two countries are D_A and D_B. It is assumed that the world supply W is perfectly elastic at price P_w. Country A, which has no domestic production of this commodity, restricts its imports by a tariff, so that its domestic tariff-inclusive price is P_A and its volume of demand and imports is Q_1. Country B's decreasing average-cost supply curve is S_B, which displays economies of scale.[2] However, B's market is small and does not allow the volume of production which

---

[2] We have assumed that, in the presence of increasing returns to scale, B's firm will follow an average-cost-pricing policy. Otherwise, a non-discriminatory marginal-cost pricing would result in losses because at that volume marginal cost is lower than average cost.

would have led to minimum cost. Therefore, before the CU with A, country B also protects its production by a tariff, thus reserving the domestic market for the domestic supply with price P_B and equilibrium output Q_3.

When the two countries set up the CU, country B's producers can increase their production to supply the entire market, and as a result the (average) cost of production falls. In Figure 1.3, we assume for the sake of convenience that the CU market allows volume of production that exactly matches B's cost with that of the world market, $P_w = P_u$. Therefore, at CU price P_u and combined demand curve $D_A + D_B$, B's production will be Q_5, of which $O'Q_4$ will be allocated to domestic consumption and $Q_4Q_5 = OQ_2$ to exports to A. Country A's welfare effect of trade creation is the standard consumer's surplus, b, which it could also have gained on its own by unilateral trade liberalization (see Appendix A1). After setting up the CU, increased demand and increased production help country B to get its domestic supplies at a lower cost of production. The resulting welfare gain $(d + g)$ is a cost-reduction effect derived from exploiting economies of scale. This is similar, but not identical, to trade creation: it is not the outcome of a movement to a lower cost source of supply but rather to a cost reduction of an existing source of supply (Corden, 1972). Formation of the CU provides a guaranteed access to a larger market that facilitates producers to exploit economies of scale. The large market makes possible the investment in large-scale production which would lead to trade and to specialization according to comparative advantage. Therefore, mutual trade liberalization among the partners in the union is superior to unilateral trade liberalization.

A problem associated with the analysis of economies of scale is that they are not compatible with perfect competition. Increasing returns mean that the firm with the largest market share can charge lower prices than other firms in the industry and thus further increase its market share by driving out its competitors, until it becomes a monopoly. Therefore, if in each country production is undertaken by a monopoly, establishing a CU will bring about either competition between the monopolies until only one of them survives, or a cartel. It could thus be concluded that integration reinforces imperfect competition. But this is not necessarily the case (Krugman, 1990). In the real world, many markets are monopolistic rather than perfectly competitive, among other reasons because of economies of scale. The monopolistic firms in these markets, however, are not price-setters because of international competition. Integration increases the degree of competition among such firms across the countries of the union. Therefore, the elements of *economies of scale* and *oligopolistic structure* of markets add an important source of benefits from integration over and above the benefits from *comparative advantage*:

■ Integration provides opportunities for *rationalization* by exploiting economies of scale.
■ Integration operates as an *anti-trust policy*, curbing monopoly power.

Factor mobility: common markets

In the analysis of trade and CUs we have assumed that factors of production are available at given supplies, are fully employed and are perfectly mobile (and costless) between industries within a country, but immobile between countries. In other words, we have assumed that countries trade internationally commodities (and services) but not factors of production. But common markets (CMs) entail the free mobility of factors of production (capital, K, and labour, L) between their members. In this section we analyse the basic causes and effects of international labour mobility but similar considerations apply to the case of capital mobility.

Figure 1.4 shows two countries, A and B, which produce the same commodity, Y, using identical production technology and two factors of production, capital, K, and labour, L. Country A is plotted from left to right with origin O, while country B is plotted from right to left with origin O'. Since only one commodity is produced, Y, international trade does not occur. Initially, there is no international factor mobility. We assume the available quantities of the two factors are fixed but different in the two countries. Country A's quantity of labour is OL, and country B's quantity of labour is $O'L$, so that the total quantity of labour in the

Box 1.4 ■ Factor mobility

If the markets for commodities, services and factors of production are perfectly competitive and certain conditions are met (for example, no transport cost and identical production technology), then free trade equalizes internationally not only commodity prices but also the prices (or rewards) of the factors which are employed to produce these commodities: labour wages and capital rents. From this aspect, therefore, commodity trade is a substitute for factor trade and the international mobility of factors of production is not necessary for international factor price equalization. In the real world, however, many of the conditions necessary for factor price equalization are not satisfied. For example, transport costs do exist and production technologies differ between countries. Therefore, factor prices only tend to converge but not equalize. Therefore, at the limit, if the factors of production were allowed to move between countries freely and perfectly, then their prices would be the same internationally even without commodity trade. This implies that a simple way to show the effects of free factor mobility is to reverse the previous analysis and instead of commodity trade with factor immobility, to consider factor trade without commodity trade, as illustrated in Figure 1.4.

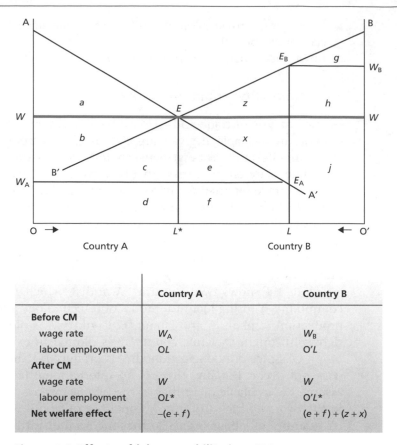

Figure 1.4 Effects of labour mobility in a CM

	Country A	Country B
Before CM		
wage rate	W_A	W_B
labour employment	OL	$O'L$
After CM		
wage rate	W	W
labour employment	OL^*	$O'L^*$
Net welfare effect	$-(e+f)$	$(e+f)+(z+x)$

two countries together is $OL + LO' = OO'$, the length of the horizontal axis. The vertical axes measure the marginal product of labour, MPL, and the wage rate, W, in each country. With given production technology and quantity of capital in each country, A's demand for labour is the line AA', which is the marginal product of labour, MPL_A, that declines as labour employment rises while the quantity of capital remains fixed. Similarly, B's demand for labour is the line BB', tracing the MPL_B. Equilibrium with full factor employment (and profit maximization behaviour) is reached in each country when the marginal product of labour equals the market wage rate, $MPL_A = W_A$ and $MPL_B = W_B$. This occurs at points E_A for A and E_B for B. Thus, country B, which has relatively less labour than A, $LO' < OL$, attains full employment at a higher wage rate than A, $W_B > W_A$. The conditions of perfect competition underlying the construction of the diagram also provide the following information:

(a) Each country's national income (or national product = the total output of Y) equals the area under the MPL curve up to the point of equilibrium, the areas $(a + b + c + d + e + f)$ in A, and $(g + h + j)$ in B; therefore in the two countries together total income is the sum of these areas.

(b) The national income of each country is distributed between the two factors of production. Therefore: (i) in A, labour income is the wage bill, *wage × workers* = $(d + f)$; and capital income is the rest, *total Y − wage bill* = $(a + b + c + e)$; and (ii) in B, the labour income is $(h + j)$, and the capital income is g.

Now suppose that, after the two countries progress from a CU to a CM, workers can move freely between A and B in search of a better paid job. Since $W_B > W_A$, workers from A will be attracted to move to B. This movement will reduce A's labour force and increase B's, raising A's wage rate and reducing B's. This process will continue until the wage rate in the two countries is equalized, $W_B = W_A$, and therefore the marginal product of labour in the two countries is the same, $MPL_A = MPL_B$. In Figure 1.4, this occurs at point E with common wage rate W and labour employment OL^* in A and L^*O' in B. The reallocation of the labour force between the two countries has the following effects:

(a) A's income falls to $(a + b + c + d)$, and B's rises to $(e + f + g + h + j + z + x)$. Therefore, there is a net increase in the CM's total income equal to the area $(z + x)$, captured by B which also gets area $(e + f)$ from A.

(b) The income of labour employed in A rises to $(b + c + d)$ and, therefore, the income of capital falls to a.

(c) The income of labour originally employed in B falls to j and, therefore, the income of capital rises to $(h + g)$, because in B more labour is employed but at a lower wage rate than before CM.

Therefore, as for commodity trade, in purely economic terms the free international mobility of labour is beneficial for the CM because it has increased total income by $(z + x)$ but some member countries and income groups gain, others lose.[3]

A general conclusion from this analysis is that, to the unification of commodity (and services) markets which customs unions (CUs) establish, common markets (CMs) add the unification of factor markets of the participating countries. Therefore, the advance of integration from CU to CM intensifies the tendency towards a single price for each commodity

---

[3] This is one of the reasons some argue in favour of redistribution of the CM benefit by, for example, a central budget, so that all social groups and participating countries get a share in the increased prosperity.

(or service) and a single price for each factor, just as in the case of a unitary state. The most important aspect of this process is that common markets improve the allocation of factors of production across country borders as well as efficiency and welfare.

Economic unions and economic growth

The *dynamic effects* of economic integration come about in the longer run after the *static effects*. Therefore, the static effects on their own should not be decisive as to whether countries should proceed with economic integration or not. The static effects occur only once at the time of trade liberalization and their size is neither a good predictor nor a necessary precondition for dynamic efficiency. Most important are the dynamic effects which arise from the intensification of competition and the opportunities offered by the integration of markets. A large market can induce more specialization leading to cost reductions from fuller utilization of plant capacity, improved productivity by the diffusion of technology and knowledge, optimality in the allocation of resources, exploitation of economies of scale, induced investment and accelerated growth. Economic growth in the real world is a complex procedure. In this section we will analyse the basic concepts of integration and growth using a simple theoretical model.

Basic concepts

Production function is the technical relationship between output and inputs of a production unit, such as a firm, an industry or an economy, using the existing technology. A country's *aggregate production function* describes the level of real national output, Y, which can be produced by the input of (usually two) factors of production, the capital stock, K, and labour employment, L, which we write as:

$$Y = g \ (K, \ L).$$

For simplicity, we assume that the production function displays two properties:

(i) *diminishing marginal productivity (dmp)*: holding one factor input constant and increasing the other results in more output, but in declining amounts; and

(ii) *constant returns to scale (crs)*: increasing inputs by a certain proportion, x per cent, increases output by the same proportion, x per cent.

But output can also rise with no increase in factor inputs by technological progress or *improved efficiency* in the utilization of resources, which raises total factor productivity. Representing technology/efficiency by a parameter $A > 1$, we can write the aggregate production function as:

$$Y = Ag\ (K, L).$$

For a further simplification, we assume that the labour force, L, remains constant. Therefore, output Y is produced with the constant L and the variable K, and varies only with changes in the capital input, according to the simpler production function:

$$Y = Af\ (K). \tag{1}$$

Equation (1) points to two causes of long-term economic growth:

(i) an increase in the stock of capital, raising K;
(ii) improved efficiency, raising A.

But in the process of production capital equipment wears out or *depreciates* over time. Assuming for simplicity that every year the depreciation is a fixed proportion of the capital, dK, investment equal to the depreciation of capital will be necessary, $I = dK$, if the existing capital stock is to remain intact. But, in order to invest, the economy must save. Assuming for convenience that saving is a fixed proportion, s, of national income, the annual national saving available for investment will be sY and, using equation (1), $sY = sAf(K)$. Therefore, in order to maintain the capital stock constant, there must be saving to cover investment equal to the depreciation of capital:

$$I = sAf(K) = dK. \tag{2}$$

The economy will settle at the point where the capital stock is constant, and this is the point of national income equilibrium.

Figure 1.5 illustrates this model. The vertical axis measures national income, Y, and the horizontal axis measures capital, K. The production function is represented by the curve $Af(K)$ which is rising but gradually flattening due to the *diminishing marginal productivity (dmp)* of capital. The curve $sAf(K)$ displays the investment and saving associated with the levels of income shown by the production function. The straight line $0dK$ represents the depreciation of capital. Investment is equal to the depreciation of capital at point a which corresponds to point b on the production function. At this point there is stable long-run equilibrium with stock of capital K^*, income Y and rate of growth zero. Investment above the depreciation level will increase the stock of capital. But a larger K entails larger depreciation requiring extra investment. Therefore, after a certain level of income is reached, further investment ceases to stimulate further economic growth because of diminishing returns which increase income but have only a transitory impact on the growth rate. It is only the rate of improved efficiency, A, that can keep the economy's long-run growth rate increasing. But in the production function (1) technology/efficiency

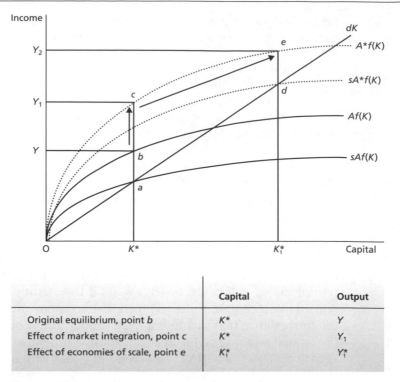

	Capital	Output
Original equilibrium, point b	K^*	Y
Effect of market integration, point c	K^*	Y_1
Effect of economies of scale, point e	K_1^*	Y_1^*

Figure 1.5 **Integration and economic growth**

A is an *exogenous* parameter and, therefore, it remains unexplained by the model.

Increasing returns to scale, integration and growth

Increases in output may also occur if the returns to scale are not constant, *crs*, but increasing, *irs*. If the borders of countries impose economic barriers that restrict the size of markets and therefore of the firms in these markets from operating at optimum size, then the integration of markets would offer the opportunity to exploit economies of scale which would result in higher output and welfare.

Figure 1.5 shows the effects of these factors on growth. Assuming that the integration of markets causes an immediate positive improvement in efficiency, from A to A^*, where $A < A^*$, the production function will shift upwards to the dashed curve $A^*f(K)$, with corresponding saving-investment curve $sA^*f(K)$. As a result, the short-run effect of integration under the existing capital stock, K^*, will increase the level of equilibrium income, from Y to Y_1.

Another effect on growth may come about by the impact effect of trade liberalization on capital accumulation. If trade liberalization expands the market and thus raises the returns on the existing capital, it can induce new investment and, if saving becomes available, new capital formation which would raise output. Trade liberalization in the market for goods, services, capital and labour, combined with diffusion of technological knowledge in the enlarged market increase efficiency and mean that the dynamic benefits of economic integration may be very high. In Figure 1.5, this is shown by the increase in capital from K^* to K^*_1 which determines equilibrium output Y_2.

Endogenous growth

The parameter A is a *residual term*, a catch-all of the factors that affect the quantity of output, besides physical capital, K, and labour, L. One such factor is human capital, H, which is defined as the level of human skills and knowledge acquired by training and education. As in the case of physical capital, the higher the level of human capital, $H > 1$, the higher the level of output. Like K, human capital is subject to wear and requires investment to replenish it. Excess investment in human capital over replacement investment can increase the stock of human capital. Therefore, the rate of change of physical capital, K, labour, L, human capital, H, and improved efficiency, A, all contribute towards the rate of growth of an economy: $Y = AHf(K, L)$.

The addition of human capital does not change the nature of economic growth: there are limits to growth because of diminishing factor returns. New theoretical research has shown, however, that under certain conditions investment in research and development (R&D) has positive externalities, or social effects, over and above the direct private benefits accruing to firms. These social effects can instigate further R&D, thus setting in motion a pattern of *endogenous growth*. In this way, the rate of technological advance and therefore the economy's long-run rate of growth becomes endogenous and is explained within the model. For example, human capital can enhance productivity through additional experience, resulting in constant rather than diminishing returns to investment. Therefore, diminishing returns can be avoided and increases in both physical, K, and human, H, capital combined with improved efficiency can direct the economy not only to a permanent rise in income but also in the growth rate. All these mean that private and public investment in K and H can raise the long-run growth rate. Moreover, countries with high physical and human capital per worker could move by integration to a permanently higher growth path.

Unfortunately, the empirical evidence relating to the endogenous growth hypothesis is incomplete and mostly unsupported: no country has experienced continuous growth. Similarly, the evidence about the existence and extent of economies of scale is sparse and controversial. In contrast, there is strong evidence that the aggregate level of technology

Box 1.5 ■ Other effects of economic integration

Economic integration can have additional effects which, however, are not or cannot be of general applicability or their size may be small. Among these effects are the following.

Terms of trade

One of the obvious flaws of the analysis of welfare gains from CU formation, as presented above, is the assumption that the member states are small. Small countries face given prices, or *terms of trade*, in their foreign trade (exports and imports) because they lack (monopolistic and monopsonistic) power to change them. In reality, some individual countries on their own or in combination with other countries in a CU have enough power to alter their terms of trade to their advantage and thus improve their welfare. However:

■ The benefit for the country or CU which exploits its power to benefit from a terms-of-trade improvement is gained at the expense of a third party which loses much more than the country or the CU gains.
■ Countries in the rest of the world may react to a terms-of-trade policy by adopting retaliatory policies of their own against the country or the CU that initiated the selfish policy.

For these reasons, in general there is no practical interest in exploiting terms-of-trade effects. However, international cartels of firms or countries aiming at the increase in prices and profits for a product they supply which has no close substitutes, do exist and operate successfully, e.g. the OPEC petrol cartel.

Bargaining power

An increase in bargaining power by association with other countries may be the origin and the objective of many regional trade associations. This objective may be purely political but with economic repercussions and effects. For example, the EU began after the Second World War when the nation states of western Europe realized that only by coming together could they hope to reconstruct their economies and to exert some influence on the two superpowers, the USSR and the USA, and on world affairs. By setting up the customs union (1958) and integrating their foreign trade policies, they also gained 'one powerful voice' in multilateral negotiations, such as the rounds for world trade liberalization, which had both economic (trade and protection) and political (influence on trade partners, e.g. the less-developed countries) implications.

Insurance

Smaller countries may join a CU as an insurance against future events, such as a generalized trade war or the possibility that the discriminating trade liberalization among the partners of a CU may affect their trade if they are left out. This is the strategy of 'if you can't beat them, join them'. For example, the fear of a 'fortress Europe' committed to a reduced outflow of foreign investment and increased protectionism may partly explain why a large number of countries have applied for membership in the EU.

The insurance may be political rather than economic. Greece, Portugal and Spain, which were formerly governed by authoritarian regimes, joined the EU for economic reasons but also for stable membership in the European political system of liberal democracy. Many of the central and eastern European applicants for membership in the EU may share similar concerns.

is not the same in all countries (Crafts, 1996) and, therefore, improved diffusion of new technology should have positive effects on growth. What is not in doubt is the importance of human capital and the exploitation and adaptation of technical innovation which in an environment of market liberalization and expansion under conditions of free trade and fair competition can amplify the positive effects of economic integration.

1.3 Conclusions

Countries form regional economic associations (REAs) for economic, political, strategic and other reasons. The main economic impact of these associations is market enlargement and enhanced competition by trade liberalization. This has static economic effects which occur in the short and medium run and can be positive or negative. Further economic integration causes dynamic effects which occur in the longer run by changes in the economic structure of the participating countries and affect the pattern and rate of their growth.

APPENDIX A1 Free trade versus restricted trade

This section explains basic analytical concepts used in the analysis of trade theory and trade policy which are useful for understanding the foundations of the theory of economic integration in this and subsequent chapters.

Efficiency

Within a country, economic efficiency comprises *production efficiency, consumption efficiency* and *allocative efficiency*. Production efficiency occurs when all producers face the same *producer price*, P_p, for the same good or service, whether it is an input or an output. Consumption efficiency occurs when consumers face the same *consumer price*, P_c, for the same good or service, whether they buy it for consumption or sell it as an input to production. Allocative efficiency occurs when producer prices are the same as consumer prices, $P_p = P_c$. A resource allocation is efficient if there is no other way of assigning the economy's resources that would make someone better off and none worse off. Economic efficiency and optimal resource allocation ensue when all the conditions necessary for perfect competition occur. Therefore, government policies, such as taxes and subsidies, in a perfectly competitive economy distort the efficiency conditions. Alternatively, if the economy is already distorted, for example by imperfect competition, government policies may attempt to increase economic welfare by correcting for or removing the distortions.

International trade

In a trading world, optimality requires that a country's prices are equal to world prices, P_w. Theory shows that, if the efficiency conditions are satisfied, $P_p = P_c = P_w$, not only can every country benefit from engaging in international trade but also that free trade is the *best* (= welfare-maximizing) policy. However, in the real world, because not all the necessary conditions are met or for several economic and non-economic reasons, most countries intervene in their foreign trade sectors, usually to protect their producers from foreign competition. Protection drives a wedge between domestic prices and international prices, $P_p = P_c > P_w$, which provides domestic producers with an advantage over lower-cost foreign producers. From the world point of view, this policy causes inefficiencies and welfare loss by misallocation of production and, therefore, it is undesirable.

Effects of protection

The commonest form of protection involves levying a tariff on imports. The tariff is a tax charged most often on the import price (= ad valorem) or sometimes per unit of the good (= *specific*). Tariffs discriminate in support of domestic production and against the foreign production of competitive goods.

For the (partial equilibrium) analysis of tariffs we consider the market for a commodity X in a small price-taking country under conditions of perfect competition in commodity and factor markets. We also adopt the following assumptions:

1. Production factors (labour and capital) are available at given supplies, fully employed and mobile between industries within a country, but immobile between countries.
2. Transport costs are ignored.
3. There are no distortions or trade impediments other than the policy-imposed tariffs.
4. The commodity X is homogeneous: the domestic production and imports supply the market with identical units of the good, but the domestic supply takes priority over imports. Therefore, imports, M, satisfy the *excess demand*, the difference between the domestic demand, D, and the domestic supply, S, that is $M = D - S$.

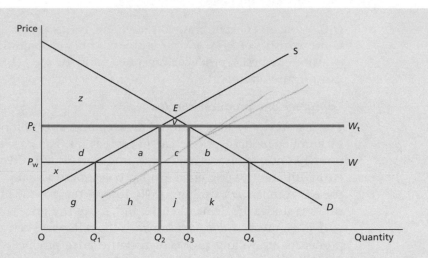

Variable	Free trade	Tariff	Subsidy
Price	P_w	P_t	P_w
Tariff rate	–	$(P_t - P_w)/P_w$	–
Subsidy rate	–	–	$(P_t - P_w)/P_w$
Demand	OQ_4	OQ_3	OQ_4
Supply	OQ_1	OQ_2	OQ_2
Imports	Q_1Q_4	Q_2Q_3	Q_2Q_4
Consumer surplus	$z+v+d+a+c+b$	$z+v$	$z+v+d+a+c+b$
Producer surplus	x	$x+d$	$x+d$
Tariff revenue	–	c	–
Subsidy paid	–	–	$d+a$
Welfare loss	–	$a+b$	a

Figure A1.1 **Free trade, tariffs and subsidies**

Figure A1.1 illustrates this case. The domestic demand curve D measures the consumers' *willingness to pay* for the good X, the domestic supply (the long-term marginal cost) curve S measures the producers' *willingness to sell* the good X, and the perfectly elastic world/foreign supply curve W measures the foreign suppliers' *willingness to export* the good X. Under free international trade, the domestic market reaches equilibrium at price P_w, which is also the domestic price of the good, $P_p = P_c = P_w$. At equilibrium, the domestic producers attain marginal cost = price, while the domestic consumers attain marginal benefit = price. Therefore, in Figure A1.1 at market equilibrium the quantity demanded is Q_4, the quantity supplied by domestic producers is Q_1, and imports are

Q_1Q_4. Consumer expenditure on buying X is $P_w \times Q_4 = x + g + h + j + k$, which consists of $P_w \times Q_1 = x + g$ expenditure on domestic production – hence, domestic producer revenue – and $P_w \times (Q_1Q_4) = h + j + k$ expenditure on imports.

Consumer and producer surplus

The measure of welfare achieved by exchange at equilibrium price (or by a policy-induced price change, such as tariffs, taxes, etc.) is based on the concepts of consumer and producer surplus. *Consumer surplus* is the difference between the price consumers actually pay and the price consumers are willing to pay to buy the good. This is equal to the area under the demand curve and above the price, $z + v + d + a + c + b$ in Figure A1.1. *Producer surplus* is the difference between the price producers are willing to accept and the price producers are actually paid for their sales. This is equal to the area above the supply curve and below the price, x. Therefore, the country's total welfare effect from exchange is $z + v + d + a + c + b + x$. The area under the supply curve, g, is the domestic supply's cost of production.

Effects of tariffs

Next, the government decides to restrict imports by levying a tariff on import price, for example because it wishes to increase the share of the domestic supply in the market, to save foreign exchange spent on imports, to raise tariff revenue, etc. In general, any restriction on imports will raise the domestic price of the commodity, forcing consumers to reduce their purchases, and domestic producers to increase their supply. Thus, protection will reduce consumer welfare and raise producer welfare.

Formally, levying an *ad valorem* tariff of t per cent shifts the foreign supply curve upwards from W to W_t with the following effects:

1. *Price effect*: in this small price-taking country, the domestic price, P_t, rises by the full percentage of the tariff: $P_t = P_w(1 + t)$. The tariff is a distortion causing divergence between domestic and free trade/international price:

$$P_p = P_c = P_t > P_w.$$

2. *Demand effect*: the higher price induces consumers to reduce their demand from Q_4 to Q_3. The utility value of this reduction is represented by the area $(k + b)$, where k is the social value of the reduction in demand and b is the social waste caused by the tariff's consumption distortion.

3. *Production effect*: higher market prices (and factor rewards) attract domestic resources from the production of other commodities to the production of X. The domestic supply of X rises to Q_2, thus increasing the revenue received by the producers by $(d + a + h)$ at an increase in total production cost by the area $(h + a)$, and thus increase in profits by the area d. However, the overall effect of the increase in production is welfare-reducing. The area h is equal to the world cost of producing the quantity $Q_1 Q_2$, while a is the excess cost of producing this quantity at home instead of importing it from W. Therefore, a is a waste caused by the tariff's distorting effect on the relative price, $P_t/P_w > 1$.

4. *Import effect*: the decrease in domestic demand and increase in domestic production imply that the excess demand directed to imports is reduced by precisely the sum of the demand and production effects, $(Q_1 Q_2 + Q_3 Q_4)$. Thus, the tariff policy leaves only the quantity $Q_2 Q_3$ to imports from foreign sources.

5. *Foreign exchange saving effect*: reduction in the volume of imports under the constant import price P_w implies that expenditure on imports is also reduced. In Figure A1.1, this reduction at domestic currency valuation is equal to $(h + k)$.

6. *Tariff revenue effect*: the tariff on imports yields revenue to the government, the area c, which is equal to the tariff per unit of imports *times* the import quantity. Under our assumption of a price-taking country, the tariff is a tax on the domestic consumers of the imported commodity, directed to the coffers of the government of the country.

7. *Distribution effect*: the tariff has changed the total consumers' expenditure on X from $(P_w \times Q_4)$ to $(P_t \times Q_3)$. This expenditure exceeds what consumers would have paid for the same quantity of X under free trade conditions by the area $(d + a + c)$. This area is in fact the increase in the price of the commodity (i.e. the tariff per unit) *times* the total consumption of the commodity, that is $P_w \times t \times Q_3$. As we have seen, the tariff revenue c is a transfer from consumers to the government, while a is a waste of domestic resources. The remaining area d is a rise in domestic producers' profit, an increase in *producer surplus*. So area d is also an income transfer from the consumers to the producers. Therefore, the tariff policy and the consequent re-allocation of expenditure between imports and domestic production cause income redistribution: the consumers lose $(a + b + c + d)$ from their surplus, while the two other economic groups, the producers and the government, gain.

8. *Welfare effects*: summing up the costs and benefits for consumers, producers and the government from levying the tariff, two items remain unaccounted for: $-(a + b + c + d) + d + c = -(a + b)$, that is the resource waste a and the social waste b. They make up the net welfare loss of the distorting effects of the tariff on the economy, in this case the consumers' surplus.

Tariffs in general foster domestic production, but at a higher real cost than competing imports. The price of the domestically produced good is equal to cost at the margin, P_t, whereas the domestic price of the competitive imported good exceeds its supply cost by the import tariff, $(P_t - P_w)/P_w = t$ per cent. If the tariff does not discriminate between foreign suppliers, then it does not interfere with the source of imports which will be the lowest-cost foreign producer.

Quotas

Under conditions of perfect competition, quantitative restrictions on imports, or *quotas*, have effects on prices and quantities identical to those of tariffs. Therefore, in this case the quota and the tariff are *equivalent* by yielding the same import level and the same divergence between foreign and domestic prices.

Since tariffs and quotas have many effects, it is not always easy to identify the exact reasons for their use in government policy. Nevertheless, their relatively large negative welfare effects mean that in general what tariffs or quotas can do, other policy instruments can do better. Assuming, for example, that the specific objective of the policy is to support domestic production, the subsidy is a better policy instrument than the tariff.

Subsidies

In Figure A1.1, a t per cent tariff raised domestic production from Q_1 to Q_2. The same increase in production can be achieved by subsidizing the domestic production at rate s per cent = $(P_t - P_w)/P_w$. The following results hold under the subsidy policy:

1. Consumer prices remain unchanged at the level of world prices, $P_p = P_w$, but producer prices rise to P_t. Therefore, demand remains at the free trade level, Q_4, and domestic production rises to Q_2.
2. Imports are reduced by the quantity Q_1Q_2 with saving of import expenditure equal to area h in domestic currency terms.
3. There is no tariff revenue for the government which instead incurs an extra budgetary expenditure equal to $(d + a)$ for financing the subsidy.

4. There is no direct transfer from the consumers to the government and the producers. Of course, the budgetary cost of the subsidy is ultimately paid for by the taxpayers (some of whom may not be consumers of this commodity).
5. The welfare effect of the subsidy is still negative but restricted to the loss of the area *a* only, which is the waste caused by the distorting effect of government intervention in the production side of the market.

It seems, therefore, that protection by tariffs or quotas is an inferior policy for promoting domestic production. However, the comparison between subsidies, tariffs and quotas must also include the cost of financing the subsidy and the administrative costs of operating each policy. Subsidies in general involve higher costs of administration than import duties which are relatively inexpensive to collect and provide the government with a revenue bonus.

Other policy instruments

Other policy instruments of effects similar to those of tariffs are the following:

1. *tax discrimination* in favour of the domestic producers;
2. *variable levies* which are tariffs adjusted to keep the domestic price of imports at some target level;
3. *production subsidies* which reduce the production costs of the domestic producers, providing them with advantages in the competition with foreign producers;
4. other *non-tariff barriers* to trade, such as e*xchange controls*, *import prohibition* of certain goods, *administrative red tape* and similar bureaucratic devices (such as discriminatory enactment of sanitary and safety regulations, different specifications of standards, quality controls, buy-at-home campaigns, etc.), which discriminate against imports.

Questions

1. What are the static and dynamic effects of trade liberalization in a customs union?
2. Under what specific conditions are the static effects of trade creation and trade diversion (i) large, and (ii) positive?

3 Why are the static effects not as important as the dynamic effects of economic integration?

4. Discuss the following quotation: 'To every trade diversion corresponds a production increase. Hence, within a customs union trade diversion is not necessarily bad.'

5. Explain why domestic producers of imported goods lose while consumers gain from the static effects of a customs union.

6. Under what conditions would a country as a whole derive a large positive welfare effect from participation in a customs union (i) in the short run, and (ii) in the long run?

7. Country A has no domestic production of good X which it imports under tariff protection from the world market at price P_W. After participation in a customs union with country B, country A imports good X from B at a higher price, $P_B > P_W$. Show the static effects of the customs union on A's imports.

8. After the formation of the customs union above, country A starts to export the commodity Z to its partner country B. Show the static effects of the customs union on A's exports.

9. Assuming that for country A above the overall static effects from participation in the customs union with B are negative, would you advise it to leave the customs union?

10. 'The traditional customs union theory concentrates on trade creation and trade diversion effects that are likely to be trivial and ignores those that are likely to be crucial in determining the net gains/losses from economic integration.' Discuss.

11. Show that a country will gain positive welfare effects from participating in a customs union if before the union its market was supplied by a domestic profit-maximizing monopoly charging a market price well above the union price.

12. Explain the following statement: 'The integration of capital markets allows countries to benefit from improved allocation of resources, while at the same time generating income distribution and adjustment problems that may be problematic politically.' Would the integration of labour markets within an economic union cause similar problems?

Further reading

For a comprehensive review of the theory of economic integration, start with recent surveys of the literature, such as Hine (1994), Pomfret (1997) and Panagariya (2000).

Structure of the European Union:
objectives, policies and constraints

2

This chapter provides answers to the following questions:

1. What is the European Union and who is in it?
2. How is it governed?
3. What is its relative economic size?
4. What are its objectives?
5. How does it attempt to reach them?

2.1 The European Community and the European Union

Introduction

The *European Union (EU)* started as a customs union, comprising three communities:

- the European Coal and Steel Community (ECSC), set up by the Treaty of Paris on 18 April 1951;
- the European Atomic Energy Community (EAEC or Euratom), set up by the Euratom Treaty; and
- the European Economic Community (EEC), set up by the Treaty Establishing the European Economic Community (TEEC, the Treaty of Rome).

The last two were signed in Rome on 25 March 1957 and entered into force after ratification by national parliaments on 1 January 1958. Signatories of these treaties were the original six EC members (EC-6): Belgium (B), the Federal Republic of Germany (D), France (F), Italy (I), Luxembourg

(L) and the Netherlands (NL). The 'Merger' Treaty (1965) set up common institutions for all three communities, the 'Council of the European Communities', the 'Commission of the European Communities' and the 'Audit Board', from 1 July 1967. In 1978 the European Parliament designated the three communities 'the European Community, EC'. With the Treaty on European Union (TEU), agreed at Maastricht in December 1991, the EC member states decided to establish a European Union (EU) founded on the European Community and guided by democratic principles.

The basis for EU law is the Treaty Establishing the European Economic Community (TEEC, the Treaty of Rome 1957), which has been modified and supplemented by the subsequent treaties and acts:

- the Single European Act (SEA, 1986);
- the Treaty on the European Union (TEU, the Maastricht Treaty, 1992);
- the Treaty of Amsterdam (TA, 1997);
- and the Treaty of Nice (TN, 2001).

The TEU relaunched the European Union as a structure based on three main elements or pillars:

1. the *European Community, EC*, rooted in the Treaties of Paris (1951) and Rome (1976) as modified by the Single European Act (1986);
2. *common foreign policy and security policy, CFSP*, which is based on inter-governmental cooperation;
3. *cooperation in justice and home affairs, CJHA*, which is also based on intergovernmental cooperation.

The Treaty of Amsterdam consolidated each of the three pillars of the EU. The member countries agreed that progressive economic and monetary integration via the EU must be complemented by similar moves for a

---

Box 2.1 ■ References to the treaties

The discussion in this chapter is based on the current (2002) EU legislation in force, that is on the Treaty Establishing the European Community (TEEC) as amended by the Treaty of European Union (TEU) and the Treaty of Amsterdam (TA). References are given by Titles (= headings) and articles of the TEEC (as renumbered by the TA). For example, TEEC, VII, 98 means: Treaty Establishing the European Community, Title VII, article 98. The Treaty of Nice (TN) has amended the existing treaties and the composition of the EU institutions in preparation for enlargement of the EU to include (at least 12) countries of central and eastern Europe, the Mediterranean and the Baltic. It will enter into force only after it is ratified by all the EU member states (probably by 2003). Important changes introduced by the TN will be noted.

common foreign and security policy and a common interior and justice policy, 'including the progressive framing of a common defense policy, which might in time lead to a common defence' (TEEC, I, 2). Therefore, the term *European Union* is wider than the term *European Community* and the abbreviation EU has replaced all others. If not otherwise indicated, EU and Community will be the terms used in this book.

The EU Treaty declares that 'any European State may apply to become a Member of the Union' and called 'upon the other peoples of Europe who share their ideal to join their efforts'. The preconditions for considering applications for entry are three:

1. The applicant state must be European.
2. It must be democratic.
3. It must accept the political and economic objectives of the EU.

The United Kingdom (UK), Irish Republic (IRL) and Denmark (DK) joined the EC on 1 January 1973 (first enlargement, EC-9). Greece (GR) became an associate member in 1962 and full member on 1 January 1981 (second enlargement, EC-10). Portugal (P) and Spain (E) joined on 1 January 1986 (third enlargement, EC-12). Austria (A), Finland (FI) and Sweden (SE) joined the EU on 1 January 1995 (fourth enlargement, EU-15). Applications for membership by new candidates are addressed to the Council 'which shall act unanimously after consulting the Commission and after receiving the assent of the European Parliament' (TEEC, VIII, 49).

2.2 EU institutions

The treaties entrust the operation of the Community to five principal institutions: the Council, the Commission, the Court of Justice, the European Parliament and the Court of Auditors (TEEC, II, 7). The first two make up the administrative branches of the EU; the Court of Justice and the European Parliament are, respectively, the judicial and the legislative bodies of the Community; the Court of Auditors investigates the Community accounts. The Council and the Commission are assisted by the Economic and Social Committee and the Committee of the Regions. The financial institutions of the Community are three: the European Investment Bank, the European System of Central Banks and the European Central Bank. As a rule, the Community has limited powers as 'conferred upon it by this Treaty and of the objectives assigned to it therein' (TEEC, II, 5). In the following we describe the composition and tasks of the principal European institutions.

The Council of the European Union

The Council of the European Union is the institution in which the governments of the member states are represented and therefore in which the real power of the Union is vested. The Council is the leading institution for decision-making but is limited to exercising only the powers and functions conferred on it by the treaties. Apart from limited cases, however, the Council can only decide on the basis of a Commission proposal and in consultation with the European Parliament (EP), the Economic and Social Committee (ESC) and the Committee of the Regions (CR). The Council consists of one representative of each member state at ministerial level, authorized to commit the government of that member state. General Council meetings deal with major issues and are attended by the foreign ministers of the member states. Specialist Council meetings deal with sectoral issues and are attended by other ministers, depending on the subject under discussion. These Councils are known by subject, for example the Agricultural Council, the Transport Council and so on. The office of the presidency of the Council is held in turn by each member state for a term of six months 'in the order decided by the Council acting unanimously'. It usually rotates among the member states, in alphabetical order, every six months commencing on 1 January and 1 July. It is customary for the member state holding the presidency to work closely with the member states whose term precedes and follows it, a combination known as the 'troika'. Since the presidency controls the chair at all Council meetings, it can have a considerable influence on policy. Therefore, care is taken to ensure that the presidency falls to every member state in the first half of the year, since this period is most important for policy-making (such as the budget and agricultural price support).

In the Council there are three voting procedures, requiring different levels of agreement before a proposal can be adopted:

1. *Unanimity* means that a proposal is rejected if one member state votes against it. Unanimity is required in several areas of importance to the development of the Union (such as the common foreign and security policy, police and judicial cooperation in criminal matters, asylum and immigration policy, economic and social cohesion and taxation). Each member state has a *veto* (introduced by the *'Luxembourg compromise'* of 29 January 1966) on Union measures in these sectors.

2. *Qualified majority voting* has become the rule for decision-making on the most important EU policies (such as the completion of the internal market, transport, research, the free movement of workers or capital, and on acts requiring cooperation with the European Parliament). Under the current system, this procedure requires 65 votes in favour from the 87 votes available to member states, allocated according to

size (see Table 2.1). If there are 62–4 votes in favour of a proposal then negotiations continue to see if an agreement can be reached commanding 65 votes. However, in the end 62 votes are enough if further negotiations prove unsuccessful. The Treaty of Nice (TN) extended qualified majority voting for decisions on 30 articles of the treaty that previously required unanimity (such as judicial cooperation in civil matters) and adjusted the weighting of votes from January 2005 (after the forthcoming enlargement).

3. *Simple majority voting* applies where the treaty does not specify any other procedure.

The Council meets about five times a month. A large part of the groundwork for these meetings is carried out in the Committee of Permanent Representatives (Coreper) of the member states, which is assisted by panels of civil servants from the appropriate member states' ministries. The Council is assisted by a General Secretariat, under the direction of the Secretary-General. Since 1999 the Secretary-General of the Council also is 'High Representative' of the EU's common foreign and security policy.

The European Council

The European Council is not one of the Community decision-making institutions set up by the Treaty of Rome. However, during the 1960s occasional summit meetings of the heads of government of the member states became necessary. The first two summits were held in 1961 at Paris and Bonn when leaders of the Six agreed to meet 'at regular intervals to exchange views, to concert their policies and to arrive at common positions in order to facilitate the political union of Europe'. The next summit meeting took place six years later on the occasion of the tenth anniversary of signing the Treaty of Rome. At the Paris summit of December 1974, it was decided that a summit meeting would be convened regularly to consider outstanding issues holding back progress in Community policy. Finally, the *European Council* was made a formal institution of the Community (TEEC, I, 4), comprising heads of state (France) or government (all other members) of the member states and the President of the Commission. They are assisted by the ministers for foreign affairs of the member states and by a member of the Commission. The European Council meets at least twice a year, under the chairmanship of the head of state or government of the member state which holds the presidency of the Council of Ministers. The European Council deals with major Community matters arising from the treaties and with general economic and political cooperation. It usually lays down strategic guidelines but does not normally take formal decisions. It delegates this role to a separate meeting of foreign ministers which is convened immediately after the summit. Since the 1990s, the European Council has played a central role in the direction and progress of EU integration.

The Commission

The Commission is the executive of the Union and has six main roles:

1. It acts as Community guardian to ensure that treaty and Community decisions are applied by the member states, with recourse, if necessary, to the Court of Justice.
2. It has sole right to propose new legislation by submitting proposals to the Council; it drafts the detailed measures needed for its implementation; and it steers legislative proposals through the European Parliament.
3. It acts as a mediator at meetings of the Council, often amending its own proposals to reach a compromise acceptable to all the member states.
4. It negotiates for the Community on certain common policy issues, for example in matters of international trade.
5. It has certain powers in administering Community rules, and limited power to legislate, mainly in the detailed implementation of the Common Agricultural Policy.
6. It administers the budget and manages Community programmes.

The Commission is based in Brussels and currently consists of 20 members – two each from D, E, F, I and the UK, and one from each of the other ten member countries – who are proposed by the governments of the member states for a renewable five-year term of office. At the head of the Commission are the President and one or two Vice-Presidents who hold office for a two-year renewable term. The Treaty of Amsterdam strengthened the legitimacy of the President of the Commission by submitting his nomination for approval to the European Parliament (TEEC, 214). Under the new provisions, the members of the Commission are now also nominated with the consent of the President, rather than simply after consulting him or her, and are subject to approval by the European Parliament. The Commission, which is strictly independent of national governments, runs an administration currently divided into 23 Directorates-General (D-Gs), each responsible to one of the Commissioners. Its decisions are taken by simple majority. The Commission is collectively accountable to the European Parliament.[1] The Treaty of Nice (TN) limits the Commission

---

[1] For the first time in the EU's history the Commission resigned *en masse* in March 1999 after a committee of independent experts appointed by the Parliament found it responsible for specific cases of 'fraud, mismanagement and nepotism' that had occurred during its term of office.

to one national per member state, with effect from 2005. Moreover, after the Union reaches a membership of 27 states by enlargement to countries of central and eastern Europe,

> the members of the Commission shall be less than the number of member states . . . [and they] shall be chosen according to a rotation system based on the principle of equality . . . The number of members of the Commission shall be set by the Council, acting unanimously.

The Court of Justice

The Court of Justice (CJ) deals with the interpretation, application and development of Community law. It comprises 15 judges and nine advocates-general, appointed by common accord of the governments of the member states. They hold office for a renewable term of six years and serve the Community in their own capacity but do not represent the member states. The role of the Court is to ensure observance of the law in interpreting and applying the treaties and on legislation stemming from them. The Court has jurisdiction over disputes between member states on Community matters, between member states and Community institutions and over actions brought by individuals against the Community. It also has the right to review the legality of directives or regulations issued by the Council or the Commission. In general, primary Community law in the fields covered by the treaties constitutes an autonomous legal system, independent of the legal systems of the member states. Community law is not incorporated into any national law but has direct applicability to the member states with precedence over national law. In areas of conflict EU law is supreme over national law. At the request of national courts, the Court of Justice gives 'preliminary rulings' on questions of interpretation of Community treaties and Community law. An objective of the Union is 'to maintain in full the *acquis communautaire* – the rights and obligations deriving from the EU treaties, laws and regulations – and to build on it' (TEEC, I, 2). The Treaty of Amsterdam widened the CJ's powers by including under its field of competence:

- fundamental rights, as guaranteed by the European Convention on Human Rights;
- asylum, immigration, free movement of persons and judicial cooperation in civil matters;
- police and judicial cooperation in criminal matters.

The Treaty of Nice stipulates that the CJ, which in the enlarged Union will continue to consist of one judge from each member state, may sit in a Grand Chamber of 13 judges instead of always meeting in a plenary session attended by all judges.

Under the treaties (TEEC, 249), the Community makes use of five legal instruments:

1. *Regulations*, which are laws binding in their entirety, directly and uniformly applicable in all member states to legal parties under Community law (member states, citizens or firms). As Community law, regulations apply directly in all the member states, without requiring a national act to transpose them.
2. *Directives*, which are laws addressed to member states and binding as to the result to be achieved, but leave the form and method of implementation to national governments. Therefore, directives must be transposed within a pre-specified time period to national legislation in the appropriate form of each member state.
3. *Decisions*, which deal with specific problems and are binding in their entirety upon those to whom they are addressed, which are member states or natural or legal persons.
4. and 5. *Recommendations* and *opinions*, which have no binding force and do not establish any rights or obligations for those to whom they are addressed. They merely state the view of the institution that issues them.

The term *mutual recognition* refers to legislative acts which are national responsibilities but are recognized and are enforceable under Community law. Therefore, mutual recognition is a decentralized form of legislation, typically applicable to standards and norms.

Since 1989, the Court of Justice has been assisted in its task by a supplementary institution, the *Court of First Instance (CFI)* which consists of 15 judges, one from each member state. They are appointed for a renewable term of six years. In contrast to the Court of Justice, which, as a rule, sits in a plenary session, the Court of First Instance sits in chambers of three or five judges.

The Community, and its agent the Commission, does not have its own police force to see that Community rules are respected in the member states. Enforcement of the rules is left to national governments and national law enforcement agencies. In addition, the Commission depends on individuals, companies, pressure groups and the governments of the member states to report dubious practices or infringements of the law. Then the Commission discusses further the case with the member state in question or takes the matter up with the Court of Justice. Every citizen of a member state is also a citizen of the Union and has the rights and obligations emanating from national and Community law. Therefore, every EU citizen whose privileges are infringed by national law can under European law bring a government before the Court of Justice.

The European Parliament

The European Parliament (EP) 'which shall consist of representatives of the peoples of the states brought together in the Community, shall exercise the powers conferred upon it by this Treaty' (TEEC, 189). Thus, while the Council represents the states, the Parliament represents the people. Until the TEU, in comparison with the national parliaments of the member states, the Parliament had limited advisory and supervisory powers and mostly acted as a consultative body which could inspect, but not initiate legislation. Draft proposals from the Commission went to the Parliament for its opinion and suggestions, which were not binding but were in general incorporated in final proposals. It had, however, certain decision powers which enabled it to influence the outcome of decision-making by legal means, such as the right: (a) to force the Commission's resignation (but not the resignation of individual Commissioners) by passing a motion of censure (as it did in 1999); (b) to approve the appointment of a new Commission in its entirety; (c) to adopt or reject the budget or amend the non-obligatory expenditures of the budget; and (d) to give or refuse assent to treaties such as the accession of new member states, association with third countries, the organization and objectives of certain budgetary funds and the tasks and powers of the European Central Bank. The Parliament also had the power to set its own agenda to debate any issues it considered important, to put questions to the Council, to set up committees of enquiry and to send delegations and fact-finding missions to third countries. Thus, through time the Parliament gained influence in policy-making and international relations beyond the limits formally allocated to it by the treaties. Under the SEA, the Parliament won the limited but significant power to reject or amend Council decisions about the single market. It also has the right of second reading, or re-examination of proposed directives, after Council has reached a common position, and to reinstate amendments which it had put forward in its first reading.

With accelerating progress towards European integration, many EU countries expressed their concern about the democratic process and accountability which had not kept up with the lessening of national sovereignty. This left a democratic deficit because Europe's peoples through their national parliaments had little influence on Community legislation, while the European Parliament had only limited powers of amendment. Therefore, the TEEC recognized and to some extent rectified this deficiency, declaring that the heads of government of the contracting European countries 'Resolved to continue the process of creating an ever closer union among the peoples of Europe, in which decisions are taken as closely as possible to the citizen' (Preamble), and affirmed that 'the European Parliament shall participate in the process leading up to the adoption of

---

Box 2.2 ■ Consultation, cooperation and co-decision

The three main procedures used to decide Community action are consultation, cooperation and co-decision. The *consultation procedure* requires an opinion from the Parliament. Under the consultation procedure, the Commission presents a proposal in consultation with the Parliament, the Economic and Social Committee and the Committee of the Regions. The decision is then taken by the Council, either by qualified majority voting (e.g. in the field of agriculture) or unanimity (e.g. in the field of taxation). The *cooperation procedure* allows Parliament to improve proposed legislation by amendment. The *co-decision procedure* shares decision-making power equally between the Parliament and the Council. Under the co-decision procedure, used, for example, for decisions on the internal market, transport policy, environmental policy or research programmes, the Commission presents a proposal, often after consulting the interested parties. Where appropriate, the Committee of the Regions and/or the Economic and Social Committee are consulted. The text is adopted if it secures the agreement of both the Parliament and the Council, acting by qualified majority voting.

These arrangements are a step in the right direction but much remains to be done to make the enhanced powers of the Parliament more democratically accountable to the citizens of the Union. To this end, the relations between national parliaments and the European Parliament are stepped up by the exchange of information. For this, national parliaments will receive Commission proposals for legislation in good time for information or for possible examination. It is also proposed that the European Parliament and national parliaments will meet in a Conference of the Parliaments to consider the main issues facing the Union.

Community acts' (TEEC, 192). This resulted in the *co-decision procedure* by which the Council and the Parliament jointly decide on legislation in areas such as research, health and culture. Henceforth, the Parliament acquired three kinds of legislative power: *consultation, cooperation and co-decision*.

The Treaty of Amsterdam considerably increased the Parliament's responsibilities by making the co-decision procedure the general rule. The European Parliament now has the power to amend and if necessary to reject EU legislative decisions, mostly those which are decided in Council by a majority. The Parliament may also set up a Committee of Inquiry to investigate alleged contravention or maladministration in the implementation of Community law (TEEC, 193). For the same reasons it was decided that from 1995 the Parliament would appoint an Ombudsman to safeguard European citizens' political, civil and social rights and investigate their complaints (TEEC, 195). Every person residing in the EU also has the right to address, individually or in association with others, a petition to the Parliament on matters relating to the Union's activity. By the Inter-institutional Agreement (1993), the Council and the Parliament have joint responsibility for deciding the Community budget on the basis of proposals from the Commission. More recently, the Parliament has also established the right to interrogate the Central Bank president at regular hearings.

Despite these advances, there has been growing concern about the lack of sufficient democratic controls over increasingly important decisions taken by a centralist bureaucracy removed from public opinion. Although this is an exaggeration (since the democratically elected governments of the member states through their representatives at the Council are the decision-makers), the Union agreed at the Nice European Council (2001) to bring forward the prospect of new institutional reforms to 2004 preceded by an open discussion on European governance. In this context, *governance* defines the rules, processes and practices that affect the way in which European powers are exercised, particularly with regard to accountability, clarity, transparency, coherence, efficiency and effectiveness. This will involve an overhaul of the European democratic set-up and the balance between EU institutions, the member states and the people in the decision-making process.

The direction of the European Parliament is in the hands of the President and 12 Vice-Presidents, elected every two and a half years. Much of the Parliament's work is done by specialist committees. The Parliament's administrative seat is Luxembourg, but plenary sessions are now held in Strasbourg. The parliamentary committees normally meet in Brussels. Since 1979, the Members of the European Parliament (MEPs) have been selected by direct elections for a fixed term of five years. The current member country representation in the Parliament is presented in Table 2.1. The Treaty of Nice (2001) set the limit of MEPs to 732 and allocated seats between member states and candidate countries (with effect from the next elections for the existing EU member states and after accession of the candidate countries to the EU).

The Court of Auditors

The Court of Auditors is the taxpayers' representative and was set up by an amendment treaty in 1975, on the initiative of the Parliament, to monitor the Community's accounts, examining the legality and regularity of revenue and expenditure in the Community budget and ensuring sound financial management. The EU institutions, national, regional and local administrations which manage Community funds, and recipients of EU aid, inside and outside the Union, must also satisfy the Court that all is in order. After the audit, the Court of Auditors provides 'the European Parliament and the Council with a statement of assurance as to the reliability of the accounts and the legality and regularity of the underlying transactions' and it 'shall draw up an annual report after

Table 2.1 **Members of the European Parliament (EP), the Economic and Social Committee (ESC) and the Committee of the Regions (CR)**

Country	EP		Qualified majority	ESC and CR memberships
	MEPs	MEPs*		
Austria AT	21	17	4	12
Belgium B	25	22	5	12
Germany D	99	99	10	24
Denmark DK	16	13	3	9
Spain E	64	50	8	21
France F	87	72	10	24
Finland FI	16	13	3	9
Greece GR	25	22	5	12
Italy I	87	72	10	24
Ireland IRL	15	12	3	9
Luxembourg L	6	6	2	6
Netherlands NL	31	25	5	12
Portugal P	25	22	5	12
Sweden SE	22	18	4	12
United Kingdom UK	87	72	10	24
Total	**626**	**523**	**87**	**222**

* Treaty of Nice: the 12 candidate countries are allocated 209 MEPs out of a total of 732.

the close of each financial year' (TEEC, 248). The Court consists of 15 members, one from each member state, appointed for a six-year term and eligible for reappointment. The Treaty of Nice set the number of Auditors to one national per member state.

The Economic and Social Committee

The Economic and Social Committee (ESC) currently has 222 members: 'representatives of the various categories of economic and social activity . . . and . . . of the general public' (TEEC, 257), including employers, trade unions, farmers and the professions. The members are appointed by the Council from lists supplied by the member states according to country quotas (see Table 2.1). The members of the ESC serve in their personal capacity and are not bound by any mandatory instructions. The ESC is convened, at the request of the Council or the Commission, to issue advisory opinions on matters of legislative procedure as laid down in the treaties. It also has the power to undertake its own investigations and to draw up opinions on every Community issue. The *Consultative Committee* carries out similar tasks for ECSC affairs. The Treaty of Nice has set the limit of ESC members to 350 after the enlargement of the EU.

The Committee of the Regions

The Committee of the Regions (CR) has an organizational structure similar to that of the ESC, consisting of representatives of regional and local governments. The members of the CR are independent of their governments, serving the general interest of the Community in their private capacity and they advise the Council and the Commission on matters concerning the regions at European level (TEEC, 263–5). With a view to enlargement, the Treaty of Nice set the limit of the CR to 350 members which must have an electoral mandate from the authorities they represent or be politically accountable to them.

The European Investment Bank

The European Investment Bank (EIB) was set up to promote economic and social integration. It operates independently as a public non-profit-making organization. The bank's task is to contribute 'to the balanced and stable development of the common market in the interest of the Community' (TEEC, 267) by supplying loans and issuing guarantees facilitating the financing of capital projects. Within the EU, the bank finances projects:

- for developing less-developed regions;
- for modernizing or developing activities contributing to the progressive establishment of the common market;
- of common interest to several member states which are of such a size or nature that they cannot be entirely financed by individual countries.

The bank's resources consist of reserves, capital subscribed by member states and funds raised (that is, borrowed) on capital markets inside and outside the Community. The EIB does not normally contribute more than 40 per cent of the cost of any project, the rest being contributed by the recipient country or countries. By permission of the Board of Governors, the bank may grant investment finance for projects in a country or group of countries under association or cooperation agreements with the Community. Most of the finance is in the form of loans at subsidized interest rates.

The European Bank for Reconstruction and Development (EBRD)

This was established in 1991 to foster the transition towards open market-oriented economies and promote private and entrepreneurial initiatives in the countries of central and eastern Europe. To reach its objectives, it provides loans, equity investment (shares) and guarantees.

To facilitate the transition to Economic and Monetary Union (EMU), the Community set up (1994–8) the European Monetary Institute (EMI) as the precursor of the EMU institutions, the European System of Central Banks (ESCB) and the European Central Bank (ECB). The ESCB and the ECB were set up in 1999 'to maintain price stability', 'support the general economic policies in the Community' and 'act in accordance with the principle of open market economy with free competition, favouring an efficient allocation of resources' (TEEC, VII, 105). We describe the functions and the roles of these institutions in Chapter 6, which deals with monetary integration.

2.3 The EU in the world

The EU is the most successful economic integration scheme in the world with economic consequences for both its member states and the world at large. It is the largest international trader and this has repercussions beyond its frontiers, giving it responsibilities in the international trading system and the world economy due to its size and the 'externalities' it can cause.

Table 2.2 presents basic economic statistics for each of the EU 15 member states. These statistics reveal big differences between the countries making up the Union, as regards the following:

1. *Physical size* (area, population). The smallest member in both area and population is Luxembourg, the largest in area is France and the largest in population is Germany. The EU-15 make up a market of nearly 380 million people, almost a third more than the population of the United States (277 million) which is almost 2.5 times larger in area than the EU.
2. *Economic Size*. With GDP per head taken as a measure of economic welfare and development, the least developed member (Greece) reaches only 67.2 per cent of the EU average level, while Luxembourg's is by 88 per cent higher than the average. In general, ten countries occupy places above, and the remaining five below, the EU-15 average GDP per head. This is also illustrated in Figure 2.1. The 15 economies together have a combined GDP accounting for more than 29 per cent of global GDP. But, as Table 2.2 shows, four of the 15 member countries (D, F, I, and UK) account for 72.4 per cent of the total Community GDP, one of them (D) for a quarter of the total.

Table 2.2 Basic statistics of the European Union

Member country	Area 1000 sq. km	Population 2001 (millions)	Gross value added by branch, 1999			GDP per head 2000: EU = 100 PPS	GDP growth 2000	GDP share 1999	Foreign trade, GDP %		Member country
			Agr.	Ind.	Serv.				Imp.	Exp.	
AT	83.9	8.1	3	25	72	111.8	3.5	2.5	41.4	40.9	AT
B	30.5	10.2	2	25	73	110.7	3.9	2.9	68.9	72.5	B
D	357.0	82.1	1	28	71	106.4	3.1	24.9	26.0	26.6	D
DK	43.1	5.4	2	22	76	117.9	2.6	2.1	31.6	36.4	DK
E	506.0	39.5	4	27	69	83.0	4.1	7.0	23.9	23.0	E
F	551.5	60.8	3	23	74	99.0	3.3	17.0	22.1	23.7	F
FI	338.3	5.2	3	29	68	103.6	4.8	1.5	28.6	34.8	FI
GR	132.0	10.6	7	21	72	67.2	4.1	1.5	26.9	18.9	GR
I	301.3	57.7	3	26	71	98.8	2.9	13.7	21.7	24.3	I
IRL	70.3	3.8	5	33	62	118.8	10.5	1.1	64.9	75.6	IRL
L	2.6	0.4	–	–	–	188.0	7.8	0.2	97.5	110.7	L
NL	41.5	16.0	3	23	74	114.1	4.3	4.7	53.7	58.9	NL
P	92.1	10.0	4	27	69	75.3	3.0	1.3	37.6	29.6	P
SE	450.0	8.9	2	29	69	103.3	4.0	2.8	33.2	38.2	SE
UK	244.1	59.9	1	25	74	103.0	3.1	16.8	27.3	26.3	UK
EU	3244.1	378.6	2	26	72	100.0	3.4	100.0	28.7	29.8	EU

Note: The trade figures are for intra- and extra-EU trade, 1991–2000 average.
Sources: Data from Commission (2000c) and World Bank (2001a).

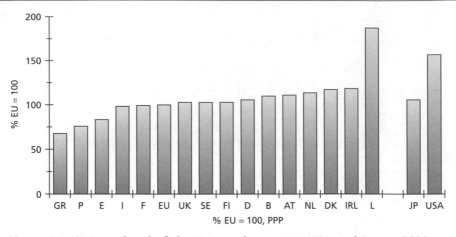

Figure 2.1 GDP per head of the EU member states, USA and Japan, 2000

Source: Data from Commission (2000c) and World Bank (2001a).

3. *Composition of value added.* Services dominate European economic activity. Agriculture, which was still important for some countries in the 1990s, contributes 7 per cent in Greece, 5 per cent in Ireland and between 4 and 1 per cent in all other countries. Similar trends are also observed in the structure of labour employment. Commercial services (which exclude government services) now account for around a half of the EU's employment and GDP.

4. *Openness to trade.* Here, the smaller more developed countries are also the more open to trade. Thus Luxembourg, Belgium and Ireland are the most open, while Greece, France, Italy and Spain are the least open economies of the Community.

These statistics confirm that, in general, the 15 members of the EU do not form a homogeneous group. Diversity in their physical characteristics and in their economic structures, both of which may imply diversity in economic interests, mean that the search for common objectives and common policies within the Community is not an easy course. The crawling pace of European integration over the last 40 or so years attests to these facts.

Table 2.3 shows the economic importance of the EU relative to two other large economies, the USA and Japan. The comparative statistics and Figures 2.2, 2.3 and 2.4 confirm the dominant size of the three economies in the world. The EU share in world GDP is 30 per cent, in merchandise trade (external) 19 per cent, and in trade in services 25 per cent. It also has the largest share in the outflows, and the second largest in the inflows of the world's foreign direct investment (45 per cent and 19.4 per cent respectively).

Table 2.3 The EU in the world

	EU	USA	Japan
Population, mil. (2001)	378.7	276.6	127.2
GDP per head (2000)			
EU = 100	100.0	157.2	106.0
World trade[1] (1998)			
(i) merchandise	18.7	18.9	7.8
(ii) services	24.9	20.1	8.6
Foreign direct investment (FDI) (1998)			
Inflows	19.4	37.4	0.6
Outflows	45.0	28.0	5.0

Notes: [1] [exports + imports]1/2.
Sources: World Bank (2001b) and WTO (2000), available at www.europa.eu.int/comm/trade

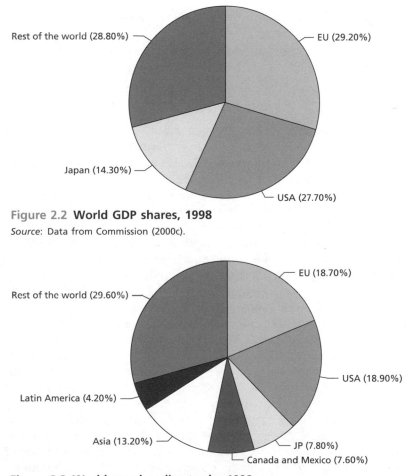

Figure 2.2 **World GDP shares, 1998**
Source: Data from Commission (2000c).

Figure 2.3 **World merchandise trade, 1998**
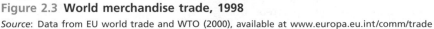
Source: Data from EU world trade and WTO (2000), available at www.europa.eu.int/comm/trade

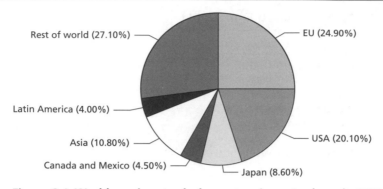

Rest of world (27.10%)

EU (24.90%)

Latin America (4.00%)

Asia (10.80%)

Canada and Mexico (4.50%)

Japan (8.60%)

USA (20.10%)

Figure 2.4 **World services trade (exports + imports shares), 1998**

Source: Data from EU world trade and WTO (2000), available at  www.europa.eu.int/comm/trade

---

Box 2.3 ■ Variable geometry

The successive enlargements of the EU increased the degree of heterogeneity between the countries that composed it from two points of view:

1. level of development
2. willingness to go further with integration.

With the member states' short-run objectives diverging, it proved difficult to reach agreement on common targets and a common course towards integration. This obviously impeded and often delayed Community progress towards achieving its set objectives. Therefore, from time to time it has been proposed that the strategy of a *multi-speed Europe* should be adopted, so that those who can would move ahead faster towards integration, and the others would follow if and when they are able to do so.

But such a strategy is against the Community's philosophy of 'overall harmonious develop-ment' (TEEC, XVII, 158) and it has not been seriously considered to this day. Instead, with regard to economic development the Community has undertaken to accelerate the process of cohesion, solidarity and convergence by 'reducing disparities between the levels of development of the various regions and the backwardness of the least favoured regions, including rural areas' (TEEC, XVII, 158). Nevertheless, with the impending enlargement of the EU to central and eastern European countries, there are many who argue that in order to achieve a flexible and strong EU, a key element of the integration strategy must be to permit and even encourage the *variable geometry* or *multi-speed* approach – though not in the form of *à la carte* choice – led by an inner hard core of countries which would accelerate the *deepening* before the *widening* of the EU. Enlargement would mean greater diversity and, therefore, increased inability of the laggards to follow the pace of the leaders. The present EU-15 states are effectively already divided into two broad camps, the core and the periphery. The core, led primarily by Germany and France, sees moving ahead as a voluntary arrangement for common action. Therefore, they favour flexibility as the means for sidestepping the potential objections of the reluctant Europeans towards faster economic and political integration.

2.4 The EU's stages of integration

Since its foundation, in order to reach its objectives, the Community has gone through three legal stages of integration: those of customs union (CU, established by the TEEC, 1958), common market (CM, established by the SEA, 1985) and economic union (EU, established by the TEU, 1992) towards reaching its objectives. In this section we will examine the EU's stages of integration and in the next we will define the EU objectives.

The customs union, 1958–85

The EU does not fit easily into any of the standard forms of regional economic associations (as presented in Chapter 1). It clearly started as a customs union but with an executive separate from national governments, the Commission, and certain sovereign rights to manage common policies using its own budgetary resources. Therefore, the EU is unlike other international organizations, which are financed by subscriptions from their member states.

As a customs union, the six EU countries removed customs duties and quantitative restrictions on their trade and adopted a common commercial policy (CCP) with common external tariffs (CET) on imports from third (i.e. non-member) countries. The countries that became members of the Community by successive enlargements took up the policies of the Union.

The TEEC provided that, besides external trade, two other sectors, agriculture and transport, would come under common policies exercised by the Community. This was soon applied to agriculture, and to a lesser extent to transport. Moreover, in certain areas of economic activity the Community also displayed some features of an economic union, such as some degree of coordination and harmonization of members' other policies, but the integration of economic policy remained on the whole minimal.

The common market, 1985–92

The Community intended from the beginning to integrate the internal market by adopting common competition rules and removing the technical obstacles to trade which arise from disparities between the laws, regulations and administrative provisions of member countries. Indeed, the Treaty of Rome asserted that the common market would be established within 12 years. However, this objective remained elusive and market segmentation on national lines continued because of the existence of different national standards, regulatory barriers to market entry and restrictions on the trade of goods, services and factors of production, border formalities and discriminatory practices.

A new date for the unification of markets was set by the Single European Act (SEA) for the end of 1992. The Act came into force on 1 July 1987 and entailed the simultaneous implementation of a six-point programme:

1. attainment of a large market without internal frontiers;
2. economic and social cohesion leading to greater convergence;
3. a common policy for scientific and technological development;
4. strengthening the European Monetary System;
5. introduction of a European social dimension;
6. coordinated action for protection of the environment.

After a slow start, implementation of the SEA measures quickened after 1988 with significant progress in removing capital controls, furthering labour mobility, liberalizing road transport, harmonizing technical standards and reducing customs formalities.

The objective of the SEA was to set the foundation of People's Europe. The Act declared that 'the completion of the internal market will provide an indispensable base for increasing the prosperity of the Community as a whole', while its 'social dimension' specified that 'all citizens, whatever their occupation, will have effective access to the direct benefits expected from the single market as a factor of economic growth, and as the most effective means of combating unemployment' (*Bull. EC*, 12, 1988). It also summoned the EU countries 'jointly to implement a European foreign policy' and 'to transform relations as a whole amongst states into a European Union' (Commission 1987).

The SEA introduced important changes in the Community's strategy for integration by:

■ limiting the requirement for harmonization, accelerating the process of integration by the systematic implementation of mutual recognition of national norms and regulations;
■ establishing a faster and more efficient decision-making process by extending the scope of qualified majority voting, which makes it much more difficult for an individual member state to block progress;
■ increasing the role of the European Parliament in the integration process;
■ reaffirming the Community's objectives and stressing the need for economic and social cohesion for their realization.

As planned, most of the necessary legislation for integrating the market for goods, services, capital and labour was completed by December 1992. In this way the economic frontiers between the member states were removed and progress towards the single market ensued, increasing the potential for improved allocation of production and exchange. Thus, after the long interval of 35 years since its foundation, the Community was well on the road leading to its first important target, the single market. This turned the Community into a large economic power, acting in world trade as a single unit.

The single market aimed at efficiency by specialization of each EU country and region in the activities of their comparative advantage. The enlarged market provides opportunities of cost reductions by economies of scale, promotes competition and presents the consumer with a wider choice. Therefore, the single market is the means for realizing the aim of economic integration: the increase in economic welfare and the rate of growth for the benefit of the Union's peoples. The Community declared that it would pursue this aim within a system of free markets and perfect competition with external and internal stability in order 'to promote economic and social progress' (TEEC, I, 2), consisting of:

- full employment of productive resources and stable prices in the short term; and
- an accelerated growth rate along a stable growth path in the longer term.

Economic union: 1992 and beyond

The progress of the single market encouraged the Community next to attempt even more ambitious projects. Economic and monetary union and political union were from the beginning two of the long-term EU objectives, the details of which were at last examined at two parallel intergovernmental conferences – one covering economic and monetary union (EMU) and the other political union – which started their deliberations in December 1990. Their reports, which were considered by the European Council at Maastricht in December 1991, led to the Treaty on European Union (TEU) which marked a step forward on a par with the Treaty of Rome. The TEU, which was formally signed in February 1992 and came into force in 1993 after ratification by the member states, amended the TEEC and set the course of the Union. It also provided for another intergovernmental conference (IGC) to be convened in 1996–7 to focus on three main issues: (1) making Europe more democratic, effective and relevant to its citizens; (2) enabling the Union to work better and preparing it for enlargement; and (3) equipping the Union with the resources to conduct a proper common foreign and security policy and a common defence policy. This IGC was duly assembled and was concluded with the signing of the Treaty of Amsterdam (1997).

The treaties also created citizenship of the Union (TEEC, II, 17–22). Anyone with nationality of a member state is a citizen of the Union, with rights and duties conferred by the treaties. Union citizens have the right to move and reside freely within the territory of the member states. Citizens living in a member state of which they are not nationals have the right to vote and stand as candidates in municipal elections or elections of the European Parliament in that country, under the same conditions as national of that state (European Parliament, 1998). The Union, which is founded on the principles of liberty and democracy,

> shall respect fundamental rights, as guaranteed by the European Convention for the Protection of Human Rights and Fundamental Freedoms [which is independent of the EU] . . . and as they result from the constitutional traditions common to the member states, as general principles of Community law. (TEEC, I, 6)

The Community also promises to contribute to the flowering of the cultures of the member states (TEEC, XII, 151), 'while respecting their national and regional diversity', by encouraging cooperation to improve understanding and dissemination of the culture and history of the European peoples and to conserve and safeguard cultural heritage of European significance.

2.5 The objectives of the European Union

It is commonly thought that the Community's main function is political: to preserve peace and security in Europe by means of closer economic cooperation. This was the explicit objective of one of its precursors, the European Coal and Steel Community (ECSC, 1951), which was established by the same original six EU member states who: 'resolved to substitute for historic rivalries a fusion of their essential interests to establish, by creating an economic community, the foundations of a broad and independent community among peoples long divided by bloody conflicts'. But although economic integration seems to be the means by which the political objectives would be reached (see Appendix A2), right from the beginning it was only the economic objectives that were made clear in the treaties. But what exactly is the ultimate EU objective?

The Treaty of Rome declared that the contracting parties decided to create the Community:

> to ensure the economic and social progress of their countries by common action to eliminate the barriers which divide Europe, affirming as the essential objective of their efforts the constant improvement of the living and working conditions of their people. (Preamble)

The TEU went further by making the aims of the Community more specific and the means for achieving them more explicit:

> The Community shall have as its task, by establishing a common market and an economic union . . . to promote throughout the Community a harmonious and balanced development of economic activities, sustainable and non-inflationary growth respecting the environment, a high degree of convergence of economic performance, a high level of employment and social protection, the raising of the standard of living and quality of life, and economic and social cohesion and solidarity among Member States.   (TEEC, II, 2)

It can also be argued that the ultimate objective of the EU is the economic and political unification of Europe in a federal form, *the United States of Europe*. But, if this is the aim of the EU, it is nowhere spelled out in the treaties. It is 'the ever closer union among the peoples of Europe' that drives the process of economic integration towards 'the desirable objective', that of 'establishing . . . a European Union' (TEEC, I, 1). But the basic question is whether the EU would remain a Europe of nations in a pluralistic community, a loosely knit alliance of independent sovereign states, or transform itself into a federal European superstate with its own government rising high above the governments of the member states. Some fear that the EU is going federalist by stealth, adopting its own flag and a European anthem and creating an identikit European personality. For others, all those features that define Europeanness, such as shared culture and values in common, a sense of democracy, a respect for one's fellow citizens and their rights and a constant process of questioning in order to innovate and make progress, are strong characteristics of the European peoples. Therefore, economic and political integration are desirable and the idea that Europe can be nothing more than a customs union is insular and absurd.

2.6 Towards the common target: EU policies and constraints

The EU is an organization of independent states which have waived part of their national sovereignty to establish an association aspiring to economic integration. It is not a federal state because its sovereign privileges are limited to specific areas and it lacks the right to create new powers. Its prerogative is limited to clearly defined areas, the *primary* powers conferred to it by the treaties and the *derived* powers devolved on it by the Council. Therefore, the EU objectives can be realized only by the action of the member states which must apply two sets of policies, *national* and *common* at the EU level 'based on the closed co-ordination of Member States' economic policies . . . and conducted in accordance with the principle of an open market economy with free competition' (TEEC, II, 4).

Cooperation, coordination, harmonization and mutual recognition

There are three channels of economic interdependence between nations: (a) international trade in commodities and services; (b) capital market linkages; and (c) labour migration. Economic integration means increasing economic interdependence. As we have seen (in Chapter 1), interdependence causes externalities by cross-country spillovers and feedbacks arising from the exercise of national economic policy, and this advances the need for the internalization of the externalities by closer cooperation and coordination between the member states. Cooperation refers to the consultation and exchange of information between countries. Coordination refers to agreements, formal or ad hoc, between countries for joint policy-making in pursuit of shared objectives. But both of these policies come at a cost: the loss of national sovereignty and rising independence. In an attempt to alleviate these problems the countries may adopt harmonization, consisting of mutual adjustment of the member states' objectives and policies in recognition of their economic interdependence. While coordination can be discretionary or rule-based, harmonization entails common rules and consistent policies which inevitably lead to a greater uniformity across the members of the economic union. In contrast to harmonization, which is a negotiated solution to the problems arising from different systems, policies and national standards, mutual recognition removes the obstacles to integration by competition in the marketplace. Ultimately, the countries of the economic union may realize that the only or the best solution to achieve their common objectives speedily and efficiently is to adopt common policies at the level of the union.

Common policies

The interdependence among the EU countries through trade and capital and labour movement is high and rising as economic integration is increasing. Therefore, after passing through the stages of integration, the EU countries proceeded with the adoption of common policies. The EU member states agreed to implement common policies or activities to achieve a harmonious and balanced development throughout the Community by establishing a single open and competitive market. This required action on specific sectors and policies (enumerated in TEEC, 8), on which the Community has competence to take action, such as:

(1) free movement of goods, (2) agriculture, (3) free movement of persons, services and capital, (4) transport, (5) competition, taxation and approximation of laws, (6) economic and monetary policy, (7) common commercial policy, (8) social policy, education, training and youth,

(9) culture, (10) public health, (11) consumer protection, (12) trans-
European networks, (13) industry, (14) cohesion, (15) research and
technology, (16) environment and (17) development.

(European Parliament, 1998)

Constraints

The exercise of strictly national policies is, of course, subject to the
constraints imposed by (a) membership in the EU and the primacy of
Community law, and the obligation 'to maintain in full the *acquis
communautaire*' (TEEC, I, 2); and (b) respect of the general provisions of
the treaties which include: 'The Union shall provide itself with the means
necessary to attain its objectives and carry through its policies' (TEEC, I,
6) and 'Member States shall conduct their economic policies with a view
to contributing to the achievement of the objectives of the Community'
(TEEC, II, 98).

These constraints are well recognized by the treaties which provide
general principles for the regulation, coordination and harmonization of
national economic policies. Their aims are to strengthen the effectiveness of measures taken nationally, to highlight the need for concerted
action aiming at a speedier progress towards integration, and to reduce
the possibility of incompatibility between the objectives of policies
applied by different member states: 'the activities of the Member States
and the Community shall include . . . the adoption of an economic policy
which is based on the close coordination of Member States' economic
policies' (TEEC, II, 4). In pursuing their common objectives, 'Member
States shall regard their economic policies as a matter of common concern and shall coordinate them within the Council' (TEEC, II, 99).

Competence and subsidiarity

In general, the process of setting up the EU causes four types of effects
on the powers of the national authorities:

1. It leaves them unchanged.
2. It modifies them – thus the need for consultation and coordination
   among the members.
3. It limits them, by binding constraints.
4. It abolishes them, by the introduction of common policies.

With coordination, harmonization, mutual recognition and common
policies, problems may arise about competence: the legal authority of
different levels of government to act in the field of policy. Given that in
the EU there are three basic layers of government, local, national and

Community, the allocation of responsibilities became important. The answer was found by recourse to the principle of *subsidiarity*. The relevant statutes state that:

> The Community shall act within the limits of the power conferred upon it by this Treaty and the objectives assigned to it therein. In areas which do not fall within its exclusive competence, the Community shall take action, in accordance with the principle of subsidiarity, only if and in so far as the objectives of the proposed action cannot be sufficiently achieved by the Member States and can therefore, by reason of the scale of effects of the proposed action, be better achieved by the Community. Any action by the Community shall not go beyond what is necessary to achieve the objectives of this Treaty.   **(TEEC, II, 5)**

The term *exclusive competence* refers to certain areas in which the Community is the only appropriate level for taking the action needed to achieve the objectives of the treaties, such as 'establishing the internal market' (TEEC, II, 14) and 'a common organization of agricultural markets' (TEEC, II, 34). In contrast, *competence shared* refers to specific areas where the best result is achieved by collaboration between the Community and the member states, while *national competence* refers to acts which are in the exclusive competence of the national authorities of the member states.

The Treaty of Amsterdam confirmed (in an annexed protocol) that the principle of subsidiarity:

- does not call into question the powers already conferred to the Community which 'shall provide itself with the means necessary to attain its objectives and carry out its policies';
- allows the Community to undertake expanded action where circumstances so require or to discontinue it if it is no longer required;
- specifies that the Community is also expected to carry out those activities which by their magnitude transcend the frontiers of the member states or can be attained better at the level of the Community than at the level of the individual member state. Moreover, the means employed by the Community should be proportional to the objective pursued (principle of proportionality).

2.7 Conclusions

The EU countries have decided that their best interests are served by partnership and cooperation between them rather than by war and strife. We will understand EU policies better if we consider that they are not solely about an economic objective defined by private consumption concepts of welfare economics, but a political one, that of establishing a European Union. This entails short-run costs according to traditional concepts of economics, but it may bring about social and political benefits and economic gains which in the longer term may prove important for the people of Europe. Subject to this caveat, we can state that the main economic objective of the EU and its policies is:

■ *'the raising of the standard of living and quality of life'* (TEEC, II, 2), *'the constant improvement of the living and working conditions of their* [member states'] *people'* (Preamble);
■ by the application of policies *'based on the closed coordination of Member States' economic policies . . . and conducted in accordance with the principle of an open market economy with free competition'* (TEEC, II, 4), *favouring an efficient allocation of resources'* (TEEC, VI, 98);
■ within *'an internal market characterized by the abolition, as between Member States, of obstacles to the free movement of goods, persons, services and capital'* (TEEC, II, 8).

As we will see in subsequent chapters of this book, 'open market economy with free competition' is the recurrent theme running through every economic policy proposed or adopted by the European Community. It is the leitmotiv of the EU.

Box 2.4 ■ Objectives of the treaties

■ The avowed intentions of the founders of the ECSC were that it should be merely a first stage towards a 'European Federation'. The common market in coal and steel was to be an experiment which could gradually be extended to other economic spheres, culminating in a 'political' Europe.
■ The aim of the European Economic Community was to establish a common market based on the four freedoms of movement – of goods, persons, capital and services – and the gradual convergence of economic policies.
■ The aim of the Euratom was to coordinate the research programmes already under way or being prepared in the Member States [p. 9].
■ The European Community's task is to promote a harmonious and balanced development of economic activities, sustainable and non-inflationary growth respecting the environment, a high degree of convergence of economic performance, a high level of employment and social protection, the raising of the standard of living and quality of life, and economic and social cohesion and solidarity between Member States [p. 13].

European Parliament (1998)

APPENDIX   A2 The political rationale of integration

The economic approach to integration begins from the static and dynamic effects on members and non-members of the association to explain why the urge to internalize the ensuing externalities propels regional associations to advance and to expand. But what is missing from this analysis is the political dimension of regional economic associations which may well be more important than the economic effects.

Economic and political integration is characterized by a decrease of the sovereign power of the member states and an increase in the influence of the Union. Depending on the extent of power-sharing between the member states and the authority of the Union, there are many degrees of integration and different ways to reach it. Four political economy approaches to integration have been suggested to explain why European countries 'voluntarily mingle, merge, and mix with their neighbors so as to lose the factual attributes of sovereignty while acquiring new techniques for resolving conflict between themselves' (Haas, 1971, p. 6) and to predict where this process might lead.

The *pluralist approach* recommends a form of loose association based on sovereign states which envisage integration as a 'pluralistic community of states' developing links of international cooperation. The aim of the participating states is a form of loose 'political union' by intergovernmental cooperation at the level of heads of state or government, while 'the international organization has no real will of its own and no power to create a new political entity apart from the wishes of its members' (Pentland, 1973, p. 51). This is the *Europe de patries* (a Europe of states rather than the United States of Europe) vision of the EU which favours a minimum degree of integration to attain certain limited economic and political objectives, principally trade liberalization in an environment of peace and security.

The *functionalist approach* argues that in the modern world technological, economic and social forces create a complicated network of economic interrelationships between states which cause problems of international dimensions, such as price and exchange rate fluctuations, transboundary pollution and depletion of scarce resources. Therefore, the objective of maximizing economic welfare transcends the boundaries and abilities of nation-states. The pressure of these inexorable problems makes functional cooperation unavoidable and this might ultimately lead to economic and political union. Thus political integration follows in the steps of economic integration.

The proponents of this course believed that, starting with market integration, the EU would establish a web of international functional institutions which would progressively lead to some form of political integration:

> *it is difficult to believe that six countries can combine their resources, opportunities and capabilities to a greater degree, can integrate and dovetail their interests more and more, without one day setting up a political authority to crown this economic organization.*
>
> (P.-H. Spaak, quoted in Camps, 1965, p. 128)

The *neofunctionalist approach* argues that the need for economic and political integration comes about through the interaction of economic and political forces rather than from functional needs or technological change. In every society, interest groups pursuing their own gain seek to exploit the pressures which international economic linkages and interdependencies exert on countries. In such a system of shared problems, the interests of various groups in society converge. Therefore, to deal with these problems, countries delegate certain of their shared duties and policies to supranational problem-solving institutions, which slowly develop to a decision-making authority attracting the loyalty and support of beneficiary groups. The outcome is a mixed system in which the common supranational institutions and the national governments share responsibilities and shape the form of integration, the terminal point of which may be some form of federation. The course of integration evolves around the 'spillover', or forward linkage, from customs union through common market and economic union and their technical and political implications. Alternatively, if the partners are not content with the consequences of integration, there will be a retraction of the commitment and extent of the integration process by *spillback*, or reverse linkages.

In neofunctionalism, integration develops not through a predetermined process (as in the functionalist approach) but from the need to resolve the conflicts arising between competing interest groups which realize that more can be gained by cooperation than from discord. For the neofunctionalists the EU institutions constitute the beginnings of a supranational state. Consolidation by the EU approach (the *Community method*) gradually unifies the markets of the participants by *negative integration*, removing internal barriers to trade, and by *positive integration*, adopting common policies.

Progression through the stages of dynamic integration increases the interdependence of the participants and thus enhances the power of the common institutions. The *federalist approach* advocates as the next step a more advanced form of integration by setting up a *federal authority* which will assume some of the constituent states' sovereign rights and obligations. How the economic, political and legal powers would be shared between the member states and the federal government is decided by a constitutional conference which will set the rules of multi-level governance. In a federation of national states the participating states remain independent in internal affairs and retain the principal powers of decision-making, but the increasing transfer of powers to the central authority eventually leads to a federal union.

The federalist approach to European integration is supported by the *pragmatists* who seek to integrate national states and the *regionalists* who endeavour to decentralize them. Both groups argued that the EU's slow progress towards integration proved that *gradualism* failed to produce anything resembling federalism and that ripe political and social conditions existed for convening an intergovernmental conference (IGC) to speed up integration. For a long time, the Community remained static and hesitant. But it finally entered the IGG stage, starting with the two intergovernmental conferences gathered at Maastricht (1991), and following with a third at Amsterdam (1997) and a fourth at Nice (2001).

Questions

1. Analyse the concepts of policy cooperation, coordination and harmonization.
2. Consider the advantages and disadvantages of *ex ante* harmonization by institutional arrangements (centralization) and *ex post* harmonization by the market process (decentralization). Where does mutual recognition belong in this case?
3. Discuss the proposition that the subsidiarity principle does not apply to competition since a common competition policy cannot evolve from competition among national competition policies.

Further reading

The TEEC, SEA and TA are found in Euroconfidentiel (1999). For the implications of the Treaty of Amsterdam see EC (1999). Cram et al. (1999a) trace the course of developments in the EU. Armstrong and Bulmer (1998) deal with the issue of governance in the EU.

Web guide

- The integrated server of the EU institutions is Europa available at www.europa.eu.int/

- Basic information about EU institutions and policies is available at www.europa.eu.int/abc.en.htm

- Information on the EU economies, including national statistics (Eurostat) is available at www.europa.eu.int/comm/eurostat/

The single market

3

The EU has decided to reach its objectives by opening and liberalizing the markets for goods, services, labour and capital. To protect the enlarged market from distorting uncompetitive behaviour the EU adopted a common competition policy. In 1985, the EU passed the Single European Act (SEA) for completion of the single market by 1992. The Single Market Programme (SMP) was expected to produce three types of effects:

- allocation effects, which consist of the impact of integration on the static, short-run allocation of resources;
- accumulation effects, which encompass the impact of accumulation of productive factors inducing medium- and long-run growth effects;
- and location effects, which comprise the geographical allocation of resources across the member states and/or the regions of the Community.

For the EU, all these effects have been calculated to be positive and high.

3.1 Opening the EU market

Introduction

The Treaty of Rome affirmed that the EU would pursue its objectives by establishing a common market and progressively approximating the economic policies of member states. The common market, however, did not take shape in the time anticipated. The economic climate of the 1970s – the recession following the oil price shocks of 1973 and 1978, and the high rates of inflation and unemployment – prompted the member states to focus on domestic economic problems rather than on market liberalization. Many observers then attributed this inactivity to advanced 'Eurosclerosis'. But economic recovery in the 1980s revitalized the quest for economic integration, which also started to be seen as the means for sustaining the economic improvement so far achieved and for fostering further growth. It was through direct action, enacting the Single European Act (SEA), that unification of the market could be completed in 1992, 35 years after the Treaty of Rome was signed.

A single market is defined as 'an area without internal frontiers in which the free movement of goods, persons, services and capital is ensured' (TEEC, II, 14). Therefore, for creating a single market, two elements are necessary: (a) removal of barriers to trade of commodities, services and factors of production; and (b) an effective competition policy backed up by a common competition law rigorously enforced. In this chapter we review the progress made towards the single market before and after enactment of the Single European Act. The basic rules of competition in the Community are described in Section 3.2. The Community's estimates of the expected benefits of the single market are presented in Section 3.3. The nature and aims of Community policies are the subject of ensuing chapters of this book.

Trade liberalization

The liberalization of EU commodity trade entailed the removal of tariff and non-tariff barriers between the Community partners. Despite the progress made since starting the Community in 1958 by removing tariffs on commodity trade and adopting a common tariff on external trade, many of the original non-tariff barriers remained effective, and some new ones sprang up. Among these barriers were varying product regulations, technical and safety standards, quality controls, health and environmental requirements, standards for consumer protection and restrictive public procurement practices as well as differences in indirect taxation affecting trade between the member states. These impediments to free trade and assorted legal, fiscal and administrative hindrances kept the Community market fragmented along national lines, distorting production and trade volume and patterns. Attempts to liberalize the market were many, but the member states failed to agree on a common approach to overcome national differences. The solution to this problem came forth after the *cassis de Dijon* case, which concerned German attempts to block the import and sale of a blackcurrant liqueur produced in France on the grounds of low alcoholic content. The Court of Justice judgment stated that any product lawfully manufactured and marketed in a member state should in principle be admitted to the markets of any other member state. The Court of Justice affirmed that:

> a measure having an equivalent effect to a quantitative restriction means any measure, whether a law or regulation, administrative

practice, or act of or attributable to a public authority that is capable of hindering, directly or indirectly, actually or potentially, intra-Community trade.

(Judgment of 20 February 1979, Case 120/78, ECR 649)

Accordingly, national norms apply automatically to all other member states on the principle of *mutual recognition*. However, despite this judgment, the volume of trade within each country remained 10–20 times larger than that between countries, suggesting that the political boundaries between countries continued to be a serious obstacle to trade and that substantial room remained for policy moves to expand trade through a process of harmonization of laws and institutions. Thus it became clear that the free movement of goods in the single market should be based on three complementary elements:

- mutual recognition
- prevention of new barriers to trade
- technical harmonization of standards and specifications.

In general, the move from 'non-Europe' to an integrated Europe without frontiers requires the enforcement of a legal structure which would provide the conditions necessary for integrating the market. This objective was pursued by:

1. removing technical differences that create barriers to market unification;
2. converging fiscal barriers, such as tax systems and tax rates, by harmonization;
3. mutually recognizing national standards.

As we have seen, intra-EU commodity trade had been partially liberalized since 1968 by abolishing tariffs. Services, which account for about two-thirds of the value-added to the Community economy (Table 2.2), are also important in international trade. But despite provisions in the Treaty of Rome requiring, within a 12-year transitional period, the abolition of restrictions preventing Community nationals from establishing and providing services in other member states (TEEC, 49–55), the free flow of services remained incomplete. This was explained by the procrastination and intransigence of some members to opening national markets to competition by harmonizing different national regulations for the supply of services, such as transport, insurance and banking.

The member states had agreed the basic principles on the free movement of labour and the professions from early on. However, in practice certain obstacles (such as administrative procedures for granting residence permits, comparability and mutual recognition of qualifications and the right of establishment of the self-employed) continued to restrict the mobility of labour. A decision for the mutual recognition of higher education diplomas was enacted only in 1988, and a proposal for the mutual acceptance of vocational training qualifications was adopted even later.

Some progress was also made in liberalizing capital movements. Nevertheless, it was the completion of the internal market and the drive towards Economic and Monetary Union (EMU) that propelled the liberalization of capital markets. The free movement of capital would necessarily spur a single market for financial services, commercial banking and insurance and an integrated European stock market.

3.2 Competition rules

The treaties provide for the institution of common rules of competition in the unified European market. The principal objective of the common competition policy is to harmonize the rules governing competition among the members to ensure unification of the European market for the benefit of all – producers, traders, consumers and the economy in general. The common competition rules seek to prevent enterprises and governments from distorting trade by abusing their market power and postulate what action will be taken against anti-competitive practices which are 'incompatible with the common market'. Since 1994, the EU competition rules apply also to trade agreements concluded between the EU and other European countries (the *Europe Agreements*).

The common competition rules apply only on trade between the member states and do not, in principle, annul the national competition legislation and policy which are the prerogatives of national governments. However, if national laws differ, the Council, acting unanimously, can issue directives 'for the approximation of such laws, regulations or administrative provisions of the Member States as directly affect the establishment or functioning of the common market' (TEEC, 94). In general, the Community competition law takes precedence over national anti-trust legislation but does not replace it automatically. Where the Commission finds that an inconsistency between the legislative and administrative rules of a member state hinders competition in the Community by producing distortions, it consults the member state concerned. If settlement is not reached, the Council issues the necessary directives and takes any other appropriate measures provided for in the treaties for the elimination of the distortion (TEEC, 96). The treaties postulate that, as a rule, the national courts of the member states should implement and enforce Community law, while the Court of Justice (CJEC) should play a residual yet a guiding role (TEU, 234). Competition rules in the form of regulations are directly enforced by the Commission.

The TEU contains the basic competition law in articles 81–9 which deal with infringement of the rules of competition by agreements between enterprises (81–6) and by state aid (87–9). These provisions have been interpreted, clarified and extended by subsequent legislation and by rulings of the Court of Justice which has the power to rescind or amend any formal Commission decision. National anti-trust laws exist to varying degrees in every country. The Community anti-trust law applies to the common market: free trade overrides every other consideration. The approach followed in the Treaty is first to define the prohibited agreements and then to provide for exemptions in certain specific circumstances: *prohibition with exemptions*. Thus certain practices, such as colluding to fix prices, are prohibited, but exemptions are allowed if it can be shown that there are substantial benefits from the practice.

Collusion

Article 81 is an anti-cartel instrument. It refers to agreements (= *explicit collusion*) and concerted practices (= *implicit collusion*) between enterprises that by their restrictive nature 'may affect trade between Member States and which have as their object or effect the prevention, restriction or distortion of competition within the common market'. Normally, trade between states is interpreted to include 'all economic activity between the Member States that might prejudice the aim of the single market', and thus a variety of cases can fall within the EU rules. The general term *restrictive practices* refers to collusive arrangements between firms which ultimately aim at price-fixing for market exploitation. These agreements can be horizontal, between firms at the same level of production, or vertical, between producers and dealers. Market exploitation does not necessarily mean that the implicated firms aim only at profit maximization. It may well be that their intentions include some degree of market stability, defence of their market share and gaining competitive advantage over other, domestic or foreign, firms.

Article 81 has three parts: 81(1) contains the basic prohibitions; 81(2) declares the prohibited agreements void; and 81(3) describes the specific exemptions. The following agreements are specifically prohibited: price-fixing and market-sharing; limit or control of production, markets, technical development or investment; discrimination, collective boycotts (market prevention) and tie-in clauses (= when you purchase one good or service, you are compelled to buy another unrelated good or service). The list of restrictions in article 81 is illustrative only. Under specific conditions, other forms of collusive agreements for buying or selling goods or services may be deemed incompatible with perfect competition, for example joint purchasing, joint selling, exclusive distribution or purchasing, and so on. These prohibitions apply to vertical agreements between manufacturers and the retail sellers of their goods, and to horizontal agreements between producers of the same goods. The competition rules cover in principle all firms operating in the common market irrespective of whether they are established within it or outside it. The conditions for exemptions from these rules are specifically enumerated in article 81(3). They are that the agreement must contribute 'to improving the production or distribution of goods or to promoting technical or economic progress, while allowing consumers a fair share of the resulting benefit'.

Besides these specific conditions, council regulation 17 (1962) gave the Commission sole power to authorize exemptions from the rules for agreements with economic benefit. If an agreement satisfies the conditions of article 81(3), the Commission grants dispensation either by an individual decision or by *block exemption*, that is by an act covering a whole category of similar agreements. Block exemption has been granted to the following types of agreement which are mostly concerned with *vertical restraint*: specialization in production, exclusive distribution, exclusive purchasing, patent licensing, research and development cooperation and, temporarily, certain categories of motor vehicle distribution.

Dominant position

Article 82 is an anti-monopoly instrument. It outlaws 'Any abuse by one or more undertakings of a dominant position within the common market or in a substantial part of it . . . in so far as it may affect trade between Member States'. Dominant position here means concentration or monopoly power which enables the firm or firms to influence, by independent action as a buyer or seller, the outcome of the market. However, following the precedence of national legislation, the article does not define what degree of concentration, or size of market share, constitutes a dominant position, since this may vary from product to product. The emphasis is not on the existence of a dominant position but rather on the abuse of power, primarily in trade between member states. Dominant enterprises are prohibited from committing price or personal discrimination in their interstate purchases or sales.

Certain forms of cooperation agreements between enterprises, which are considered beneficial for the consumers by improving production, distribution, or technical progress, are deemed not to restrict competition and therefore they are exempted. Cross-border concentrations of Community interest, regardless of whether they are brought about by agreement or by takeovers, are also exempted. Following a Court of Justice decision, the Commission had until recently based its powers of control over mergers and acquisitions occasioning dominant positions on article 82. But one major drawback of article 82 as an instrument of

Box 3.1 ■ Case study 1: Dominant position

(1) In June 2001 the European Commission decided to impose a fine of €19.76 million on French tyremaker Michelin for abusing its dominant position in replacement tyres for heavy vehicles in France during most of the 1990s. After a careful and lengthy investigation, the Commission has come to the conclusion that Michelin's complex system of quantitative rebates, bonuses and other commercial practices illegally tied dealers and closed the French market to other tyre manufacturers. The infringement is all the more serious in that this is the second time that Michelin has engaged in similar anti-competitive behaviour in Europe (the first was in 1996).

Michelin is Europe's largest tyre manufacturer. According to publicly available information, Michelin has a market share in excess of 50 per cent of the market for new replacement tyres for heavy vehicles in France. As regards the French retread market, its share is even higher. None of its competitors are comparable in size. It can, therefore, be considered that Michelin holds a dominant position in France.

In setting the fine, the Commission took into account the fact that the infringement was of a serious nature, that it went on for a considerable number of years and that it had an appreciable effect on the European market. Michelin had two months to pay the fine or lodge an appeal with the European Court of First Instance.

(2) The European Commission decided in October 2001 to impose a fine of €71.825 million on DaimlerChrysler AG, one of the world's leading car manufacturers, for three infringements against article 81 of the EC Treaty. The Commission decision concerns measures adopted by DaimlerChrysler AG in order to impede parallel trade in cars and limit competition in the leasing and sale of motor vehicles. This is the fourth Commission decision imposing a fine against a car manufacturer that does not respect EC competition rules. The Commission identified three types of infringement of EC competition rules. The first one consisted of measures by DaimlerChrysler that constituted obstacles to parallel trade. The company instructed the members of its German distribution network for Mercedes passenger cars, roughly half of whom are agents, not to sell cars outside their respective territories. In a second infringement, DaimlerChrysler in Germany and Spain limited the sales of cars by Mercedes agents or dealers to independent leasing companies as long as these companies had not yet found customers ('lessees') for the cars concerned. As a consequence, it restricted the competition between its own leasing companies and independent leasing companies because the latter could not put cars in stock or benefit from rebates which were granted to all fleet owners. Finally, DaimlerChrysler participated in a price-fixing agreement in Belgium with the aim of limiting the rebates granted by its subsidiary Mercedes Belgium and the other Belgian Mercedes dealers to consumers. The amount of the fine takes into account the gravity of the infringements and their duration. The fine must also have a sufficient deterrent effect on DaimlerChrysler and other companies.

Source: http://europa.eu.int/rapid/start/cgi/

merger control was that it could be activated only after a merger has taken place; pre-emptive action by the Commission was not possible.

Mergers

A common policy on mergers empowering the Commission to block or authorize them was at last approved at the end of 1989, thus ending 16 years of protracted negotiations. What finally convinced the EU partners to sign the agreement was the expected boom in cross-frontier mergers, as companies had started to challenge the emerging single market. Under the new merger regulation, which came into force in 1990 and was amended in 1997 (regulations 4063/89 and 1310/97), the Commission is empowered to intervene to assess the compatibility of all mergers with a Community dimension of:

- combined worldwide turnover in excess of €2.5 billion;
- in each of at least three member states, combined turnover in excess of €100 million;
- in each of these three countries, the total turnover of at least two of the companies concerned in excess of €25 million;
- the aggregate Community-wide turnover of each of at least two of the undertakings concerned in excess of €100 million.

Proposed concentrations with a Community dimension must be notified to the Commission for assessment. Smaller mergers – or larger ones where each company has over two-thirds of its Community turnover in the same member state – must apply to the national monopolies and mergers authority for approval, but the Commission may intervene at the request of one of the member states involved. Large companies incorporated outside the EU, but generating at least €100 million of their annual business in the Community, are also subject to the EU merger regulation, if a merger between them threatens to distort competition on the Community market. Special rules apply for banking and financial and insurance institutions. Enactment of the new regulation means that the Commission has effectively renounced all existing powers under the competition rules over mergers below the threshold of €2.5 billion, unless explicitly asked by national governments to intervene. The agreed thresholds for intervention apply for four years, after which they may be varied by qualified majority vote in the Council of Ministers.

State aid

The importance of rules and surveillance over state aid can be seen by considering that, on average in the late 1980s, subsidies to manufacturing in the Community amounted to about 4 per cent of the value added.

Box 3.2 ■ Case study 2: Mergers and acquisitions

(1) In March 2000 the European Commission blocked Swedish truck and bus maker AB Volvo's $6.95 billion merger with rival Scania, citing the dominant share that the combined company would have: 90 per cent in the Swedish market and 75 per cent in the Nordic market, but only 30 per cent in the EU market. Volvo's top executive objected to the EU's move to block the merger on a country-specific basis, rather than looking at the European Union as a single market. The ruling amounts to a regulatory stall in the global vehicle market that has been quickly consolidated through deals such as the merger of Daimler-Benz and Chrysler last year and the cross-investment pact between Fiat and General Motors agreed the previous week. The deal would have made Volvo-Scania Europe's biggest heavy truck maker. DaimlerChrysler is Europe's largest truck maker overall with Volvo second.

(2) Following detailed investigation, the Commission decided in October 2001 to prohibit the merger of Schneider Electric and Legrand, the two main French manufacturers of electrical equipment. The merger would have considerably weakened the operation of the market in a number of countries, particularly in France, where the rivalry between the two companies has hitherto been the mainstay of competition. The Commission's investigation showed that there were substantial overlaps between the activities of Schneider and Legrand in the markets for electric switchboards (where the combined share would have been between 40 per cent and 70 per cent depending on the country); wiring accessories (where combined market shares ranged from 40 per cent to 90 per cent); and certain products for industrial use. In France, the merger gave rise to particularly serious problems over virtually the whole range of products concerned, but competition problems were also identified in Denmark, Spain, Greece, Italy, Portugal and the United Kingdom.

Source: http://europa.eu.int/rapid/start/cgi/

Therefore, one of the duties of the Commission is to ensure that in the single market no member state provides its own firms with a competitive advantage over the firms of other member states. National aids to industry are controlled by the Commission under articles 87 and 89. As a rule, all government aid to business is forbidden under article 87:

> Save as otherwise provided in this Treaty, any aid granted by a Member State or through State resources in any form whatsoever which distorts or threatens to distort competition by favouring certain undertakings or the production of certain goods shall, in so far as it affects trade between Member States, be incompatible with the common market.

The forms of aid prohibited include direct subsidies; tax exemptions; preferential interest rates; guarantees or loans on especially favourable terms; acquisition of land or buildings either gratuitously or on favourable terms; indemnities against losses and other means having equivalent effect; preferential ordering; preferential discount rates; dividend guarantees; and deferred collection of fiscal and state guarantees (Council 20.502/IV/68). However, some types of aid, such as transparent region-specific development subsidies, are exempted. Governments are compelled to report any plans to introduce new aid schemes or alter existing ones to the Commission. The Commission then decides whether these are acceptable under the Treaty. If the aid is found to be incompatible with the Treaty, the Commission has the power to ask the member state to amend or end it. For example, credit facilities which favour exporters have been terminated at Community instigation. The Commission may authorize certain forms of aid, if it considers that any distortions of competition they might cause are offset by advantages to the Community. For example, the Commission has relaxed the competition rules on state aid for companies engaged in high technology research and has granted derogations for certain less developed regions or countries, for example Greece and Portugal. Aid which does not affect trade between member states does not come under this law.

Public procurement

Progress has also been made on the issue of liberalizing public procurement which has been subject to extensive discriminatory practices. Countries favour domestic firms in the awarding of government contracts, particularly military contracts. In general, purchases of goods and services by national or local authorities and by public enterprises (energy supply, post and telecommunications, railways, etc.) cover more than 15 per cent of national economic activity in most member states and have been marked by specifications preserving them exclusively to domestic sources of supply, usually public enterprises. But such schemes closely resemble production subsidies. In the run-up to 1992, the Commission set out the main points of reform needed for completing the internal market in public procurement. They included increased transparency, rules for direct-agreement contracts, harmonization of technical standards and guaranteed means of redress. This led to several directives on public supply and works by state, regional or local authorities and legal persons governed by public law and expanded to sectors not previously covered (telecommunications, energy, water and transport). They are intended to ensure practical compliance with Community rules on contract award procedures. The opening of the public procurement market to intra-Community competition pertains to contracts of a fixed minimum threshold of expenditure. The coordination procedures of public works and public supply contracts consist of the publication of notices in the *Official Journal of the European Communities* for the invitation of tenders, the selection of which is based on identical criteria, published in advance. The Commission has also increased the monitoring of compliance with Community law. Widening the EU rules on public purchasing and works, coupled with an effective compliance regime, was expected to open up a market equal to 12 per cent of Community GDP.

Implementation

Articles 83–6 deal with procedures covering implementation of the rules of competition. In general, national courts implement the competition rules of the TEEC. However, running parallel to this option, the Commission is entrusted with powers, exercised independently of the Council, to investigate, to declare restrictive arrangements by companies or governments void, to order the parties to terminate them, and to impose fines and penalties (of up to 10 per cent of the firm's worldwide turnover) for infringement of the competition rules payable to the Community budget. However, the Commission can act only if the relevant agreement has a perceptible, actual or potential, restrictive effect on trade between member states. Restrictive agreements, whose effects are purely domestic, are a matter for the laws of the member states concerned.

Anti-competitive behaviour can be investigated by the Commission on its own initiative 'and in co-operation with the competent authorities in the members states'. Alternatively, infringements can be brought to the attention of the Commission by interested parties as a complaint. Commission decisions can be challenged at the Court of Justice, which has the power to confirm, cancel, reduce or increase fines and penalty payments or to annul Commission decisions (TEEC, 230).

In practice, the competition law has developed through experience and Court rulings, which in general have tended to support the Commission's reasoning, and thus the Commission has lost few cases. However, the Commission has been criticized for its preoccupation with excessively bureaucratic procedures which delay decisions for many years. The Court of First Instance (CFI) has been specifically established to relieve the Court of Justice of such cases as competition law, which involve complex facts needing lengthy examinations.

3.3 Benefits of the single market

Introduction

Completing the single market in the European Community entails much more than removing tariffs and quantitative restrictions on trade between the member states (the theoretical aspects of which we discussed in

Chapter 1). It also includes the abolition of all the barriers that prevent market integration by constraining competition, efficiency and the optimal utilization of resources. In this section we examine the nature of these barriers in the Community and present quantitative estimates of the economic effects of their abolition.

Market barriers

As we have seen, most tariffs and quantitative restrictions on trade between the member states were removed during the first few years of the Community. The next stage for completing the Single European Market (SEM) included 'the abolition of barriers of all kinds, harmonization of rules, approximation of legislation and tax structures, strengthening of monetary cooperation and the necessary flanking measures to encourage European firms to work together' (EC, 1985a). The Single European Act was followed by a detailed programme for attaining this objective, the Commission's White Paper *Completing the Internal Market* (Commission 1985). This paper listed 300 specific areas for action, aimed at the removal of the remaining physical, technical and fiscal barriers to the internal market by the end of 1992. Two types of barriers were distinguished: cost-increasing barriers on trade; and market entry restrictions and controls. Cost-increasing tariff and non-tariff barriers on foreign and intra-EU trade included the following:

1. *Tariffs and quantitative restrictions.* Border taxes or subsidies existed on trade of agricultural products. Production quotas were reintroduced for steel and some agricultural commodities. National quotas on imports from outside the EU (such as on textiles from less-developed countries and on cars from Japan) were still prevalent. Market-sharing arrangements (such as on air transport) were maintained and had effects similar to those of trade restrictions.
2. Different *norms and technical regulations* between the member states.
3. *Border controls.* Customs formalities and other administrative burdens causing frontier delay, such as those arising from different tax rates and tax systems, agricultural trade subsidies, different health regulations for plant and animal products, different licensing qualifications, and so on.
4. *Market-distorting subsidies* at Community and national levels. These were kept under control by the Community's competition policy, but certain markets were still distorted by price controls and specific taxes.

Market entry restrictions included:

1. *Protectionist public procurement practices.* The public authorities in the EU countries granted preferential treatment to domestic suppliers of

goods and services. This was done in many ways, including procedures through which bids were invited and contracts were awarded, most often to public enterprises.

2. *Differing regulation of services.* The service industries, such as transport (air, freight) and especially finance (banking, insurance, stock markets, etc.), were subject to national regulations. Restrictions existed on the freedom to engage in certain service transactions, or to set up certain service activities in other Community countries.

3. *Controls on the movement of capital.* Eight of the twelve EU countries maintained some degree of control over capital flows to or from other member states.

4. *Lack of a common legal framework for business.* Diverging national laws and regulations caused complications in cross-border business activity involving mergers, joint ventures, patents, copyrights, and so on.

These barriers segmented the European markets along national lines, exposing their smallness which caused weak competitiveness and encouraged oligopolistic structures. Evidence of this was the observed large price difference between countries. Across countries in 1985, the average before-tax price variation from the EU mean price was 15.2 per cent for consumer goods and 12.4 per cent for capital equipment. Much wider were the price differences in the service sectors: 28 per cent in road and rail transport, 42 per cent in electrical repairs and 50 per cent in telephone and telegram services. Many of these differences were sustained by the walls of barriers which prevented interstate trade. It was predicted, therefore, that price convergence by free arbitrage across countries would lower the average price level. Market integration offered great potential for the rationalization of production and distribution, leading to improvements in productivity and reductions in cost and prices.

Effects of barrier removal

The removal of internal market barriers and the harmonization of national rules and regulations were expected to bring about cost reductions from the following:

1. strengthened competition, leading to greater allocative efficiency;
2. economies of scale from optimizing the size of production units and enterprises;
3. specialization of production and trade according to comparative advantage;
4. improved access to the flow of innovation, new processes and new products.

These cost reductions were expected to lead to reallocation of production and trade across the EU, improved efficiency and increased competitiveness, leading to a better performance in international trade.

The quantitative evaluation of these effects and of the overall economic gain from completing the internal market is complex and inexact. Moreover, completion of the internal market was to be gradual and, as the necessary measures were implemented through time, some effects would occur instantly while others would be delayed. Furthermore, any quantification is subject to conjectures about long-term economic conditions in the EU and the rest of the world and depends on several assumptions about policy considerations. For this reason, the estimation of the effects is based on the assumption that all changes are completed instantaneously. Therefore, all estimates of this nature are no more than an illustration and a rough approximation of orders of magnitude.

The quantitative estimates presented in the following are those made by the EU (Emerson et al., 1988). Two types of effects were distinguished:

1. *'Barrier removal' effects* which are the static welfare effects of reducing the price differences between member states caused by the tariff and non-tariff barriers listed above.
2. *'Integration' effects* which are the quasi-dynamic effects of increased technical efficiency (or reduced X-inefficiency stemming from a failure to maximize), erosion of oligopoly profits and increased consumer choice. All these effects come about from improved market access leading to greater market integration and increased competition, as listed above.

The genuine dynamic effects, which arise from technical progress and from improved allocation of capital, labour and production in the integrated market that lead to specialization according to comparative advantage, are not easily quantifiable and the EU did not attempt to estimate them.

Static effects

The static effects were estimated by partial equilibrium analysis, separately for each barrier and for each economic sector. The sum of these effects is the total static effect of market liberalization. A drawback of this technique is that it ignores the extent to which the barriers overlap and economic sectors are interconnected. Therefore, no account was taken of spillover and interactive reactions between sectors which occur as barriers are removed and relative prices change, nor of the effects of integration on factor prices. If the necessary information is available, all these effects can be estimated by general equilibrium analysis.

The method of estimating the costs of tariff and non-tariff regulatory barriers is basically that of the consumer and producer surplus as employed in calculating trade creation and trade diversion in customs unions (described in Chapter 1). The analysis is based on the following assumptions:

1. The export supply curve is not perfectly elastic, so if a member state increases its demand for imports the supply price will rise.
2. Goods and services may be imported from both other Community countries and the rest of the world.
3. Completing the internal market removes only the non-tariff barriers between the Community countries while the common external tariff (CET) and non-tariff barriers remain intact against imports from the rest of the world.

Economies of scale

Removing cost-increasing trade barriers and production and market distortions has an impact effect and a delayed effect. The impact effect arises from reducing economic rents (wages and profits) and improving efficiency after abolishing protection. The delayed effects will come about from restructuring production, investing in new technology and exploiting economies of scale. Scale economies will be most probable and more significant in industries that before barrier removal operated in national markets which were imperfectly competitive and not large enough to accommodate optimum size plants for reaching minimum cost and maximum efficiency. The effects will be much larger if, in the member states, protection, different national standards and diverse technical specifications have contributed to development of non-competitive markets. If that is the case, then there are barriers both to entry of firms in industries and to trade. Therefore, if the domestic market is small, exports cannot provide an outlet for reaching an efficient scale of production, and the pro-competitive effects of economic integration will be large.

At the customs union level, both internal and external economies of scale may have positive effects on total output. External economies of scale will occur at the level of the industry from technological spillovers which are expected to increase the productivity of one firm when the output of other firms rises. In general, market integration provides the opportunity for greater specialization and efficiency leading to rising output. Competition in the integrated market will, of course, oust the less efficient firms and even industries, causing transient waste and unemployment. But this is an inevitable outcome of moving towards optimal reallocation of resources across the EU, which in the longer run will benefit the member states by increasing output, employment and welfare.

The costs of customs formalities, different technical regulations, entry restrictions, public procurement and X-inefficiency were estimated by industry case studies and market research. Estimates were also made of the effects of removing the remaining controls on capital flows and unifying the financial markets under the European Monetary System (EMS).

Methodology

The total microeconomic impact of fully integrating the Community market was calculated by two methods under two different assumptions:

1. The *price-convergence approach* which takes no account of the response of production to rising demand, stimulated by price reductions, or cost reductions from economies of scale.
2. The *welfare-gains approach* which, besides the secondary demand effects, considers losses that might be suffered by some currently protected producers.

The microeconomic partial-equilibrium estimates of direct and induced effects were supplemented by macroeconomic analysis, which focused on the repercussions of the single market on major components of GDP, taking into account intersectoral relationships and interdependencies, such as multipliers and accelerators, income distribution, price competitiveness, inflation mechanisms, capital accumulation and growth potential. The effects were calculated under two different assumptions: first, that in the run-up to the single market macroeconomic policy would remain passive; and, second, that active macroeconomic policy would exploit the new opportunities as they emerged from liberalizing the market.

Abolishing internal frontiers may, however, cause transient problems of adaptation to the dynamics of competition, reallocation of production and loss of employment as industry adjusts to the new conditions. But it is also expected that, as the restructuring process of production goes on and real incomes rise, many new jobs will be created, increasing total employment in the medium and long term.

Results

Taking account of all these changes, the potential economic impact of the completion of the internal market was estimated in the Cecchini Report (1988). Using a microeconomic approach the report found welfare gains in the range of 2.5 to 6.5 per cent of Community GDP (Figure 3.1, the *Cecchini effect*). Macroeconomic simulations showed that these gains imply a medium-term increase in GDP of 4.5 per cent, a

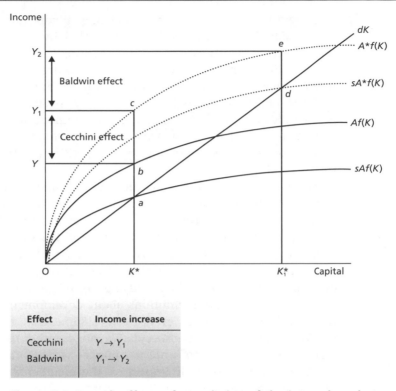

Effect	Income increase
Cecchini	$Y \rightarrow Y_1$
Baldwin	$Y_1 \rightarrow Y_2$

Figure 3.1 **Growth effects of completion of the internal market**

decrease in the price level of 6 per cent and an increase in employment of 1.5 per cent, which is equal to almost two million jobs. However, by combining market liberalization measures with the relaxation of economic constraints – improved public and external balances and reduced inflationary pressures – the GDP gain could be 7 per cent and an extra five million jobs created.

Later studies have shown that the Commission's estimates might have been on the low side. For example, they would be higher if before 1992 most markets in the member states of the Community were oligopolistic. Two characteristics found in the Community markets support this hypothesis: (a) prices for the same commodities (and services) differed significantly between states; and (b) there was widespread market segmentation by regulations and other institutional means which allowed oligopolistic price discrimination by preventing consumers from buying from the cheapest source of supply. The single market objective was not confined to just removing trade barriers. It was a general programme of deregulation to promote competition in a genuinely unified market by removing the sources of distortions and price divergence between different national markets. Therefore, the pro-competitive welfare benefit of integrating the market and abolishing oligopolistic practices could exceed significantly the estimates presented by the Community. The total effect would consist of price reductions from strengthening competition, increasing product variety and reducing profits. It is, of course, possible that under these circumstances the number of firms in the industry would drop through exit and mergers. But more concentration in an industry, which is observing the competition law of the single market, may lead to larger firms and cost reductions from increasing returns to scale, thus improving the competitive position of EU firms in the international markets.

Against this optimistic conclusion, critics argued that 'the Commission's estimates, for obvious political reasons, err on the high side. Therefore, they should be identified with the *potential* rather than the *realistic* outcome of the internal market which could fall short of the predicted effect' (Peck, 1989). The Commission's estimates were indeed presented as an attempt to measure the costs of not having a single market, thus divulging *'information on the potential gains'* (Commission 1988a, p. 155) under certain critical assumptions about developments in the EU and the world economy. But even if we assume that the Commission's numerical estimates denote speculative ranges rather than accurate point predictions, enlarging the internal market would undoubtedly have a significant macroeconomic impact on the member states and, by their extensive international trade links, on the rest of the world. Since the effects are estimates derived from comparisons with a counterfactual theoretical construct and not a prediction which can be corroborated *ex post*, the outcome of EU market integration can never be established precisely. Therefore, the general conclusion should be that the net overall effect of European market integration is likely to be positive.

Allocation effects

The estimated gains from completing the internal market are aggregates for the Community as a whole. The study offered no quantitative estimates of their distribution among the countries in the Community. It stated, however, that all the member states of the Community, irrespective of existing inequalities and regional imbalances, must and should benefit from the internal market programme. But it anticipated that proportionally larger gains will emerge in countries which in the past protected their domestic market with relatively high barriers and so developed industries dominated by small uncompetitive firms. Similarly, lower-wage countries will gain if they can attract new investment. Thus there is a possibility that, with the removal of trade barriers, the low-wage southern countries of the Community may become attractive locations of production (Neven, 1990). They will have more chances to realize these gains if they can supply a workforce possessing the necessary skills to match the productivity performance of the high-wage countries of the Community. But against this prediction of high gains it can be countered that the southern European countries are relatively the least developed members of the Community, requiring to do much 'catching up' to compete effectively in the internal market. Therefore, with the removal of obstacles to factor relocation and the possible concentration of investment and production in more privileged regions, they may as well suffer large losses before adjusting to the new competitive environment of the single market.

The next question concerns the effects of the single market on the rest of Europe and the world. The agreement reached in 1991 to form the European Economic Area (EEA) comprising the EU and EFTA countries created a free trade zone, which went some way towards extending the single market over a large part of Europe (which happened more decisively after three members of the EFTA joined the EU in 1995). If market integration would yield the predicted improvements in economic performance, then the rising EU income could induce more imports and thus stimulate higher levels of economic activity in the rest of the world. Therefore, the benefits of 1992 were expected to be a bigger boost to world trade by the EU becoming more open, so that the overall outcome of the single market would be trade creation. The Community stated that it 'will seek a greater liberalization of international trade: the 1992 Europe will not be a fortress Europe but a partnership Europe'. Therefore, increasing economic activity in the Community would provide opportunities for more foreign trade and for sharing the benefits of market integration within and outside the European Union.

Growth effects

Completing the internal market by a one-off removal of barriers will lead to a one-off static gain of a higher level of output and employment, spread over several years. Time is a key element in securing this gain. But a one-off efficiency gain does not necessarily change the dynamic effects and the rate of economic growth. It is, however, possible that the static benefit of market integration could exert a positive influence on growth by generating extra savings and investment and increasing the rate of capital accumulation, technical innovation and productivity. The medium-run growth effects of a one-off rise in investment and increasing returns to scale have been estimated to be at least as large as the static effects, giving an overall (static + medium-term) welfare gain from completing the internal market equal to 15.3 per cent of GDP (Baldwin, 1989), approximately equal to doubling the static efficiency gains (Figure 3.1, the *Baldwin effect*). But, if the partners in the Community take on the challenge to exploit scale economies and technological spillovers, the one-off market enlargement effects could turn into a permanent sustainable increase in the growth rate of the Community equal to an additional 1 per cent (Baldwin, 1989). If we consider that during the period 1984–9 the annual growth rate of Community GDP at constant prices was 3.1 per cent, the long-run effect of such an increase in the rate of growth will be much larger than the estimated static effects. Although these estimates rest on specific assumptions and are by their nature imprecise and indicate the potential rather than the expected effects of the internal market, they suggest that the most important impact of 1992 may well be its dynamic effect on growth, not the static effects of resource allocation.

Evaluation

The *ex post* verification of these predictions is, of course, a different story because in the intervening years from 1985, when the Single Market Programme (SMP) started, to 1992, when it ended, many conditions changed both in the EU countries and in the outside world. Nevertheless, the European Commission did undertake this investigation. The results showed that in 1994 the EU GDP was 1.1–1.5 per cent above the level that would have prevailed in the absence of the SMP, with 600,000 additional employment posts generated. The least developed member states (E, GR, IRL and P) benefited from the SMP relatively more than the developed member states (Commission, 1996a).

3.4 Conclusions

The Community has instituted a common competition law to safeguard the liberalization of its enlarged market. Enactment of the Single European Act (SEA) in 1985 also led to completion of the internal EU market in 1992. The Commission and independent observers estimated the gains from the single market which consist of the static effects of increases in potential income with given endowments of labour and capital and the dynamic effects of increases over time of the capital stock in response to efficiency gains. Although the evaluation of these effects is difficult and inexact, the prediction is that, under specific conditions, the economic effect of the completion of the EU internal market will be large.

Actually, 1992 showed the first phase of completion of the single market. As we will see (in Chapter 6), it took the EU another ten years to complete the second phase of the single market by monetary unification.

Box 3.3 ■ The human cost of 'non-Europe'

The Commission (1988a, 1988b) estimated the economic 'Costs of Non-Europe'. But the costs of non-Europe extend beyond economics. The importance of a united Europe is much more than an economic gain, whatever its size. It is about the devastations and the waste of millions of lives in Europe's past, and about a better future. The two internecine World Wars of the twentieth century were started by European countries, and it was Europe that paid a high price for them:

European losses during two World Wars (estimates)

	First World War	Second World War
Military	8 427 000	14 362 000
Civilian		27 078 000

In 1914 Europe's power and prestige were unrivaled: Europeans led the field in almost any sphere one cared to mention – science, culture, economics, fashion. Through their colonial empires and trading companies, European powers dominated the globe. By 1945, almost all had been lost: the Europeans had fought each other to the point of utter exhaustion. (Davies, 1996, p. 899)

It was after the Second World War, which 'reduced much of Europe and Asia to rubble, exhausted national exchequers, destroyed industries, and left millions homeless or even stateless, [whereas] America was intact' (Bryson, 1994, p. 399) and emerged as the unchallenged world economic leader, that the European nations realized it was better to attempt to resolve their differences around a table rather than on the battlefield.

Questions

1. Consider the following quotation: 'Many expect – or at least hope – that the removal of remaining barriers to movements of goods, services, people and capital within the EU will not only provide a one-off boost to EU output but will set EU incomes on a permanently higher growth path.'
   (a) What are the 'one-off effects' and the probable 'growth effects' of the single market?
   (b) How have they been estimated?
   (c) What criticisms have been directed against these estimates?
2. Analyse the effects of the Single European Market (SEM) for a firm experiencing increasing returns to scale.
3. What is the 'growth effect' of the SEM and under what specific conditions could it be realized?

4. 'Competition policies are set against monopolies in general. But monopolies can be beneficial for the consumers, and this fact must be taken into account.'
   (a) Under what conditions can monopolies be beneficial for the consumers?
   (b) Has EU legislation taken account of this possibility?

Further reading

For a lucid and informative survey of EU competition law see Cini and McGovan (1998). The EU's massive study of the 'Costs of Non-Europe' (Commission, 1988a, 1988b) is a detailed multi-volume investigation of the effects of the single market. The results of this study are summarized in two general reports, Cecchini (1988) and Emerson et al. (1988). For the probable effects of the single market on growth see Baldwin (1989, 1992). Commission (1996b) presents the results of the *ex post* calculations of the single market effects.

Web guide

- 'One-stop shop' for EU law, treaties etc. is available at www.europa.eu.int/eur.lex
- For competition policy, see www.europa.int/pol/index_en.htm

  http://europa.eu.int/comm/dgs/competition/index_en.htm

  http://www.eubusiness.com/competit/index.htm

The budget of the European Communities

4

The *general budget* of the European Community is an account of revenues and expenditures. The budget is relatively small and the narrowness of structure results in unequal *net contributions* among the member states, which in the past caused disputes that threatened to halt the progress of European integration. Although a series of reforms has temporarily settled the Community finances, monetary unification and the imminent accession of lower-income central and eastern European countries mean that the budget will soon require further restructuring and expansion.

4.1 Introduction

As we have seen, the EU objective is integration and enlargement of the market, with mainly market-determined solutions to economic problems. The emphasis on the market mechanism does not mean that the EU would abstain from using economic policies. On the contrary, integration requires the active participation of the central authority in policy-making, particularly when the objective of a common policy is a Community target, and the process of integration involves costs or brings benefits which must be shared among the participating countries. One of the most important instruments of national economic policy is the budget. The budget is also a major instrument of economic policy in regional economic associations and in the EU. In the following we examine the principles governing budgetary policy and the structure and objectives of the Community budget.

The budget is an estimate of government revenues and expenditures for the period of a financial year. In general, the budget is a statement of the objectives of the government in power and reflects the extent of public activity in the economy. Analysis of the structure of the budget is the study of the following:

1. the *origin* of government financial resources. The taxation of personal and corporate incomes and of expenditure is usually the most important source of government revenue.
2. the *destination* of these resources. This is determined by government expenditure on direct consumption and investment and on transfer payments to persons and firms.
3. the *effects* of the composition of revenues and expenditures and of the overall position of the budget: the budget *surplus* or *deficit*.

In any financial year, the government is not constrained in its spending by its income. It can borrow from domestic or foreign sources and it can levy more taxes. Normally, the government has a real choice of whether to balance its budget or run a deficit or surplus. This choice is based on the objectives of the government and on consideration of the benefits and costs of its policies. This directs us to the question of the proper role of the government in the economy.

In general three approaches to the question of the degree of government involvement in economic affairs can be discerned, which are based on concepts partly theoretical and partly ideological and political:

1. The *minimum*: government action is required only when the private sector cannot do the job. This is the traditional view of neutrality according to which the state should refrain from any interference with the market economy and therefore only a limited number of tasks should be assigned to it.
2. The *medium*: the government must play an active role by interventionist economic policy. The argument here is that the market mechanism is not always able to attain the community's social goals and therefore state intervention is necessary. In particular, the market mechanism may not lead to an optimal allocation of society's resources (the *allocation problem*) or it may fail to achieve a distribution of income satisfying some generally accepted standards of equity (the *distribution problem*). Similarly, the price mechanism may not ensure full employment with external and internal stability and a satisfactory rate of economic growth (the *stabilization problem*). Therefore, state interference for resolving these problems is often not only acceptable but also desirable.
3. The *maximum*: the government plays the main role in the economy – the socialist approach. The most active policy for the government occurs when the state owns the means of production and undertakes most of the functions which the private sector performs in market economies.

Under the first approach, the government is required to operate in the market economy only as a provider of collective or public goods, and to intervene only in the case of market failure. The distinguishing characteristic of public goods is the indivisibility of their services among persons: they are supplied to a group of people rather than personally and cannot be withheld from individuals who refuse to pay for them (the free-riders). Defence, law and order, foreign policy and environmental control are such goods. Market failure occurs when there is divergence between private and social costs or benefits, causing external economies or diseconomies. An example of external economies is education which benefits not only the individual but also the society in which the educated individual lives and works. An external diseconomy is pollution. The government is also expected to intervene in natural monopolies – industries in which technical factors preclude the efficient existence of more than one producer, such as public utilities (electricity, gas, water and railways, the supply of which requires a network).

A more active role for the government includes the exercise of fiscal and monetary policy to prevent depression and inflation, to induce investment and growth, and to redistribute income by welfare and social security policies. In contrast to the private sector, where decisions are made through the market mechanism, in the public sector decisions are reached through the political process.

In general, different budgetary measures (taxation and expenditure policies and the size of the budget surplus or deficit) have a different incidence on the economy as a whole and on its constituent sectors (households and firms; production, consumption, investment, balance of payments, etc.). As a rule, there are certain commonly invoked criteria of organizing a fiscal system: that is, deciding the tax and expenditure structure of a country. These criteria entail aspects of *equity* and *efficiency*. Fiscal equity, or fairness, is the principle of equal treatment for equally placed economic agents (individuals or firms) for the allocation of burdens or the distribution of benefits (*horizontal equity*), and proper division of the budgetary burden according to ability to pay (*vertical equity*). Economic efficiency concerns the allocation of resources and the goal of optimality, and is based on the rule that the operations of the public sector should cause the least price distortion in the market.

While some criteria raise no conflict-of-interest issues, others produce sharp differences of opinion among different social and economic groups. Thus the budget mirrors the ideology and the political, economic and social aims of the government in power. For the economists, the budget is the fiscal policy instrument which is used by the government to pursue economic objectives relating to:

- the allocation of resources between public and private uses, consumption and investment, and geographic regions;
- the distribution of income;
- stabilization;
- economic growth.

Ultimately, these objectives form a part of the more general target of the economic policy of the government – the improvement in social welfare.

In general, the relative importance of the budget as an instrument of policy is to be found in the following:

1. the *size* of the budget: whether it is large or small with reference to national income;
2. the *structure* of the budget: the composition of its credit and debit sides;
3. the *net position* of the budget: whether it shows an overall surplus or a deficit;
4. the *incidence* of the budget: the net transfers from the rest of the country to particular industries, regions or population groups.

4.2 General characteristics of the EU budget

Background

One of the basic aims of the Treaty of Rome (TEEC) was 'to establish the foundations for an ever closer union among the European peoples': an economic and political union rather than another international organization. To reach this objective, the member states must gradually confer on the Community certain functions and the powers to operate them. These will be the common targets which will be pursued by common policies at costs shared by all the participants. Therefore, under the terms of the Treaty of Rome, the Commission was given an operational budget and the task of administering the Social Fund and the Agricultural Fund. The ECSC (Treaty of Paris, 1951) and the Euratom (Treaty of Rome, 1958) also started with their own budgets, financed by national contributions. Following the 'Merger Treaty' (1967), the budgets of the three communities were brought together in a single budget, the general budget of the European Communities.

Initially, the budget consisted of financial resources made available, and expenditures allocated, according to decisions taken in common by the contracting parties. The budget was specific with revenues derived from fixed financial contributions by the member states on an agreed scale, and expenditures directed to clearly specified activities. An extra constraint was (and still is) that 'the revenue and expenditure shown in the budget shall be in balance' (TEEC, 268). Thus, unlike national budgets, deficits, financed by borrowing, are not allowed. So this budget was not much different from the budgets of other international organizations, which usually have more moderate aims than those of the EU.

To pursue successfully the objective of economic integration by common policies, the authority of the economic union needs the power to choose what revenues to collect and how to spend them: that is, its own budget. Just as in a federation of states, community financing means the transfer of resources from the national to a common supranational level. In the EU, the target of this process is to provide the Community with resources which would be used in operational activities geared to integrate different policies of different countries and peoples. Therefore, although in political terms the EU is not a federation of states, it has specific objectives which, in many respects, are similar to those of federations and can be realized in common only by access to an adequate central budget. But progress in this direction has been slow.

Under the terms originally agreed, the Council decided in 1970 to replace gradually the direct contributions of member states to the budget by revenues accruing to it automatically from suitably allocated revenue sources. An advantage of a budget 'financed wholly from own resources' (TEEC, 269) is that the Commission has gained a certain degree of power by loosening its financial dependence on the member states which cannot default on payment, but made sure that the sources of revenue and the direction of expenditure are strictly kept within predetermined narrow margins. As a result, at the current phase of European integration the budget is still based on narrow foundations and remains relatively insignificant in size.

To a large extent, the budget of the EU is still functioning as an account of revenues from specific resources and expenditures for specific purposes, in *ex post* balance as required by the treaty. But if the ultimate policy objective of the contracting parties is to establish a European political and economic union, the present small budget cannot function as an effective policy instrument. That role can be played only by a larger, more ambitious, and independent central budget, which could progressively absorb many of the functions currently coming under the jurisdiction of the national budgets, just as in fiscal federations. However, fiscal federalism is not one of the explicit objectives of the Community.

The current state of the EU budget thus reflects the stage and state of economic integration in Europe. There is so far no question about using this budget as an instrument for pursuing Community policies at large, other than those explicitly specified in the treaties. For example, with integration of monetary policy under European Monetary Union (EMU, discussed in Chapter 6), direct cooperation between the member states is necessarily increasing, but general macroeconomic policy is still considered to be the prerogative and responsibility of the national governments.

Budgetary procedure

The budget, which is denominated in euros, is drawn up annually for a calendar year. Supplementary budgets are added during the year, whenever necessary. Under the treaty, the Council and the European Parliament are the 'budgetary authority' and have joint responsibility for deciding the Community budget on the basis of proposals from the Commission. The Interinstitutional Agreement on budgetary discipline and improvement of the budgetary procedure (1993) sets out the way the three institutions will exercise their responsibilities in accordance with the TEEC (268–80), respecting the revenue ceilings which are laid down in the own resources decision. In preparing and adopting the budget, the three institutions adhere to the following procedure and 'pragmatic timetable':

1. From estimates submitted by five Community institutions (the Council, the Commission, the Parliament, the Court of Justice and the Economic and Social Committee), the Commission prepares the preliminary draft budget which it presents to the budgetary authority by 15 June.
2. The Council, acting by a qualified majority, prepares the draft budget and forwards it to the Parliament for a first reading by 15 September.
3. The Parliament amends (non-compulsory expenditure), proposes modifications (compulsory expenditure) or rejects the draft budget and returns it to the Council for a second reading and changes.
4. The Council acts on the proposed amendments and modifications and returns the draft budget to the Parliament for a second reading by 22 November.
5. The Parliament declares that it adopts the budget by the end of December or rejects it as a whole and requests submission of a new draft.

The final adoption of the budget is the prerogative of the President of the European Parliament. Although 80 per cent of expenditure is managed by authorities within the member states, the Commission has overall responsibility for implementing the budget, 'having regard to the principle of sound financial management', and is responsible to the European Parliament for making certain that the budget is effected as voted (TEEC, 274).

After the end of the budgetary year, a sixth Community institution, the Court of Auditors, scrutinizes all Community revenue and expenditure accounts and decides whether financial management has been sound and regular. Finally, after the Parliament has examined the accounts, deliberated on the report of the Court of Auditors and considered the recommendations of the Council, it grants *parliamentary discharge*, endorsing the Commission's management of Community funds.

This is a simplified version of a complex procedure which often causes delays in approving the budget beyond the completion deadline (usually December). In the past, the complications often arose from the classification of expenditure as compulsory or non-compulsory. Compulsory is 'expenditure necessarily resulting from this Treaty or from acts adopted in accordance therewith' (TEEC, 272). This vague definition caused many demarcation disputes between the Council and the Parliament, which has the power to decide only the non-compulsory expenditure, and only within pre-specified limits, while the Council has 'the last word' on compulsory expenditure. Finally, the matter was settled by the Interinstitutional Agreement (1993) which clarified the role of each institution in the budgetary procedure.

4.3 Structure of the general budget

In 2000 the general budget was €89 590 million (*payment appropriations*, in 1999 prices). This is equal to about 1.2 per cent of EU GNP. The national budgets of the EU member states average more than 40 per cent of their GNP. Although comparisons between the EU budget and national budgets are inappropriate, because the former does not include expenditures for defence, education, health, etc., there is no doubt that the EU budget is small. Moreover, its narrow structure of revenues and expenditures affects its incidence on member states. For example, the budget has often caused unplanned inter-country income redistribution, which since the 1970s has propelled the Community into acrimonious crises that threatened to slow down European integration. These problems arise from the members' net contribution, the difference between each country's contribution to and payment from the budget. For some member states (notably the UK) the net contribution was regularly positive and 'excessive' relative to their prosperity. This inequity was caused by aspects of the budgetary process which originated from both the revenue and the expenditure sides of the budget. In the next two sections we examine the structure of the budget and briefly review the crises and reforms.

Budgetary revenues and expenditures

At the beginning of the 1980s, when the crisis reached its peak, the EU budget was financed by its 'own resources' which consisted of: (a) customs duties, agricultural levies and sugar levies on imports from non-EU countries; and (b) the members' contribution based on value added tax

(VAT). This is based on hypothetical revenues calculated by applying a notional VAT rate of 1 per cent – raised to 1.4 per cent in 1985 – to a notional common VAT base (range of goods and services), and it is unrelated to the actual VAT system. As an indirect tax, VAT is regressive and does not reflect ability to pay. In certain cases, therefore, the reliance on a common VAT base caused an imbalance between a member's high contribution to the budget and relatively low prosperity (e.g. the UK).

The budgetary expenditure on Community policies was (and still is) dominated by a few items which caused different distributional effects among the partners: (a) expenditure on the Common Agricultural Policy (CAP), which until the mid-1980s accounted for more than two-thirds of the total and went mostly to member states with relatively large surpluses of heavily subsidized agricultural commodities (e.g. Denmark, while Germany and the UK were net importers of agricultural products and thus low recipients of CAP spending); and (b) the 'structural funds' for regional development and social policy, which accounted for less than 20 per cent of the total and, by being thinly spread among the member states, were unable to balance the allocation of expenditure. The excessive weight of farm spending in total expenditure was the main cause of the problem faced by the UK, which paid according to its relative prosperity but received according to its relatively insignificant agricultural sector. Therefore, the UK government asked for a large cut to its contribution. In an attempt to reach agreement, the Community linked the budget debate with cuts in CAP expenditure by setting up production targets which, if exceeded, were subject to a 'co-responsibility levy' paid by the producers. But this device did not solve the budgetary problem. After strong demands by the UK government, the 1984 European Council at Fontainebleau decided that any member state which was bearing excessive budgetary costs in relation to its relative prosperity would benefit from a correction. On this basis, the UK's VAT contributions are abated by two-thirds of its net contribution to the EU budget. The Council did not change the 'own resources' rules but simply decided that the cost of the UK abatement should fall on the other member states, with the largest net contributor to the budget, Germany, paying the most.

Reforms

This arrangement dealt with some of the problems but left the budget still structurally unsound. Since the budget is drawn up each December, its largest item of expenditure, for the CAP, is only a guestimate subject to a wide margin of error (due to fluctuations in the volume of output, which is produced later in the year, and the uncertainty of international prices). As a result, deficits often developed between planned and actual compulsory expenditures which the member states had to finance by extra emergency contributions during the financial year. These caused resentment and delays in both payments and receipts from the annual budget. After a long period of staggering from one financial crisis to another, the commitment to complete the single market programme by 1992 and to move towards EMU finally compelled the Community to implement the long overdue radical overhaul of Community finances. This was based on the proposal that an upper limit should be placed on the amount the Community can raise from member states. The own resources ceiling was set to 1.21 per cent of GNP in 1995, and raised in stages to 1.27 per cent of GNP in 1999. The uniform VAT rate was gradually reduced from 1.4 per cent to 1 per cent in 1999 with the VAT base capped at 50 per cent of GNP. In practice, these reforms meant that in addition to the 'traditional own resources' comprising agricultural levies (now replaced by fixed tariffs), sugar levies and customs duties, and the 'third resource' based on VAT, a new topping up 'fourth resource' was introduced, based on members' GNP and thus reflecting each country's 'relative wealth and income of its citizens'. As a result the members' contributions to the budget have become more equitable. Whereas in 1992 the VAT-based resource represented 61.6 per cent of the total revenues, in 1998 it went down to 41 per cent and is set to drop to about 33 per cent with a corresponding increase of the GNP-based resource (which reached 43 per cent in 1998). The Community also decided to restructure the expenditure side of the budget by (i) increasing expenditure by about 22 per cent in real terms during 1993–9 to help promote 'economic and social cohesion' between the EU member states and regions for accelerated progress towards EMU; and (ii) increasing the allocation of funds to the Structural Funds by 40 per cent and to agriculture by 9 per cent in real terms. The agreement concerning the UK rebate was left intact. These developments changed the structure and the size of the general budget with the CAP share of expenditure declining to 46 per cent and that of the Structural Funds increasing to 32 per cent.

But by 1998 the remodelled budget continued to create imbalances in 'net positions' by shifting the inequities from country to country, and

Box 4.1 ■ Cost of the EU

The European Commission's report yesterday on the financial contributions of member states is a response to two specific problems. First, the UK's special rebate, negotiated by Lady Thatcher in 1984, is becoming anomalous. Second, plans to admit poorer countries into membership will put the present system under extra strain.

Of these, the special rebate is the more difficult. The main justifications for it were that the UK paid in substantially more than it received from the EU and that it was poorer than its neighbours. But now the UK's national income per head is about equal to the EU average and will be above average after enlargement. Moreover, four other countries have budget deficits with the EU greater than that of the UK as a proportion of their gross domestic products. Naturally, they want similar rebates, albeit on a less generous formula.

But if Germany, the Netherlands, Austria and Sweden claim refunds, the burden on the remaining countries would rise significantly. Since the rules cannot be changed without a unanimous vote, a long and unedifying session of horse trading can be expected. This will inevitably widen to include disputes about enlargement.

Before this starts, it would be well to consider a few simple principles suggested by the Commission's report. The most important is that the method of financing the EU should be simple, transparent and fair. The present system, which increasingly relies on a VAT levy and payments proportional to countries' GDP, broadly meets the fairness criterion. It might be improved, perhaps, by putting more emphasis on a VAT levy, but complicated formulae for making rich countries pay proportionately more should be resisted. They would be obscure and open to endless dispute.

The main difficulties arise on the expenditure side, particularly from anomalies created by the common agricultural policy. Root and branch reform must be the long-term aim. Meanwhile, the Commission suggests a more modest adjustment. The EU's contribution to CAP income support would be reduced from 100 per cent to perhaps 75 per cent, with members paying the balance to their producers. This would not get rid of budget anomalies and economic distortions, but it could help to reduce them. It might also curb the desire to invent a higher mathematics of special rebates, and help to moderate the appetite for CAP handouts.

These are the minimum conditions for successful enlargement, and the Commission's proposals are a signpost towards a sensible path.

Financial Times, 8 October 1998

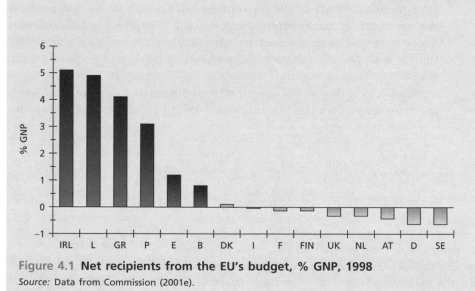

Figure 4.1 Net recipients from the EU's budget, % GNP, 1998
Source: Data from Commission (2001e).

the Commission had to admit that 'the budgetary imbalance of the UK is no longer unique' but extended to Germany, the Netherlands, Sweden and Austria, which have budget deficits with the EU greater than that of the UK as a proportion of their GNP so that they, naturally, wanted similar rebates. But a generalized system of abatements based on the current UK rebates would be very costly for the budget. The Berlin European Council (1999) therefore decided, first, to reduce the shares of these four countries in the financing of the UK correction to 25 per cent of its normal value; second, that any windfall gains to the UK, caused by enlargement or other future events, would be neutralized; third, that the maximum call-in rate for the VAT resource would be cut to 0.75 per cent in 2002 and 2003 and to 0.50 per cent in 2004. Therefore, by 2004 the largest contributions to the budget will be calculated as a proportion of GNP.

At the moment the Community finances are settled. But the forthcoming accession of central and eastern European countries, the completion of EMU, and other political and economic developments in Europe and in the rest of the world confirm that the size and the structure of the budget are inadequate for the role the EU is expected to play and, therefore, further reforms and a fairer system of corrections will be necessary in the near future.

4.4 The financial perspective, 2000–6

Community expenditure is constrained by a framework covering a number of years, known as *the financial perspective*, which forms part of the Interinstitutional Agreement. The financial perspective for the period 2000–6 sets out annual ceilings for seven categories of expenditure:

1 agriculture, for the CAP and rural development;
2 structural operations, for the Structural Funds (regional and social) and the Cohesion Fund;
3 internal policies, such as research, energy, and transport;
4 external operations, mostly development and humanitarian aid to associate and other countries;
5. administration;
6. reserves (monetary, emergency aid, and loan guarantee);
7. pre-accession aid, for agriculture, structural instruments, and the PHARE programme for applicant countries.

Figure 4.2 shows the composition of the revenue and expenditure sides of the general budget in 2002. In the revenue side, the GNP resource, which is the dominant one since 1998, and the VAT resource account

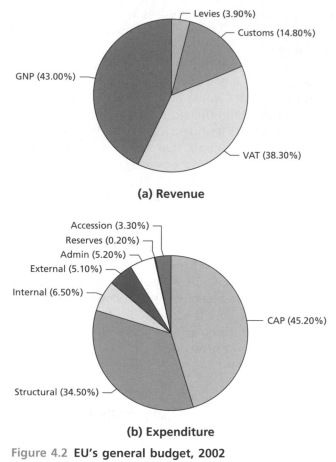

(a) Revenue

(b) Expenditure

Figure 4.2 **EU's general budget, 2002**
Source: Data from EC (2002).

for almost 82 per cent of the total. With world trade liberalization, including agricultural products, the revenue contributions of customs duties and agricultural levies will diminish further, while the importance of the GNP source will rise. The expenditure side of the budget shows that agriculture still absorbs 45.20 per cent. Although this is a remarkable improvement relative to budgets of the past, when 70–80 per cent of the expenditure was directed to agriculture in 1960–80, it is nevertheless still quite high. The Structural Funds (for regional and social development) constitute the second-highest item, while all the rest get about 20 per cent of the total.

Table 4.1 presents the financial perspective for the years 2000 and 2006. In preparing this perspective, the Commission took into account the possible accession of six new member states from 2002 onwards and attached an indicative financial framework for a 21-country Union with

Table 4.1 **Financial perspective for EU-15, 2000 and 2006**

	million euros		%	
	2000	**2006**	**2000**	**2006**
1. Agriculture	40 920	41 660	44.5	46.2
CAP costs	*36 620*	*37 290*		
Rural development	*4 300*	*4 370*		
2. Structural operations	32 045	29 170	34.8	32.3
3. Internal policies	5 900	6 200	6.4	6.9
4. External operations	4 550	4 610	4.9	5.1
5. Administration	4 560	5 100	5	5.7
6. Reserves	900	400	1	0.4
7. Pre-accession aid	3 120	3 120	3.4	3.4
Total commitment appropriations	**91 995**	**90 260**	**100**	**100**
Total payment appropriations	**89 590**	**89 310**		
Available for accession		14 220		
Ceiling for payment appropriations	89 590	103 530		
Ceiling for own resources (% GNP)	**1.27**	**1.27**		

Note: Calculations based on expected GDP growth of 2.5 per cent per annum and 1999 prices.
Commitment appropriations refer to amounts which can be legally committed for payments over several years; payment appropriations refer to amounts which by law must be paid out in the year.
Source: Compiled from data presented in EC (1999b).

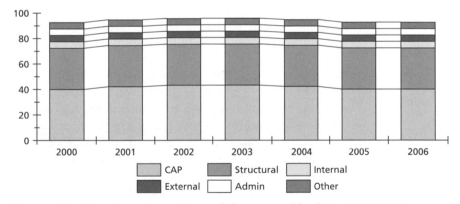

Figure 4.3 **Allocation expenditure of the general budget, 2000–2006**

an additional item of expenditure, 'Available for accession'. Under the constraint of the 1.27 per cent of GNP financial ceiling, the allocation assumes stabilization of budgetary expenditure at broadly the 2000 real terms level. This is confirmed by Figure 4.3, which illustrates the composition of the budgetary expenditure for each of the years of the financial perspective, with little variation between them. However, these are plans based on current situations and on assumption of GDP growth of 2.5 per cent a year for existing member states and 4 per cent a year for new member states over the period of the financial framework. For example, the cost to the EU of enlargement will depend upon which countries accede, when they accede, and the stage of their development on accession. It will also depend on the nature and extent of reform of EU policies, most particularly the most important items of budgetary expenditure, the CAP and the Structural Funds which are bound to be changed by developments in the EU, such as enlargement, and in the outside world, such as further trade liberalization.

The conclusion is that reforms in the finances of Europe will be inevitable, and this will bring to the forefront discussions about the necessity of introducing some form of federal finance. The next section deals with this problem.

4.5 Principles of fiscal federalism

Subsidiarity

The EU is an economic association but it displays some characteristics that are commonly found in federations. In a federal system, there are public sectors in the constituent states and the central authority. For example, in a federal structure with tripartite vertical division of power the public sector consists of local, state and federal levels of government. The problem raised in such a system is the proper assignment of functions between the different levels of government. Similar considerations apply to the case of two or more sovereign states which have decided to develop closer cooperation in an economic union. They would have to decide what fiscal functions, if any, the member states should transfer to the central authority. The dominant answer to this problem maintains that the allocation of fiscal responsibilities should be based on efficiency criteria so that each level of government would take charge of what it can do best. The issue of the assignment of responsibilities for budgetary (tax and expenditure) policy invokes the principle of subsidiarity in a multi-level government.

Subsidiarity in fiscal federalism is associated with decentralization, which aims at decision-taking at the level of government that would reflect most accurately citizen preferences and interests. Most federal structures of government include some sharing of fiscal capacity combined with member-state autonomy over local taxation and local public expenditure. As we have seen (in Chapter 2), the TEEC embodies a presumption in favour of decentralization. But since the structure of every federation presumably expresses the wishes of the constituent states and their citizens, different federal structures require different forms of fiscal federalism and different rules of subsidiarity. This is displayed in federal budgets that are based on elaborate systems of constitutional rules governing the origin of budgetary revenues and the destination of budgetary expenditures. As a rule, the federal government should deal with the provision of federal public goods and other policies which entail a uniform distribution among individuals and can be performed more efficiently centrally rather than at state or local level (for example, defence and foreign policy). Similarly, the central authority should have control over fiscal functions that cause externalities between member states or yield large-scale economies.

Expenditure assignment

On the expenditure side of the budget, the federal approach assigns two fiscal functions to the central government: stabilization policy and redistribution policy because (a) centralization eliminates the large spillover effects (externalities) which uncoordinated national macroeconomic policy might have on the members of the union; and (b) population mobility within the union may restrict the ability of national governments to make independent choices about redistribution priorities. The assignment of these functions to the higher level of government requires the transfer of sovereignty over macroeconomic policy from the member states to the central authority of the union.

The approach is different for the supply of local public goods, such as fire services and public transport, which provide benefits and entail costs restricted to certain geographic areas. In this case the allocation function is delegated to subcentral levels of government and may differ between jurisdictions, depending on the preferences of their citizens. The state or local authorities are supposed to be better informed about local needs and respond to them, and to have better control over administrative 'slack'.

Revenue assignment

Fiscal federalism also deals with the vertical structure of the budgetary revenue system, the tax assignment. Taking account of the externality or market failure arguments for fiscal centralization subject to efficiency and equity considerations, the tax assignment 'principles' (Musgrave, 1983) between levels of government include the following general rules:

1. Highly progressive taxes, such as personal income and corporation taxes, which can cause perverse mobility (of factors of production and firms) if they are levied at different rates by different state or local authorities, should be centralized.

2. Taxes on tax bases distributed across jurisdictions, such as deposits of natural resources, should be centralized. Decentralized governments should levy taxes on relatively immobile tax bases (such as property or land) and eschew taxes on highly mobile tax bases.

3. User taxes and fees, which in principle do not create potentially distorting incentives for mobility between jurisdictions, should be decentralized.

These general principles for the assignment of fiscal responsibilities in a federal system of government may, however, give rise to an imbalance between the members of the fiscal union. For example, the fiscal revenues at one level of government can fall short of the required spending. In this case, if the aim is to achieve national objectives or standards, the difference is made up by financial transfers from other levels of government. Intergovernmental transfers or grants are, in fact, a prominent feature of fiscal federalism. Most of the revenues of state and local levels of government in a federation usually come from a share in the revenues in each of the major federal taxes. Intergovernmental grants are instituted for the following purposes:

- to correct for interjurisdictional spillovers
- to promote interregional redistribution for equity, cohesion and balanced economic development
- to compensate for welfare losses resulting from central government initiatives
- to correct vertical fiscal imbalances
- to promote interpersonal equity.

These general principles of fiscal federalism are normative; they are rules which should be observed for welfare improvement in an ideal setting. In practice, historical and political factors determine both the vertical structure of government and the degree of fiscal centralization of each country, association of countries and federation of states. Therefore, in the real world both the fiscal functions and the fiscal instruments with which these functions are pursued differ between countries and between levels of government within countries (Oates, 1991). So, when previously independent sovereign countries come together to form a fiscal federation, the process is beset with problems and difficulties.

4.6 Towards a federal EU budget

A question the partners in the EU have faced since the early 1970s is whether evolution towards Economic and Monetary Union (EMU) calls for a federal central budget. This problem was examined by the MacDougall

Committee which concluded in its report (EC, 1977) that no sufficient 'political homogeneity' existed to justify such a move at that time. The report argued, however, that a distinct sense of common destiny prevailed in the EU which justified a slow progress towards fiscal federalism which was considered necessary for monetary union. A three-stage approach was recommended:

1. *pre-federal* integration, with a Community public sector taking up 2–2.5 per cent of Community GDP
2. *federation* with a small Community public sector, 5–7 per cent of GDP
3. *union* with a large Community public sector, 20–5 per cent of GDP.

However, the immense political implications of adopting a federal objective has meant that the EU did not adopt any such strategy. The question is whether the EU has to move towards a federal budget. There are no clearcut grounds from theory or practice for or against a federal budget in Europe. Over the last quarter of the twentieth century existing federations and unitary states have displayed a trend for fiscal decentralization by delegating some of the central government's allocating goals to local governments (a top-down process, e.g. the USA, Canada, Belgium, Spain). At the same time, the EU is completing monetary unification with a single currency from 2002. This development has prompted many discussions about whether fiscal policy should also be centralized in step with monetary policy. Among the many arguments for and against such a move are the following:

- *Redistribution*: the process of EU integration causes externalities which call for compensation (= internalization) by a higher level of government. The Structural Funds essentially play that compensatory role. Therefore, the EU budget is already developing along fiscal federalism lines (Wildasin, 1990).
- *Constraints imposed by economic and monetary integration on national fiscal policies*: a federal and larger EU budget is necessary to compensate for the constraints imposed by (i) EMU on the members' fiscal policy (the *Stability Pact*, see Chapter 6); and (ii) tax harmonization on the ability of member states to raise revenue by increasing their taxation. We will examine these issues under monetary integration (Chapter 6).
- *Non-homogeneity of countries and peoples*: the marked economic and social heterogeneity of the countries and the peoples of the EU (such as per capita GDP, the role and size of the public sector, culture, language, geography) has resulted in different preferences for public services and differences in the levels of taxation and public services. Therefore, levelling the different preferences by moving to a federation would reduce efficiency and distort economic activity.

■ *Relative immobility of labour*: a federal budget is required for the internalization of externalities caused by high factor mobility within the union. But in the EU labour mobility is very low and it is not expected to rise in the immediate future. Therefore a federal budget is unnecessary.

■ *Democratic deficit*: a federal budget with increased power in spending and revenue-raising will require more democratic accountability than that provided in the EU treaties. Therefore any move towards a federal budget should follow in the steps of a genuinely democratic federal structure of government, i.e. only after the European Parliament takes full responsibility for it.

4.7 Conclusions

The general budget of the European Communities is an instrument for attaining common objectives relating to economic integration. Moreover, its structure and size, which have been proved inflexible and inadequate for the functions and initiatives the budget is expected to assume, may come under additional pressures after the accession of new and less prosperous member states, which will reverse the process of convergence. The changing conditions and the pressures of advancing integration will call for different policies which will hasten the need for new budgetary reforms. It is argued that some of these reforms should be along the lines of federal finance. But what is most important is that the European Union would soon need a substantially larger budget. Whether it will be called federal or not, makes no difference.

Questions

1. What are the structure of revenues and expenditures and the functions of EU's general budget?

2. Why are the United Kingdom and Germany net losers from the general budget?

3. 'Quite simply, the problem of the EU budget is that equals neither contribute equally to it nor do they benefit equally from it.' Does this imply that the Community budget should be governed by the principle of 'fair return'?

4. Why is the EU arguing that now is the time to reconsider the structure of the EU budget 'including the position of the UK'?

5. If the EU were to move towards fiscal federalism, on what particular principles should it be based?

6. How would a federal budget deal with the budgetary problems of the Community?

Further reading

For recent developments concerning EU finances see Begg and Grimwade (1998) and Laffan (1997).

The Commission's opinion is in Commission (1997, 1998).

Web guide

www.europa.eu.int/comm/budget/en/budget/index.htm

Tax harmonization

5

Different tax systems and tax rates distort trade and factor movements between the member states of a common market. Therefore, during market integration it becomes necessary to introduce policies aiming at tax coordination and harmonization. The European Union never had the intention to apply overall tax harmonization. However, a high degree of harmonization is desirable in the indirect tax field because indirect taxes may create obstacles to the free movement of goods and services within the single market. In 1998, the Commission set out a broader vision of tax harmonization and laid down three categories: income taxes, which would never be harmonized; VAT and excise duties, where more harmonization is desirable; and business taxes, where the Commission would be willing to act.

5.1 The problem

Abolition of trade barriers among the members of the customs union does not necessarily mean that a common, perfectly competitive market has been completed. Impediments to the smooth functioning of the competitive markets for commodities, services and factors of production are still many. Differences between the tax systems of the members of the customs union are one of the most important of these impediments and one of the most difficult to alleviate. This has also been the case in the EU. Therefore, we discuss the problems of tax harmonization rather extensively.

The nature of tax harmonization

Tax systems may differ between countries in many ways associated with (a) what is taxed – the *tax base*; (b) by how much it is taxed – the *tax rate*; (c) what particular sort of tax is levied – the *tax type*. Even if the tax base, rate and type are the same, tax compliance and tax enforcement may differ across countries.

Tax harmonization is the process by which the tax systems of different countries are aligned with each other so that tax considerations do not influence the movement of goods, services and factors of production between countries. Tax harmonization is required when there are fiscal externalities between member states whereby one state's fiscal decisions affect other states. Tax harmonization attempts to *internalize* these effects by making different tax systems compatible with each other and with the objectives of the economic union. The aim of tax harmonization is 'to encourage the interplay of competition in such a way that integration and economic growth . . . may be achieved simultaneously and gradually' (Commission 1963, p. 188). The scale of compatibility ranges from nil to perfect and exactly what degree of compatibility/tax harmonization is ideal for a particular economic union will depend on the extent of integration the members aim at. In a free trade area, where only trade barriers between the members are removed, the required tax harmonization is minimal. But even fully independent states may choose to coordinate their tax systems to reduce the likelihood of tax avoidance, double taxation and so on. In a regional economic association aimed at economic and political integration, some form of tax coordination is inevitable. This comes about by tax harmonization or by the market process.

5.2 Principles of tax harmonization

Significant differences in tax or fiscal systems between different countries can affect trade in commodities and services, capital movements, labour migration, and the location decisions of firms. Optimality requires that international trade, factor movements and the location of production should not be guided by tax considerations. It is argued, therefore, that for this reason inter-country fiscal affairs should be based *on tax neutrality*: the flows of goods, services, persons and capital and the international specialization in production should be the same with and without taxes. This condition for optimality can be met by adopting the *destination principle* of taxation for international trade and the *residence principle* of taxation for border-crossing interest income flows. Similar considerations apply to the fiscal affairs between the members of an economic union.

Therefore, trade tax harmonization should be considered under these principles.

Trade and taxation

Indirect taxes and their changes affect relative prices within an economy and therefore the terms of trade between countries, and thus the direction, pattern and volume of trade may be affected. Tax-induced changes in the terms of trade cause income redistribution between (a) the citizens of the country, (b) the country and its partners in the economic union, and (c) the economic union and the outside world. The effects of tax changes implemented by tax harmonization are similar to those derived from changes in tariff structures and cause trade creation and trade diversion.

Indirect taxes are levied on traded commodities according to the *origin* or *destination* principles of taxation. Under the origin principle, taxes are levied at the production stage and the country of production gets the tax revenue. Therefore, exports of identical-cost products from a low-tax country to a high-tax country enjoy an artificial comparative advantage, thus distorting the specialization of production and trade. Under the destination principle, which is used worldwide, taxes are levied at the consumption stage and the country of consumption gets the tax revenue. Therefore, countries have to make border tax adjustments, levying domestic taxes on imports and removing domestic taxes on exports. Countries can gain an unfair advantage by taxing imported products at rates higher than those levied on similar domestic products, and by refunding taxes on exports at levels higher than those actually paid. This amounts to placing disguised customs duties on imports and subsidizing exports, and therefore it is specifically banned by international agreements (such as the GATT, see Chapter 8) and forbidden in common markets (TEEC, 90–1).

The destination principle of taxation, which (barring unfair practices) treats imported and home-produced goods alike, ensures that firms compete on the basis of prices net of taxes. Thus, the destination principle does not distort comparative costs and international competition. Therefore, under conditions of perfect competition in international trade, production will be located in the country with the lowest cost ex-tax. In contrast, the origin principle of taxation entails tax-induced trade distortions, so the pattern of pre-tax trade is different from post-tax trade. The origin principle would have effects equivalent to those of the destination principle only if all trading countries apply a single tax rate to an identical tax base. But, since in practice tax bases differ and tax rates are many, the equivalence between the two principles is only a remote theoretical possibility, of no interest to the real world.

Countries forming customs unions start with the existing destination system of taxation. But when they proceed to a common market and remove border controls from the member states, geographically they will be similar to a country and its regions. The regions of a country operate a common tax system and tax rates and, therefore, in interregional trade they apply the *origin* principle with tax revenues accruing to the national treasury. It is therefore suggested that the members of a common market should adopt the *restricted origin principle*, whereby the origin principle applies on internal trade and the destination principle remains in force on trade with the outside world. But there is an important difference between the regions of a country and the members of a common market: the latter apply different tax systems and tax rates and the proceeds of taxation accrue to different national treasuries. Therefore, the application of the restricted origin principle in a common market is impractical for as long as the tax systems and tax rates of the member states differ substantially. Since border controls have been removed, the only way out of this dilemma is to proceed with tax harmonization until the tax differences between the member states are erased.

In general, the change from one principle of taxation to another will have effects on competitiveness and tax revenues (and so on budgets). It may also affect relative prices and therefore trade, specialization and the location of production: *allocation efficiency*. For example, if the member states of an emerging common market applied different indirect tax rates under the destination principle, with national markets separated by tax borders, and decide to unify the market by adopting the restricted origin principle, trade flows will be affected by tax considerations. In this case, optimization would be reached only by forming a *tax union* and adopting a uniform tax system which would provide the necessary tax neutrality. Therefore, in common markets and economic unions indirect tax harmonization becomes a necessity.

International income taxes

For income taxes in an international context there are two polar principles: the residence of the taxpayer and the source of income. According to the first principle, the residents of a country are taxed equally, regardless of whether the source of their income is domestic or foreign. Therefore, if capital can move freely between countries and all countries adopt the residence principle, then capital income taxation does not disturb the optimality rule which requires equality of the marginal product of capital across countries, and the international allocation of capital remains optimal. According to the source principle, a country's residents are taxed only on income from domestic sources. Therefore, if the tax rate is not the same in all countries, the marginal product of capital will differ between countries and the international allocation of capital will be non-optimal.

The residence principle accords with tax neutrality, making investors indifferent between domestic and foreign assets if the interest rates are the same. If the residence principle is not universally applied within an economic union, then capital flows will be governed by tax considerations and therefore tax harmonization will be necessary.

Tax harmonization

There are two approaches to tax harmonization within economic unions: the equalization approach and the differentials approach. There are also two methods of implementing them: the administrative method and the market solution.

The equalization approach favours standardization by uniformity of tax base and tax rates among the members of the union. Standardization can be reached with or without unification of the tax system under a single fiscal policy authority. The equalization approach is supported mainly for two reasons: (a) it accords with the aim of economic unions to 'enhance competition on equal terms'; and (b) it is favoured by those who consider tax harmonization as one of the driving forces for economic and political integration, where equalization of rates and uniformity of taxes are deemed necessary.

The problem of tax harmonization under the equalization approach consists of selecting and implementing the set of taxes and tax rates which will direct the economic union to realize its objective. This objective is economic integration and maximization of welfare for the economic union as a whole.

The differentials or fiscal diversity approach is based on the principle that the tax system of each country acts as an instrument of policy for attaining major economic objectives. It is argued, therefore, that the same principle should apply at the scale of the economic union, with the prerequisite that the externalities of each country's tax system on other countries should be minimized. This can be achieved by close collaboration among the members, achieved by a minimum degree of tax harmonization implemented administratively. The differentials principle is based on the presumption that private (members') benefit and social (economic union's) benefit coincide. Since the sum of the members' welfare adds up to the welfare of the economic union, the differentials approach consists of each participant selecting the taxes and tax rates which would optimize its own welfare.

A variant of the differentials approach asserts that administratively imposed tax harmonization is an unnecessary interference with the price system. The convergence of tax systems in an economic union should instead be left to market forces and tax competition based on the recognition that states differ in: (a) preferences for one tax over another; (b) perceptions of the role of taxation; (c) acceptability and feasibility of various taxes; and (d) preferences for public sector size. Therefore, taxation should be based on residence, which in an economic union depends on subjective choice. Then, like participants in the marketplace, governments will have to compete for scarce resources – tax revenues. This will restrain the inherent tendency of governments to overtax and overspend, promote efficiency in the public sector and lead to the necessary convergence of tax systems through harmonization by the market process. More often than not, in practice this is wishful thinking (see Box 5.3).

It is obvious from the discussion so far that tax harmonization encompasses both the equalization approach and the differentials approach. Tax harmonization ranges from the one extreme of zero change in taxes and tax rates and the other extreme of unification of taxes and complete equalization of rates, with all the variations in between. The differentials approach covers most of the cases, while the equalization approach occupies only the upper limit of this range.

In general, tax harmonization is multidimensional, influencing all the functions of the tax system, allocation of resources, economic stabilization, economic growth, income distribution, the balance of payments and tax revenue. The equalization approach gives precedence to the common goals of the economic union, placing them above the goals of the individual members. Therefore, moves towards a uniform tax system, with common tax rates, imply that the members endorse the transfer of fiscal policy power from the national to the union's authority. This means that the members decided that the ultimate objective of the economic union is economic (and political) integration, and that a common tax system based on tax (fiscal) neutrality is a direct way towards achieving that goal.

Under the differentials approach the presumption is that the economic association will not move further towards full integration and, specifically, that fiscal policy will remain in the domain of each member state. In this case, they will cooperate to overcome the tax obstacles to cross-border economic activities by *tax coordination*, without giving away much of their fiscal sovereignty.

5.3 The state of EU tax harmonization

The tax systems of the six signatories of the Treaty of Rome were dissimilar, reflecting important differences between the members' economic and social structures and policy objectives. *Sales taxes* were in the form of value added tax (VAT), cumulative turnover tax and taxes on gross value. *Excise taxes* were applied to different goods in different countries, at different rates and means of evaluation. Different systems of *corporation taxation* had different implications on capital mobility and investment. The personal *income tax* system differed in rates, allowances, administrative procedures, compliance and enforcement. The *social security taxes* and the social benefits were also diverse. All these differences constituted serious obstacles to the integration of markets and were dealt with by the treaties.

The Treaty of Rome specifies that 'the harmonization of legislation concerning turnover taxes, excise duties and other forms of indirect taxation' (TEEC, 93) is a principal objective of the Community, and that laws in general – including tax law – should be approximated to the extent necessary for the 'establishment or functioning of the common market' (TEEC, 94). The general aim of tax harmonization was fiscal neutrality, defined as equal treatment for domestic production and imports from member countries. The Commission clarified that tax harmonization 'is not an attempt to design an ideal fiscal system for the Community, but a blueprint for abolition of fiscal frontiers' (Commission 1987). But details about what tax harmonization and coordination involve are not provided in the treaty. They are specified by special study committees and submitted to the Council by the Commission as proposals. If the Council approves them, then they are issued as directives binding on the member states.

Tax harmonization in the EU has aimed at two objectives: (a) competition on equal terms among the EU partners, implying abolition of tax frontiers; and (b) acceleration of the process of integration and unification of the market. In practice, tax harmonization has proved more difficult than envisaged. The complexity of the problem and the widely held democratic principle of *no taxation without representation*, which makes tax sovereignty one of the fundamental components of national sovereignty, meant that little could be achieved, and at a slow pace. Taxation in EU countries is based on the principles of:

■ *national competence*, whereby policy is exclusively a matter for member states if the Community does not have competence under the treaty;
■ *subsidiarity*, whereby action should only be taken at Community level where the objectives cannot be sufficiently achieved by member states and can be better achieved by the Community (TEEC, 5);
■ *unanimity*, whereby EU-wide taxation matters can only be adopted by a unanimous vote of member states.

Figure 5.1 shows the structure of taxation, or *the relative tax burden*, in EU countries as revealed by the ratio of tax revenue on GDP (the *effective tax*

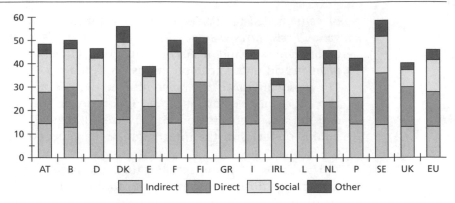

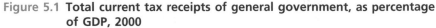

Figure 5.1 Total current tax receipts of general government, as percentage of GDP, 2000

Source: Data from Commission (2000c).

rate) and the shares of indirect, direct and social security taxes. Ireland displays the lowest tax burden (33.9 per cent) and Denmark and Sweden the highest (56.8 per cent and 58.6 per cent) among EU countries. Both indirect taxes and direct taxes are most important for government revenue in Denmark (17.3 per cent and 29.5 per cent), while the highest ratio of social security taxes on GDP is in Germany and France (18.6 per cent and 18.4 per cent). Despite many years of economic cooperation and several attempts at tax harmonization, the data reveal significant differences between the EU countries in both the total tax burden and the composition of tax revenues. These attempts and their results we examine in the following sections.

5.4 Indirect taxes

Indirect taxes enter the final prices of goods and services on which they are levied. Therefore, under similar production cost conditions, different principles and levels of taxation will be reflected in different market prices.

Tax harmonization in the Community has followed a pragmatic approach. The objective of indirect tax harmonization entails a three-stage process: (a) fiscal neutrality in intra-Community trade; (b) simplification of administrative procedure in this trade; and (c) creation of a single market by abolishing fiscal frontiers. In the following we examine the nature of indirect tax harmonization in the Community's integrated market.

Sales tax harmonization

First attempts

When the first moves towards trade liberalization among the members of the Community had started, the Commission appointed a group of experts, the Neumark Committee, to review the fiscal systems of the member states and to recommend methods for harmonizing them. The Committee's report (Commission 1963) recommended the introduction of a common sales tax, the value added tax (VAT) and the *restricted origin principle* which would promote integration by abolishing fiscal frontiers between the member countries. The Community accepted the VAT proposal. It declared, however, that, although it formally adhered to the introduction of the origin principle and the abolition of border controls, for as long as the process of building up the common market was in progress, the destination principle of taxation should apply. This was considered essential to reassure the member states that the revenues from indirect taxation would continue to accrue to the country of consumption of the good.

From 1969, six directives have set up VAT as the common sales tax of the Community. Tax harmonization at the going phase of integration in the EU meant adopting only a common structure, but no attempt was made to introduce a common VAT rate. The sixth directive of 1977 aimed at a uniform VAT base by a common list of taxable activities and a common *tax threshold* – a lower limit of exempted transactions. An important simplification was also made by replacing an abundance of national customs papers by a single common administrative document for traded commodities.

VAT has several advantages over other forms of sales taxes (turnover, single stage, etc.):

Box 5.1 ■ VAT

It is important to emphasize that VAT is a method of taxation and not a new type of tax. VAT is a general sales tax, levied on all stages of business activity, from each stage of production through to sales to final consumers. If there is a single VAT rate, then the tax is on the value added – the difference between the value of inputs and output in each stage of production and distribution. Businesses credit tax paid on their purchases of inputs against the tax due on their sales of output. Thus the tax payments accumulate at each intermediate transaction and the final tax burden is precisely equal to that which would have been levied under a single-stage sales tax applying only at the retail stage. To show how VAT works we assume a simple three-stage production from wool to yarn to a pullover. In Table 5.1, the first two columns show the 'no tax' situation, and the next three columns how the VAT would be charged at 10 per cent. Firm A supplies wool to firm B

Table 5.1 **The calculation of VAT**

Firm	NO TAX		VAT at 10%		
	Purchase price + value added	Selling price	Purchase price less VAT + value added	VAT	Selling price
A	nil		nil		
wool	1000	1000	1000	100	1100
B	1000		1100		
yarn	400		−100	−100	
	1400	1400	+400	+140	1540
			1400	net 40	
C	1400		1540		
pullover	600		−140	−140	
	2000	2000	+600	+200	2200
			2000	net 160	
+ retail stage tax 10%	200	2200	total VAT	200	2200

Note: Value added = labour cost + capital cost + profit.

at pre-tax price 1000 and pays tax of 100 which it adds to its selling price. Firm B is entitled to be repaid the 100, so it deducts it in arriving at its pre-tax selling price of yarn, which is therefore 1400. Tax on that is 140. Therefore, its total selling price to firm C is 1540 and the net amount of tax it owes is 40 (i.e., 140 − 100). Firm C deducts the tax of 140 and its pre-tax price is 1400. With value added 600, the pre-tax selling price of the final product, a pullover, is 2000. Tax on that is 200 and therefore the price charged to the consumer for a pullover is 2200 with the net amount of tax C owes at 60 (i.e. 200 − 140). Total tax revenue = 200.

The example shows that, even without 'exemptions' and 'multi-rates', VAT is complicated, among other reasons because it charges one firm in the chain of production, only to repay the same tax to the next firm. It would be possible and less complicated, therefore, just to charge the tax at the retail stage and collect the same revenue with less fuss, 2000 × 0.10 = 200 tax revenue. But this solution entails the risk that the government may suffer a high loss if the retailer were to evade the tax. In contrast, by taxing at each stage of production the government introduces a self-policing control which helps tax collection.

If a good is VAT-taxed and traded under the destination principle, the customs know exactly the amount of tax which they must rebate on export at the border. For example, if yarn is exported, the rebate is 140 and the net export price is 1500. If yarn is imported, the tax charged is 10 per cent on the import price. But, after 1992, the EU has had no border customs controls on internal trade; hence the changes in the system introduced by the single market. The Commission believes that the present VAT system has a number of defects, because it is complicated, susceptible to fraud and out of date, and therefore it must be improved and updated.

- It provides neutrality about saving, investment and work decisions, especially if the tax base is wide and there is a single tax rate.
- It is neutral between production by vertically integrated enterprises and production by several independent firms.
- Under the destination principle of international taxation, it promotes unambiguous border tax adjustments by the exact refunding of taxes on exports and the precise non-discriminatory levying of taxes on imports. Therefore, trade taxes are transparent and cannot be used as a disguised subsidy to exports or tariff on imports in support of domestic production.
- But VAT may involve heavy administrative costs for both the tax authorities and the taxpayers. Therefore, exemptions are usually granted to small firms since collection costs may exceed the tax revenue.

VAT is a tax on consumer spending. It is usually assumed that a general single rate (or *flat rate*) consumption tax is regressive, and that tax rate differentiation can change it into a progressive one. Therefore, in some countries a variety of sensitive goods, with a relatively large share in the budget of low-income consumers (such as food, clothing, etc.), either are not taxed at all or are taxed at a lower rate, while luxury goods are taxed at a higher rate. Moreover, VAT is made more complicated by 'exemption' of certain kinds of business which are difficult to fit into the scheme of tax, e.g. banking, insurance and some property transactions. These operational principles and complications are also observed in the countries of the Community.

The single market

The decisive stage for completing indirect tax harmonization in the Community started with the move for unification of the market and the Single European Act (SEA). A single and free internal market 'without internal frontiers in which the free movement of goods, persons, services and capital is ensured' requires the abolition of fiscal frontiers, which anyway cannot work without border controls. For this reason, federal states with a VAT system allocate all control over the definition of the VAT base and the rates to the central government, i.e. they apply *tax equalization*. In contrast, outside observers and certain EU states argued that frontier obstacles can be eliminated without aligning tax rates, as for example in the USA (which does not apply the VAT system). This argument expresses more an unwillingness to move to market integration rather than a realistic proposal for creating a single internal market. In the USA, different states apply different sales taxes without having border controls. But the evidence suggests that only tax differences of about 5 per cent are as much as can be sustained without causing large-scale tax-dodging and 'cross-border shopping'. In other words, in an economic union tax harmonization is indispensable, but this does not imply the complete equalization of tax rates.

Consenting to this argument, the Commission proposed market unification from 1993 with tax harmonization under the restricted origin principle of taxation. The first step would consist of 'VAT approximation' by squeezing the operational VAT rates in the Community within two bands, a 4–9 per cent reduced rate for necessities and a 14–20 per cent standard rate for other goods and services. But the Council, representing the member states, objected that this proposal would cause difficulty for countries with very high (Denmark) or very low (Luxembourg) indirect tax rates, or for those that rely for their revenues mostly on indirect taxes (Ireland). As usual, certain member countries protested in principle against the proposed harmonization, arguing that it would impose unwarranted constraints on their fiscal sovereignty. Since changes in taxation law require unanimity, the member states' unwillingness to face the problems posed by the necessity to harmonize rates led only to a compromise which did not advance the process of tax harmonization and thwarted the realization of benefits from the single market. After a long period of protracted negotiations, an interim system was adopted from 1 January 1993, the Single Market Transitional System, which included the following main points:

1. All member states applied a legally binding minimum standard VAT rate of 15 per cent.
2. Member states had the option of applying up to two reduced rates of not less than 5 per cent; reduced and zero rates of VAT continued in those states which applied them before 1993.
3. The destination system remained in operation, but, without border controls, the taxable event of 'importation' was replaced by 'acquisition'. This means that exporters do not charge tax, as under the old system, but importers from other member states pay the exporting country's tax and claim it as a liability on their VAT returns. Next, they charge the domestic VAT rate and deduct in the same way as if they had purchased the good from domestic producers (see Box 5.1).
4. Tax revenues would be allocated to the country of consumption by setting up a central 'clearing house' for settling tax credits and debits between countries in accordance with the value they added to traded goods.
5. Individuals buying goods from another country of the union by post or telephone are charged the VAT of their own country as if the goods are imports. But they have the opportunity to buy them personally 'in unlimited amounts' by crossing the border and paying the VAT of the country of purchase.

The Council decided that 'the transitional arrangements shall be re-placed by a definitive system for the taxation of trade between Member States based in principle on the taxation in the Member State of origin of the goods or services supplied' (Sixth Directive, Article 281).

The transitional system for VAT proved to be costly, administratively complex and discriminating between intra- and interstate transactions, thus creating barriers to intra-Union trade and distorting the operation of the single market. But while plans are devised for its replacement, the transitional system still remains in operation.

VAT rates

Table 5.2 presents the VAT rates of the EU member states. It can be seen that there exist marked differences between both the number of rates and their levels. There is a single rate in Germany, Denmark, and the Netherlands, and two in every other country; 15 per cent standard rate in Luxembourg and 25 per cent in Denmark and Sweden. Differences also exist with regard to what range of items are classified as sensitive (e.g. food, medical products) and are subject to reduced VAT rates on grounds of regressiveness. In the extreme, some items are zero-rated (subject to a zero VAT rate and receiving credit for tax paid on inputs) in B, DK, FI, I, IRL, SE and UK. Owing to different exemptions, the VAT coverage of private consumption is only 35 per cent in Ireland and 44 per cent in the United Kingdom, whereas in most of the other member states it is about 90 per cent. Therefore, a uniform base has not yet been

Table 5.2 **VAT rates in the Community, %, 1 May 2001**

Country	Standard	Reduced
Austria AT	20	10, 12
Belgium B	21	0 and 6
Germany D	16	7
Denmark DK	25	0
Spain E	16	4 and 7
France F	19.6	2.1 and 5.5
Finland FI	22	0, 8 and 17
Greece GR	18	4 and 8
Italy I	20	0, 4 and 10
Ireland IRL	20	0, 4.2 and 12.5
Luxembourg L	15	3 and 6
Netherlands NL	19	6
Portugal P	17	5 and 12
Sweden SE	25	0, 6 and 12
United Kingdom UK	17.5	0 and 5

Source: Data from Commission (2001d).

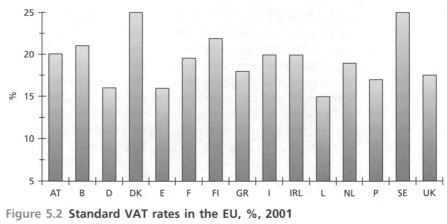

Figure 5.2 Standard VAT rates in the EU, %, 2001
Source: Data from Commission (2001d).

reached. Figure 5.2 shows the divergence of standard VAT rates in the EU countries.

Excise tax harmonization

First attempts

Excise duties are *specific* taxes levied on certain products which are characterized by their relatively high share in consumers' expenditure (up to a fifth) and low price elasticity of demand. Excises are levied mainly for revenue-raising reasons, but sometimes also to discourage the consumption of harmful products for public health reasons, for example tobacco and spirits.

The systems of operating and enforcing excise duties in EU countries displayed wide diversity. Some countries operated controls based on strict production supervision and distribution through a network of bonded warehouses, while others affixed tax stamps on the product itself at the production stage. The tax rate varied from country to country, but in general was (and is) very high, three to four times higher than the standard VAT rate. High rates mean that excise taxes have a high incidence on prices and, in general, a wide economic impact. Therefore, differences among the members in the structure, rates and administration of excise taxes have serious effects on competition on equal terms. The significant divergence between the excise duty systems was maintained by strict frontier controls that insulate domestic markets from duty systems abroad. As a result, trade was affected by inter-commodity and inter-country discrimination.

In assessing the proposals for harmonization of excise taxes, the most important consideration is the revenue effect. In some members of the

---

Box 5.2 ■ Excise tax discrimination

The European Commission has decided to send a formal request to Sweden to end tax discrimination against wine in comparison to beer. The Commission considers that the Swedish tax system affords undue protection to beer, mainly produced domestically, in comparison to wine, which comes from Member States. Thus, for example, a beer of 3 per cent alcohol by volume content (abv) will be taxed 441 SEK [Swedish Krona] per hl [hectolitre], whereas a wine of the same strength will be taxed at 934 SEK per hl. The effect of the discrepancy is aggravated because the final retail prices of beer and of wine include 25 per cent VAT, which is charged on the combined pre-excise price and excise tax charged. In the Commission's view, this discriminatory tax regime violates EC Treaty rules (Article 90) that forbid Member States to impose higher taxes on products from other Member States than on competing domestic products.

Source: Commission *DN: IP/01/819*, 6 December 2001 (draft paper)

Community, excise taxes contributed more than 25 per cent of the total receipts from taxes and social contributions. Furthermore, in certain countries some commodities, which are subject to excise duties, were also traded by state monopolies (for example, tobacco in France and Italy and alcohol in Finland) and some others (such as mineral oils, tobacco and alcohol) are inputs to further processes whose output is subject to different systems of taxation.

The harmonization of excise duties in an economic union attempts to remove distortions to competition and fiscal frontiers. The first steps for a common policy concerned agreement on the tax base to decide which excise duties were to be retained and harmonized. Traditionally three broad groups of commodities are subject to excise taxes in most countries: hydrocarbon oils, manufactured tobacco and alcoholic beverages. In the EU, as in many other countries, most of the revenue from excise duties is collected from 'the big five': tobacco products, beer, spirits, mineral oils and wine. However, a variety of other commodities were subject to excise taxes in different countries (e.g. sugar in Belgium, spices in France, coffee in Germany, matches in Italy, and even cars in Denmark). Besides the tax base, there is also variation in tax rates. Among the EU countries Denmark, Ireland and the United Kingdom had the highest tax rates.

Over the years the Commission put forward many proposals, mostly about harmonizing tax structures rather than tax rates. However, progress was slow mainly because of the budgetary impact of excise tax harmonization which for certain countries would have been considerable. This of course is another facet of the conflict between national priorities and Community targets. After long deliberations, the member states agreed on a compromise system which sets a minimum tax rate made up by a

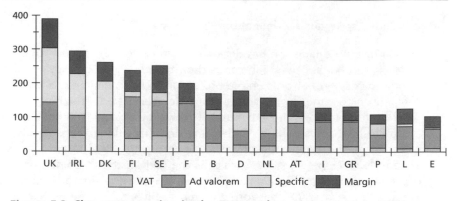

Figure 5.3 Cigarette taxation in the EU member states, January 2000

Note: 1. Most popular price category in each member state.
2. VAT + *ad valorem* + specific + margin = retail price (in £pence).

Source: Data available at www.thetma.org.uk/statistics/eu_cig.htm

combination of VAT, *ad valorem* and excise duties. But the rates remained widely diverging between the countries. Figure 5.3 illustrates these differences for the case of cigarettes.

The single market

The Commission argued that the single market required uniformity throughout the Community in structure, rates and administration of excise taxes as a precondition for abolishing frontier controls. Therefore, it proposed that only the three principal excise taxes should remain after 1992 (alcohol, tobacco and mineral oils) and that duty rates should be standardized at about the average of national rates. Problems resurfaced from the proposed uniformity of excise duties, which could affects consumption, social habits, health policy and tax revenues. Finally, excise tax harmonization was settled by a general and definitive agreement. Since 1993, the EU interstate trade of products subject to excise taxes has gone through interconnected bonded warehouses. On leaving the warehouses, taxes are levied by the country of consumption which also appropriates the tax revenue according to the destination principle. When individuals purchase goods for their own consumption in other EU member states, they pay the excise tax in operation at the point of purchase. Therefore, significant differences in excise tax rates may give rise to cross-border shopping. Competitive goods entering the EU from third countries are subject to excise taxation at the point of entry.

As predicted, the agreed system induced extensive cross-border shopping, particularly between the UK and France, Sweden and Denmark, and Denmark and Germany, but without any tendency for tax rate convergence from the operation of tax competition.

Box 5.3 ■ Taxation, tax competition and cross-border shopping

The convergence of tax systems by market forces and tax competition has proved impractical. Alcohol purchased in France by a UK citizen means typical savings of £1.16 (€2.69) on a bottle of wine, £1.65 (€2.66) on champagne, £5.48 (€8.84) on spirits and £3.40 (€5.48) per packet of 20 Embassy cigarettes. Many of the warehouses offer further discounts on top. This wide divergence between the high UK and low French taxes and market prices has brought about a booming cross-Channel 'booze cruise' trade, which is costing £4bn (€6.45bn) a year in lost revenue to the UK Treasury. But these losses have not led to any approximation of the two tax systems. Instead the UK's Chancellor of the Exchequer is spending an extra £209m (€337) on surveillance equipment and 1000 more customs officers in a new purge on the smugglers. The number of vehicles confiscated by customs staff at Channel ports has trebled in three years. Customs officers hand out leaflets with what are described as 'EU guidelines', limiting people to 800 cigarettes, 1 kg of rolling tobacco, 110 litres of beer and 90 litres of wine. However, the operators of the giant cash-and-carry warehouses in and around Calais complain that the customs crackdown is discouraging legitimate customers who wrongly believe that a trip to France to stock up their wine cellar could cost them their car. It has also drawn criticism from the office of the European Commissioner for the internal market, which argues that travellers should not be limited in moving goods around the single market unless there is proof that they intend to sell them on the black market. The UK's Brewers and Licensed Retailers' Association is unconvinced that the day of the Calais cash-and-carry is over. It believes that more than a million pints of beer are still being brought into Britain every day and thinks that the government should be cutting the duty on alcohol instead.

Source: Compiled from current news items, i.e. BBC news (27/11/2000), 'Cigarette smuggling "costs £4bn"', available at www.news.bbc.co.uk/english/business

5.5 Other taxes

The Community has decided that, as far as direct taxation is concerned, no harmonization but at least a certain level of coordination is required to ensure the smooth functioning of the internal market. Without concerted action on these taxes, market integration could result in unrestrained tax competition for mobile factors and limit member states' freedom to choose the tax structure which they consider most appropriate. In this section, we will study the attempts of the Community to instate cooperation in the field of direct taxation and certain other taxes.

Business taxes

Corporation tax affects the incentive to invest, the riskiness of investment, and the volume of business saving, and thus the supply of investment funds. Differences in corporation taxation between countries create tax arbitrage opportunities which can influence the international mobility of capital. In turn, if capital is induced to move between countries by tax motivations and not by financial and investment considerations, there will be distortions on allocative efficiency and on the allocation of tax revenue between states. This problem becomes more complex if companies registered in one country have subsidiaries in other countries and thus are subject to different tax jurisdictions. In principle, foreign-owned companies should not be discriminated against or favoured in matters of taxation. However, this is what often happens by using taxation to induce domestic or to attract foreign investment. Economic efficiency requires taxation to be neutral with respect to the nationality of the company and its decision on where to invest.

Efficiency in capital markets is achieved if two conditions are met:

(i) If the value of the marginal product of capital is the same across countries. This condition is met if firms are competitive, capital mobility is perfect, and investors are taxed at the same effective tax rate on investments at home and abroad.

(ii) If the marginal rate of substitution between present and future consumption (which determines savings) is equated across countries. This condition is met if the after-tax rates of return on savings are equalized across countries.

Thus, regarding capital mobility and taxation, two notions of capital neutrality are distinguished:

a. *capital export neutrality* (CEN) which holds if the effective tax rate on an investment is independent of its location and, therefore, the same after-tax return on investment is obtained. This accords with condition (i) above.

b. *capital import neutrality* (CIN) which holds if savers in different countries receive the same post-tax rate of return on their savings. This accords with condition (ii).

Unless effective tax rates are the same in all countries, CEN and CIN cannot be achieved simultaneously. In that case, it is usually argued that CEN, which guarantees production efficiency and is consistent with horizontal equity in taxation, should have precedence over CIN, which is consistent with consumption efficiency. Neutrality, however, does not always hold in practice where distortions and economic inefficiencies do occur. Harmonization is required because of different corporation tax systems and different tax rates. Corporate tax harmonization aims at integration of the capital markets and therefore at optimization in allocating capital and investment. In a common market with harmonized corporation taxes capital will gravitate where the rate of return is highest.

Among the EU partners there are many differences in corporation tax, especially on the following:

1. *liability* to corporation tax and tax base (e.g. limited companies are taxed, but sole proprietors are usually not liable to it);
2. *assessment* (e.g. exemptions, incentives);
3. *rate* of tax;
4. *system* of taxation. Most of the EU countries apply the *partial imputation system* which is designed to avoid, partially, the double taxation on dividends by imputing part of the corporate profit tax to the personal tax liability of shareholders. But taxable profits are calculated differently in different countries.

Repeated attempts by the Commission to harmonize at least the tax base proved fruitless. Anticipating the single market, the Commission renewed its long-standing interests in these issues and appointed a committee of experts to examine:

- whether the differences in taxation between the member states cause major distortions, and
- what measures could usefully be taken to reduce them and to encourage international business activity within the EU.

The Ruding Committee (Ruding Report, 1992) found that all member states' tax systems discriminated in one way or another between domestic and non-domestic investment. It concluded, therefore, that market integration could accentuate these differences and cause large tax distortions which the interplay of market forces and competition between national tax regimes were not likely to smooth out. In view of the global character of capital markets, EU tax policy should also take account of the international interdependencies. Following the report, the Commission proposed, and the Council adopted, a code of conduct which aims at tax cooperation but is not a legally binding instrument. The code is specifically designed to detect only such measures as unduly affect the location of business activity in the Community by offering discriminatorily favourable tax treatment. At the moment, effective marginal tax rates in the EU vary between 13.74 per cent (Greece) and 40.71 per cent (France) on the level of the corporation while the average in the EU is 24.30 per cent. But there are doubts about the congruity of tax bases and effective tax rate among the EU members. Therefore the Commission argues that what is needed first is the harmonization of the accounting methods used to calculate taxable profits. The hope is that this would help make business in the EU more competitive and more open.

Personal income tax

The Community has not included personal income taxes among those intended for harmonization. In effect, it is tacitly agreed that harmonization should not directly impinge on this tax which should remain exclusively subject to national sovereignty. In an economic union, the bases for direct taxation become very 'mobile' and therefore more sensitive to tax differentials. Significant differences in personal tax rates may influence personal saving and investment decisions, migration and, indirectly, the location of corporation headquarters. This means that income tax rates have to converge. However, the EU member states are likely to retain considerable flexibility and freedom of manoeuvre for a long time to come. The strong linguistic and cultural differences between countries mean that labour mobility is weak and that personal tax differences will not have any significant effect on it. For some internationally mobile professions, however, this might not be the case. For example, when senior executives can choose in which European country to take up residence, it becomes no longer possible for their personal taxation rates to differ widely.

Social security taxes

Personal income taxes and social security contributions and benefits affect the take-home pay and the social insurance of labour. Thus, they are among the factors affecting production costs and prices, as well as the mobility of labour between occupations and countries. Therefore, as with capital and the harmonization of corporation tax, there should be a move for coordination of benefits and taxes on labour. However, with the exception of certain agreements on social policy (see Chapter 10), nothing else has happened in this field.

Taxation of savings

At the moment, withholding tax rates on savings income vary widely between EU states. Differences also exist in the taxation of capital income (bonds and dividends) and, since it is difficult to arrange to receive such income in low-tax countries, this can lead to tax distortions and tax evasion. The Commission made a proposal in 1998 aimed at guaranteeing a minimum of effective taxation of savings income within the Community by common consent between the member states and applying a *withholding tax* of 20 per cent for all EU countries on interest paid to non-residents. Alternatively, they could make the payments untaxed, but exchange information with the tax authorities of the recipients' home country. However, this proposal was unacceptable to countries which are international banking centres, such as the UK and Luxembourg, and the chances are that only the exchange of information might be accepted.

Questions

1. (a) Why is it argued that tax harmonization is necessary in economic unions?
   (b) Could the same outcome be reached by tax competition between the member states?

2. (a) What are the destination, origin and restricted origin principles of indirect taxation?
   (b) Which of these principles has the European Union adopted and what has the introduction of VAT to do with it?

3. Consider whether and under what conditions the following statement is valid: 'Tax coordination is generally preferable to tax competition in neutralizing distortions caused by fiscal differentials, while preserving diversity in fiscal choices among jurisdictions.'

4. 'The destination principle of taxation ensures that, despite international tax differences, competition will be based on comparative advantage and there will be a tendency to equate the producer price ratios of any two commodities in all the countries that participate in the common market, thus ensuring that the requirement of an efficient international specialization is satisfied.' Discuss.

5. 'The only way to ensure that net-of-tax prices are equated across borders is to harmonize tax rates within a band sufficiently narrow that the origin and destination principles roughly coincide':
   (a) Should tax harmonization aim at price equalization?
   (b) Would this objective be reached more efficiently by tax competition?

Further reading

Economic analysis of sales tax harmonization in economic (or tax) unions usually deals with the equivalence of different principles of taxation; see Lockwood et al. (1995). For tax harmonization in the single market see Keen and Smith (1996), and for corporate taxation Devereux (1992) and Cnossen (1996). For a market-based harmonization proposal see Cnossen

(1990). The Commission's proposals for a common system of VAT are in Commission (1996a).

Web guide

'*A note on tax policy in the European Union – priorities for the year ahead*' (2001) is available at www.europa.eu.int/comm/taxation and www.minfin.nl/uk/ taxation/TaxCompetition

Monetary integration

6

> So much barbarism, however, still remains in the transactions of most civilised nations, that almost all independent countries choose to assert their nationality by having, to their own inconvenience and their neighbours', a peculiar currency of their own.
>
> *(John Stuart Mill, Principles of Political Economy, 1848)*

From early on the European Union set monetary integration as one of the essential elements of market integration. In the past, it attempted to reach this target by means of fixed exchange rates which led nowhere near European Monetary Union (EMU). Finally, the objective of monetary integration was reached by establishing a new currency, the euro (€), and a new central bank, the ECB, which together with the national central banks of the member states constituted the new monetary authority of the European Community, the 'Eurosystem'. The most important task of the Eurosystem is to ensure price stability. In the context of European monetary integration, this chapter describes the institutional structure and the stability-oriented policies available to the Eurosystem which would enable it to reach its objective, and analyses issues relating to its operations.

6.1 Definitions and principles

Introduction

Rising economic interdependence between sovereign countries often leads them to coordinate their macroeconomic policies. In the field of monetary policy, 'externalities' caused by interdependence may steer them towards some form of international monetary collaboration. Within economic unions, rising interdependence and closer monetary coordination among the member states may propel them towards *monetary integration*.

Economic unions, such as the EU, adopt the standard four fundamental principles of an open market:

- free trade in goods
- free trade in services
- free mobility of capital
- free mobility of labour.

These are the building blocks of an integrated competitive market, which by means of common prices across the union arrived at through market competition would lead to optimal allocation of resources, increasing welfare and economic growth. But the existence of separate national currencies, which are often subject to erratic exchange rate changes, causes random price fluctuations which obviously disturb the integration process. For example, assume that the exchange rate between the French franc (FF) and the UK pound (UK£) is FF6 = £1 and the production cost of a good X in France is FF9 while in the UK it is £1. In the circumstances, the good would be exported from the UK to France. Next, either by market forces or by a devaluation of the FF (or revaluation of £) the exchange rate changes to FF12 = £1. Then the price of the good X in France is FF9 = £0.75, and in the UK £1 = FF12. Hence, trade is reversed by France now exporting the good X to the UK. The exchange rate shift has changed the direction of trade, which in turn may affect the balance of trade and other macroeconomic variables in both economies, disturbing the comparative advantage by a monetary (= nominal) fluke. This is one of the reasons monetary integration might become a necessary component of economic integration. The problem is that in an economic union the economic policies of one member state cause externalities on other member states. The solution to this problem is to internalize these externalities. But any move in this direction is complicated because monetary integration affects three of the most important instruments of national economic policy: monetary, fiscal, and exchange rate policy, which are basic components of every county's 'national sovereignty'.

Assuming that the members of the union agree to integrate their monetary sectors, in ascending order of national sovereignty loss they would proceed by:

- coordination
- harmonization
- unification,

of the policies that cause the externalities. Monetary integration, which requires the complete liberalization of capital movements between the participating states, can be implemented by two methods.

Box 6.1 ■ Exchange rates

We will define the exchange rate, S, as the price in domestic currency of one unit of foreign currency. Assume, for example, that in the EU you pay €1.05 to buy $1. Then, in Europe the exchange rate between the euro and the dollar is $S_{eu} = €/\$ = 1.05$. In the United States it will be the reverse: you pay $0.95 to buy €1, and the exchange rate of the dollar for the euro is $S_{us} = \$/€ = 1/S_{eu} = \$0.95$. According to this definition, a rise in the exchange rate S means a lower value of the domestic currency, or *depreciation*, e.g. $S_{eu} = €/\$ = 1.10$. Conversely, a fall in the exchange rate S means a higher value of the domestic currency, or *appreciation*, e.g. $S_{eu} = €/\$ = 1$.

The foreign exchange market is worldwide and open, and its participants are foreign exchange dealers (brokers and other agents), commercial banks, central banks, retail clients (businesses, traders, etc.) and speculators. The *spot* exchange rate is the price quoted between two currencies for immediate delivery. The *forward* exchange rate is the price quoted between two currencies for future delivery in one month, three months, six months, etc.

The *nominal* exchange rate is the one prevailing at a given date, $S_{eu} = €/\$$. The *real* exchange rate is the nominal exchange rate adjusted for relative prices between the two countries $S_{eu}^* = S_{eu}P_{eu}/P_{us}$, where in our example P_{eu} is the EU's price index and P_{us} is the US price index.

The exchange rate system is *flexible* and the exchange rate *floating*, when the authorities do not intervene to buy or sell their currency in the foreign exchange market and, therefore, its price fluctuates freely in response to changes in supply and demand. The exchange rate system is *fixed* when the authorities fix the price of their currency relative to another, the *key* currency (or to gold). To keep the currency steady at the fixed exchange rate the authorities have to supply any excess market demand for their currency or buy back any excess supply, using foreign currencies (and/or gold) from their *reserves*. Therefore, a fixed exchange rate system requires the monetary authority to hold *exchange* (and gold) *reserves*. The monetary authority can change the exchange rate, or the *parity value*, of their currency by *devaluation* (= depreciation) or *revaluation* (= appreciation). Devaluation decreases the country's export prices and increases its import prices in terms of foreign currency. Therefore, devaluation is used to improve a country's competitiveness by a simple stroke without any restructuring and cost reduction. But the success of devaluation is based on several assumptions which are not always met and therefore make it only a last-resort short-term remedy with serious side effects. The Bretton Woods system of fixed, periodically adjustable, exchange rates was set up in 1944 and lasted until 1972, supervised and monitored by the International Monetary Fund (IMF). Each country's currency was assigned a central parity against the key currency, the US$, with permitted margins of fluctuations ± 1 per cent. In the case of 'fundamental disequilibrium' causing persistent deficits in the trade account, the system permitted a country to devalue its currency. The US dollar itself was fixed to the price of gold at $35.0875 per ounce. In the 1960s, expansion of US expenditures abroad (e.g. from financing the Vietnam War), caused dollar oversupply and exchange rate instability in international markets. Balance of payments crises became increasingly frequent in many countries, leading to speculative attacks and devaluations. In the early 1970s, these crises became massive and free convertibility of the dollar to gold was suspended. This finally brought down the fixed exchange rates system. Its successor, adopted by most countries nowadays, is that of floating or managed floating rates.

There has been much discussion in the past on the relative merits of the two exchange rate systems, which differ significantly in both targets and operational rules. The floating system has apparent attractions with regard to resource allocation, similar to those of a free market mechanism. It provides countries with monetary policy autonomy and symmetry in financial affairs, and allows swift adjustment by automatic stabilizers. But experience has shown that it also reduces discipline, encourages destabilizing speculation, causes high exchange rate volatility, and increases uncertainty harmful for trade and international investment. In general, exchange rates are not just a price between two currencies. Their fluctuations and changes have important implications for trade, the balance of payments, inflation and national income as well as expectation formation and the credibility of monetary institutions and their policies. When international economic cooperation breaks down, no exchange rates system functions well.

1. Irrevocable fixing of exchange rate parities and irreversible convertibility of the union members' national currencies. After this stage is completed successfully, a prominent characteristic of the monetary union will be the multiplicity of currencies joined together in a fixed exchange rate system run by collaborating national central banks.
2. Replacement of the national currencies by the introduction of a new *common currency*, leading to integration of the financial and monetary sectors of the participating countries under a *common central bank*.

The problem of the first route to monetary integration is that countries have to give precedence to external rather than domestic economic issues. If they renege on their commitment to do so, e.g. by mounting domestic pressures requiring devaluation of their currency, then the system comes under tension which may affect its survival. The second method requires the full commitment of the participants to the union's objectives and thus entails the loss of a large chunk of national sovereignty. The EU followed the first method with the European Monetary System (EMS), but transformed it to the second method with European Monetary Union (EMU). Since EMU and the euro, €, are now a reality, we shall describe and analyse primarily the second method for reaching and operating monetary integration.

Benefits and costs

Clearly, monetary integration brings benefits, but it also entails costs. It is therefore suggested that the rationale of monetary integration should be based on a comparison of the benefits and costs of a common currency. The benefits are positively associated with the openness of a country within a large competitive market and its volume of international trade. They include:

- price transparency across borders which will encourage arbitrage between price discrepancies, inducing market integration, increasing the volume of trade[1] and enhancing competition;
- efficiency of a single currency as a unit of account and store of value;
- elimination of the transaction costs of changing one currency into another in inter-country trade;
- savings through holding lower international reserves;
- improved allocation of resources by elimination of the uncertainty which unpredictable exchange rate volatility causes in market prices and trade;
- standardization and lowering of interest rates, inducing investment within a more stable market;
- increased policy credibility from the elimination of devaluations.

But a single currency involves risks too, which are negatively associated with the openness of a country to international trade: the higher the intra-union volume of trade, the higher the country's dependence on the union's economy, and the lower its autonomy and effectiveness in the use of national policies. The members of a monetary union give up:

- the right to use their own monetary policy and the option of moving exchange rates against each other, e.g. by devaluation, to counteract asymmetric[2] shocks by changes in relative prices;
- the use of seigniorage, or 'inflation tax', as a source of budgetary revenue;[3]
- the rising interdependence of other national policies within the union (e.g. budgetary policies) which are constrained by the common monetary policy.

Figure 6.1 places together the benefits, line BB, and the costs, line CC, of monetary integration (Krugman, 1990). At the intersection point, E, the costs and benefits are equal. The vertical line HH through E divides the area of the diagram into two sectors: to the left of HH, the costs exceed

---

[1] Rose (2000) argues that a country conducts on average three times as much trade with its partners in a common currency union than with other equidistant countries.

[2] Asymmetric or idiosyncratic exogenous shocks (or business cycles) affect only the country concerned. Therefore, in a monetary union they would not solicit a response from the central bank of the union.

[3] Inflation tax or seigniorage means raising revenue for the government budget by monetary expansion (which may cause inflation). This source of revenue was unimportant in the EU countries.

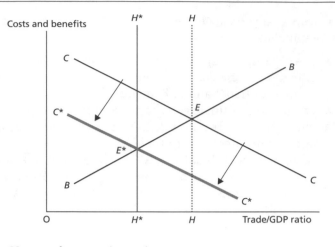

CC = costs of monetary integration
BB = benefits of monetary integration
E = point of benefits = costs
C*C* = shift in costs after monetary integration
E* = point of benefits = costs after monetary integration

Figure 6.1 **Benefits and costs of monetary integration**

the benefits, C > B; and to the right of HH, the benefits exceed the costs, C < B. Therefore, on static benefits–costs consideration, a country ought to join a monetary union only if its openness places it to the right of HH. In a common market, factor movements and increased trade expand competition which induces wage and price flexibility. Therefore, through time a country's membership in a common market would expand its openness, increasing its potential benefits and decreasing its costs from monetary integration. This is shown in Figure 6.1 by the shift of the costs curve to the left, C*C*, which increases the area of net benefits to the right of H*H*.

6.2 Optimum currency areas and monetary unions

OCA criteria

The standard theory of *optimum currency areas* (OCAs) sets up the criteria which the prospective members of a monetary union must meet for reaching maximum benefits and minimum costs within the union. As a rule, the more the member states resemble the regions of a single country, which do share a common currency, the greater the possibility that they will derive net gains from integrating their monetary sectors. The regions of a single country display two essential interregional characteristics:

1. price flexibility, in the prices of goods, services, capital and labour;
2. factor mobility, of both capital and labour.

By meeting these two conditions, all regions of a country display common prices because any discrepancy between them will be eliminated by trade arbitrage. The OCA criteria for the formation of a beneficial monetary integration between two (or more) countries are based on the interplay of these two interregional characteristics. By combining them, we can therefore distinguish the following four cases:

Case	Price flexibility	Factor mobility
1	Yes	Yes
2	No	Yes
3	Yes	No
4	No	No

Case 1. *Price flexibility* and *factor mobility* both exist. When both countries display flexible prices, then their real exchange rates are also flexible. Therefore, the countries would not lose by fixing their nominal exchange rates. Under these conditions, market competition ensures that productive resources and the production of output will be allocated optimally according to comparative advantage, while consumers will also gain from supply at optimal cost conditions.

Case 2. *Price flexibility* does not exist but *factor mobility* does. If the countries' prices are sticky (i.e. change very slowly), while both labour and capital can freely move from one country to the other, then again the nominal exchange rate can be fixed without undue costs to the two economies. For example, if a country-specific shock, such as a switch in demand from domestic suppliers to imports from the other country, were to reduce its demand for labour and capital and raise it in the other, equilibrium would be re-established by labour and capital moving in the country experiencing the increased demand (Mundell, 1961). This is identical to what is supposed to happen between the regions of a country. Therefore, the two countries can form a common currency union expecting to derive net benefits.[4]

---

[4] In other words, the members of the OCA must be (or become) homogeneous. It is also argued that, since national economies are the aggregates of their constituent regions, OCA theory's homogeneity condition should also apply at the interregional level (Thirwall, 2000). But the persistence of interregional economic disparities means that few countries of the real world meet the interregional homogeneity condition to justify the existence of a national single currency. The homogeneity condition should mean that each region should have its own currency.

Case 3. *Price flexibility* exists but *factor mobility* does not. This case is similar to case 2. For example, if commodity prices are flexible and trade is free, then commodity price equalization is assured. The theory suggests that commodity trade operates as a substitute for factor trade. Therefore, through time, factor prices will also tend to equalize.

Case 4. Neither *price flexibility* nor *factor mobility* exist. If the two countries have sticky prices and wages and low factor mobility or none at all, they should be advised to keep their own currencies and independent monetary policies, particularly if they are also affected by country-specific shocks. If these conditions prevail, changes in the nominal exchange rate can substitute for domestic price and wage flexibility, facilitating adjustment. Devaluation of a country's currency would operate as a 'shock absorber', restoring its price competitiveness without recession and unemployment. But even in this case the two countries could form a favourable currency union, if it is possible for them to set up a system of risk-sharing (or co-insurance), such as a central budget big enough to facilitate adjustment through fiscal transfers, just as a national budget does between the regions of a country. Access to a common capital market can operate in a similar way.

As we will see in the following, newer research has scrutinized the standard OCA criteria which are now greatly qualified.

Trade conditions

Since the benefits from monetary integration mostly arise from a reduction in transaction costs, the greater the volume of international trade between the members of the monetary union the greater the cost savings. If countries are very open, then they are also dependent on each other's economic conditions, and the positive and negative externalities caused on each other. Therefore, if they share the same objectives of price stability and growth, comparable degrees of openness and interdependence between the partners of the union accord with monetary integration.

Symmetric and asymmetric shocks

The discussion so far implies that in practice no single, overriding criterion can be used to assess the desirability or viability of a currency union. Furthermore, the application of these criteria to prospective common currency areas reveals factors working both for and against success. Attention has therefore turned to analysing the nature of shocks or business cycles affecting the prospective candidates of a monetary union, especially whether these shocks are *symmetric* or *asymmetric* (they hit countries in the same way or differently). For example, a general decline in the demand for industrial output will hit countries with similar industrial structures in the same way (symmetrically) and a mainly agricultural country differently (asymmetrically). Therefore, the more similar (or homogeneous) the countries forming the union are the better, and this is the general condition for benefits from economic integration at large (as shown in Chapter 1).

Summary

Monetary union only makes sense under three broad conditions:

- when asymmetric regional supply or demand shocks do not occur or are rare;
- if and when a negative shock does occur, either out-migration or a fall in nominal wages prevents unemployment staying persistently high;
- if the union has introduced a system of co-insurance.

Endogeneity of the OCA criteria

But the most important problem is that the OCA criteria are *jointly endogenous*: if a customs union establishes a single market and progresses to an economic union, its internal trade intensity and interdependence between its members rise and become increasingly correlated with symmetry in business cycles as member countries progressively become more similar (Frankel and Rose, 1998). Therefore:

- Judging the desirability of a prospective monetary union on the basis of past experiences and the use of historical data is invalid.
- Comparisons between an old-established monetary union, such as the USA, and an emerging one, such as the EU, are fruitless and invalid.
- Moreover, the standard OCA analysis is based on a fixed-price assumption, while a strong incentive for monetary union is the assurance that competition will reduce costs and prices (and that the union's inflation rate will be low: see Tavlas, 1993).

Therefore, if two or more countries form a currency area without meeting the standard optimality criteria *ex ante*, they will meet them endogenously *ex post*, ending up as an OCA (Hitiris, 1988). The members of the currency union can speed up this process by adopting measures to facilitate economic convergence with a greater degree of internal goods, services, capital and labour market flexibility and cross-border trade and mobility.

Political considerations

In general, the incentive for monetary integration comes from the potential improvements of efficiency in resource allocation and exchange by the use of a single currency in the interregional trade of a unified market. If two or more countries form an economic union and their ultimate objective is to integrate the market for goods, services and factors of production and to proceed with some form of political unification, there are not many valid arguments against establishing a monetary union. It is possible that initially some countries, which meet the standard criteria for participation in an optimum currency area and ought to join, are not members of the economic union, while other countries, which should not be included in the currency area, are included. However, as economic integration progresses and openness to trade and factor mobility rises, the OCA conditions are progressively fulfilled. Undoubtedly, a single currency is also a public symbol of political unification. For example, in the EU *'the euro is much more than just a currency . . . It is a symbol of European integration in every sense of the word'* (Duisenberg, *Financial Times*, 31 August 2001). Even if the expressed goal of the contracting parties is simply stated as economic integration, monetary integration is

---

Box 6.2 ■ The euro = EUR = €

The voluntary transfer of monetary sovereignty from the national to the European level is unique in history. However, it should not be seen as a single, isolated event. The introduction of the euro is part of the process of European integration . . . The aims of European integration are not only, or even primarily, economic. Indeed, this process has been driven and continues to be driven by the political conviction that an integrated Europe will be safer, more stable and more prosperous than a fragmented Europe.

Wim Duisenberg (First president of the European Central Bank, in a speech at the National Bank of Poland, 4 May 1999, available at www.ecb.int/key/sp990504.htm)

The euro is much more than just a currency . . . It is a symbol of stability and unity; countries from a continent which, throughout the ages, has so often been ravaged by war, have together vowed to uphold the values of freedom, democracy and human rights, forever replacing the horrors of past conflict.

On January 1, 2002, 300 million people will for the first time be able to cross 12 national borders and discover that the currency which their neighbours are using is the same as the one they are using at home . . . Europeans will realise they are at home throughout Europe.

In addition to the economic and political benefits the euro brings, it will, I believe, help to change the way in which we think about one another as Europeans.

Wim Duisenberg (reported in the Financial Times, *Friday, 31 August 2001, p. 6)*

In memoriam: Austrian schilling, ATS; Belgian franc, BEF; Finnish markkaa, FIM; French franc, FRF; German mark, DEM; Greek drachma, GDR; Italian lira, ITL; Luxembourg franc, LUF; Dutch guilder, NLG; Portuguese escudo, PTE; Irish punt, IEP; Spanish peseta, ESP.

implied because market unification without monetary integration is not conceivable.

Is Europe an OCA?

The underlying premise of the optimal currency areas (OCA) theory is that in order to reduce the costs and maximize the expected benefits of monetary integration there should be a high degree of economic homogeneity amongst the countries setting up the currency area. Homogeneity is usually evaluated with reference to (a) the volume of trade; (b) the intensity of labour and capital mobility; and (c) the degree of synchronization of business cycles. If these are high, then it is inferred that the degree of homogeneity amongst the countries is also high and therefore they can safely proceed to monetary union. At first sight, Europe falls short of the standard OCA conditions. Compared with the USA, employment shocks are distributed less symmetrically across regions, labour markets are less able to absorb them and people are less inclined to migrate. However, the problem with these tests is that there is no standard benchmark for deciding what score is high, low or just right. Comparisons with the scores of existing federal states which were established a long time ago, such as the USA, are a priori meaningless and invalid. But we can analyse some of the variables which may inform us about the current degree of EU progress towards achieving homogeneity:

Volume of trade

We concluded earlier that the greater the volume of trade between the members of a union the greater the potential benefit from monetary integration. A high volume of trade indicates that the economies of the member states are closely integrated and complement each other consistently. In the EU, the ratio of internal trade on EU GDP is about 17 per cent, which is high but much lower than, for example, trade between US states. However, the euro has only just started to circulate while the dollar has a long history behind it. Since interregional trade intensity within countries is more than 20 times higher than between countries (McCallum, 1995), there is plenty of room for trade within the EU to grow *endogenously*. Since the bulk of member-state commercial and financial transactions already take place with the Union's other member states, the recent introduction of the single currency suggests that EU internal trade may expand further in the near future.

Intensity of capital and labour mobility

The more mobile the factors of production between regions, the more likely these regions are to constitute an OCA. While capital mobility within the EU is high, labour mobility is not. Moreover, under the prevailing European conditions, it is not expected to grow to the level of labour mobility of the USA. Differences in language and culture discourage the mobility of labour between European countries. Even interregional labour mobility within EU countries is low, despite the existence of vast differences in unemployment rates and the opportunities open to those who might choose to move. But, in general, labour mobility will rise after EMU by the ease of comparing interstate factor rewards.

Degree of synchronization of business cycles

Synchronicity of external shocks is one of the requirements for countries contemplating a monetary union. However, even if the countries experience broadly similar business cycles, different policy reactions to them by the countries' policy-makers could lead to asymmetries. Despite these issues, research has found 'considerable synchronicity between [EU members'] business cycles (the UK being a partial exception)' even before EMU, indicating the emergence of a 'European business cycle' which will become more dominant in future years[5] (Artis et al., 1999, p. 25). Even if European cycles are not yet very synchronized, the endogeneity of OCA criteria implies that an increased degree of synchronicity should be expected to follow the advent of monetary integration.

Conclusion

At the moment, the EU meets some of the OCA criteria but not all of them. But this does not mean that the EU countries should not have proceeded to EMU: the endogeneity of the OCA criteria suggests that, if these criteria are not completely met before EMU, they will be met through EMU.

6.3 Moves for monetary integration in the EU

Treaty provisions and procedures

The Treaty of Rome did not refer to monetary integration. The international monetary system in operation at that time consisted of the

---

[5] The tests were applied, however, on historical data of mostly the pre-EMU period. This is not a valid procedure for predicting the future of the EU because EMU has created its own 'new regime' based on a single currency which has no foundations in the past performance of the quasi-fixed exchange rates under the EMS.

dollar-based fixed exchange rates (see Box 6.1), which effectively made the whole world a common currency area. Therefore, there was no specific need for the EU to include monetary integration as one of the components of market integration. However, in the late 1960s and early 1970s increasing pressure on the dollar (arising from the global financial and strategic commitments of the USA) and general exogenous shocks and disturbances in world markets (such as oil embargoes) caused diverging inflation rates across countries which in turn induced frequent exchange rate changes by devaluations and revaluations. Finally, the fixed exchange rate system collapsed and, in an attempt to insulate domestic policy from external constraints, many countries floated their currencies. But the system of floating exchange rates brought chaos, not the 'sensible market-led adjustment' that its champions had promised. Soon after, inflation rates rose well above what they used to be under the fixed exchange rate system. The concurrent high exchange rate volatility that followed the breakdown of the fixed rate system started to unsettle mostly the countries which were open to world trade and payments, such as those comprising the EU.

Meanwhile, the EU had already started to pursue its integration objectives by common policies. The most important among them was the CAP which guaranteed EU farmers minimum support prices for their products, expressed in the European *unit of account (ua,* initially set at 1ua = US$1). However, this mode of setting prices led to problems: when exchange rates within the EU were realigned relative to the dollar, some countries' farmers found that the real value of their support prices had risen, while farmers in other countries were in the opposite position. The continuing exchange rate turbulence caused many such asymmetric repercussions among EU states, and this forced some of them to change their priorities by resorting to the use of policies selected on purely domestic considerations rather than on their external obligations in the common market. For example, in 1969 France devalued the franc by 11.1 per cent, and soon after Germany revalued the Deutschmark by 9.29 per cent, thus changing the intra-Community parity rates (and the gap between the agricultural prices of the two countries) by more than 20 per cent.

These developments had an impact on economic performance and inflation rates which started to diverge significantly between the EU countries. This confirmed that the foundations of the common market – free trade in goods, services and factors of production, competition on equal terms, coordination of policy instruments and targets, and common policies for common objectives – under national currencies and monetary policies could not be sustained except with the support of a fixed exchange rate among the Community partners. Under this externally imposed pressure, the EU started to examine how to continue its course towards economic integration. This brought forward several political and economic arguments for and against monetary integration and provoked many disputes among the EU partners about what degree of monetary integration was necessary and how it should be implemented. Finally, the Hague summit (1969) appointed P. Werner, the prime minister of Luxembourg, to head a committee to outline a plan for the elimination of intra-EU exchange rate turbulence. The Werner Report, adopted by the EU in 1971, proposed the establishment of European Monetary Union (EMU) in stages by 1980.

The first attempt: the 'snake in the tunnel'

The Council decided that the first stage of EMU should be implemented in 1972 in the form of a 'European band' of currency fluctuations or the 'snake in the tunnel'. This was a variant of the adjustable fixed exchange rate system with the US dollar in the centre (as under the previous fixed exchange rate system) and margins of permitted fluctuations around it of ±2.25 per cent. Thus the Community currencies could float together as a band relative to the dollar in a quasi-fixed relationship. The system was monitored and administered by the European Monetary Cooperation Fund (EMCF), while the margins of permitted fluctuation were defended by coordinated monetary policy, short-term credit facilities from the Fund and the concerted action of the member countries' central banks. As a last resort, if the fixed rate could not be defended, the participants were allowed to withdraw from the system, temporarily or permanently.

The narrowing of exchange rate fluctuations was rapidly achieved. But in March 1973 the dollar was set free to float and thus, without an anchor, the 'tunnel' caved in, leaving the snake just a joint float of the participants. This event, combined with the quadrupling of the oil price, meant the demise of the system which was abandoned and rejoined by committed participants 18 times while the 'fixed' parities were altered by devaluation 31 times. By the end of 1977 only the Deutschmark, the Dutch guilder, the Belgian franc, the Luxembourg franc and the Danish krone remained in the 'snake', and thus Europe was no nearer to EMU than in 1969.

The second attempt: the EMS

When worldwide inflation, high unemployment and turbulence in the currency markets proved the snake system unworkable, the EU set up a new scheme for monetary integration in 1979, the *European Monetary System, EMS*. This system was based on fixed, though adjustable exchange rates relative to a central currency standard, the *European currency unit* (*ecu*) which was a composite currency of unit value equal to a basket of specified amounts of the national currencies of all the EU states. These amounts broadly reflected each country's weight in the EU economy (e.g. share in EU GDP and intra-EU trade), and were normally revised every five years to keep up with economic changes. Germany was the strongest economy in the EMS and therefore its currency, the Deutschmark (D-Mark or DM), was assigned a dominant one-third share in the composition of the ecu. The exchange rate of each EU currency was defined in terms of the *ecu central rate* which in turn determined the bilateral exchange rates between the EU currencies. Participation in the *Exchange Rate Mechanism* (*ERM*) of the EMS required countries to maintain their currency within specified margins of permitted fluctuations around the ecu central rates and each other of ±2.25 per cent. If in the financial markets an ERM currency tended to move outside the margins, the country concerned was expected to intervene by taking appropriate monetary and fiscal measures to keep it within them. Policy adjustment was intended to be *symmetric*: all countries were expected to help each other by direct intervention in the foreign exchange markets. If, for example, Italy's lira was to appreciate against the French franc, the Bank of France was expected to buy francs for liras, and the Bank of Italy to sell liras for francs until the exchange rate between the two currencies returned to the ERM band.

Financial help for intervention was provided by the EMCF, which was the central monetary institution of the Community, administered by the Governors of the EMS members' central banks. In the case of 'marginal interventions' the ERM participants had recourse to a 'very short financial facility' (VSFF). For broader interventions, funds were made available directly by the EMCF. But, if there were indications that the disequilibrium between exchange rates had arisen from more permanent misalignments caused by changes in economic conditions (such as trade imbalances and diverging inflation rates), then a realignment was implemented by a mutually agreed devaluation/revaluation of central rates. Thus, the EMS was a system of irrevocably fixed rather than managed exchange rates, subject to periodic adjustments by collective decision and a common procedure. During 1979–90 12 realignments were implemented which were relatively small and therefore did not cause speculative crises. The system operated smoothly and achieved its objectives of long-run nominal and real exchange rate stability and low inflation (from 12.7 per cent in 1988 to 4.3 per cent in 1992), leading to closer cooperation between the central banks of the ERM members and a significant degree of monetary policy convergence (MacDonald and Taylor, 1991). Some researchers, however, attribute a large part of the stability of the EMS to the protection afforded by exchange and capital controls that during this perod were still prevalent in most ERM countries (Artis, 1988).

All member states of the Community automatically became members of the EMS but not of the ERM. Spain joined the ERM in June 1989, the UK in October 1990 and Portugal in April 1992, but Greece decided to remain outside. Of the new members, Austria and Finland joined in January 1995, while Sweden opted out of the ERM.

Although the EMS was conceived as a *symmetric system* with all the countries cooperating and agreeing together the policies applied in common, the most successful ERM economy with high employment and low inflation was Germany. Therefore, when the other member states decided to 'borrow credibility' from the German Federal Bank (the Bundesbank) by committing themselves firmly to fixed exchange rates and following its lead, they implicitly elevated Germany to the unofficial leadership of the EMS, which implicitly became an *asymmetric* system. This was in accordance with the international currency markets, which viewed not the ecu but the D-Mark as the *de facto* anchor of the ERM. However, the economic policies of Germany continued to target primarily domestic and not EU-wide issues. Through time, these developments inevitably led to a clash between Germany's economic objectives and policies and those of other member states. In the meantime, the EU's commitment to completion of the internal market by the end of 1992 also included the lifting of all controls to capital mobility. But with the controls gone, the credibility of the EMS fixed exchange rates suffered from the possibility that speculative capital movements could destabilize the system. In the end, speculation proved to be one of the major forces that destabilized the EMS.

The crisis started after the unification of Germany which induced the federal government to undertake massive public expenditure in the former East Germany that caused a large fiscal deficit. As a result inflation in Germany started to rise and the authorities reacted by raising the interest rate. The rest of the EMS countries were suffering from recession and needed a cut in their interest rates to stimulate aggregate demand, but in order to remain in the ERM they were instead required to raise their interest rates above the German one. Speculators realized that under these conditions the financially weakest EMS countries (such as Italy, Spain and the UK) would not be able to support such a policy for long, and put their bets on impending devaluations against the D-Mark. This precipitated the crisis and, despite the massive intervention by national central banks, devaluations and the reintroduction of capital controls were implemented, undermining the ERM, which from 1 August 1993 in effect ceased to be the chosen instrument for achieving monetary integration in the EU.

Box 6.3 ■ EMS asymmetry and the 1992 crisis

The unification of Germany in 1990 induced massive public expenditure from West Germany to the former East Germany. This caused a large fiscal deficit which raised the inflation rate from 1.3 per cent in 1988 to 4.8 per cent in March 1992. The Bundesbank reacted with its standard inflation-fighting policy of raising the interest rate to the historically high level of 9.75 per cent. This intensified the demand for the D-Mark and caused tension in the EMS because it forced the other ERM countries to tighten their monetary policies in line with Germany in an attempt to convince investors to hold their currencies. Meanwhile, the United States was hit by a recession and the Federal Reserve cut the interest rate to 3 per cent. The unprecedented gap of 6.75 percentage points between German and US interest rates induced capital to flow from New York to Frankfurt. To stay within the ERM exchange rate band, the rest of the EU countries had to raise their interest rates above Germany's, although they had been suffering from recession for more than a year (e.g. Spain, Italy and the UK) and would have preferred to cut rather than raise their interest rates. These events convinced the financial markets that the weak currencies would be devalued and therefore that the days of fixed exchange rates in the ERM were numbered. In August 1992, the foreign exchange markets induced a dollar fall to a historic low against the D-Mark despite the intervention of 18 national central banks which tried to prop it up by support-buying. Sweden and Finland, which had fixed their currencies to the ecu in preparation for joining the EU, were the first to be hit by all-out speculative attacks. Sweden defended its currency successfully by raising its interest rates on overnight loans to 500 per cent. The markets next picked out the weakest of the ERM currencies, the Italian lira and the UK pound, and despite massive coordinated intervention by the Bundesbank and other central banks, they forced them to depreciate by free fall below the ERM floor. Italy devalued the lira and on 'Black Wednesday' 16 September 1992 the UK pound was allowed to float after the Bank of England lost billions defending it. Despite the devaluation, the lira came under attack again and Italy suspended it from the ERM. Spain, Portugal and Ireland devalued their currencies while some countries also reimposed exchange controls to slow reserve losses. In the spring of 1993, Portugal devalued for a second time and Spain for a third. The French franc also came under strong speculative attack twice, threatening to force it out of the ERM by devaluation despite prolonged intervention by both the Bank of France and the Bundesbank. Since the franc along with the D-Mark lay at the heart of the ERM, the system was in imminent danger of collapse. Therefore, in an attempt to restore the ERM's stability, abate speculative attacks and give governments more room to spur their economies out of recession, the EMS countries reluctantly decided on 1 August 1993 to widen the EMS flexibility by increasing 'temporarily' its bands from ± 2.25 to ± 15 per cent. This brought calm to the markets and the speculation attacks finally ceased.

The events of 1992–3 convinced many Europeans that the EMS was fundamentally flawed. The wider bands only meant that exchange rates could fluctuate more than before, causing wider divergences in prices and interest rates between the national markets of the countries comprising the common market, thus reversing the course towards the single market. Meanwhile, the Community had already decided at Maastricht to proceed to European Monetary Union (EMU) by a new strategy.

6.4 Establishing EMU

Introduction

The Single European Act, which aimed at unification of the EU market by 1992, specified that economic and monetary union was an objective of the Community and that the EMS was a stage towards achieving that goal. Clearly, with a free market for goods and services, the members could not at the same time have (a) stable exchange rates, (b) integrated capital markets, and (c) an independent monetary policy. As we have seen, the EMS helped the EU to achieve 'a zone of increasing monetary stability' but in many EU countries stability in domestic financial markets and protection from speculative attacks were attained only by the assistance of capital controls. Moreover, during the early years of the EMS, convergence in economic policy and performance was limited and, from necessity, parity realignments within the EMS often occurred. It became clear, therefore, that the EMS, by being focused on quite short-term exchange rate stability and constrained by the limited power of its institutions, which were not designed to bypass the sovereignty of members' monetary authorities, was not subject to the built-in evolutionary process that would have transformed it into the EMU. Although improvements were introduced, it was still felt that the EMS could not be relied upon as a durable system and as a channel to monetary integration without further institutional developments.

It was generally agreed that the growing economic interdependence between the member states would require more intensive and more effective economic policy coordination and that, without a firm commitment to irrevocably fixed exchange rates, further integration could lead to destabilization. In particular, the liberalization of trade in financial services and the integration of capital markets could be accompanied by large speculative capital flows in anticipation of central rate realignments. Therefore, monetary union started to be seen as the natural complement of the economic union which was actively pursued by the single market project.

Therefore, another important step towards monetary integration was taken at the Hanover summit (June 1988), when the European Council set up a special committee under the chairmanship of the President of the Commission, 'to study and propose concrete stages leading towards Economic and Monetary Union'. The Delors Report (Commission 1989) linked completion of the single market to a single currency, with the coordination of all macroeconomic policies and the endorsement of 'binding rules for budgetary policies'. Following the recommendations of the Delors Report, the Maastricht conference decided the strategy and the timetable for advancing towards monetary integration.

The Maastricht route to EMU

The Maastricht Treaty (1992) outlined a three-stage process for achieving EMU. The timetable and content of each stage were as follows:

Stage 1 (1990–3)

All Community currencies join the ERM on equal terms. The member states fully liberalize capital movements and improve economic policy co-ordination between them. Exchange rate realignments remained possible.[6]

Stage 2 (1994–8)

The European Monetary Institute (EMI) is set up. Monetary policy continues to be made by national central banks, while the EMI concentrates on defining the instruments and procedures which the European Central Bank (ECB) will use in the next stage, and monitors with the Commission the economic situation of the countries with regard to the criteria for admission to EMU.

Stage 3 (1999)

Exchange rates are irrevocably locked. The European System of Central Banks (ESCB) and the European Central Bank (ECB) start formulating and implementing the common monetary policy according to the provisions of the treaty which include:

1. three fundamental principles: (a) the objective: price stability; (b) independence from national governments and Community authorities; (c) democratic accountability;
2. three main tasks: (a) the formulation and implementation of the single monetary policy and the issue of the common currency; (b) exchange rate and reserve management; (c) banking supervision.

The ESCB is composed of the European Central Bank (ECB) and the National Central Banks (NCBs) of the 15 EU member states The ECB and the NCBs of the EU member states that have met the Maastricht criteria and agreed to adopt the single currency, collectively form the 'Eurosystem'. The national central banks of the EU member states that decided not to adopt the common currency are members of the ESCB but do not take part in decision-making with regard to the single monetary policy. The Eurosystem is managed by the decision-making bodies of the ECB, namely the Governing Council and the Executive Board. The Governing Council is the highest decision-making body of the ECB and consists of the

---

[6] The events of 1992 meant that this stage could not be completed on time, with some countries remaining outside (Greece) or withdrawing from the ERM (the UK and Italy).

governors of the central banks of the euro area. The Executive Board consists of the President, the Vice-President and four other members, all chosen for their expertise in banking matters, appointed by the heads of state or government of the euro area countries. In view of the primary objective of price stability, a 'no-bailout' rule forbids the Eurosystem from monetizing, i.e. buying up, the debt of member states experiencing fiscal crises. When the member states replace their national currencies by the euro, the ultimate objective of monetary unification will have been achieved.

The date of transition to stage 3 and the membership of the monetary union were conditional on the majority of member states achieving a high degree of sustainable convergence, as laid down in the convergence criteria set by the treaty (see Box 6.4). The treaty foresaw a first examination of these criteria in 1997 and stipulated that the third stage of EMU would definitely begin on 1 January 1999. It was agreed that from that

---

Box 6.4 ■ The Maastricht convergence criteria

The Maastricht Treaty laid down the following five convergence criteria which every EU country aspiring to participate in EMU had to meet:

- *Price stability*: The applicant country's inflation rate should not be more than 1.5 per cent higher than the average of the three member states with the lowest inflation rates.
- *Interest rate*: Its nominal long-term interest rate should not be more than 2 per cent higher than the average of the three low-inflation member states.
- *Debt convergence*: Its public debt should not exceed 60 per cent of GDP; if it does, it should be brought down low enough to approach the reference value of 60 per cent at a satisfactory pace.
- *Budget deficit*: Its government budget deficit should not be more than 3 per cent of its GDP; if it is higher, it should be declining 'substantially and continuously' and come close to the 3 per cent norm, or, alternatively, the deviation from the norm should be 'only exceptional and temporary' and remain close to it.
- *Currency stability*: Its currency should have been stable within the narrow band of the EMS without realignments or 'severe tensions' for at least the two preceding years.

In addition, the applicant country's central bank should become independent.

In contrast to the OCA criteria that are concerned with economic conditions in the real side of the economy, the Maastricht convergence criteria pertained to current and prospective inflation performance, the stance of fiscal policy and exchange rate stability. However, the Maastricht Treaty also listed certain 'real convergence' conditions, such as 'the results of the integration of markets, the situation and development of the balance of payments on current account and an examination of the development of labour costs and other price indices' (TEU, 121). Therefore, eligibility for EMU was made conditional on both nominal and real economic convergence.

date onwards, exchange rates would be irrevocably locked and monetary policy would be handed over to the European Central Bank. Monetary operations and the issue of new public debt would start to be denominated in the new currency which the Council decided would be named 'the euro, symbol €, official abbreviation EUR'.

Associated measures

The events of 1992–3 intensified the doubts about the ability of the EU to complete EMU on schedule. Furthermore, insufficient economic growth led to new problems and, while inflation remained low, unemployment started to rise (soaring to 11.1 per cent average rate in 1996, see Figure 6.2). To check these developments, Europe started to implement the growth initiative (agreed at summits in Edinburgh, 1992, and Copenhagen, 1993) which shifted the emphasis from deregulation to active public policy, and advocated firm budgetary and other macroeconomic measures to ensure sustainable recovery. The signing of the *Stability and Growth Pact* (SGP) in 1997 also bound all the EMU participants to strict fiscal rectitude. Budgetary discipline is required to support the monetary policy to achieve its objective of price stability, without spillover effects of unsound fiscal policies on the countries of the euro area. It does this, in part, by setting the Maastricht target for budget deficit at 3 per cent of GDP as an explicit ceiling that cannot be breached by EMU participants during normal business cycles. Where an excessive deficit persisted, a qualified majority of member states could require the transgressing country to take specific action to rectify the situation within a given time limit, and to impose financial sanctions if it failed to comply. It also strengthened the medium-term framework for surveillance by requiring member states to submit 'stability programmes' annually for an audit by the Council of Ministers.

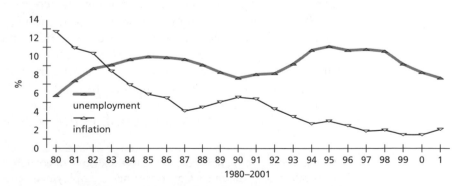

Figure 6.2 Inflation and unemployment in EU-15, 1980–2001
Source: Data from Commission (2001f).

Box 6.5 ■ Functions of the Eurosystem

The basic tasks of the Eurosystem are:

■ to define and implement the monetary policy of the euro area;
■ to conduct foreign exchange operations and to hold and manage the official reserves of the member states;
■ to issue banknotes in the euro area;
■ to promote the smooth operation of the payments system.

Further tasks of the Eurosystem are:

■ to collect the necessary statistical information either from national authorities or directly from economic agents, e.g. financial institutions;
■ to review developments in the banking and financial sector and to promote a smooth exchange of information between the ESCB and supervisory authorities.

The single money market of the euro area is based on a system of payments known as TARGET (Trans-European Automated Real-time Gross settlement Express Transfers). This links together the national payments systems of the EU member states and the ECB payments mechanism. TARGET makes it possible and safe to transfer large amounts of money between bank accounts from one end of the EU to the other within seconds.

Source of information: ECB, available at www.ecb.int

6.5 How EMU is run

The launching of EMU

European Monetary Union (EMU) came into being on 1 January 1999, with an initial complement of 11 out of 15 countries. Greece met the criteria in 2000 and joined EMU on 1 January 2001. The UK and Denmark have an opt-out clause, whilst Sweden, which was not a member of the EMS and did not express any wish to join the EMU, was judged to have failed the criteria. The people of Denmark decided by a referendum held in September 2000 that they did not wish to join the EMU at that time. However, Denmark's currency, the krone, remains pegged to the euro. The UK position is that membership in the EMU will be recommended to its citizens after the UK economy satisfied five 'economic' tests.[7] The final decision will be based on the results of a referendum.

---

[7] These wide-ranging tests are related to the degree of economic convergence and flexibility, and the impact on investment, employment and financial services exclusively in the UK. With the exception of the first, they have very little in common with the OCA criteria (Hitiris, 2001).

From 1 January 2002 onwards euro notes and coins became legal tender and the withdrawal of the old national notes and coins began. The dual circulation of old currencies and euros ended on 28 February 2002. Thus the single currency, €, which had always been seen as the vital missing piece of the single market jigsaw, the bulwark against currency speculation, and the guarantor of price stability, became a reality.

The Eurosystem

The move to EMU, which has a different task from its predecessors, has established a new regime without a prior historical track record. Therefore, the European Central Bank (ECB) started taking monetary decisions for the euro area without any previous experience of the policy applied, its effects and the reactions to them at the EU level: the ECB is writing its own history and generating its own reputation.

According to the TEEC and the statutes of the ESCB and the ECB, the primary objective of the Eurosystem is to maintain price stability. In doing so, the Eurosystem will contribute to minimizing distortions in the allocation of resources, thus fostering economic growth at the economy's productive potential. Without prejudice to this objective, the Eurosystem 'shall also support the general economic policies of the Community and act in accordance with the principles of an open market economy'.[8]

A fundamental and immediate objective of the ECB is to establish its credibility. The treaties provided the Eurosystem with clear institutional independence from (member states' and the EU's) political pressures to help development of the conditions that would deliver this credibility.

The monetary policy strategy of the Eurosystem

The treaty specifies that the Eurosystem's 'stability-oriented monetary policy strategy' aims at ensuring the maximum degree of effectiveness, transparency, accountability, forward-looking orientation, and continuity with past successful strategies of NCBs. It does so by combining the following basic elements:

- A precise quantitative definition of price stability: the year-on-year increase in the harmonized index of consumer prices (HICP) for the

---

[8] Therefore, the promotion of full employment and growth are among the implicit objectives of the ECB, which it can pursue only to the extent that this does not conflict with its primary target of price stability. In contrast, the US Congress explicitly directs the Federal Reserve to aim at two objectives 'maximum employment' and 'price stability'.

euro area of below 2 per cent per annum. Neither prolonged inflation nor prolonged deflation is consistent with this definition of price stability, which applies over the medium term.

■ A prominent role for money among the monitored variables: this is signalled by adopting a reference value for the *growth of money supply*[9] and analysing the deviations from it, which normally warrant changes in the monetary policy stance.

■ A broadly based assessment of the prospects for price stability in the euro area as a whole based on a wide range of economic and financial indicators, such as cost and price indices, the exchange rate, real economy indicators and financial market indicators (ECB, 1999a and 1999b).

The 'operational framework' of monetary policy is characterized by reliance on the self-regulating market mechanism with limited involvement of the ECB which consists primarily of open market operations, standing facilities and minimum reserve requirements.[10]

While under EMU monetary policy is centralized, primary responsibility for fiscal and structural concerns is decentralized. This is designed to enable individual countries to adapt fiscal and structural policies to their own specific problems. However, policy coordination will be enhanced further and will be subject to the surveillance instruments provided for in the treaties.

6.6 Fiscal policy and monetary integration in the EU

Introduction

When monetary integration has reached the stage of irrevocably fixed exchange rates and capital mobility has established a common interest rate in the union, fiscal expansion in one country could raise prices at

---

[9] For example, the growth rate of the monetary aggregate known as M3, which measures the amount of cash in circulation + short-term deposits + short-term interest-bearing securities, was set at 4.5 per cent for the year 2000.

[10] *Open market operation* is the purchase or sale of securities by the central bank to influence the money supply, and so interest rates and the volume of credit. *Standing facilities* are instruments for influencing overnight liquidity by lending to NCBs or borrowing from them. A *minimum reserve requirement* is an instrument for stabilizing money market interest rates and monetary expansion by the requirement for credit institutions to keep a deposit with the central bank.

union-wide scale. This implies that some of the costs of fiscal policies[11] in one country may be passed forward as *negative externalities* to other members of the union by trade.

In contrast, monetary integration with decentralized fiscal policy may impart a disincentive to member states to expand demand by their own fiscal policy. This effect could arise because a large part of the benefits of a country's fiscal expansion may accrue as *positive externalities* to fellow member states in terms of increased demand and employment. But most of the costs of the fiscal expansion would fall squarely on the country itself in terms of a balance-of-trade deficit.

Although these arguments may not be absolutely valid if capital mobility is perfect, the members of a monetary union would be better off by closer coordination of their fiscal policies or, in some cases, by adopting some degree of fiscal centralization. The latter should not mean the complete federalization of the members' national tax and public expenditure policies. Even in established federal systems, such as the United States and Canada, state and local governments maintain jurisdiction over a sizeable proportion of tax revenues and expenditures (see Chapter 4). On balance, however, monetary unification may need a parallel move towards fiscal centralization.

Constraints on national budgetary policy

While monetary policy under EMU becomes a European policy instrument, fiscal policies remain national responsibilities. This has led to worries about the possibility that some member states might abuse their fiscal policies to free-ride on their fellow member states and thus endanger the success of monetary unification. This was one of the reason the Stability and Growth Pact (SGP) was signed. This, however, raises the issue of whether member states possess the necessary instruments to pursue stabilization policies after EMU.

In the light of EU market integration for goods and services with low labour mobility and wage flexibility still imperfect, automatic adjustment to equilibrium is unsure. Therefore, without national monetary and exchange rate policy to repulse asymmetric shocks, the stabilization role of fiscal policy becomes pivotal. But the flexibility of fiscal policy, which was constrained by the debt and deficit criteria during the transition to EMU, is perpetuated by the SGP which set strict limits on how much countries can borrow and spend on anti-cyclical policies. If they exceed the pre-specified limits, they are subject to financial penalties.

---

[11] 'Fiscal policies' and 'budgetary policies' are taken to include both tax and spending policies.

Many commentators argue that, in comparison with the US Federal Reserve (the Fed), the ECB's brief is 'fatally flawed'. The Fed has to aim at price stability and maximum employment. The ECB is concerned solely with price stability. Therefore, without a national monetary policy and with national fiscal policy tied, it should be the task of a centralized common stabilization policy to act as insurance against asymmetric shocks. An adequate central budget could be used to restore equilibrium by transferring resources from the surplus country to the deficit one. But at the moment there is no official support for initiating any EU stabilization schemes. This brings forward the role of fiscal policy in monetary unions, and in the EMU.

The optimum currency literature recommends centralization of a significant part of fiscal (tax and spending) policies to enable it to play a positive role in monetary unions (Kenen, 1969). The Werner Report (1970) also envisaged a larger EU budget with tax harmonization and centralized control of national fiscal policies. Similar arguments were presented in the MacDougall Report (EC, 1977) which pointed out that, within countries, regional stabilization is provided automatically through the tax-benefit system: a depressed region pays fewer taxes and receives more benefits due to the 'automatic stabilizers'. The report suggested, therefore, that inter-country transfers through a centralized EU budget would be necessary to offset country-specific shocks. It also argued that monetary union without a significant centralization of budgetary power would lead to social tensions which could threaten the survival of the union (see Chapter 4). The counter-argument is that, compensating for the loss of the monetary policy instrument, national governments in a monetary union must turn to a more active use of fiscal policy (Kenen, 1969). This will be essential for the EU countries because their national economies will remain diverse well after EMU, and some of them may continue to experience asymmetric macroeconomic disturbances (Eichengreen, 1993). Convergence will occur but its time path may be long and erratic. This may be particularly important for the countries of central and eastern Europe (CEE) which are expected to join the EU in the near future (as discussed in Chapter 9).

Federal fiscal stabilization and co-insurance

In monetary unions, region-specific and country-specific problems can no longer be redressed by exchange rate changes. In existing federal states, the federal government is endowed with a large flow of tax revenues and expenditures to cushion downturns in regional incomes. For example, studies have found that the USA federal fiscal system offsets 30 to 40 per cent of short-term shocks to a state's income loss through automatic reductions in federal tax liabilities and increasing inward transfers

(Sala-i-Martin and Sachs, 1992). It is suggested, therefore, that a similar union-wide fiscal system should be adopted by the EU, especially because labour mobility is particularly low and regional labour markets may display imperfections. In this case, region-specific shocks can lead to unemployment and large slumps in regional personal incomes. Therefore, Europe may find that EMU may cause sharper regional cycles (Krugman, 1991) which cannot be tackled by its small central budget and its low labour mobility.

The counter-argument holds that federal states, such as the USA, started as monetary unions with a common currency long before they developed a federal budget with the capacity to redistribute resources across regions. Therefore, starting with EMU, the EU could later develop a federal fiscal structure if and when it would need to respond to problems which individual member states cannot cope with. As we have seen (in Chapter 4), the EU budget is specifically non-federal and small, and therefore by design it may lack the 'stabilization' and 'co-insurance' functions afforded by national budgets. Therefore, implicitly, these functions are left to the member states, which must fulfil them subject to the constraints imposed by the 'stability pact'. An alternative approach would have been to pre-empt any expected predicaments by starting to move progressively towards a federal budget in parallel with the monetary union.

In summary, currency unions cannot ignore the effects of national fiscal policies on the common monetary system and on other member states in the form of positive and negative externalities. The EU treaties do not provide the EU budget with 'stabilization', and 'co-insurance' functions. Therefore, if and when region- and country-specific problems arise which might endanger the smooth functioning of EMU policies, the EU should be ready to intervene with radical changes in the size and functions of its budget. After all, fiscal federalism is basically a question of politics rather than of economics.

Questions

1. What policies can countries use to maintain their exchange rates within a narrow band of fluctuations such as the one set by the EMS?

2. What were the exchange rate realignments of the EMS? If for an EMS currency a realignment meant devaluation against the ECU, what did this imply about the value of this currency against the US dollar?

3. Critically evaluate the following quotation: 'Europe is less of an optimum currency area (OCA) than its North American counterparts. Therefore, it should not attempt an EMU until it becomes an OCA.'

4. (a) Analyse the arguments for and against budgetary centralization in a monetary union.
   (b) Explain how unsustainable national fiscal policies in a member state create negative externalities to the monetary union, and suggest possible solutions to this problem with reference to EMU.

5. A major argument against European Monetary Union (EMU) is that the single currency and the common interest rate would mean 'one-size-fits-all' monetary policy.
   (a) Explain this argument and consider whether and under what onditions it might be important.
   (b) Countries also apply 'one-size-fits-all' monetary policy with respect to their own regions. In what ways does this differ from EMU in the European Union?

6. 'Many people are claiming that a single currency will infringe fiscal sovereignty and therefore monetary integration makes fiscal integration inevitable. But it is simply false to argue that – as a matter of economics – the one implies the other. Since it would be necessary to forfeit room for manoeuvre in national monetary policy, it would be necessary to reserve the right to take specific action on the national budgetary side.' Discuss.

Further reading

For the costs/benefits of one currency see *The Economist* (1998). Eichengreen (1993) argues that Europe is not an OCA; Frankel and Rose (1998) argue that it does not matter. Eijffinger and De Haan (2000) review the EMU policy options. Levin (2002) has a good short guide to the euro and Issing et al. (2001) discuss monetary policy in EMU.

Web guide

The ECB's site is available at www.ecb.int; information on the euro is available at www.europa.eu.int/euro; worldwide daily news about the euro and EMU is available at www.dailynews.yahoo.com/fc/World European Monetary_Union. See also www.amue.If.net. The member states have their own euro sites, e.g. the UK's is available at www.euro.gov.uk; Italy's at www.tesoro.it; Spain's at www.euro.meh.es; Ireland's at http://www.emuaware.forfas.ie

Agriculture

7

Agriculture and trade are the two sectors that the EU integrated right from its beginnings. The Common Agricultural Policy (CAP) replaced the national agricultural policies of the member states but in the process created new problems which had important implications across the Community and to the outside world. In more recent years, under the combined pressures of consumers, taxpayers, international competitors and world trade liberalization agreements the EU agricultural policies have been slowly but steadily restructured 'in accordance with the principle of an open market economy . . . with free competition, favouring an efficient allocation of resources'.

7.1 Introduction

Agriculture is historically considered special for economic, social, political and strategic reasons. Accordingly, in almost every industrial country and in many less-developed countries governments intervene in the agricultural sector, attempting to modify its course and to regulate its production and trade. Intervention is usually justified by the belief that an institutional structure rather than the free market will move the sector in preferred directions. The specific objectives of government intervention in agriculture are mainly four:

1. the desire to maintain a certain *degree of self-sufficiency* in agricultural products, especially food, because of the risk of interruption or curtailment of foreign supplies, for example by war;
2. *saving foreign exchange* by supplying agricultural products for domestic consumption from domestic sources rather than imports;

3. *stabilizing prices* at levels reasonable for consumers and producers, as the means for reducing hardship and uncertainty, and for encouraging investment and growth in the agricultural sector;
4. the desire to improve efficiency and productivity in the agricultural sector as the means for *raising* the level and the rate of growth of *agricultural incomes*.

The last two of these reasons are loosely based on the assumed incidence of market failure and, in developed economies, are often used as the dominant excuse for government intervention in agriculture. Governments often assert not only that farming is riskier than other enterprises, but also that conventional private markets provide limited mechanisms for hedging that risk. A more recent excuse for intervention in agriculture is the recognition of another form of market failure associated with resource conservation and general environmental awareness. Differences often exist between the interests of society at large and the farmers about land use and water resources, pollution, erosion and common property problems.

However, more often than not, the agricultural sector is supported for political, economic and social reasons, both domestic and international. It is commonly alleged that in most developed countries agricultural support policies often reflect vested interests and rent-seeking behaviour. Therefore, they originate from the relative power of sectoral lobbies and the influence of special and political constituencies rather than from purely economic considerations. Although this may be so, we will concentrate mostly on the economic rationale for agricultural policy, beginning with an examination of the structure of the agricultural sector and the markets for its inputs and outputs.

7.2 Problems of the agricultural sector

A general characteristic of the agricultural sector is that the markets for its output, free from intervention, possess most of the features of the competitive market model. Specifically, the number of firms is large, entry of new firms in the industry is unrestricted, and the output of each commodity is on the whole homogeneous. However, information about the future quantity and prices of output and production techniques is imperfect. Although these are problems shared by most markets, they are made more complicated in agriculture than in other sectors by certain features of the short- and long-term demand and supply in the markets of both agricultural commodities and factors of production. Furthermore, agricultural problems can be both economic and social. Although some farm enterprises are big agribusinesses and their output dominates the market, even in developed countries the majority of farms are typically small family units in which all or most labour is supplied by the family, and the proprietor is the sole supplier of risk capital. Since farmers normally live on the farm, farming is a way of life rather than a modern business, and at the limit (e.g. hill or island farming) it is hardly different from subsistence agriculture. Many countries also believe that rural communities based on family farms constitute a form of social organization which preserves proper values, such as social solidarity and community care. All these characteristics in a way make government intervention in the agriculture sector almost inevitable.

The most obvious display of the peculiarities of the agricultural sector is that agricultural incomes on the whole are relatively low and fluctuate widely, and their rate of growth lags behind the national average. Specifically for these reasons government intervention is often defended on considerations of relative national welfare, such as the premise that, left on its own, the market does not lead to a 'fair' distribution of national income between agriculture and the other sectors of the economy. Moreover, it is also asserted that without a positive policy, economic growth makes the gap between agriculture and other sectors wider.

In the following we examine: (a) how the markets for agricultural products set prices and quantities; and (b) the characteristics of factor markets of the agricultural sector.

Determination of prices

Supply

The supply of agricultural products is characterized by short-term fluctuations and long-term trends which work against agriculture's contribution to and share of national income. The reasons for this situation are that, compared with other sectors of the economy such as manufacturing, the prices of agricultural products are flexible and the quantities of output can vary widely from year to year between gluts and shortages. Furthermore, in the longer term, technical progress brings about cost reductions which, owing to the competitive structure of the sector, and contrary to the experience of other industries, are passed on to the consumer in the form of lower prices.

Fluctuations

Short-term fluctuations in production are caused by the crucial dependence of agriculture on:

- natural conditions such as the soil, climate and weather;
- the incidence of pests and diseases affecting both crops and animals;

■ biological constraints which cause concentration of the flow of output into certain years or seasons within a year.

Since in agriculture the output of many subsectors is often input to other subsectors (e.g. cereals as animal feed), generalized fluctuations in the volume of agricultural output are common. Moreover, the relatively long time-lag between committing resources to production and gathering the output, a process which once started is not easily reversed, means that the supply of agricultural products is in the short term unresponsive to changes in market conditions. Fluctuations in short-term supply are therefore common and unpredictable. Since the agricultural sector has important links with other industries (e.g. the food industry or the chemical industry for fertilizers), its instability can affect many other sectors.

Trends

Longer-term trends in modern agriculture are characterized by rapid technical and economic change, both of which increase factor productivity. Technical innovation in agriculture increases the use of capital, limits the need for more land and decreases the use of labour. Economic improvement occurs from specialization and the move towards more optimal plant size displaying economies of scale, and from cost-reducing advances in organization and management. These developments also tend to accelerate mechanization and the displacement of labour by capital. As a result, in the longer run more is produced with less factor input and the cost per unit of output falls through time. Allegedly, the competitive nature of agricultural markets means that these cost reductions do not necessarily lead to more profits or higher agricultural wages, but to lower prices for the consumer. This is in sharp contrast to the manufacturing industry, where the manifest oligopolistic structure of markets for both commodities and factors of production ensures that technical innovation does not so much lead to lower consumer prices but rather to higher factor rewards.

Demand

The demand for agricultural products is characterized by low price and income elasticities. A *low price elasticity* of demand means that, at a given income, a fall in the price of a commodity will induce a proportionally smaller increase in the quantity bought. Thus, producers' revenue from the sale of output will fall. A low price elasticity of demand makes farm prices and incomes very sensitive to supply shocks and, therefore, a technical innovation or a good crop can reduce farm prices and incomes drastically. A *low income elasticity* of demand means that, at a given commodity price, as economic growth raises personal incomes, the demand shifts increasingly against the purchase of staples (i.e. resource-based products). So the proportion of income spent on purchases of these products, food in particular, falls as income rises.[1] Therefore, if productivity grows at the same rate in all sectors of the economy, the growth of income will cause the demand to shift from food to luxuries, or, in general, from agricultural products to manufactures. Thus the price ratio of agricultural products over manufactured products (i.e. the relative price) falls to the detriment of farmers' incomes.

Income

Agricultural incomes are affected adversely by both the special characteristics of the demand and the problems of the supply sides of the market. Rapid technical progress, causing rapid growth in the supply of agricultural products, and declining demand depress agricultural prices and aggravate the difference between the incomes of the agricultural sector and the rest of the economy. Agricultural incomes thus lag behind the rate of growth of national income without any prospect of ever catching up. Fluctuating production, depressed product prices and increasing costs may also cause farm income instability. Therefore, in times of growth and rising prosperity, farmers do not share in the increasing wealth of the nation at large.

Factor market problems

Yield and price fluctuations suggest that the agricultural industry is subject to uncertainty. Since many agricultural products are perishable, it is difficult and costly to build up stocks as a buffer against erratic short-term fluctuations of the supply. In the longer run, any solution to the problems of agriculture would entail implementing structural changes which would shift resources – surplus manpower in particular – from agriculture to activities offering employment and higher rewards. Ideally, this reallocation of resources should be initiated by market forces. But although resource migration from agriculture does occur, its pace is often slow and uncoordinated, and thus the divergence of factor rewards between sectors persists and widens. The slow mobility of factors of production employed in agriculture is caused by both economic and social reasons. An important economic reason is the high specificity of the land, capital and labour that are engaged in agriculture which means that their employment in other sectors is neither instantaneous nor costless.

---

[1] The statement that, with given tastes or preferences, the proportion of income spent on food diminishes as income increases is known as *Engel's law* (after Ernst Engel, 1821–96).

Extra problems arise because the transfer of factors of production from agriculture to other sectors is almost always characterized not only by occupational limitations but also by the necessity for geographic mobility. This requirement gives rise to the social causes of relative factor immobility. Farmers in particular will only reluctantly abandon their 'way of life', independence and abode in search of new employment and higher rewards, most probably in an urban environment. They prefer instead to continue living on the land in their traditional ways, often reacting to the fall in revenues by increasing their production. More often than not, this form of individual behaviour collectively leads the sector to yet more increases in supply, falling prices and a further erosion of agricultural incomes.

7.3 Policies and effects

Policies

The preceding discussion shows that the agricultural sector may be subject to certain singular types of *market failure*. If this is the case, then the aim of government policy should be to restore the operations of the free market as the means for achieving optimal allocation of resources. However, certain types of agricultural market failure cannot be corrected by intervention, for example weather conditions and biological limitations operating on the supply side of the market, and the low price and income elasticities on the demand side of the market. Regardless of these limitations, for many strategic, political, economic and social reasons governments intervene in agriculture to make it reach a target level of production or a target level of income for the factors engaged in the sector. These objectives are usually pursued by a variety of intervention policies in the markets for factors of production and commodities, which attempt to stabilize prices and to minimize unwarranted fluctuations in output. Since governments use agricultural policies to attain different economic, social and political objectives, there is no single policy which is superior to all the others under all circumstances. The right policy depends on the problem in hand, the nature of the target in the short and the long run, and an array of economic, social and political constraints. Since the targets are manifold, governments usually apply not one but a combination of policy instruments to achieve several objectives. In general, government intervention considers broadly the interests of both the consumers and the producers of agricultural commodities. However, in the field of pressure-group politics of developed economies, the farmers' lobby is relatively more homogeneous, compact, organized, vociferous and, more often than not, more powerful than the discordant and disorganized consumers' group, and it usually (some would say invariably) wins.

The policies available to governments differ in effectiveness and in their implications on income distribution and resource allocation. The latter as a rule is affected negatively, in directions other than those which the free market would have dictated. This is often justified as a temporary expedient within a spectrum of objectives among which 'efficiency' is not ranked high in the government's list of priorities. The effects on income distribution arise from the direct and indirect costs of financing the policy. As a rule, policies that raise the market price of the protected commodity directly affect (i.e. are paid for by) the consumer of that commodity, while policies that do not raise the commodity's market price involve budgetary transfers and are paid for by the taxpayer, who may not be a consumer of the good. Significant differences may also exist in the cost of implementing and administering the different policies (see Appendix A7).

Effects

If the economy is not operating efficiently and the objective of government policy is to remove existing distortions from the agricultural sector, then the key question is, which specific policy is the best for attaining optimality. But even that sort of policy can have unwarranted side effects. For example, if society's objective is to increase incomes or employment in the agricultural sector, then direct income supplements or employment subsidies are the most efficient policies to adopt. However, if there is a disparity between farm and non-farm incomes arising from misallocation of resources which allow the retention in agriculture of excess manpower, then policies designed to raise farmers' incomes will not improve resource allocation. If agriculture is competitive, while manufacturing industry is oligopolistic and protected from international competition by trade barriers, then attempting to correct the misallocation of resources by applying concerted policies to the agricultural sector will be a misguided exercise which most probably will not improve the situation. The problem of operating a policy in a suboptimal world is that if all the conditions for maximum efficiency are not met simultaneously, then satisfying some of these conditions will not necessarily increase welfare – another facet of *the general theory of second best* (see Chapter 1).

If the economy is operating efficiently and the government intervenes in the agricultural sector to improve it, then the outcome would be distorting welfare. By restricting imports and promoting domestic production and exports of agricultural commodities, government policies adversely affect the production and trade of other sectors of the economy and the country's international comparative advantage. This occurs because the policy promotes the growth of the agricultural sector and agriculture-related industries at the expense of other sectors and national welfare. This policy would also have international repercussions.

7.4 The Common Agricultural Policy

Foundations

A recurrent theme in our analysis is that the main objective of the EU is to integrate the market, preferably in its free form, where supply and demand would determine prices and the allocation of resources. However, the market is the means to an end, and this does not exclude the possibility of departures from market-determined solutions. For example, if the structure of the market is imperfect or the prices of commodities and factors of production adjust sluggishly to changing market conditions, then intervention may be needed to lift the distortions and to assist the operation of the market mechanism. Yet the principle of competition on equal terms, which common markets promote, suggests that whenever intervention is deemed necessary, it must be general, applied equally to each member state. This rule implies that, since in the EU an agricultural policy was deemed necessary, the existing national agricultural policies of the member states had to be replaced by a common agricultural policy. Unequal relative size and development of the agricultural sectors in the member states, different natural environments and diverse social, political and economic objectives meant that the first six countries that set up the EU had earlier followed different, but strongly interventionist national agricultural policies. Nature and government policies shaped the structure of agricultural production and prices in each country, in such a way that the members' agricultural sectors made up a markedly heterogeneous group. Therefore, when the Six decided to address the agricultural problem by setting up a Common Agricultural Policy (CAP), they embarked on a task of huge economic and social implications. Despite the difficulties which this venture has caused right from the start, and which still bedevil the Community, many observers argue that on the whole the EU succeeded in establishing the first fully fledged common policy, but at a great cost. For a long period, the CAP reflected a balance of interests and a compromise among the original six members, which were developed industrial countries but continued to have vested social and economic concerns in their relatively small agricultural sectors.

Objectives

The main objectives of the Common Agricultural Policy are defined (in TEEC, 33) as follows:

(a) to increase agricultural productivity by promoting technical progress and by ensuring the rational development of agricultural production and the optimum utilization of the factors of production, in particular labour;
(b) thus to ensure a fair standard of living for the agricultural community, in particular by increasing the individual earnings of persons engaged in agriculture;
(c) to stabilize markets;
(d) to assure the availability of supplies;
(e) to ensure that supplies reach the consumers at reasonable prices.

The policies which the Community would apply to reach these objectives are broadly outlined in the treaties (TEU, 34–8) which emphasize: (a) the social structure of agriculture; (b) the need to implement the appropriate adjustment gradually; (c) the links between agriculture and the other sectors of the economy. But it was left to the institutions of the Community, following agreed procedures, to work out the details of the common policy. This was duly done at a conference of agricultural ministries and farmers' organizations held at Stresa, Italy, in 1958, and shaped the direction of the CAP for the ensuing five decades.

Principles

The CAP is founded on three principles which have guided it since the beginning:

1. establishing a single market for agricultural commodities;
2. Community preference for domestic production by reducing international competition through protection;
3. financial solidarity in support of agriculture.

A *single market* means the free movement of agricultural produce within the Community by removing every distortion on competition, harmonizing legislation and operating a common intervention system. The latter required centralization of the administration, policies and market organization which would bring about common prices. Community policy is to set these prices in a way that will achieve its objectives, principally to provide the farmers with remunerations at levels comparable with those enjoyed by other sectors of the economy.

Community preference within an integrated domestic market means protection from external influences, such as competitive imports and price fluctuations in the world markets. Protection is necessary because the production conditions in the Community are inferior and the costs higher than those in the large exporting countries outside Europe. Market prices are also higher than those of the international markets because the Community manages them as the main policy instrument for attaining its specific objectives. Since the aim of the CAP is not self-sufficiency and in the world market many prices are also set by interventionist policies, the principle of Community preference also extends to embracing policies for export promotion.

Financial solidarity means sharing the cost of the CAP between the member states and centralizing the necessary funding. This task was assigned to a specially created Community organization, the *European Agricultural Guidance and Guarantee Fund (EAGGF)*. The *guarantee* section of the Fund finances the intervention policies of the CAP, while the *guidance* section manages funds intended for policies of structural reform.

During the operation of the CAP, more objectives emerged reflecting the inadequacies of the existing policies or new trends in public affairs. Thus, the Community has increasingly paid attention to problems of regional inequalities in the agricultural sectors of member states, to concerns about the links between agriculture, conservation and environmental protection, and to the urgency of protecting certain rural areas from depopulation. These issues affect the nature of policies dealing with agriculture by introducing more constraints in the implementation of the CAP.

Method

The CAP covers all the quantitatively important agricultural products of the EU. The policy mechanism varies to some extent from product to product, depending on its nature (storable, non-storable or transformable) and the nature of its market. For some goods, which can be produced in the EU in large quantities, the CAP support price normally does not allow any competing imports to enter the market. For other goods, imports are normally allowed but in reduced quantities. We can study the basic characteristics of the first group of goods in the market for cereals which, from the beginning of the CAP, is regarded as 'the model'. Cereals occupy a central role in the agricultural sector of the Community, first, as a quantitatively important final product of the sector and, second, as an input to further processes within the sector, for example as food for livestock. For the second group of goods, which includes, for example, oranges which are produced in the EU and are also imported from third countries, the analysis is similar to trade under tariff protection (see Appendix A1). For both groups, the CAP policy and its implications are presented here with the help of a diagram (Figure 7.1) which is based

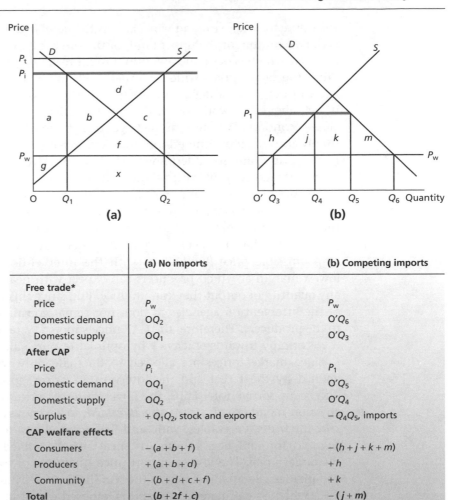

	(a) No imports	(b) Competing imports
Free trade*		
Price	P_w	P_w
Domestic demand	OQ_2	$O'Q_6$
Domestic supply	OQ_1	$O'Q_3$
After CAP		
Price	P_i	P_1
Domestic demand	OQ_1	$O'Q_5$
Domestic supply	OQ_2	$O'Q_4$
Surplus	$+ Q_1Q_2$, stock and exports	$- Q_4Q_5$, imports
CAP welfare effects		
Consumers	$-(a + b + f)$	$-(h + j + k + m)$
Producers	$+(a + b + d)$	$+h$
Community	$-(b + d + c + f)$	$+k$
Total	$-(b + 2f + c)$	$-(j + m)$

Figure 7.1 Effects of the Common Agricultural Policy on a product's market

Note: * Free trade is used here as a benchmark. The CAP did not replace free trade but national intervention policies.

on oversimplified assumptions, but at the same time draws attention to key aspects of the problem.

No import competition

In Figure 7.1 (a) the EU supply curve of cereals is sloping upwards, suggesting increasing costs of production, while the world supply of cereals is low-priced and perfectly elastic. After considering local price differentials arising from transport costs and storage, the EU Council of Ministers of Agriculture fixes yearly a *target price*, P_t (known as the *guide price* for beef, veal and wine, and as the *norm price* for tobacco). This is the maximum, or the upper limit, of the price for a standard quality of produce, which is desirable or 'optimum' for realizing the CAP objectives. Thus, the target price, which is usually set for each commodity in the 'zone of the greatest deficit' between domestic production and demand, is well above the world price, P_w, and the price for equilibrium in the closed economy. Therefore, at the target price there will be excess domestic supply and threat of competition from imports, both of which will reduce market prices, and so undermine the policy objective of the Community. These threats are dealt with by the policy.

The permissible minimum, or lower limit, of market price fluctuation is the *intervention price*, P_i (known as the *basic price* for pig meat) at which the Community halts the downward pressure of domestic supply on prices by purchasing the excess quantity. Therefore, the CAP fixes a band of permissible price fluctuations with the intervention price P_i as the lowest margin at which producers can expect with near certainty to sell any quantity of output they can produce. But, since this is at the demand of the intervention agencies, it does not signal consumer requirements to the producers. Therefore, the CAP price support system does not guide the economy towards efficiency by optimal resource allocation.

Since market prices are allowed to fluctuate only within the range defined by the target and the intervention prices, foreign trade plays only a supportive role. Thus, the lowest internal price for imports from any non-member country is the *threshold price* (known as the *reference price* for fruits, vegetables, wine and fishery products, and as the *sluice-gate price* for pork, eggs and poultry meat), which is fixed at or just above the target price. The lowest import price (inclusive of transport, storage and incidental costs) is raised to the threshold price by an import *levy*, $P_t - P_w$, which is calculated daily and is imposed on all imports regardless of source and cost of supply. Thus imports are charged a *variable levy* which acts as a tariff equalizing the minimum current international price with the fixed domestic target price. However, if for any reason the EU domestic price rises above the target price, imports become competitive, enter the market and keep the domestic price steady at the threshold price. In this way the CAP assures the consumer that market prices will never exceed the threshold price.

By fixing producer prices above the market equilibrium price the CAP encourages excess supply. The CAP organization stipulates that the quantities bought by the intervention agencies will be used as buffer stock for maintaining the market price within the permissible limits of fluctuation. Stocks over this requirement are usually sold, either in the domestic market at reduced prices for specific purposes (e.g. schools, hospitals), or abroad as EU exports at world prices. Aspiring to encourage direct exports of the excess supply by the producers (and to save on storage costs), the policy provides export *refunds* or *export restitution*, which compensate the exporters for the difference between world and Community market prices. Thus, at a given world price P_w, the compensation/subsidy on a unit of exports varies between a minimum of $P_i - P_w$ and a maximum of $P_t - P_w$. If for any reason world prices rise above the threshold price, the domestic producers will export their output rather than sell it to the EU intervention agencies. The CAP specifies that in this case the export refund will become an export levy to ensure that domestic supplies first reach the EU consumer at a reasonable price (the threshold price P_t) and only surpluses are exported. Theoretically at least, Community preference extends to cover both producers and consumers. In Figure 7.1 (a) the financial and welfare effects of the policy are high and affect the consumers and the Community budget (and thus the taxpayers of the member states) negatively and the producers positively, but to a smaller extent.

Market organization similar to that for cereals applies to roughly 70 per cent of the EU agricultural output (dairy products, meat, sugars, table wine, etc.). Another 25 per cent of agricultural production (eggs, poultry, flowers, etc.) is covered by a looser organization confined to external protection without significant support measures in the internal market. A few other commodities, which are of limited production, geographically and quantitatively, or are subject to international agreements preventing extensive protection, get production subsidies (durum wheat, olive oil, tobacco, etc.). They cover about 2.5 per cent of total EU agricultural production. Finally, for certain specific products covering less than 1 per cent of the total agricultural output, the CAP provides flat subsidies by hectare of cultivation or by volume of output.

Competing imports

Some agricultural commodities are produced in the EU but their quantities fall short of domestic demand. The producers of these commodities are also protected by the CAP by price support which increases the quantity they supply but not enough to match the domestic demand. Therefore, imports are allowed to enter the market subject to a variable levy, as shown in Figure 7.1 (b). As a result, domestic producers are subsidized directly by the consumers while the Community also gains revenue from agricultural import levies, which constitute one of the 'own resources' of the general budget (see Chapter 4). The net welfare effect of this policy is negative overall.

Structural policies

Common prices policy and common trading policy are the two principal features of the EU common market in agricultural products. The third task of the CAP is to shape the future of Community agriculture by a common structural policy. As we have seen, structural diversity was, and still is, one of the main characteristics of European agriculture. But a uniform price and trading policy would take little account of interstate and interregional disparities. It may instead aggravate the structural differences and slow down the economic growth and modernization of the integrating sector. These problems can be met only by direct intervention, undertaken by a central organization with the task of restructuring Community agriculture, aiming at improved efficiency and competitiveness. The Community assigned this task to the *Guidance Section* of the EAGGF which was instructed to: (a) modernize the sector; (b) implement technical progress; (c) rationalize production; and (d) improve the processing and marketing of agricultural products.

These assignments are pursued by capital investment, the supply of grants and loans for agricultural development and the dissemination of modern production methods among the agricultural populations. The EAGGF also provides support for the relocation of labour shifting from agriculture to other sectors of the economy by financing retraining and related costs.

7.5 European Community agriculture under the CAP

Qualifications

We must now examine the main features of the Community's agricultural sector to evaluate the cost-effectiveness of operating the CAP.

The CAP has had successes and failures which in a way have contributed to the present shape of EU agriculture. However, not everything good or bad in EU agriculture can indisputably be attributed solely to the CAP. There are many other factors that influence economic developments and it is not always easy to disentangle the complexity of the real world and to ascribe specific outcomes to specific causes. Often several policies are applied simultaneously to achieve different (and sometimes contradictory) primary objectives and, therefore, cause and effect cannot be easily identified. Changes in the constraints and in the general economic environment within which the policy is applied mean that both the targets and effects of the policy are not fixed but variable.

Trends in EU agriculture

As we have seen, the treaties specify five main objectives of the CAP (TEEC, 33). It is therefore opportune to examine the trends in EU agriculture under five relevant headings, presenting arguments and statistics both in favour and against particular aspects and features, as they emerged during the operation of the CAP. Certain key features of EU agriculture changed through time as the Community expanded from the original Six to 15 members. Moreover, under internal EU pressures and international agreements, reforms were gradually implemented in the CAP. We will review the changes in the agricultural sector of the Community to form a picture of the situation it has reached today.

Structure and productivity

The importance of the agricultural sector as a contributor to the Community's gross value added and as an employer of factors of production is relatively small and declining. In 1999, agriculture accounted for only 2 per cent of the EU's GDP against 3.4 per cent in 1980 and 5 per cent in 1973. This declining trend is caused by both the relative contraction of agriculture and the expansion of other sectors of the economy. However, important differences still exist between the member states. For example, the contribution of agriculture to the 1999 gross value added was 7 per cent in Greece and 5 per cent in Ireland, but only 1 per cent in Germany and the United Kingdom (Table 2.2). In all member countries, agriculture accounts for a larger share of employment than it does for production, thus confirming agriculture's relatively lower labour productivity. But the workforce employed in agriculture has also declined from about 11 per cent in 1973 to 5 per cent in 1999. Between 1990 and 1999 the agricultural labour force in EU-15 fell by 2.5 million. However, agricultural employment still occupies a significant share in rural areas, ranging from 20 per cent in Greece and 13 per cent in Portugal to 2 per cent in the United Kingdom.

During 1961–90, the average labour productivity growth in the Community's industry was about 3 per cent a year, while in agriculture it was more than 5 per cent. This rapid increase in productivity came about mostly because of the restructuring of the agricultural sector towards larger farms and a faster pace of mechanization. But smallholdings still predominate in the south. In Greece, Italy and Portugal the average farm size is between 5 and 9 hectares of utilized agricultural area. In contrast, the biggest holdings, averaging 70 hectares, are in the UK, where around 17 per cent of holdings are bigger than 100 hectares, compared with only 1 per cent in Greece, Italy, the Netherlands and Finland. Consequently, labour productivity varies considerably from one member state to the next. In the UK, it takes two full-time workers to farm 100 hectares; in Greece nearly 16, with an EU average of 5. Therefore, despite the progress, in value terms productivity in agriculture is only 50 per cent of that of other economic sectors.

Standards of living

The second objective of the CAP is to ensure a fair standard of living for the agricultural community by increasing the earnings of persons employed in agriculture. The CAP pursued this objective mainly by producer price support in the form of fixing high output prices, P. But net income, Y, is the revenue from sales, R, *minus* the cost of production, C. Since revenue is the quantity sold *times* the sale price, $R = Q \times P$, the net income is $Y = R - C = Q \times P - C$. Of these three variables, cost, quantity and price, only price is controlled by the CAP. Therefore, farmers' incomes will be variable if the quantities of output or the production costs are variable. Thus CAP's price support directly linked farmers' revenues to the quantity produced, providing 'a permanent open-ended incentive to greater production and further intensification' (Commission, 1991), causing overproduction and unsold surpluses. To raise production, farmers brought into cultivation marginal lands, and thus the price of land and the cost of production also increased. In the end, increased production did not necessarily raise farmers' net incomes.

Income per agricultural worker has risen slightly as a result of the steady fall in the agricultural labour force in all the member states. Despite the price-support policy which insulates the EU market from the instability of world markets, agricultural prices have declined relative to the general price level in the EU economies, while productivity was not high enough to prevent farm incomes from falling. Thus, in real terms, the prices of agricultural products fell by almost 25 per cent between 1985 and 1999. In contrast, production costs (depreciation, interest, rents) increased while the prices of intermediate consumption goods and services (such as fertilizers and animal feedstuffs) fell by about 5 per cent. In contrast, the consumer price index rose by 20 per cent. Therefore, agricultural real incomes still lagged behind those of other sectors of the economy. This outcome is in direct contradiction to the intended objectives of the CAP, reinforcing the conclusion that the price support policy is not an efficient method for closing the gap between agricultural and non-agricultural factor rewards.

Another defect of the price support policy for raising living standards is that it induces farmers to increase their supply, irrespective of market demand, which under this sort of policy is irrelevant. A consequence of this is that higher support prices benefit disproportionately the large producers who realize economies of scale and in general are not those in dire need of better living standards. It is estimated that 80 per cent of the CAP support accrues to the richest 20 per cent of the farmers. These are the large producers of output which takes up the largest share of CAP expenditure, as shown in Figure 7.2. Their output consists of products in excess supply which the Community accumulates in *mountains of*

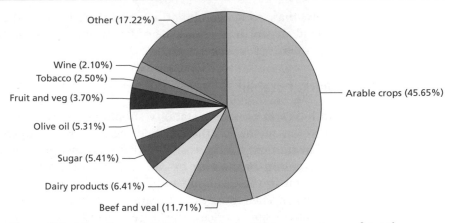

Figure 7.2 Allocation of CAP spending in 1999, percentage of total

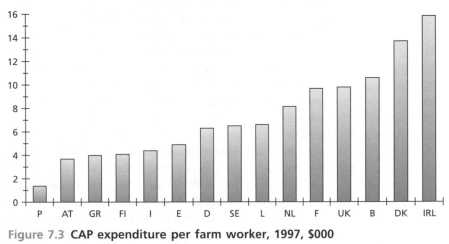

Figure 7.3 CAP expenditure per farm worker, 1997, $000
Source: Data from Eurostat (1999).

surpluses that can only be sold abroad at prices much lower than the costs of production. Clearly, a non-discriminating, 'universal' price support policy that aims at a fair standard of living for the agricultural community cannot make farmers' incomes converge or be equalized throughout the Community. In fact, a characteristic of EU agriculture is the marked disparity in farm incomes between the member countries. Thus the richest 'average' farmer (in the Netherlands) has an income two and a half times higher than the Community average and is more than five times better off than the poorest farmer (in Greece). Among the reasons for these disparities are the productivity of the farm, the extent of CAP support and the actual price received by the farmer. Figure 7.3

shows that, from a combination of all these reasons, the farm workers of Ireland are the most and those of Portugal the least favoured by the CAP expenditure.

Market stability

An indicator of market stability should be the stability of market prices. However, in the EU the prices of agricultural products are set high as the instrument for increasing agricultural incomes. During 1973–84 the intervention prices rose by about 7 per cent yearly. After 1984, with problems in the Community budget, they started to fall by 0.2 per cent annually. Therefore, in comparison with the Community's inflation rate in consumer prices, the price increases of agricultural output were moderate.

An implication of the policy of administered prices is that the Community prices of agricultural products were more stable than the world prices. But this was attained by the high-price support policy, with the result that the Community prices of most agricultural commodities were much higher than world prices. This was happening at a time of plentiful supplies, while expenditure on food takes up a small and shrinking share of consumers' income. But the simple comparison between EU and world prices should be regarded as unreliable evidence for the case against the CAP, because the Community's prices of agricultural commodities are high by design. Furthermore, the world prices (which are not the domestic prices of any particular country but the offer prices of exports, i.e. of low-priced surpluses of countries which most probably also intervene in their agricultural sectors) are low, among other reasons because in these markets the EU, first, was no longer a buyer of these products and, second, it was a seller of its own surpluses. What the world prices would have been without the CAP cannot easily be guessed. Despite the CAP, the Community remains an important buyer in the world markets of agricultural products.

Availability of supplies

Security of supply of agricultural products in the Community was ensured by the CAP through an increase in self-sufficiency, an intensive storage policy and a stable import policy. For several products domestic supplies far exceed the domestic demand of the Community, without of course any particular effects on market prices. The long-term increase in the volume of EU agricultural production is about 2.0 per cent a year, while consumption is increasing only by 0.5 per cent a year. Therefore, for the principal farm products more than self-sufficiency was achieved and the Community relied increasingly on exports for the disposal of excess production: exports of agricultural products accounted for about 10 per cent of extra-Community trade. Despite the increase in EU agricultural production and stocks, the Community remains the world's largest importer of food.

Reasonable prices for the consumer

Consumer prices were on the whole much higher than producer (farm gate) prices and there is no close correlation between the two. The increase in consumer prices over the last few years has lagged behind the inflation rate. Therefore, although the prices of agricultural output within the Community did rise, those who produced this output did not cause the observed inflation, they lost from it. However, the poorer consumers, who spend a large part of their income on food, lost from the high price policy. Thus the CAP caused not only massive income transfers from surplus-producing countries to deficit countries within the EU but also from consumers to producers of food within and between member countries. Since the CAP has failed to concentrate on the needy poorer farmers, the problem was not only that the poorer people of Europe were paying disproportionally for the costs of the CAP, but that those who benefited from the policy were the richest farmers of the Community.

International repercussions

The EU's high import restrictions on some agricultural commodities and its switch from buyer to seller in the international markets of certain other commodities came under intense attack by agricultural producing countries who attributed three major defects to the CAP policies:

1. The CAP led to excess production. With growing world production and no matching increase in world demand, the EU's rising farm output and subsidies to exports depressed world prices.
2. The CAP's variable import levies and export subsidies insulated the EU markets from external price fluctuations, thereby amplifying the variability of world commodity prices.
3. Depressed prices and price instability in world markets caused farmers in developing countries to reduce their production and exports, thereby lowering their incomes and reducing their prospects of economic growth.

The EU is not, of course, the only culprit, but with the United States (which is by far the most important net exporter of agricultural produce in the world) it is one of the largest offenders in world agricultural trade. As Figure 7.4 shows, the EU is a more modest supporter of its farmers than the Unites States. Almost all industrial countries pursue agricultural

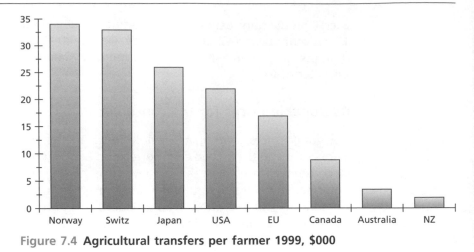

Figure 7.4 **Agricultural transfers per farmer 1999, $000**

policies leading, to a greater or lesser degree, to distortions in resource allocation at domestic and worldwide level. This has created a strong feeling among the traditional agricultural exporters (Australia, New Zealand, Canada, Argentina) who resent the aggressive encouragement of agricultural production and the unloading of surpluses on the world markets. Of course, not every country loses from cheap exports: those who are net importers of subsidized exports gain.

Until very recently, international disputes concerning agricultural subsidies and countervailing duties often ended in open trade warfare (mostly between the EU and the USA) which led to demands for liberalization of trade in agricultural products under the auspices of the GATT (and later the WTO). The first step in this direction was taken at the Uruguay Round of trade liberalization which aimed to achieve 'a fair and market-oriented agricultural system' and began replacing all non-tariff barriers to trade, such as the variable CAP levies, by fixed and transparent tariffs ('tariffication' agreement) subject to agreed maximum rates. The next trade liberalization round (in 2002) will aim at a further reduction in this protection.

7.6 Reforms of the Common Agricultural Policy

The problem

The CAP replaced the national agricultural policies of the member countries, achieved certain of its objectives and, to a large extent, unified the EU market for agricultural commodities. However, the CAP was far from perfect, and since the mid-1970s mounting criticism was directed against it within the EU with regard to the following issues:

1. The CAP kept prices above world prices.
2. It caused significant financial expenditures which required budgetary transfers between the member states.
3. It led to income redistribution from consumers to producers within and between countries.
4. It raised the collective protection of EU agriculture to such high levels that large surpluses of some important commodities were generated.

The surpluses of skimmed-milk powder and butter were notorious. These surpluses, further to the initial costs of collection and storage, caused new problems when they were disposed of within the Community or outside as exports at prices below cost. Therefore, a series of reforms of the CAP was introduced, some of which alleviate certain of the problems but mostly temporarily, while others caused new and unforseen complications and side effects. Under mounting external and internal pressures, more radical reforms have been introduced in the last few years.

In general, all reforms come under two broad categories:

1. adjustments in the structure of the CAP which would leave administered prices to meet the target of income support, but reduce production surpluses and budgetary expenditure;
2. replacement of the price support mechanism as the principal instrument of the CAP by more efficient methods, such as direct income support payments.

Economic theory would consider the second type of proposal as the most efficient method for achieving the CAP objective of 'a fair standard of living for the agricultural community'. However, farmers usually regard high prices as a right and direct income payments as a socially demeaning charity.

At least the Commission cannot be accused of not trying to change the CAP. However, it is the consent of the Council, representing the member states, that counts. The first attempt at reform was the Mansholt Plan in 1968 which reached the conclusion that the twin objectives of stabilizing production at the level of demand while ensuring farmers a fair income could not be met. It proposed, therefore, radical restructuring of the CAP based on 'reasonable incomes, reasonable prices and increased productivity', followed by agricultural trade liberalization in line with the treaty. However, political opposition to the plan, arising from diverse interests between the members meant that the proposed reforms were not accepted.

The Commission presented to the Council a second major plan for reform in 'Guidelines for European Agriculture' (EC, 1981). This plan aimed specifically at a reduction of production by gradually lowering prices to bring them in line with world prices. The Community recognized that at a time of changing world economic conditions and scarce financial resources 'it is neither economically sensible nor financially possible to give producers a full guarantee for products in structural surplus.' Following these guidelines, target levels of output and 'guarantee thresholds' were introduced for several products, with entitlement to full CAP benefits limited to prespecified levels of output. When these levels were exceeded, the policy took one of the following forms: (a) the target and intervention prices were reduced; (b) aid paid under the market regulation was limited; (c) the producers participated in the cost of disposing of surplus output by a 'coresponsibility' levy; (d) production quotas applied at the national or the enterprise level.

However, these measures did not solve the fundamental problem of 'how to reconcile the social objectives of the CAP with real market conditions.' Production continued to exceed self-sufficiency with long-term growth for most products at least three to four times higher than the annual rate of growth of their intra-EU consumption, while the markets for agricultural exports proved to be unreliable long-term outlets for surpluses. The CAP problems worsened after Greece, Portugal and Spain became members of the Community which increased the CAP budgetary expenditures and worsened the balance between supply and demand of agricultural products. Therefore, the Community set up a framework for a series of reforms of the CAP.

Pre-1992 reforms

The measures advanced during this period proposed primarily the freezing or reduction of administered prices and subsidies with the aim of complying with 'budgetary discipline'. After bitter arguments, the Council (1988) agreed on a formula for funding the EU budget and introduced 'budget stabilizers', leading to automatic CAP price cuts. It also introduced complementary measures, such as 'coresponsibility levies' and 'milk quotas', which were supply controls based on previous volumes of output, and attempted to alleviate budget crises by penalizing excess production without correcting the price distortions which continued to inflict high welfare losses on consumers and taxpayers. The 'budget stabilizers' were potentially promising in terms of allocation effects but they were not extensive, nor were they fully implemented. A straight cut in support prices would have been the most direct and more effective policy for removing the inefficiencies forced upon EU agriculture by the CAP but political considerations and the influence of the farming lobby did not allow this approach.

The 1992 reforms

The budget-inspired reforms proved ineffective. Meanwhile, pressures were mounting from:

- the EU decision to complete the single market by 1992;
- the GATT Uruguay Round for trade liberalization.

Therefore, in 1992 a far-reaching restructuring of EU agricultural policy was undertaken which was finally approved in December 1993 (the MacSharry reforms). The GATT agreement marked the full integration of agriculture into the 'rules and disciplines' of international trading relationships for the first time. The EU reforms aimed to slash overproduction by reducing the guaranteed prices by up to 30 per cent and switching the CAP policy from *price support* to *compensatory payments* in the form of direct income supplements linked to farm size and average yields. To qualify for these payments arable farmers of all but the smallest holdings were compelled to *set aside* 15 per cent of their land and with the help of generous grants to turn land over to forestry and ecological or recreational uses ensuring protection of the environment and natural resources. The agreement aimed to bring CAP prices closer in line with world levels so that export subsidies would fall, thus reducing the CAP distortions in international trade and increasing market access for competitive third-country producers. Guaranteed prices and Community preferences continued, though at a lower level, but the Community agreed to change protection from variable levies to fixed tariffs, thus re-establishing a link between EU prices and world market prices. Therefore, in contrast to the reforms originating from budget crises, the GATT-inspired reforms were welfare-improving by shifting the agricultural problem towards market-oriented solutions. These changes reduced price support and lowered consumer prices. But by shifting the burden from consumers to taxpayers with direct payments from the EU budget, they increased total guaranteed CAP spending by about 25 per cent. For the first time, they also included environmental considerations, by linking payments of farm support to compliance with some pre-agreed environmental improvements. Moreover, since environmental payments, afforestation and structural measures in agriculture are all targeted actions, responsibility for their implementation was moved from the Commission to local authorities with the costs shared equally by the member states and the CAP budget.

   With these reforms the EU governments took a big step towards market liberalization of the agricultural sector by separating the economic from the social functions of the CAP, and thus finally admitting that the revered price-support system could not raise farmers' incomes and at the same time bring the agricultural markets into balance.

Box 7.1 ■ **Incoherence and inconsistencies in the CAP**

The CAP is an unbalanced policy. The imbalance at the broadest level is its gross over-dependence on the use of market policy at the expense of structural, environmental and rural development measures. The incoherence also shows up between elements of the policy, between market and environmental policy, and between structures and environmental policy. This is also evident within each of these three stands of policy. Many of the inconsistencies are the result of years of adding and elaborating measures to deal with successive problems encountered. Rarely have categories of instruments or regulations been removed altogether, almost always new regulations were added to existing ones. This is usually done in politically balanced packages of measures in which there are enough decision variables to allow differentiation and exceptions enabling each Member State to achieve some of its own interests. However, this political balance has been obtained at the cost of an extremely complicated and increasingly incoherent policy.

EC (1997b)

The 1999 reforms

On top of these changes a new agreement for reform of the CAP was signed in 1999, which the Community declared as 'the biggest ever negotiated for EU's Common Agricultural Policy'. These reforms were required for 'deepening and extending the 1992 reform through further shifts from support to direct payments and developing a coherent rural policy' (Commission, 1997) and were induced for four main reasons:

1. budgetary constraints caused by the closer link of budgetary revenues and GNP;
2. the difficulties of extending the current CAP into central and eastern European countries after EU enlargement;
3. EU commitments under the World Trade Organization (WTO, which replaced GATT) agreements regarding export subsidies and the forthcoming start of further trade liberalization talks;
4. the reform of the EU structural funds which included the funds financing CAP expenditures.

The new reforms introduced further direct payments and cuts in support prices on top of those already implemented, in some cases reducing them by more than 50 per cent. As a result, agriculture's share in the budget, once two-thirds of the total, fell to under half. The Commission also attempted but without success to ease the 'budgetary imbalance' of the big contributors to the EU budget – Germany, the Netherlands, Austria, Sweden and the UK (see Chapter 4) – by a partial 'renationalization' of farm spending which would have cut down the EU's contribution to the CAP income support from 100 per cent to 75 per cent, with members paying the balance to their own producers. The drawback of co-financing is that it may hit some of the poorer farm producers in the less-developed EU countries (GR, E, IRL, P) and that it contains the costs of the CAP to the EU budget by transferring some of the spending to national budgets, without perceptible reduction to total costs. Proposals by member states to cut direct payments to farmers, which account for nearly 65 per cent of the annual CAP budget rising to 68 per cent in 2006, were also abandoned. Therefore, without further reforms, the expansion of the EU to Mediterranean and central and eastern European (CEE) countries in 2003–4, will require extending the system of direct payments to their farmers. Without these payments, it will be impossible to implement supply control mechanisms such as requiring farmers to set aside land. Therefore, the problem of production surpluses, which the EU has managed to bring under control, could re-emerge after enlargement with sharp budgetary implications. All these mean that another review of the CAP agreement will be necessary just before the next EU enlargement.[2]

7.7 The Common Fisheries Policy

Fish are a natural, biological, mobile, and renewable common resource. Fish mobility means that every fisherman is vulnerable to the actions of others. Therefore, as a common resource, fish stocks are common heritage and property subject to common problems that require common management. In Europe, the fishing sector's contribution to national output is generally less than 1 per cent but, by being concentrated in certain coastal areas with no other opportunities, its impact on employment is significant.

The fishing industry of the EU countries has been in prolonged crisis, as it has in most fishing countries of the world. Overfishing has led to smaller catches, smaller landings and smaller incomes. After protracted negotiations, which started in 1966, the Community introduced a Common Fisheries Policy (CFP) in January 1983. The policy aimed to ensure 'optimal exploitation of the biological resources of the Community Zone' by improved efficiency in both the structure and marketing of the sector and 'equitable exploitation of these limited resources between member states'. In particular, the objectives of the policy were as follows:

---

[2] For the latest Commission proposals regarding the extension of the CAP to new EU members after enlargement see Chapter 9.

1. *on the structural side*
   (a) rational use of resources;
   (b) no discrimination among nationals of the EU member states employed in the industry;
   (c) conservation of resources.
2. *on the marketing side*
   (a) secure employment in the industry, especially in certain coastal regions traditionally specializing in fishing;
   (b) a fair income for those employed in the industry;
   (c) improvement in marketing and marketing standards;
   (d) adequate supply adjusted to market requirements;
   (e) reasonable prices for the consumer.

The necessity for a CFP became more urgent because of developments in the international field which took place during the 1970s, when many countries introduced economic exclusion zones (EEZs) of 200 nautical miles (320 km). The CFP is based on article 32 of the TEEU, which explains that the term 'agricultural products means the products of the soil, of stockfarming and of fisheries and products of first stage processing directly related to these products'. Therefore, the objectives of the CAP (TEEU, 32–8) apply also to the CFP. The methods for achieving the CFP objectives are broadly similar to those of the CAP. In the fishing industry the instruments of policy are as follows:

1. *Access arrangements* which determine exactly where fishermen may fish. These also provide 12-mile (19-km) national fisheries zones for each member country, with limited access for other member countries, and a 200-mile exclusive Community zone with members' quotas of catches. Several third countries have signed agreements for reciprocal fishing and trade arrangements with the Community (Norway, Canada, etc.).
2. *Marketing arrangements,* which are designed to promote 'rational disposal' of fishery products and to bring some degree of stability to the industry and the incomes of those employed in it.
3. Quotas (*total allowable catches, TACs*), technical conservation measures (minimum size for certain species of fish, minimum mesh size, etc.) and surveillance. These are instruments of policies aimed at stock preservation, based on the recognition that the biggest threat to fish stocks is overfishing. The Commission has set up a special inspectorate to supervise member states' enforcement of the CFP regulations (such as mesh size, minimum landing size, closed areas, and closed season areas). However, each member country is responsible for policing the waters under its nominal jurisdiction and for ensuring the terms of the CFP are adhered to.

4. *Structural policies* which aim at contraction of the industry which suffers from overcapacity, a better allocation of resources, increased productivity and long-term development. Structural expenditures are financed by the Financial Instrument of Fisheries Guidance (FIFG, which plays a role similar to that of the EAGGF).

As in the CAP, for the CFP a target price and a guide price were set yearly at the start of each fishing season. A withdrawal price also applied. However, the withdrawals were limited to a maximum of 20 per cent of the permitted annual catch, so a degree of coresponsibility was attached to the supply. The CFP also provided export refunds and import duties, but the Community depends on imported fish products, which now account for almost 60 per cent of total consumption. In contrast to the CAP which was based on guaranteed prices designed to ensure farmers a fair income, the CFP helped to stabilize the market and to shelter fishermen from falling prices. But it did not attempt to regulate the upper bound of price fluctuations, so fishermen benefited from the peaks of prices and were protected from the troughs.

The Mediterranean member countries were covered by the CFP for market organization, structural change and financial matters. The Community also proposed measures on inshore fishing and the conservation of resources. However, there are no 200-mile zones, quotas or TACs established there so far. The treaties provided for all businesses and workers – including fishermen – to practise their trade anywhere in the single market of the Community.

Every year the European Commission, on advice from a panel of national scientists, redoubles its insistence that stocks are overfished and that TACs must be reduced further. Where governments are forced to accept that stocks are depleted, they still attempt to win as big a quota as possible of the TACs. New regulatory measures, along with TACs and quotas, include limits on fishing days, the number, size and engine power of vessels and specifications of fishing gear for national fleets. These measures aim at less fishing which, together with smaller catches of immature fish, would allow the stocks to rebuild.

The Community attributes the continuing fisheries crisis to structural factors, such as fleet overcapacities, overfishing, low productivity and inappropriate commercial structures. Therefore, the solution it proposes includes improved resource management and the control of catches, the elimination of overcapacity, and better market management. The conservation measures introduced by the Community aim to establish zones in which fishing is prohibited or restricted; to limit exploitation rates; to set quantitative limits on catches; to limit time spent at sea; to fix the number of fishing vessels; and to introduce incentives to reduce overcapacity and promote more selective fishing. The next review of the CFP will be carried out in 2002.

The problem of overfishing and stock preservation is international. Since fish swim the seas in blissful ignorance of international boundaries, what is required is an international agreement involving cooperation, regulation and enforcement.

7.8 Summary

The CAP is based on three principles:

■ unity of markets, by removing barriers between the member states;
■ community preference, by trade protection at external borders;
■ financial solidarity through the Community's participation in the costs of agricultural policies.

Five broad types of agricultural policy are in use:

■ price support by market price guarantee;
■ market support payments, including storage costs, premiums for cessation of production, subsidies to consumption, etc.;
■ compensatory payments as direct income transfers to producers;
■ supply controls by production quotas and restrictions on factor use (set-aside land and early retirement of farmers);
■ environmental programmes, such as payments for afforestation.

Following international agreements on agricultural trade liberalization, import protection changed from variable levies to fix tariffs. This restored the links between world market prices and EU market prices.

The importance of agriculture in the EU-15 is diminishing. The agricultural sector contributes today less than 2 per cent of the GDP and employs just 5 per cent of the workforce. These elements and the combined effects of consumer and taxpayer pressures, further trade liberalization and the scheduled enlargement of the Community to countries of central and eastern Europe (CEE) mean that the character and coverage of the CAP would be altered by devolution based on subsidiarity. Thereafter, the Commission's role would be to monitor and supervise the member states' agricultural support schemes to ensure their compatibility with the common objective of economic integration.

APPENDIX A7 Agricultural policies

Two general categories of agricultural policies can be distinguished: price stabilization policies and income support policies.

Price stabilization policies attempt to raise prices and to remove their unwarranted fluctuations. They take the form of price controls and quantity controls and their cost is mainly borne by consumers. *Price controls* are applied directly to market prices to change them, or to prevent them from changing by market forces. They include:

1. *Price fixing*, which is sustained by removing from the market any disequilibrium tendencies by buying for stock all excess supplies, and supplying (from stock or imports) all excess demands. Stockpiling carries a budgetary cost.
2. *Tariffs and levies* on imports, which raise the domestic prices, if the country is a net importer of the relevant commodity. Restrictive sanitary requirements and other administrative devices of a similar nature have similar effects on the volume of imports. An alternative policy is to define a threshold or minimum import price – and so a domestic price – by placing a *variable levy* on import price.

Quantity controls directly alter the quantity of supply in the market as the means for changing market prices. They take the form of:

1. *Building up of stocks* as a buffer between production and consumption, at budgetary cost. The stocks are augmented when supply exceeds demand, and run down when supply falls sort of demand, so short-term price fluctuations are minimized. This policy applies to commodities with inelastic demand and variable supply, provided they can be stored without excessive deterioration or at prohibitive cost.
2. *Quota controls* on imports, which reduce the supply and raise prices like tariffs.
3. *Supply controls*, such as destroying a part of the available output to reduce the quantity entering the market, thus removing the pressure on prices to fall.
4. *Production controls*, such as acreage quotas, licensing and diversion or land set aside for reducing the supply of output at the production stage and thus raising commodity prices.
5. *Export subsidies*, which can be included here as an indirect measure for controlling the residual quantity of output remaining available for supply in the domestic market and thus raising the domestic price. This policy affects both the taxpayer, who carries the burden of financing the subsidy, and the domestic consumer, who pays higher prices.

Income support policies have a budgetary cost and are subdivided into indirect and direct. *Indirect* income support policies raise the price the producers receive for their output as the means for increasing their revenue and income, leaving the domestic market price unaffected. They take the following forms:

1. *Production subsidies*, as fixed payments per unit or unit price of input or output, which reduce the marginal cost of production and raise producers' income.
2. *Deficiency payments* by the state making up the difference between a guarantee price and the average price received by the producers from selling their output in the unprotected domestic market.

Direct income support policies are lump sum transfers related to or independent of the volume, price, revenue or income of agricultural activity. Naturally, this policy is the most effective for reaching a target level of income for the agricultural population. However, this is a *social policy* that may carry high administrative costs, while leaving the domestic prices of agricultural commodities unaffected.

Besides these policies the government may operate long-term policies to change the structure and productivity of the agricultural sector, e.g. by investment in physical infrastructure, research and development.

Questions

1. Why does the European Union support its agricultural sector?
2. Evaluate the following quotation: 'The CAP consists of one major instrument, yet it is attempting to achieve five major, and to some extent contradictory, objectives; it cannot possibly succeed.'
3. Describe the objectives and policy of the CAP. Show what effect the following have on the efficiency losses and gains of CAP support pricing: (a) a higher support price; (b) a more elastic supply curve; (c) a more inelastic demand curve.
4. Analyse the effects and relative efficiency of price fixing, direct income support, primary factor subsidies and deficiency payments as methods of support for agriculture.
5. Taking into account the objectives and the main policy instruments of the CAP, analyse the effects of the following:
   (a) a higher support price;
   (b) a more elastic supply curve;
   (c) a more inelastic demand curve.

6. 'There are too many boats and too few fish. There are only two choices. One, the classical free market choice, to abolish all regulation. The fish stocks would be wiped out within a decade. Alternatively, some form of regulatory system which protects stocks and allocates them fairly' (Commissioner Emma Bonino, 1996). Comment.

Further reading

A survey of the costs of the CAP on the EU and its adverse effects on international trading relations is given in Gylfason (1995). Comparisons between various agricultural policies are in Munk (1989) and OECD (1990). For a comprehensive review of the CAP and the case for reform see Commission (1997) and Ingersent et al. (1998). A critical review of recent reforms is in Ackrill (2000), and of the fisheries policy in Song (1995).

Web guide

Information on agriculture and the CAP can be found at:

■ www.europa.eu.int/comm/agriculture/index_en.htm
■ www.europa.eu.int/comm/fisheries
■ www.agra-net.com

Trade policies

8

Customs unions start with integration of their trade policies. The EU's Common Commercial Policy (CCP) began with the liberalization of internal trade and the integration of the foreign trade policies of the member states. In spite of its stated commitment to free trade and to multilateralism, the EU has followed protectionism in its agricultural trade and bilateralism in its commercial relations with third countries, based on a system of diverse trade preferences. These arrangements often brought the EU into conflict with many developed and less-developed countries, and with international organizations aiming at multilateral trade liberalization. But after consolidating its internal 'single market', which made the EU the most important trading bloc in the world, the EU has become a strong supporter of multilateral trade liberalization under the auspices of the World Trade Organization (WTO), in which it cooperates fully with similarly disposed countries.

8.1 Trade, protection and liberalization

Protection

International trade increases world efficiency by specialization in production and exchange according to comparative advantage. Under conditions of perfect competition, given technology, constant returns to scale, and the absence of externalities, free trade maximizes these efficiency gains for all the participants. However, in many countries free trade is the exception rather than the rule. Developed industrial countries have used trade intervention policies with the following intentions:

1. to preserve or encourage mature industries, such as steel and shipbuilding;

2. to promote sectors strategic for growth, such as high-technology industries;
3. to cater for the special characteristics of disadvantaged sectors, such as agriculture;
4. to protect sectors important for national security and defence;
5. to correct persistent trade imbalances causing macroeconomic problems;
6. to protect the employment of labour, thus averting the high social and budgetary cost of unemployment;
7. to avoid exchange-rate changes precipitating instability;
8. to offset the 'unfair' trade actions of other countries;
9. to operate profit-maximizing strategic trade policies.

Income distribution

An issue of contention is the income distribution implications of trade policies and the relative power of different groups in society (farmers, trade unions, industrialists, consumers, and so on) to influence trade policy-making. Protection and liberalization do not benefit or harm all the residents of a country to the same extent, so there is always some group with interests in protection or anti-protection. In general, while consumers are better off by trade liberalization and producers by protection, free trade brings about a net collective benefit to society as a whole (see Appendix A1). However, if the costs of protection are spread over a large and diverse group, such as the consumers, while the benefits are concentrated on a relatively small, well-organized group that can exert political pressure, such as the producers, protection may be adopted despite its adverse net effects on society. Therefore, certain influential economic groups may engage in 'rent-seeking' activities, using the power of the state to increase their share of national income rather than create wealth. Trade restrictions are often used to redistribute income in favour of some disadvantaged group, such as the farmers. It is unlikely, however, that a foreign trade policy is the best way of dealing with the domestic problem of income inequality. Domestic market failures should be corrected by domestic policies aimed directly at the source of the problem.

Instruments

Protection takes the direct form of tariffs on imports or non-tariff measures, such as quantitative restrictions, subsidies, government procurement practices, and technical barriers to trade. Multiple exchange rates (e.g. high rates on imports and low rates on exports) can have effects similar to those of a system of tariffs on imports and subsidies on exports. In a wider sense, a whole range of interventionist government policies (such as grants and loans for industrial development, terms attractive to foreign investors, promotion of R&D, regional subsidies, public procurement, and preferential allocation of defence contracts) have wide implications for foreign trade. Therefore, governments adopt such policies at least in part for protection and promotion of domestic production. In general, industrial and trade structures and policies are intertwined, and different industry structures incite different trade policy incentives and instruments. Thus, the most recent argument for protection (that of strategic policy interaction, (9) above) is that in the real world of imperfect competition and increasing returns to scale, firms can make excess profits or generate externalities that create a divergence between private and social benefits. Therefore, a strategic trade policy, which includes protection, is required: (a) to shift the terms of international competition to the domestic industry's advantage; and (b) to promote sectors yielding external economies. The problem with these arguments is that all too easily they may be used to justify protectionism leading to international confrontation and retaliation which in the end may cause more harm than benefit.

During the 1970s and 1980s, slow growth and the rise of unemployment in industrial countries and, probably, shifts in competitiveness and comparative advantage induced a proliferation of non-tariff trade barriers. They usually took the form of quantitative restrictions, subsidies on production and exports, and discriminating administrative measures, which were collectively known as the 'new protectionism'. The most widespread of these measures of protection were trade-limitation agreements, either informal 'orderly marketing arrangements' (OMAs) or formal 'voluntary export restraints' (VERs). These were temporary quantitative restrictions on exports of a product, agreed bilaterally at government or industry level, between exporters and importers. They were usually administered by the exporting country which often raised its sale price, thus improving its terms of trade.

Exporting countries sometimes attempt to alter the pattern of their production and trade by resorting to export subsidies and other discriminating policies, such as low interest loans and preferential taxation, which reduce the producer cost of exports. Price discrimination in international markets is in general called 'dumping'. If the foreign demand is more elastic than the domestic demand and the two markets are separate, dumping aims at profit maximization by price discrimination. A different sort of dumping, which allegedly has become more prevalent in recent years, consists of exports priced below marginal cost, 'subsidized' by high-priced sales in a tied-up and protected home market. In this case dumping may aim at achieving economies of scale in production by increasing the volume of output and reducing unit costs. Whatever the reasons for initiating dumping, the resulting lower export prices benefit the consumers of the importing country. However, many countries impose penalties against goods they believe are dumped in their markets by their foreign competitors. These penalties or anti-dumping duties are levied on imports to offset the competitive advantage gained by either price discrimination between exports and domestic sales of a product (= anti-dumping duties) or subsidies in the exporting country (= countervailing duties). An alternative policy is to compel the accused exporting firm to raise its offer price by the dumping margin. In general, the 'anti-dumping' argument for protection is valid if the dumping is 'predatory' – designed to erase competition and thereby gain for the exporter monopoly power in the foreign market. Otherwise, foreign export subsidies improve the importing country's terms of trade.

Trade liberalization

Successive rounds of world trade liberalization measures undertaken since the early postwar years under the auspices of the General Agreement on Tariffs and Trade (GATT, 1948) have lessened the importance of tariffs and quantitative restrictions, especially on manufactured goods. This task continues under the WTO, which replaced the GATT in 1995. The GATT also condemned harmful dumping as an unfair practice which is not based on a true comparative advantage and, under the International Anti-Dumping Code signed in 1967, it allowed countries to defend themselves (by anti-dumping and countervailing duties) when dumping 'causes or threatens material injury to an established industry'. However, the rules on anti-dumping and countervailing duties were rather fuzzy, and this made their misuse tempting for protectionist purposes. The multilateral trade agreement, which was reached at the Uruguay Round of trade liberalization, contains detailed rules for the determination of dumping, the criteria ascertaining proof of injury, the procedural regulations for the initiation and the conduct of anti-dumping investigations, and the implementation and duration of anti-dumping measures.

8.2 The Common Commercial Policy (CCP)

As a rule, the EU is founded on the principles of free trade, but the exceptions are many and important. The Treaty of Rome stipulated that 'the Community shall be based upon a customs union' (TEEC, II, 23), which entails liberalizing trade between the member states and adopting a common customs tariff on trade with third countries. The Community planned to implement the changes in customs duties in three stages over a 12-year period. In effect the process was speeded up and the customs union was completed a year and a half ahead of schedule in 1968.

Box 8.1 ■ The GATT and the WTO

Countries have come to realize that acting unilaterally, in what seems to be their best interests in international trade, fails to achieve the best outcome possible. Multilateral coordination of trade policies through international treaties can lead to superior results. Therefore, in 1947, a voluntary pact was concluded, the General Agreement on Tariffs and Trade (GATT), which was updated several times to keep pace with changes in the international economic order. A major overhaul of the world trade system was implemented after the Uruguay Round trade accord (1994), when the GATT was replaced by the World Trade Organization (WTO) which was established and started operating on 1 January 1995 by the agreement of more than 125 countries. The next WTO round started in Qatar in November 2001 with 142 member countries.

The GATT was providing a code of rules for the conduct of world trade and a forum for resolving disputes and reducing trade barriers by international negotiation. The agreement was based on the free market, fair competition, free trade and specialization according to comparative advantage and it was based on two main principles:

1. trade liberalization by tariff cuts and by the general elimination of quantitative restrictions and non-tariff barriers to trade;
2. non-discrimination in international trade.

Regional economic integration was permitted but: (a) the customs union's common external tariff 'shall not on the whole be higher or more restrictive than the general incidence of the duties and regulations of commerce applicable' before the union; (b) the agreements must cover 'substantially all the trade' between the parties; and (c) the customs union or free trade area must be completed 'within a reasonable [= short] length of time'. But the growth of preferential regional trade associations remains a cause for concern, particularly after the EU's single market programme and the formation of the North American Free Trade Area (NAFTA, Canada–United States–Mexico). These two blocs together count for about two-thirds of world exports and global GDP.

Through the years, the GATT kept liberalizing international trade by a series of rounds of multilateral negotiations (the 1959–62 'Dillon Round', the 1963–7 'Kennedy Round' and the 1973–9 'Tokyo Round'). The 'Uruguay Round' (September 1986 to April 1994) opened up the way to further liberalization of trade under the guidance of the World Trade Organization (WTO).

In contrast to the GATT, which was primarily designed to reduce and to regulate trade intervention *at the border*, the WTO is assigned a greater role in monitoring and management. Its mission is to accelerate trade liberalization and to settle trade disputes on multilateral rather than bilateral or unilateral basis. Whereas the GATT was an international agreement covering only trade in goods, the WTO is an international organization that covers trade in services, foreign direct investment and intellectual property.

The three members of the first enlargement (DK, IRL and UK) dismantled their tariffs on intra-Community trade and adopted the CET in 1977. The next three member states (GR, E, and P) completed the same process in 1992. The countries of the latest enlargement (AT, FI, SE) joined the common market which led to the EU-15 in 1995. Meanwhile, the Community had also made progress in dismantling the national non-tariff barriers on internal trade and the internal frontier controls for completion of the single market.

The Common Commercial Policy (CCP) began operating at the end of the transitional period in 1968. The member states provided the Community with exclusive competence to conduct the common external trade policy (TEEC, 133), to maintain 'appropriate relations' with international organizations (TEEC, 302), and to conclude association agreements with third countries (TEEC, 300, 310) and international organizations aiming at 'the harmonious development of world trade, the progressive abolition of restrictions on international trade and the lowering of customs barriers' (TEEC, 131). However, the Community and the member states shared competence for the conclusion of international agreements on trade in services.

Decisions on CCP are taken by the Council, on proposals from the Commission, by qualified majority vote. Agreements between the Community and third states or international organizations are negotiated by the Commission but completed by the Council (TEEC, 300). The Community may conclude with a third state, a union of states or an international organization 'agreements establishing an association involving reciprocal rights and obligations, joint actions and special procedures' (TEEC, 310). A Council regulation on common rules for imports (288/1982) provides the legal basis for introducing surveillance measures of limited duration or imposing quantitative restraints (safeguards) if a product is being imported 'in such greatly increased quantities and/or such terms or conditions as to cause or threaten substantial injury to Community producers'. In this context, the Commission has competence to open investigations but only at the request of member states. Affected parties are entitled to present their views. In 1984, under the CCP the Community adopted the New Commercial Policy Instrument to counter 'unfair and unlawful trading practices' which are contrary to international agreements (for example, GATT rules) or 'generally accepted principles'. Similar trade-policy tools are employed, or threaten to be employed, by other industrialized nations (such as the USA) to obtain consent for a 'voluntary' export quota from another nation. In 1990, the European Parliament adopted a resolution which made the adoption of anti-dumping measures more effective, more equitable and more transparent. The Community justified this practice by invoking a general clause in GATT which allows countries to take defensive action. However, on this issue the Community has been accused of using anti-dumping measures as a means of protecting uncompetitive companies, especially in 'strategic' industries, thus shifting the costs of adjustment onto the outside world.

After several enlargements and association and trade agreements, the Community has become one of the most important trading blocs in the

Figure 8.1 Intra-EU and extra-EU imports of goods, 1980–2000, percentage of GDP, current prices

Source: Data from Commission (2001c).

world, influencing both the volume and the direction of international trade. As we have seen in Chapter 2, the Community accounts for 19 per cent of world merchandise trade (external), and 25 per cent of trade in services.

In the course of its development, the Community faced criticisms from advocates of a more liberal economic order about its assorted tariff preferences. Problems have also arisen in the Community's relations with other trading countries, some of which welcome the EU as a large trading partner predisposed towards trade liberalization, while others have seen in the EU the emergence of an adversary which does not always play the international trade game according to the rules, particularly the trade of agricultural commodities. Many countries also feared that after completing the single market, the EU could become a more inward-looking, highly protected, and a self-sufficient economic bloc – 'Fortress Europe'. Figure 8.1 confirms that these concerns proved unfounded and that the single market benefited both internal and external trade. Nevertheless, the EU did apply discriminatory trade agreements, dispensing preferences to designated countries and territories.

8.3 The ACP–EU partnership

The TEEC (XX, 182–8) and other agreements granted associate membership to certain 'countries and territories' that had dependency and colonial ties with some of the Six. The association agreements entailed 'reciprocal rights and obligations' for establishing a free trade area with two-way free access for each other's products. The Community also set up a special institution, the European Development Fund (EDF), to supply development aid to the associate states. Soon after 1960, most of the associate overseas territories gained their national independence and started negotiations for a new agreement with the Community. This led in 1963 to the Yaoundé Convention, an agreement between the EU and each of 18 African states. The second Yaoundé Convention was signed in 1969. After the first EU enlargement it became necessary to reconsider the Community's association system for extension to developing countries with close ties with the UK through the Commonwealth. A new five-year association agreement, the Lomé Convention (1975–80), was signed in 1975 by the EU and 46 African, Caribbean and Pacific (ACP) countries. This agreement was succeeded by Lomé II (1980–5), III (1985–90) and IV (1991–2000) signed by an increasing number of ACP countries. The main provisions of the ACP conventions included:

1. *tariff preferences* for manufactures produced and exported from the ACP countries to the EU;
2. *agricultural export preferences* for products not competing with the EU's CAP;
3. *aid* from the EDF for the stabilization of earnings from agricultural and mineral exports.

Since 1995 the ACP-EU convention has been founded on 'respect for human rights and democratic principles and the rule of law'. Lomé IV was succeeded by the 20-year Cotonou Agreement between the EU and 78 ACP countries (of 640 million people), which was signed in 2000 and contains several innovations, aspiring

- to enhance the political dimension and refocus development policies on poverty-reduction strategies;
- to improve the framework for investment development and trade, including the links between environment and trade;
- to create an investment facility in support of the development of the primary sector and to base the allocation of funds on an evaluation of the requirements of each country and its policy performance;
- to introduce a new system of rolling programming, allowing the EU and the beneficiary country to adjust their cooperation programme on a regular basis;
- to decentralize administrative and, in some cases, financial responsibilities towards local level with the aim of making cooperation more effective.

The EU and its member states are by far the biggest donors of aid to less developed and developing countries (index in 1997, for EU = 100, Japan = 29 and US = 22).

Box 8.2 ■ Development cooperation

The EU with its member states together makes up the world's leading source of official development assistance, contributing nearly one-third of all aid granted to developing countries. The ad hoc arrangements at the level of the Community were strengthened and formalized by the TEEC, 177–81. The common policy, which complements similar policies within the member states, aspires to foster the sustainable economic and social development of developing countries, especially the poorest ones, to effect a smooth and gradual integration of the developing countries into the world economy. Community policy will contribute to the general objective of developing and consolidating democracy and the rule of law with respect for human rights and fundamental freedoms. The Community and the member states coordinate their policies on development cooperation and consult each other on aid programmes, complying with the commitments and objectives they have approved in the context of the UN and other international organizations. Between them, the EU and its member states provide 55 per cent of total international official development assistance (ODA) and more than two-thirds of grant aid.

In the past, however, the ACP and other developing countries have criticized the Community's aid and association scheme. They have argued that the aid provided by the EU was inadequate and not increasing in real terms or per head of population. Other developing countries which are not parties of the ACP convention, have criticized the EU's preferences for ACP countries as discriminatory and divisive for the LDCs.

8.4 Trade relations between the Community and other European and Mediterranean countries

The EEA agreement

Besides the EU, Europe had another integration scheme, the European Free Trade Area (EFTA) which began life in 1960 by the Stockholm Convention. Of the original members of EFTA, Denmark and the United Kingdom left to join the EU in 1973, Portugal in 1986, and Austria, Finland and Sweden in 1995. The remaining EFTA countries are: Iceland, Norway, Switzerland and Liechtenstein. EFTA's objective of trade liberalization in industrial products between its members was almost completed by December 1966, but agricultural products were excluded from tariff-free trade.

Proximity and historical ties meant that the EU was by far the biggest trade partner of EFTA. As members of EFTA, Denmark and the United Kingdom already had free trade in manufactures with the other EFTA countries. Therefore, when they applied for membership in the EU, an opportunity arose to negotiate the reduction of the barriers that divided western European trade. Since certain EFTA countries (Finland, Sweden,

Switzerland, Austria) were at that time against membership in the EU because of political neutrality, a merger of the two organizations was not considered. It was decided therefore to conclude bilateral agreements between the EU and each of the EFTA countries and to put them into effect from the date of the first enlargement, 1 January 1973. By July 1977, these agreements collectively set up a free trade area for industrial products throughout western Europe.

Following the Single European Act, discussions on increased cooperation between the two organizations in economic, cultural and educational matters forged the outline of a treaty, designed to draw EFTA fully into the EU's single market ahead of its completion, but without offering full membership in the Community. The agreement establishing a European Economic Area (EEA) of 18 member states (Switzerland voted against participation) and more than 380 million people came into force on 1 January 1994. The aim of the EEA was to strengthen economic co-operation between the Community and the EFTA countries by setting up 'a dynamic and homogeneous integrated structure based on common rules and equal conditions of competition and equipped with the means, including the judicial means, necessary for its implementation'. The agreement included free trade in goods, services and factors of production governed by the competition and single market law of the Community, with the exception of agriculture and fisheries. Many observers viewed the EEA agreement as a bridging mechanism leading eventually to EU enlargement, and this is essentially what has happened. While for practical purposes EFTA was wound up in 1995, the EEA agreement between the EU and Norway, Iceland and Liechtenstein is still operating constructively.

Central and eastern European countries

Czechoslovakia, Hungary, Poland, Romania, Bulgaria, the USSR and the German Democratic Republic (GDR) were until 1990 members of the Council for Mutual Economic Assistance (CMEA or Comecon) which was founded in 1949 with the objective of accelerating economic growth and establishing a more rational division of labour based on 'state-trading' among its member countries. The EU and individual members of the CMEA had signed bilateral trade and cooperation agreements. But after the political changes in these countries, the unification of Germany and the demise of CMEA, the Community signed bilateral 'Europe Agreements' with the Czech and Slovak republics, Hungary, Poland, Romania and Bulgaria, and more limited agreements with Latvia, Estonia, Lithuania and Slovenia. Similar agreements have also been concluded with other newly independent states (NIS, such as Armenia, Azerbaijan, Georgia, Kazakhstan, Kyrgystan, Moldova, Tajikistan, Turkmenistan and Uzbekistan). These agreements are designed to promote trade and cooperation in industry, science and technology, energy and the environment. Partnership and cooperation agreements with Russia, Belarus and the Ukraine were signed in 1994, lifting quotas on exports and promising free trade negotiations after 1998. The Community, in coordination with other developed countries, set up and funded the European Bank for Reconstruction and Development (EBRD) to assist the economic development and the transition towards open market-oriented economies of central and eastern European countries.

The European Council has also declared its intention to examine the question of association with those independent states which have successfully and purposefully followed their chosen path of thorough economic and political reform. In 1997, the Commission proposed in 'Agenda 2000' that negotiations should start with certain central, eastern European and Mediterranean countries for possible accession to the EU (dealt with in Chapter 9).

The EU's 'stabilization and association process' is its principal instrument for the south-eastern European countries: Albania, Bosnia and Herzegovina, Croatia, the Federal Republic of Yugoslavia and the former Yugoslav Republic of Macedonia. The process includes economic and financial assistance, cooperation, political dialogue, the goal of a free trade area, the approximation of their legislation to EU law, and co-operation in areas of justice and home affairs.

Mediterranean countries

After the accession to the Community of Greece, Spain and Portugal, the term Mediterranean region (MR) refers to the following non-member countries of the Mediterranean basin:

1. the Maghreb group: Morocco, Algeria, Tunisia and Libya;
2. the Mashreq group: Egypt, Jordan, Lebanon and Syria;
3. Turkey;
4. Israel, Cyprus, Malta, and the Palestinian Authority.

For geographic, strategic and economic reasons the EU countries have always had close relations with the countries bordering the Mediterranean, which historically depended for more than 50 per cent of their trade on the EU.

The formation of the EU, the introduction of the CAP and the restrictions on imports of agricultural commodities meant that many of the Mediterranean countries could lose their most important export markets. Therefore, in an attempt to preserve their access to these markets, they asked for special trade relations with the Community. The Community responded favourably, and from early on concluded trade agreements with individual countries of the region. These agreements were different in legal structure from country to country, some taking the form of association with a view to eventual membership (Greece and Turkey), others endeavouring to set up free trade areas (Tunisia, Morocco), and others offering only certain preferential advantages (Israel, Lebanon). In 1972 the EU offered them a more uniform agreement, the 'Global Mediterranean Policy', and in 1995 followed with a 'Euro-Mediterranean Partnership' which adopted the Barcelona declaration, to create an area of peace and shared prosperity and to improve mutual understanding between the EU and its Mediterranean neighbours.

The agreements with Cyprus and Malta provided for future negotiations to set up a customs union. Both countries now belong to the group of countries negotiating for imminent accession to the EU (see Chapter 9). Similar considerations apply to Turkey, which concluded a fully fledged customs union with the EU in 1995.

8.5 Trade agreements with other developing countries

The Community has signed non-preferential agreements and cooperation agreements with Latin American (Argentina, Brazil, Paraguay and Uruguay, which in 1991 formed the Southern Common Market, (Mercosur)), Central American (Mexico, Colombia, Chile, Haiti, Guatemala, Costa Rica, El Salvador, Nicaragua, Panama), and Asian countries (Bangladesh, India, Pakistan, Sri Lanka and Vietnam). Selective trade and cooperation agreements have also been negotiated with Hong Kong, Korea, Thailand, Macao and China. Cooperation agreements have been concluded between the Community and Yemen AR, the Andean group of countries (Bolivia, Colombia, Ecuador, Peru and Venezuela) and the ASEAN group of countries (Brunei, Indonesia, Malaysia, the Philippines, Singapore and Thailand). The first agreement with the Arab countries of the Gulf Cooperation Council (GCC – Bahrain, Kuwait, Oman, Qatar, Saudi Arabia and the United Arab Emirates) was concluded in 1988.

8.6 Relations with developed countries

Introduction

The EU's trade relations with non-European industrialized countries, that is Australia, New Zealand, Japan, South Africa, Canada and the United States, are supposed to be conducted under the GATT and WTO rules. But relations have often been strained, mostly because of the effects of

Table 8.1 **Tariff barriers, 1999 (simple mean tariff, %)**

Area	All products	Primary products	Manufactures
EU	3.5	6.4	2.7
Japan	4.8	8.6	3.4
USA	4.3	4.8	4.2
Australia	5.7	1.7	6.2
Canada	4.4	12.2	8.4
N. Zealand	2.8	1.5	3.0

Source: Compiled from data presented in World Bank (2001b).

the CAP on world markets and the discriminatory trade policies of the EU with non-member countries. The early reforms of the CAP were rightly perceived by many countries as motivated by the EU's budgetary problems rather than by any desire to open its market to competition in agricultural products or to reduce its export subsidies. Thus trade disputes often occurred, but after a short war of words, they were usually resolved by recourse to the multilateral GATT and WTO dispute settlement procedure. In general, the EU has followed a liberal CCP and, as Table 8.1 shows, its common external tariffs (CETs) are among the lowest in the developed world.

Relations with Canada

The first bilateral accord between Canada and the EU was signed in 1976 with the Framework Agreement for Commercial and Economic Co-operation. Contacts became far more ambitious in 1990 with the adoption of the Transatlantic Declaration on EU–Canada Relations and then six years later with the EU–Canada Joint Action Plan. In 1998, this was extended by the signing of the mutual recognition agreement (MRA) which will encourage trade by allowing product testing and certification to be implemented in the exporting country instead of at destination. The MRA covers goods and services, government procurement, intellectual property rights, competition issues, cultural cooperation and business-to-business contacts. A Canada Europe Round Table for Business (CERT) was formally launched on 16 June 1999. The EU is the second most popular destination for Canadian direct investment after the USA (see Table 8.1).

Relations with Japan

Japan is one of the EU's major trading partners. Friction during the 1980s over trade imbalances and the difficulties European firms encountered in exporting to Japan have given way to a far more constructive relationship.

In the past, the Community claimed that Japan operated non-tariff barriers to imports from abroad, while Japan's industrial policies also provided its exporters with subsidies in the form of tax preferences and credit facilities. Therefore, disputing the pricing of Japanese exports, the Community occasionally resorted to the use of anti-dumping duties and administrative protection. Japanese exporting firms reacted by foreign direct investment in the protected markets of the EU (and the US) as a substitute for trade flows, mostly in the machine tool, electronics and automobile sectors. Foreign direct investment by Japanese firms was motivated by a desire both to overcome trade barriers affecting its exports and to share in the benefits of the 1992 programme.

Since 1985, Japan has reduced tariffs and other 'visible' trade barriers and has eased its 'invisible' barriers arising from standards, testing and certification procedures which restrict access to Japanese import markets. Since then, relations between the EU and Japan have been improving by direct dialogue at annual summit meetings which have recently focused on market access, structural reform and political cooperation. In 1991, the Community and Japan signed a Joint Declaration which sets the principles and objectives of integrated dialogue and cooperation covering macroeconomic questions, sectoral issues including services, structural obstacles, industrial cooperation, export promotion, public procurement and political cooperation. This was consolidated in 1995 by a strategy on Europe–Japan relations which was considerably extended by an action plan which the two parties agreed to develop at the Tokyo Summit in 2000. As a result of these actions, trade between Japan and the EU has been increasing. Japan is the largest economy of Asia, accounting for two-thirds of regional GDP, and the EU's third largest destination of exports and the second largest source of imports (see Figure 8.2). The EU–Japan foreign direct investment (FDI) links are also strong, with a very large imbalance in favour of Japan.

Relations with the USA

After several years of negotiations, the United States and Canada signed a free trade agreement, which became binding on 1 January 1989. A new agreement was signed in 1992 by the United States, Canada and Mexico establishing the North American Free Trade Area (NAFTA). The agreement incorporates several innovative provisions covering dispute settlement, foreign direct investment, services and some restrictions on the use of safeguard measures.

Trade relations between the Community and the United States have often become tense on several issues connected with imports and exports of both agricultural and industrial products. Volatility in the value of the US dollar and growing external deficits in the 1980s intensified

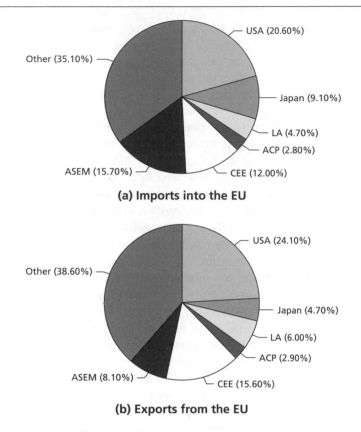

(a) Imports into the EU

(b) Exports from the EU

ASEM = Brunei, China, Indonesia,   LA = Latin America
South Korea, Malaysia, the Philippines,   ACP = African, Caribbean and Pacific countries
Singapore, Thailand, Vietnam   CEE = Central and eastern European countries

Figure 8.2 **Main external trade partners of the EU, goods trade 1999**
Source: Data from Commission (2001g).

protectionist pressures and led the United States to legislation extending the use of bilateral approaches to trade disputes (Omnibus Trade and Competitiveness Act, 1988) and increasing investigations for 'unfair' trade practices, anti-dumping and countervailing. The Act – also called Super 201 – authorized the Executive Branch to retaliate unilaterally against countries that maintain trade barriers that either violate US rights or are 'unreasonable'. Anti-dumping is also used on the excuse of 'level playing', i.e. that since the USA has enacted cost-increasing social and environmental prerequisites, it can impose a duty on imports from countries which have no such provisions. This raised the question whether the USA or other countries have the legal right to violate GATT and WTO procedures and to retaliate unilaterally – and arbitrarily – against alleged offenders.

Almost half of all US anti-dumping investigations are about trade with the EU and Japan. But in spite of the deep economic links between the triad USA–EU–Japan, the *unilateralism* of US external economic policy has been raising concerns. The USA and the EU are the two largest economies, accounting together for nearly half the goods and services produced in the world and for more than half of all foreign trade. Their relationships are particularly close on a range of issues stretching from economics and politics to foreign policy and security. With regard to trade, the USA and the EU are each other's major trading partners (for goods and services) and account for the largest bilateral trade relationship in the world: 7 per cent of total world trade. The USA accounts for 17 per cent of total EU imports and 18 per cent of total EU exports. In turn, the EU is one of the two top markets (the other being Japan) for the US, accounting for 20 per cent of US exports and 17 per cent of US imports. Furthermore, each is the other's most important source of, and destination for, foreign direct investment (FDI).

The EU and USA are the most important partners in supporting the global trading system. However, both sides make the point that trade disputes are inevitable between such competitive trading partners but that this should not detract from the high level of cooperation between the parties. Thus, despite their close cooperation, there are still several outstanding disputes between the USA and the EU which are mostly centred on a few traded commodities and related issues that account for less than 4 per cent of transatlantic trade. By mid-1995, the EU–US dialogue resulted in the New Transatlantic Agenda (NTA), an action plan for collaboration aiming at the creation of a 'new transatlantic marketplace' by breaking down the barriers to the flow of goods, services and investment between the two economic blocks. An early warning system and arrangements are now in place to try and defuse potential problems as quickly as possible. Some aspects of US–EU trade disputes are illustrated in the following three examples.

Agricultural trade

Both the US and the EU agricultural policies are mostly oriented towards domestic problems. In the past, one of the main differences between the two was in the method of protection, with EU agricultural policies (guaranteed farm prices) being relatively more transparent than US policies (top-up income payments to farmers). Both policies, however, caused overproduction which both the EU and the USA tried to unload by exporting to ('dumping' on) world markets. As a result, there were frequent disputes about what constitutes 'fair' trade and who was violating it. Until the mid-1970s the USA was the dominant producer and exporter of many key agricultural commodities such as grain, flour, and animal feed, so that the domestic US price level and the world price level were often identical. But, more recently, growing competition from other exporting countries, such as Argentina, Brazil, Australia, Canada and the EU, has squeezed the US's pre-eminence as world market leader. Consequently, the US share of world wheat exports fell from 50 per cent in 1976 to 30 per cent in 1986. These events, the EU's rise to the world's second largest food exporter and the United States' record trade deficits provided a prolific background for many disputes.

The United States objected to the EU's CAP on three issues:

1. protection of the European market which affected US exports to the Community;
2. CAP's subsidized exports which competed with US exports in the markets of third countries;
3. bilateral preferential trade agreements between the EU and other countries which discriminated against US exports.

On these issues the US brought several 'lawsuits' against the EU to the GATT adjudication procedure and retaliated by both countervailing duties on imports from the EU and the underbidding of exports by subsidizing US exporters. The excuse offered by the EU was that its subsidies were not different from the open and hidden subsidies which the US government granted to its farmers and exporters (Commission 1984). Furthermore, relative to the USA and despite the CAP, the EU is a small exporter and the biggest importer in world markets of agricultural products. These disputes were usually contained by mutual threats of action and counter-action which ultimately led to negotiated settlements rather than to escalation of economic sanctions and trade warfare.

Although the need for the liberalization of the trade in agricultural commodities had been accepted in principle, it was not clear how far it would go. The USA had called for income support to farmers, detached from price support, by switching to a compensation system that required no external protection, causing overproduction. It therefore urged the EU to reduce its farm support by 70 per cent and its export subsidies by 95 per cent over the next 10 years. The EU argued instead for action to reduce surpluses first, with subsidies possibly increasing initially to preserve current income levels. After the EU implemented the CAP reforms, the USA observed that their results fell short of the cuts required and objected to the fact that the Community offered no guarantees on improved access to the single market and no cuts of export subsidies, commenting that 'Europe exports its problems and the rest of the world pays for it'. After seven years of protracted negotiations, agreement was finally reached at the Uruguay Round for trade liberalization. For the first time, the agreement provides for the liberalization of the trade in agricultural products, guaranteed market access, gradual reduction

---

Box 8.3 ■ The US–EU banana war

The banana trade dispute of the past nine years between the USA and the EU is one of the biggest bones of contention between Washington and Brussels. It started in July 1993 after the EU adopted a new banana regime that favoured banana growers in Africa, the Caribbean and the Pacific states, many of which are former British and French colonies.

The World Trade Organization (WTO) ruled in 2000 that the EU's system unfairly favoured growers in EU territories and the Caribbean over Latin American producers, which are marketed by US multinationals. The EU decided to adopt the now disputed new banana import system in an attempt to end its long-running trade dispute with the USA. Under the new EU rules, import rights are granted as ships arrive at port, in what has been described as a 'first come, first served' system. The EU wants that system to be replaced in 2006, by a system of tariffs that EU agriculture ministers argue will comply with WTO rules. Washington dismissed this new system as unacceptable. The US government announced that it was prepared to impose sanctions worth $191m to defend American interests in the banana trade dispute. The USA already has $308m worth of sanctions in place, almost two-thirds of which are related to the banana trade. The WTO has estimated that US firms have lost $191m sales through 'unfair' competition and for first time in its history it has given its blessing to this set of sanctions.

The EU has said that if the USA decides to raise the stakes with more sanctions, the backlash will be painful. The EU would then implement billions of dollars' worth of sanctions on US imports in a dispute over US export tax breaks.

The US government and the EU Commission today announced an agreement to resolve their long-standing dispute over bananas. The two parties recognized that they had shared objectives: to reach agreement on a WTO-compliant system. The new regime will provide a transition to a tariff-only system by 2006. During the transition, bananas will be imported into the EU through import licences distributed on the basis of past trade. The agreement will end the past friction and move the USA and the EU toward a better basis for the banana trade.

Compiled by the author from news and press releases, April 2001, mainly available at www.news.bbc.co.uk and http://www.useu.be/issues

of production subsidies, and observance of export discipline (see Chapter 7). Despite the agreement, disputes between the EU and the USA about agricultural trade still flare up quite often.

Steel

Successive economic recessions since the 1970s had repercussions on the world demand for steel. Long-established steel producers also suffered extra blows from the onslaught of steel exports at competitive prices from newer entrants into the industry, such as Japan, Korea, Mexico,

India, Brazil and more recently China. The first steel dispute between the USA and the EU occurred in 1968. The EU, which is not a major competitor in the US market, had faced many problems in its steel industry and introduced reforms aiming at capacity reduction and modernization (see Chapter 14). In contrast, US steel production had remained 'a rust belt industry', highly protected from competition by the effective lobbying of the producers who 'spent 30 years with their lawyers manipulating the dumping and subsidy laws so that they can use them at any time, and in almost any slow market situation, and so they do' (AIIS, 1999). Under US law, firms sustaining the claim that their products face import competitions from subsidized foreign production have automatic recourse to anti-dumping action. The commonest form of this action is countervailing duties, which operate as import tariffs against low-priced imports, which are assessed by the US authorities as subsidized if they decide that their production costs are low relative to US costs.

The first filing of countervailing duty cases against EU steel-makers led to voluntary restraint agreements which ended in 1974. A similar procedure was followed in 1982, although imports from the EU at the time were no more than 6 per cent of total US consumption. The US official investigation estimated that in some EU member states steel producers received 20–40 per cent production subsidies and sanctioned apposite countervailing duties. The Community's reaction was to object to the US investigation which did not distinguish between operating subsidies and grants for modernization and, in response, to adopt unilaterally countervailing measures against certain US exports. The case was finally settled in 1992 by the introduction of a quota on EU steel exports to the US market.

Naturally, this was not the end of the story. In 1998, imports of (hot-rolled) steel in the USA increased by 70 per cent from the previous year and domestic capacity utilization dropped within a year from 90 to 75 per cent. Accumulation losses drove six big producers into bankruptcy, while thousands of US steel workers were laid off. This time round, the increase in steel imports and the drop in prices were attributed to three countries: Russia, Japan, and Brazil, all of which had experienced depreciation of their currencies and, therefore, lower dollar-denominated prices of their exports. The US Commerce Department responded by announcing penalty duties ranging up to 67 per cent on Japan, 86 per cent on Brazil, and 200 per cent on Russia. Diverse penalty duties violate WTO rules which provide for 'escape clause' relief by contingent protection applied identically to all foreign suppliers. The US policies also had effects on the EU, which argued that the problems of the US steel industry originated from its failure to modernize and that 'the 201 route is not the way to go'. The EU faced two effects: first, the direct decrease in its steel exports to the USA; and, second, the possibility that the reduction of US imports from the big producers could result in oversupply of low-priced surpluses in the world market which could disrupt the steel markets of every country. The EU argued that *'in such circumstances, "burden shifting" by the US onto the rest of the world would be extremely unfair and strongly resisted . . . Should safeguards ultimately be introduced, the EU would review whether they were WTO compatible and, if not, take appropriate action in Geneva.'* (EC, 2001). On 5 March 2002 the USA imposed tariffs on imports of steel of up to 30 per cent for domestic party political reasons: the forthcoming congressional elections. The EU, and other steel-exporting countries, decided to appeal to the WTO dispute settlement panel and, following WTO rules, drafted a list of US exports for potential retaliatory action.

US export subsidies, EU and WTO

This case started after the USA created the Domestic International Sales Corporation (DISC) scheme by the Deficit Reduction Act (1971) to stimulate exports and reduce the US trade deficit. But DISC was declared an illegal export subsidy by a GATT panel in 1976. Therefore, DISC was replaced by the Foreign Sales Corporation Replacement Act (FSC) scheme in 1984, which was described by the USA as 'an incentive for US exports . . . which encourages exports by reducing the tax rate on export income'. The FSC also involved across-the-board export subsidies and local content subsidies contrary to the WTO rules. The EU contested the legality of the FSC when it was adopted, but did not pursue it at the time due to the opening of the Uruguay Round trade negotiations. Following further complaints by EU companies, and in view of the increasing amount of FSC subsidies being granted by the USA, the EU resumed bilateral contacts with the USA in 1997, but no progress was made. The EU therefore took up the matter under the WTO Dispute Settlement Understanding. Consultations followed in December 1997, February 1998 and April 1998, but without resolution. The EU then requested a WTO panel to pronounce on the dispute, which reported on 8 October 1999. The FSC was found to constitute an illegal export subsidy under the Agreement on Subsidies and Countervailing Measures and (in relation to agricultural products) an export subsidy in violation of the Agriculture Agreement. The USA appealed to the WTO Appellate Body (AB), which on 24 February 2000 confirmed the panel's findings as to the illegality of the FSC scheme. The USA was given until 1 October 2000 to withdraw the FSC scheme as required by the Subsidies Agreement. Following fruitless discussions between the parties regarding the legality of the US proposals to replace the FSC scheme, on 29 September 2000 the EU decided to act reasonably and give the USA the benefit of the doubt, and concluded an agreement on procedures with the USA providing for a compliance panel to examine the WTO compatibility of the new US legislation, before countermeasures could be imposed. But the FSC Replacement Act was signed into law by the US President on 15 November 2000. As the USA failed to comply with the WTO recommendations, the EU was entitled under the bilateral agreement on procedures to have direct recourse to countermeasures. On 17 November 2000, the EU presented the request for countermeasures as required by the WTO, for an amount of $4 billion, accompanied by a broad list of products. The USA requested arbitration on the number of countermeasures requested by the EU. On that same date the EU also presented a request for consultations as the first step in the compliance panel procedure. The compliance panel was established on 20 December 2000 and the arbitration procedure on the amount of countermeasures was suspended the following day, with the agreement that it would automatically be reactivated upon adoption by the WTO of the AB's findings (28 January 2002). On 20 August 2001, the WTO compliance panel examining the FSC Replacement Act, issued its report in full support of the EU. The panel found that the FSC Replacement Act constitutes a prohibited export subsidy, although US companies established outside the USA obtain the tax reduction on all their sales and only those within the USA can obtain it by exporting. The FSC Replacement Act also violates the Agriculture Agreement, as it can be used to circumvent the commitments given by the USA not to grant, or to reduce, export subsidies on agriculture products. The USA has also been found to fail to comply with the WTO ruling and recommendations on the original FSC case, as the transitional rules under the FSC Replacement Act maintain the FSC scheme for at least two years beyond the deadline granted by the WTO to the USA to withdraw it (1 October 2000).

8.7 Conclusions

The Common Commercial Policy means that the Community has become a large economic unit with a unique, and potentially very strong, trading position *vis-à-vis* all other countries. Thus the Community has concluded several agreements with developed and developing countries over the years. A common characteristic of these agreements has been diverse discrimination which the EU applied to its trade in different commodities and different countries. These agreements conferred privileges selectively, resulting in the ranking of countries according to their place in the Community's 'pyramid of preferences'. Among the less-developed countries, the ACP associate states were placed higher than the Mediterranean countries, which were placed above the non-associate countries of Asia and South America. Among the developed countries, the EFTA members were placed above the non-European industrial countries and the central and east European (CEE) countries. The EU's discriminatory preference system was incompatible with world trade rules and caused critical comments and trade disputes with certain countries and, sometimes, with international trade organizations. The multilateral approach to trade liberalization is a principle every country and association of countries should respect and apply, and the EU has more recently clearly moved in this direction.

Many countries had feared that the single market would lead the EU to more trade protection. But concerns about creating a 'Fortress Europe' proved unfounded. The Community continues its adherence to free trade principles and its commitment to 'the progressive abolition of restrictions on international trade' (TEEC, 131), including agriculture and the services sector, under the auspices of the WTO. It has also stated that European integration should be regarded as a contributing factor to greater liberalization of international trade, beneficial to both the EU and third countries.

Questions

1. Why do countries use protection? Who gains and who loses from protection?

2. What are the main instruments of protection? What are VERs and why do exporting countries agree to their imposition?

3. What are the GATT and WTO organizations; what is their objective and who would gain if they reached it?

4. What are the ACPs and why does the EU grant them trade preferences? Who gains from these preferences and who loses from them?

5. Critics of liberal policies argue that since world markets are imperfect and the EU's trade rivals resort to unfair trade practices, the EU should do the same by introducing interventionist and strategic trade and industrial policies. Do you agree?

6. 'Protectionist measures such as anti-dumping duties and export restraints show that free trade within the EU may be accompanied by more protectionism against the rest of the world.' Comment.

Further reading

EC (1997a) gives an overall view of Community policies on trade. Issues in US–EU trade relations are examined in Hufbauer (1990). EU–Japan trade relations are discussed in Abe (1999). See also Eurostat (1998a).

Web guide

■ For the EU's trade policies and practices see <u>www.europa.eu.int/comm/</u> <u>trade</u> and for external relations see <u>www.europa.eu.int/comm/world</u>

■ For the steel trade see the American Institute for International Steel (AIIS), Inc., available at <u>www.aiis.org/html/release03 ad.htm</u>

■ For the dispute about US subsidies see the EU's DG Trade web site, available at <u>www.mkaccdb.eu.int/miti/dsu?FICHE=GO&CASE=WT/DS108</u>

Enlargement

9

Several Mediterranean and central and eastern European countries have applied for membership in the Community. The problem, however, is that the economic, political, institutional and administrative levels of development of most of the applicant states are far lower than the EU average. Therefore, the EU has bilaterally agreed with each of the applicants that their accession will be decided upon a set of criteria which they must reach by a mutually approved pre-accession strategy, and EU financial assistance. It is now expected that the first candidates for accession will meet the necessary conditions for EU membership by 2004.

9.1 Introduction

As we have seen (in Chapter 2), the treaty between the original Six members of the Community declared that 'Any European State which respects the principles set out in Article 6(1) [liberty, democracy, respect for human rights and fundamental freedoms, and the rule of law] may apply to become a member of the Union' (TEEU, 49). This is the procedure the EU has observed through successive enlargements and intends to follow with the forthcoming ones. Therefore, following applications for membership, the Commission (1997) proposed in 'Agenda 2000' that negotiations should start with Estonia (EE), Poland (PL), the Czech Republic (CZ), Slovenia (SI), Hungary (HU) and Cyprus (CY) for their accession to the EU by the year 2002. The Helsinki summit of 1999 ruled that Turkey (TR) and six other European countries could also begin full negotiations for accession in 2000: Bulgaria (BG), Latvia (LV), Lithuania (LT), Malta (MT), Romania (RO), and Slovakia (SK). Of the applicant countries, Cyprus, Malta and Turkey form one group of traditional market economies, while the rest belong to another group of *transitional* countries converting from *centrally planned* economic systems to free market economies before accession to the EU (see Chapter 8).

Turkey's application for membership in the EU is a somewhat distinct case. Turkey's formal relations with the Union started with an association agreement in 1963, and Turkey was the first of the current group of candidates to apply for membership in 1987. However, for a multiplicity of political, economic and human rights reasons the request for accession made little progress over the years. But, at the Helsinki summit (1999), the EU recognized Turkey as 'a candidate state destined to join the Union on the basis of the same criteria as applied to other candidate states', subject to fundamental improvements in its internal conditions and external relations.

The present membership of the EU is the result of four successive enlargements to countries which on the whole were not vastly different from the already existing Community members. Therefore, although delays in the process of integration were inevitable, the EU could afford the necessary time and finance to assist the economic adaptation and convergence of the new members to the standard EU-country model. This time, however, it is different because the candidate countries for accession to the EU are many, they are at levels of development far below those of the EU average, and the available EU funds for helping their convergence are limited. Enlargement has political, social, cultural and economic consequences. We will restrict our analysis to the field of economics only.

9.2 Conditions

In 1993, the member states decided at the Copenhagen European Council that 'the associated countries in central and eastern Europe that so desire shall become members of the Union' stating, however, that 'accession will take place as soon as an applicant is able to assume the obligation of membership by satisfying the economic and political conditions required'. The required conditions for membership were specified as:

- *political*: stability of institutions guaranteeing democracy, the rule of law, human rights and respect for and protection of minorities;
- *economic*: the existence of a functioning market economy and the capacity to cope with competitive pressure and market forces within the Union;
- acquis communautaire: (i) the ability to take on the obligations of membership including adherence to the aims of political, economic and monetary union; (ii) the creation of the appropriate administrative and judicial structures able to implement EU legislation effectively.

The applicants will need to show progress towards meeting the Maastricht criteria, although this is not strictly required for accession. But the applicants have to continue to reduce government involvement in the economy while dismantling monopolies, removing trade restraints, and developing flexible labour markets. In turn, the Community specified that its 'capacity to absorb new members, whilst maintaining the momentum of European integration, is also an important consideration in the general interest of the Union and the candidate countries'. Therefore, the Commission in 'Agenda 2000' (EC, 1997) presented an opinion of the effects of accession on the EU, taking into account the future financial framework beyond 2000, and the current and future performance of each candidate country.

After projecting and evaluating their expected progress, the Commission recommended that accession negotiations should start with a multilateral conference in 1998. It was decided then that all candidates would join the EU on the basis of the same conditions, which include:

- an enhanced pre-accession strategy
- the accession negotiations
- 'screening' of EU legislation
- a review procedure.

For its part, the EU will need to undertake a major review of its institutions and decision-making procedures. Therefore, the Community convened a special intergovernmental conference to address these questions and, with the signing of the Treaty of Nice (TN, 2001), it introduced the institutional series of reforms necessary for accession of the first candidates that fulfil the criteria. While the candidate countries strive to meet the criteria, the Commission monitors the situation and submits regular reports to the Council on the progress achieved by each country. To support the 13 applicants' enhanced pre-accession strategy, the Community uses five main channels of financial aid and technical cooperation:

- the PHARE programme which is concentrating its support on the adoption of the *acquis communautaire* by institution-building and investment support;
- the Instrument for Structural Policies for Pre-Accession (ISPA) which assists the alignment of the candidates' infrastructure in transport and environmental standards to those of the EU;
- the Special Accession Programme for Agricultural and Rural Development (SAPARD) which helps the candidates to deal with the structural adjustment in their agricultural sectors and rural areas;
- co-finance and special loans from the European Investment Bank (EIB) for assistance in the candidates' efforts to meet the conditions of entry;

■ loans, equity investments (shares) and guarantees provided by the European Bank for Reconstruction and Development (EBRD) which was established in 1991 to foster the transition towards open market-oriented economies and promote private and entrepreneurial initiative in all the countries of central and eastern Europe.

But these grants and loans are not on their own adequate for the convergence necessary for accession to the Community. It is left to the candidates themselves to attract more foreign private investment from the EU and third countries by putting in place the legal and institutional framework that would facilitate this.

9.3 The economies of the candidate countries

The candidates for accession differ widely in terms of size, population, level of economic development and economic problems, and thus make up a very heterogeneous group. They are also dissimilar in their relations with the EU and, therefore, the decision on the conditions and the timetable for accession will be decided bilaterally between each candidate and the Community. However, we will examine all the candidates together, comparing their economic structures with that of the EU-15 average.

With regard to GNP per head, the island states of Cyprus and Malta are the most advanced, in the case of Malta well above the EU average. Figure 9.1 shows, however, that the remaining 11 candidates are well below the EU average (= 100), within the range of 23 per cent for Bulgaria to 68 per cent for Slovenia with a group average of 38 per cent. This vast gap is the result of deep recessions, high inflation and high unemployment which these countries experienced after turning from centrally planned to market economies. The case of Turkey is different, but in recent years it has also suffered from high rates of inflation and unemployment and a low rate of growth.

Overall, the candidates will increase the total EU GNP by about 10 per cent, and the EU population by almost 30 per cent (170 million, making an EU total of 550 million), in the process reducing the average GNP per head of EU-15 to the expanded EU-28 by a considerable percentage. One of the reasons for this is that the candidates with the highest population are also those with relatively lower incomes (such as Turkey, Romania and Poland, see Figure 9.2). Another reason is that in many candidates (such as Turkey, Bulgaria and Romania) agriculture is still a major economic sector, contributing a large share to national income and employing a substantial share of the working population, but in general displaying low productivity and supplying low-quality output relative to EU standards.

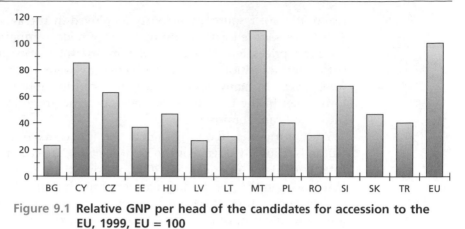

Figure 9.1 **Relative GNP per head of the candidates for accession to the EU, 1999, EU = 100**

Note: BG   Bulgaria   CY   Cyprus   CZ   Czech Republic
         EE   Estonia   HU   Hungary   LV   Latvia
         LT   Lithuania   MT   Malta   PL   Poland
         RO   Romania   SI   Slovenia SK   Slovakia
         TR   Turkey   EU   EU-15

Source: Data from Eurostat (2001d).

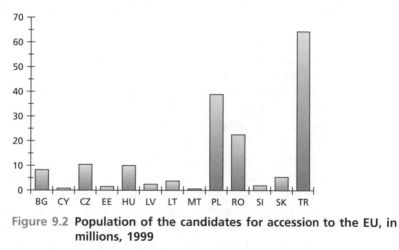

Figure 9.2 **Population of the candidates for accession to the EU, in millions, 1999**

Source: Data from Eurostat (2001d).

On average, the contribution of the applicants' agricultural sector to their national product and the percentage of their labour employment in agriculture are twice as large as those of EU-15 average.

In most of the CEE countries, agricultural income has declined significantly since the beginning of transition. One of the reasons for this has been the sharp adjustment to world market prices and the consequent reallocation of resources previously employed in the agricultural sector. This was associated with declining terms of trade as input prices rose and producer prices fell. The result has meant that farm incomes, which before the transition to a market economy were at or above national wage levels, in many countries are now considerably lower, and much lower than in the EU. These low levels of agricultural incomes translate into significant rural poverty.

As countries neighbouring the EU, the applicants' trade share with the Union is relatively large. For the EU, the candidate countries' share in its total trade was 14 per cent in 2000, making them (added together) the Union's second biggest trading partners after the United States. As for the candidate countries, the EU is now their leading trade partner, accounting for 65 per cent of their total internal and external trade in 1999. But while as a group they export mainly resource-based and labour-intensive commodities, they import advanced-technology products. As a result, they often experience balance-of-trade problems which cannot be alleviated without restructuring and accelerated economic growth.

9.4 The process of the candidates' integration in the EU

The net contributors to the EU budget believe that enlargement can go ahead without any significant increase in the budget. They argue that the underdeveloped market structure of the CEE candidates would not be able to absorb moderate funds productively (no more than 4 per cent of their own GDP) or to match structural funding by an equal domestic expenditure contribution, in accordance with current EU rules. Therefore, they maintain that with regard to enlargement there is no reason to over-expand the current budgetary expenditure. Under these assumptions, the EU has already decided the size of its pre-accession aid programme for the applicant countries in the Financial Perspective 2000–6 (see Chapter 4). In general, the sums allocated are modest. In the past, the lower-GDP-level countries that joined the EU (such as Greece, Spain and Portugal) benefited from the high budgetary expenditure of the CAP and the Structural Funds, and the Cohesion Fund specially designed for them. But the EU's budgetary reforms, which have contained these expenditures, and the planned further reforms in the CAP and structural policies, mean that the candidates for accession cannot expect that the Community's public sector can be relied upon to alleviate their exposure to the competitive conditions of the EU market. It will be left to the candidates themselves and to their success in reforming their institutions and economic structures to attract private-sector initiatives and funds to help them accelerate their passage to EU integration.

Some commentators argue that the accession of so many disparate countries is bound to dilute the cohesion of the EU and to decelerate its progress towards economic (and political) integration. They suggest, therefore, that to compensate for these setbacks the EU should go deeper into economic integration by transferring more powers from the member states to the EU authority. If this were to be the case, the burden of adaptation the candidates would have to overcome for full membership in the Community would escalate.

In general, integration boosts development by expanding the set of opportunities facing consumers and firms. Enlargement will expand these opportunities for the candidates by open access to the large and developed market of the EU in goods, services, capital, expertise and enterprise. It is left to the candidates' consumers and firms to take up the challenge and to arrange their affairs more efficiently, so that they will increase their output and income. The EU firms undertaking direct investment and production in the candidate countries will, of course, do so only if they expect benefits. For the EU member states the benefit will depend on the extent to which their firms have successfully joined in the modernization and development of the candidates and, therefore, the gain may be unevenly distributed across the Community. For the EU as a whole, the political gain will be of paramount importance.

An issue of contention is whether the accession countries will have full rights to labour migration. Most of these countries, and especially those with large populations, have a GDP per capita less than 50 per cent of the EU average, wage levels 10–15 per cent of the EU average, and high rates of unemployment. Figure 9.3 shows that the unemployment rate in the candidates ranged from 17 per cent in Bulgaria to 7 per cent in Hungary, with Malta and Cyprus well below the EU average. It is, therefore,

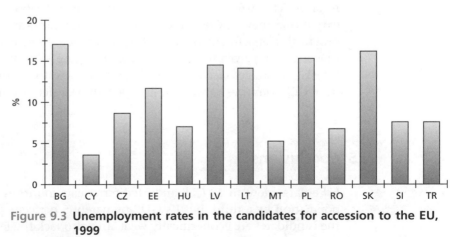

Figure 9.3 Unemployment rates in the candidates for accession to the EU, 1999

Source: Data from Eurostat (2001d).

> **Box 9.1 ■ Eastern enlargement**
>
> After a decade of prevarication, the Union will open its doors to its neighbours to the east. The empty promises and hollow rhetoric of the 1990s will become reality. Within four or five years the EU's membership will be 20 or more; within a decade it will be approaching 30. There are still hurdles to be vaulted before Poland, Hungary, the Czech Republic, Latvia and Lithuania, Malta and Cyprus take their places at the table. There could yet be further delays. But the existing members have run out of excuses to keep the doors locked. The accession negotiations with the applicant countries have become a process rather than a matter of political decision . . . By and large, the consequences have been ignored. Only now does it seems to be dawning on the political elites that the new geography of Europe will also change geometry . . . Enlargement also promises a new definition of rich and poor within the Union. At present the line is drawn between north and south. When the number rises to 20 and more, the divide will be between the prosperous west and the developing east. For now, the Union breaks down easily into those who contribute to, and those who benefit from, the Brussels budget. Before too long the present 15 will find they are all net contributors. As these familiar points of reference are swept away, we can expect a different set of dynamics in the Council of Ministers. *Financial Times*, 8 Dec 2000
>
> The German chancellor yesterday warned workers from central and eastern European countries applying to join the European Union that they would have to wait up to seven years before gaining access to jobs in existing member states . . . The chancellor's remarks prompted immediate criticism from accession candidates states, which all seek unrestricted entry to labour markets. *Financial Times*, 19 Dec 2000

possible that labour from some candidate countries will wish to emigrate to EU-15 countries in search of employment or better jobs and higher rewards. This would put excess pressures on EU labour markets to the extent that they may demand the introduction of transition periods with progressive enactment of the principle of free movement of labour. In the longer run, given the demographic and aging population problems and the skill shortages faced by the EU-15 countries, the migration of labour from CEE countries to western Europe will be welcomed and encouraged.

9.5 Conclusions

EU enlargement to 13 CEE and Mediterranean countries will increase its population by a third, but its GDP by barely 5 per cent. The majority of the candidates are economically weak and also lack the legal systems and the institutions which would have helped them to adapt to EU conditions quickly and gain from the operations of the large single market. The sector which could benefit immediately on joining the EU is that of agriculture which in the candidates' countries is a relatively large producer and employer. But, in anticipation of their accession, the EU is reforming the CAP which otherwise would have to incur vast expenditures before and after the accession. Moreover, under the latest proposals put forward by the European Commission in January 2002, farmers in the 10 countries which plan to join the union in the first instance will initially get only one quarter of the subsidies paid to their counterparts in existing member states. They will have to wait a decade before the funding becomes equal. The EU has also approved the institutional reforms which are necessary for the almost 100 per cent increase in the country membership of the Community, and it will put them into effect when the first wave of new entrants joins the Union. Given the accession criteria set by the Community and the level of development they started from, some candidates are expected to join the EU in 2004 while the majority of aspiring member states may require a long transition period before being able to assume the full rights and obligations of membership in the European Union.

Questions

1. Why do the CEE and Mediterranean countries want to join the EU?
2. What would be their costs and benefits?
3. Why does the EU support their candidacy?
4. What would be the costs and benefits for the EU?

Further reading

Baldwin et al. (1997) analyse the enlargement from the candidates' and the EU's points of view. For more information on the CEE countries consult Lavigne (1999). Annual transition reports and statistical data are published by the EBRD, e.g. EBRD (see Web guide), and also World Bank (2000) and Eurostat (2001b).

Web guide

■ European Commission available at europa.eu.int/comm/enlargement/index.htm and www.europa.eu.int/comm/enlargement/atoz.htm
■ For statistics see EBRD, available at www.ebrd.com/

Regional policy

10

Nearly 22 per cent of the EU's population live in regions with output per head 25 per cent or more below the EU average. Although the single market and EMU have helped convergence to occur, the pace at which it happens varies and different types of regions face different kinds of problems and have performed very differently. Therefore, interregional disparities persevere within countries and across the EU. For this reason, the Community in coordination with the member states has implemented regional programmes to ensure that all undeveloped regions accelerate their progress by taking full advantage of the solidarity of the Union, the benefits of the single market, and economic and monetary unification.

10.1 The nature of regional problems

Introduction

Regional problems consist of the disparities in levels of income, in rates of growth of output and employment, and in levels of economic inequality in general between the geographic regions of a country. They arise from unequal growth rates of economic activity. Higher income areas are invariably those where the centres of population, government and industry are found.

According to the neoclassical theory of regional development, free competition and factor mobility will tend to equalize factor returns across a country by moving production and employment to the regions of highest returns. Therefore, in the long run regional disparities are self-correcting. However, in practice not only is the natural process of adjustment slow and uncertain but also the conditions of the neoclassical 'convergence' theory are not always fulfilled. For instance, capital and labour might not be perfectly mobile and persistent disparities among regions may exist in production technology, economies and diseconomies of scale, and obstacles to the market mechanism. Therefore, regional disparities can be self-perpetuating and, in the absence of intervention in support of the market forces, self-reinforcing. It is also possible that the process of development may tend to favour certain regions within a country by a cumulative gravitation mechanism. Thus, new industry and trade will be attracted to where industry and trade already exist, and the necessary infrastructure, associated services and the market for selling output are more readily available than in other areas.

Polarization

This gravitation process causes intra-country polarization by which areas that are relatively developed continue to grow fast, while the relatively backward areas experience cumulative economic decline. Regional growth thus tends to cluster in 'poles of development', that is in geographic areas that provide new investment with the opportunity to exploit economies of scale, thus making it possible for them to gain a head start and to continue growing at the expense of other regions. These scale economies, which are both external and internal, are usually specified as economies of *localization* and economies of *urbanization* or *agglomeration*. Economies of localization arise from the geographic concentration of plants in the same industry and the advantages gained by linkages between them, which increases the potential for improved efficiency through specialization. Urbanization economies arise from the geographic concentration of a large number of economic activities served jointly by different facilities, such as transport, availability of a skilled labour force, financial institutions and proximity of markets for their output. Polarization causes a vicious spiral of economic growth which may assist the relatively more-developed regions in a country to grow at the expense of the less-developed regions. So the regional problems are both causes and effects of the problems of unbalanced growth within the borders of a country.

Regional inequalities have economic and social implications and costs. Interdependency between the regions of a country by their extensive trade and factor movement links means that the economic problems of some regions permeate other regions and affect the overall economic activity of the country. Regional unemployment, economic imbalances and inequity, and excessive concentration of residential, industrial and commercial activity in major conurbations cause severe costs to society. Therefore, policies are introduced to prevent their occurrence or to alleviate their effects.

Regional policy

Regional policy is the intervention by the state in designated regions in an attempt to reduce the socioeconomic disparities between different parts of the country and restore prosperity. If these disparities arise largely because of obstacles to the effective functioning of markets, as claimed by the neoclassical view, then the regional policy is restricted to the application of measures aimed at the removal of the impediments to the free play of markets. It has to be recognized, however, that because of economic and social conditions market failures arise which may imply, for example, that the required factor mobility should be greater than is realistically attainable. In this case, regional policy is based on the premises that market forces cannot be relied upon to produce the necessary degree of interregional balance within a reasonable time interval. The economic arguments in support of regional policies are always supplemented by political and social considerations. The political argument asserts the importance of equity as an essential element in the cohesion between the regions of a country. The social argument stresses that, if the national economy grows, all citizens, wherever they happen to live and work within the country, should be provided with a reasonable share of the country's increasing prosperity.

10.2 Regional problems within economic unions

Integration and the regions

The neofunctionalist approach to integration predicts that in economic unions regional convergence will occur by a process of 'peripheral ascendancy' of the less-developed regions which will make them to catch up with the developed regions. Liberalization of trade and factor movements should in principle bolster the process of confluence across regions. However, it is also likely that, once economic integration is in progress, trade liberalization in the presence of increasing returns and agglomeration economies may not accelerate convergence but intensify instead the existing problems of regional disparities. There are three reasons for this:

1. Labour productivity and wage differentials between independent states are often taken care of by adjustments in foreign exchange rates which restore export competitiveness. In effect, foreign exchange policies provide the depressed areas with a measure of protection by reducing domestic prices, and so real wages, relative to foreign prices. Economic integration, free trade, enhanced competition and freer mobility of factors of production will tend to equalize commodity and factor

prices (wages, rent of capital, etc.) between the participating states. However, productivity differentials will continue and will favour the technologically advanced firms of the developed areas within the economic union. With integration advancing and encompassing monetary unification, the low-productivity regions will no longer be protected by national exchange-rate adjustments. At the same time, regional money wage differences will lessen and therefore the low-productivity regions will face progressive comparative disadvantage.

2. Economic integration may encourage concentration of new industry and relocation of existing industry in certain industrialized areas of the economic union which offer superior infrastructure, availability of skilled labour, proximity to large markets, and lower transport costs. With enlargement of the market and enhanced competition, the most efficient enterprises will expand by the integration process, while the less efficient will contract or even be driven out of the market. Commonly, enterprises at the periphery are on the whole less efficient, with lower productivity than those at the developed centre of the union. If in the integrated market transport costs are not high, then the centripetal forces resulting from agglomeration economies of scale and externalities will exacerbate the dominance of the core, favouring concentration of economic activity in existing growth poles. Therefore, economic activity at the periphery of the union will be affected negatively by the process of integration.

3. Economic integration reduces transport and transaction costs and increases trade and factor mobility. This in turn creates new opportunities for economies of scale and specialization which generate competitive advantage but also lead to agglomeration. The key aspect of regional specialization is external economies (such as access to specialized labour, technological spillovers, and supporting institutional, financial and administrative structures). This process deepens the interregional disparity in growth and accumulation.

Besides these problems, there is always the possibility that common policies undertaken for the realization of integration objectives, and later for the economic management of the integrated area, may have profound (and often unforeseen) regional effects. Since the regions within and between countries are not homogeneous, the regional impact of a common policy may be positive for some and negative for others. Therefore, the aggregate effect of any particular common policy may be beneficial for the economic union and detrimental for one or more of its regions.

As a consequence of these reasons, the rates of growth in the developed centres will be higher than those in the less developed regions of the economic union. Different rates of growth will in turn induce geographic relocation of industry and migration of capital – and later labour – from the underdeveloped periphery to the developing centres. Although the mobility of factors and industry may in practice remain imperfect, integration may result in some unwarranted developments. Peripheral regions, which before integration relied for their growth on small-scale production units, may become unable to reach the scale advantages of integration or to face competition from large industry. Thus, with progressing economic integration, the economic and social life of the less-developed regions will lag behind the growth levels of the developed regions.[1]

Competence

The question then is: if economic integration aggravates regional problems, whose task should it be to take proper policy measures to redress the decline of the regions?

During the process of integration regional economic problems undergo changes in both dimension and severity. Economic integration may exacerbate regional inequalities, produce tendencies for polarization at the scale of the economic union, and create new problems by the different regional impacts of common policies. The process of economic integration internationalizes the problem of regional divergence by adding to the already existing trends of national regional inequality the more powerful gravitation of the developed centres of the economic union which can be well outside the borders of the country. So areas that were considered relatively prosperous before integration may end up as backward regions of the economic union. Obviously, this aspect of integration is not promoting economic and political cohesion within the economic union. Therefore, under economic integration the purely national regional economic problem of the member states is transformed into a problem of the economic union. Regional inequality thus becomes the subject of a common regional policy.

This is necessary, among other reasons, because many of the policies which a member country will be advised to adopt for its regional problem may already be incompatible with the integration agreement or ineffective under the increasing interdependence between the members of the economic union. For example, subsidies, preferential taxation, development aid, and other similar instruments of national regional

---

[1] This is not a remote theoretical possibility. Historical cases of the decline of regions after (economic and political) integration abound, like, for example, the economic decline of southern Italy after the unification of the Italian states in the 1860s.

policies operate in principle against market unification and are incompatible with competition, the free market and the convergence of intra-union economic policy. Regional economic policies, which might have been effective within a country, may become ineffective when the country joins a union. A possible way out from this conundrum would be to respond collectively to regional problems by integrating national regional policies. The effectiveness of national policies can then be restored and complemented by common regional policies aimed at a common objective. Therefore, as a first step in this direction, a union should institute a common regional policy to supplement the regional economic policies of the member states.

Conclusions

Coordination and ultimately integration of regional economic policy at the level of the economic union is required to ensure that:

1. the dynamic process of integration does not aggravate the national regional economic problems of the member states;
2. the national regional economic policies are impartial between the members and compatible with the integration agreement;
3. the costs and benefits of integration are properly shared across the countries and regions of the union.

10.3 Regional problems in the European Union

Regional disparities exist in every country of the EU, although the regional problem differs between countries in nature and intensity. In general, four main types of regional problems are found in the Community: rural underdevelopment, industrial decline, congested cities and frontier regions.

Underdeveloped rural areas

These areas depend mainly on agriculture for both employment and production. But farming in these areas is usually based on smallholdings of relatively infertile land, with low capitalization and application of technology, low productivity, low participation rates and a high incidence of disguised unemployment. Therefore these areas are in general decline, failing to achieve economic diversification and lagging behind the more prosperous regions in both income and employment. These features are common in many mountain, hill and island areas (and the

Arctic areas of Finland and Sweden) which show evidence of progressive rural decline, depopulation and land dereliction. Similar rural areas close to large towns and cities suffer instead from the effects of modern development associated with the expansion of urban centres, degeneration of the countryside and deteriorating ecological balance.

Farming areas in developed countries also suffer from regional problems. But in contrast with the case of overdependence on uneconomic agriculture, the problems of these agricultural areas have come about from applying modern technology, which has led to a fast increase in productivity, causing a rapid decline in the employment of labour. Over the postwar years declining labour employment in agriculture has been a pronounced feature of every European country. This has forced rural labour to seek employment in other occupations and other locations. Large-scale migration has occurred from rural areas to developing industrial and urban centres, both domestic and foreign. However, the decline in agricultural employment has not spread evenly among the regions of every country. It has also encouraged the migration of the relatively employable younger section of the population, with the result that those who are left behind are the older and the less productive. Moreover, in the less-developed European countries, employment in urban sectors and industrial regions has not expanded enough to offset the decline in agricultural employment, nor has the released agricultural labour always had the necessary skills to be readily employable in other occupations. Thus, despite the outflow from the problem regions, surplus labour and chronic unemployment still exist. To some extent this might be an indication of imperfect factor mobility. It is important, however, to restate that perfect mobility of labour may have undesirable effects, such as depopulation of peripheral rural areas and an excessive concentration in the urban areas.

The basic problem of regional development is not how to move resources out of the rural economy, but how to preserve rural society and economy by promoting balanced rural development, which would often encompass activities other than those related directly to agriculture. Only this will ensure improvement in the economic and social conditions of the rural population together with protection of the rural environment. Rural development is an EU objective pursued under the CAP policy.

Decline of existing basic industries

Basic industries located in certain areas within a country have declined, while wage levels remain relatively rigid. Thus problem areas have emerged which are still predominantly industrial but face increasing unemployment and deindustrialization (southern and eastern Belgium, the Ruhr,

Saar and parts of eastern Germany, northern and eastern France, and in the United Kingdom, west-central Scotland, South Wales, north and north-west England and Northern Ireland).

For historical and economic reasons certain industries (notably, textiles, steel, coal and shipbuilding) have converged on the same area over long periods of time. But, in recent years, shifts in technology, decreasing demand for output and increasing international competition have led to a declining demand for labour, and the emergence of severe regional unemployment. These problems have been aggravated by general economic depression. In a way, the problems of these industrial regions are structural. The existing industry is under threat because of rising costs associated with near-exhaustion of stocks (such as coal), the emergence of more competitive alternative sources of domestic supply and increasing competition from imports originating in newly industrializing countries (NICs) with low labour costs. Moreover, while in these declining regions the existing infrastructure is adequate for the development of alternative activity, the new industry tends to be located nearer to demand centres and away from traditional industrial poles. Therefore, industrial change and renovation which would have kept these areas prosperous have not happened and the prospects that it will materialize by market forces alone are remote. Instead, the uncontrolled expansion of the past and the current industrial decline have combined to produce only environmental degradation and desolation. Advances in labour-saving technology and the overall problem of economic recession mean that the industrial decline of these regions cannot be compensated for by the growth of new industry, which is unable to absorb the available labour surplus.

Congested areas

Regional imbalance means that within the same country regions of excess supply of labour may coexist with regions experiencing excess demand for labour. The latter, which are called 'pressured' or 'congested' regions, display the reverse characteristics of those found in depressed rural regions and areas of industrial decline. In contrast to the under-developed regions, the congested areas offer a high degree of agglomeration economies which are causing excess concentration of capital, labour and industrial production to the detriment of the declining areas. The excessive concentration of economic activity is detrimental because the rising social costs associated with overpopulation, congestion, pollution, noise and other urban problems surpass the social benefit of increased economic activity. The benefits from high growth rates of income and employment in industrialized congested conurbations often coexist with inner-city decay and pockets of poverty, generalized decline in the environment and deteriorating quality of life. These problems are a manifestation of market failure arising from interdependence, negative externalities and the divergence between private (firms) and social (public) optimum, all of which lead to misallocation of resources and welfare waste. A degree of optimality can be restored only by intervention in the form of regional policy.

Major conurbations in both the developed and the less-developed members of the Community attract large proportions of the population and economic activity. The Paris region, which is just 2 per cent of French territory, contains 20 per cent of the population and 23 per cent of the total employment, and produces 30 per cent of national output. The Randstad region in the Netherlands which has four major centres (Amsterdam, Utrecht, Rotterdam, The Hague) contains 46 per cent of the national population. London and south-east England comprises only 12 per cent of the national territory but contains 30 per cent of the population. Similar congested regions are the Rhine–Ruhr area of Germany, greater Copenhagen, Glasgow and Liverpool, and in the Mediterranean countries, greater Athens, Naples, Barcelona and many more.

The regional problem of the congested areas consists of: (a) how to divert activity away from them in order to reduce congestion and stimulate growth through renewal of the existing industry; and (b) how to stimulate enough growth in other regions to attract economic activity from the congested regions.

Frontier areas

After trade liberalization and factor mobility in the single market, regions across the internal frontiers of the Community faced a reorientation of their economic activity arising from changes in their comparative advantage. They are expected to develop closer economic links and more trade and factor movement with regions of neighbouring member states, and in the process some of them may benefit while others may lose. On the whole, regions across internal frontiers were impeded by inadequate cross-border infrastructure associated with the historical separation of national states. In this case, regional policy is required to promote the necessary infrastructure and to encourage the border regions to exploit the opportunities offered by integration. In contrast to the internal border regions, a different problem arises from the external border regions of member states, and therefore of the Community. These are the geographically peripheral regions for which economic integration may induce reorientation of trade from their natural outlets in neighbouring states to other regions within the common market. In this case, regional policy attempts to protect and cushion the impact of integration on the economies of these border regions.

A different form of regional problems is created by the regional impact of market liberalization and common policies, if they aggravate the existing regional imbalances. In this case, unless specific measures are undertaken for the gradual adjustment of the regional economy, integration may result in serious economic and social divisions. Similarly, liberalization of the transport sector, combined with abolition of national subsidies to rural transport would tend to favour the most central and metropolitan regions. Then, compensatory policies should be instituted to neutralize the negative regional impact of actions which are considered necessary for the integration of markets but have side effects on some regions. This type of regional problem may give rise to an EU centre-to-periphery and north-to-south pattern of economic divergence. The four least-developed members of the Community and many of the least-developed regions of other member states are situated at the outermost ring of peripheral areas (Ireland, Portugal, Greece and parts of Spain, Italy, Sweden and Finland).

10.4 Regional economic policy of the Community

Introduction

The Treaty of Rome (TEEC) did not deal specifically with regional economic problems, though in the Preamble the signatory nations expressed their endeavour 'to strengthen the unity of their economies and to ensure their harmonious development by reducing the differences existing between the various regions and by mitigating the backwardness of the less favoured'. In practice, the Community from early on recognized that the problem of regional disparities between the richest and the poorest areas (e.g. in Italy) threatened to disrupt the convergence of economic performance inside the EU and to delay the progress towards integration. The regional problem worsened over the years by the accession of countries with severe regional problems (such as the UK) and a general level of development well below the EU average (IRL, GR, E, P). The problem has not disappeared.[2] It will be repeated and most probably deepened by the expected accession of new member states from central

---

[2] Of the 46 regions with a GDP 75 per cent or more below the EU average, ten are in Greece, six are in Portugal, eight are new Länder in Germany, seven are in Spain, five are in Italy, four are overseas departments of France, three are in the United Kingdom, and there is one each in Belgium, Austria and Finland (Eurostat, 2000).

and eastern Europe (CEE), which, with the exception of a few large urban centres (Budapest, Warsaw, Prague, Bratislava), are beset by regional imbalances displayed by high unemployment, low productivity, and serious environmental degradation.

At the beginning, it was assumed that the regional problem was a matter of national policy which should deal with it by national schemes of regional assistance. But the issues were proved to be too big and to cause such externalities that Community involvement became inevitable, particularly after the decision to proceed to a single market and economic and monetary union. The importance of the regional problem was thus recognized (TEEC, Title XVII, *Economic and Social Cohesion*, 158–62). Social cohesion was seen as not only an important goal in its own right, but also a key factor contributing to economic success. Regions which are unable to mobilize the economic potential of large sections of their population are handicapped in the increasingly competitive global marketplace, while disparities can breed social unrest, damaging economic performance. For these reasons, the Community introduced common policies and established special institutions for the application of regional policies. Thus, in 1975, the Community created the *European Regional Development Fund (ERDF)*, which co-finances programmes covering a number of years to assist regional development, and the *Committee of the Regions (CR)* to advise the Commission on research programmes and general inter-country regional economic coordination.

Organization

The broad aims of Community regional policy are two: 'Solidarity which will ensure that all regions and their citizens can take full advantage of the single market and economic and monetary union'; and 'assistance to the weak regions to help them alleviate the restructuring pressures associated with enhanced competition in the single market'. This resulted in the 1988 reforms of the Structural Funds (EAGGF, ESF and ERDF). Two crucial developments compelled these reforms: the accession of Spain and Portugal, which led to 'doubling of the population of the least favoured regions', and the push for completion of the single market by 1992. The reforms were based on improved coordination of the previously separate structural funds with a doubling of expenditure allocation by 1993. It was also agreed that, for increasing the effectiveness of the programmes, the intervention operations of all the structural funds should be based on five principles:

1. *concentration* of the employed resources geographically and in relation to people for the benefit of those regions and groups which are genuinely in need;

2. *programme planning* drawn up by the member states and approved by the Commission;
3. *'additionality'* of the finance provided by the funds to the corresponding national measures;
4. *partnership* in carrying out the programme by the member state and the Commission;
5. *effectiveness* by monitoring and evaluation to ensure that the objectives are observed.

Additional elements in the application of the policies are (i) *consistency and complementarity* with other policies, such as competition, environmental protection, equality of men and women, and other provisions of the treaties; and (ii) concentration of expenditure on the areas of greatest need. To comply with the latter, the regions were classified under five categories (called objectives), with the bulk of spending focused on the most disadvantaged regions of objective 1.

The accession of Austria, Finland and Sweden called for modifications of the ERFD in 1993 which set the *Cohesion Fund* alongside the Structural Funds, established exclusively to provide additional structural assistance to member states with a GDP less than 90 per cent of the EU average. As a result of these changes, the Community stated in its Cohesion Report that in the period 1985–95 disparities in GDP per head between the member states 'narrowed significantly', although interregional disparities within some countries had increased.

A further reorganization of the ERDF was implemented by the Financial Perspective 2000–6 which specified that it would support programmes in the following areas:

- the development of the most disadvantaged regions (*objective 1*);
- the economic and social conversion of areas facing structural difficulties, such as industrial degeneration, rural deprivation and urban privation (*objective 2*);
- the adaptation and modernization of policies and systems of education, training and employment and in general human resource development (*objective 3*);
- community initiative programmes which are prepared by the member states;
- innovative measures, which are the only ones managed directly by the Commission and deal with pilot projects or innovative strategies for cooperation and exchange of experiences concerning local and regional development.

Resources under the Structural Funds are allocated on the basis of programming periods. Financial assistance is in the form of non-refundable grants. During the current programming period 2000–6, the allocation is as follows: objectives programmes 94 per cent, community initiatives

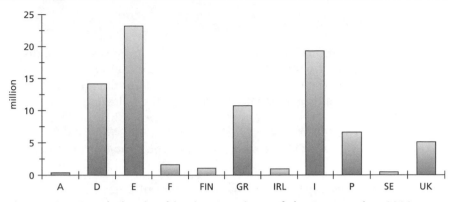

Figure 10.1 **Population in objective 1 regions of the Community, 2000**

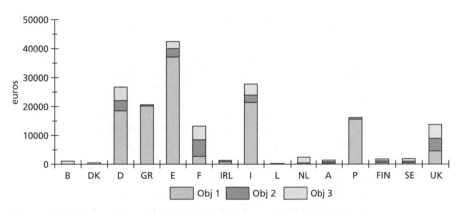

Figure 10.2 **Allocation of Structural Fund expenditure 2000–6**

Note: The Structural Funds included are: EAGGF, ERDF and ESF; the small Fisheries Instrument (outside objective 1) is not included.

Source: Data available at www.europa.eu.int/comm/regional_policy.

5.35 per cent, and innovative measures 0.65 per cent. The objective 1 regions which account for 22 per cent of the population of the Union – see Figure 10.1 – get the most because they contain Europe's poorest regions. The ERDF pays 75 per cent of the costs of economic development projects in these areas – see Figure 10.2 – with the rest contributed by the recipient state.

Community initiatives include the programmes:

■ *Interreg III*: cross-border, transnational and interregional cooperation;
■ *Urban*: social and economic regeneration of urban areas in crisis;
■ *Leader+*: rural development by local action groups;
■ *Equal*: transnational cooperation to combat discrimination and inequality in access to work.

Box 10.1 ■ Classification of the regions

For statistical purposes, Eurostat classifies the regions of EU-15 according to the *Nomenclature of Territorial Units* (NUTS) which distinguishes the regions into: 78 regions at level I, 211 regions at level II, and 1093 regions at level III. For the purposes of ERDF allocation the regions of the Community are classified under the following headings.

Objective 1: Regions whose development is lagging behind the EU average

These regions account for 22 per cent of the population of the Union – see Figure 10.1 – and consist of:

- those with per capita GDP below 75 per cent of EU average;
- Finnish and Swedish regions with extremely low population density;
- the most remote regions (French overseas departments, the Canary Islands, the Azores and Madeira).

Eligibility for objective 1 is principally defined with reference to NUTS level 2.

Objective 2: Areas facing structural difficulties

These areas account for 18 per cent of the European population and meet the following criteria:

- industrial areas with (i) an unemployment rate above the EU average, (ii) a higher percentage of jobs in the industrial sector than the EU average, and (iii) a decline in industrial employment;
- rural areas with low population density and higher employment in agriculture than the EU average;
- urban areas characterized by (i) long-term unemployment, (ii) a high level of poverty, (iii) a particularly damaged environment, (iv) a high crime rate, and (v) a low level of education;
- areas dependent on fisheries;
- other areas which (i) are rural with an ageing or declining population, (ii) are facing serious structural problems of high unemployment due to restructuring.

Objective 2 areas are generally defined with reference to NUTS level 3.

Objective 3: Development of human resources

These areas come under the new European strategy for employment (agreed at the Treaty of Amsterdam) and involve measures to:

- promote active labour market policies to combat unemployment;
- improve access to the labour market;
- enhance employment opportunities;
- promote measures which ensure social and economic changes;
- promote equal opportunities for men and women.

Other

This is covered under the Community initiatives for assistance to resolve specific social and economic problems affecting the whole of the Union and includes:

- interregional cooperation (*interreg III*), which is concerned with transnational and interregional cooperation intended to encourage balanced and sustainable development of the whole EU area;
- the sustainable development of urban areas (*urban*), which aims at the economic and social regeneration of cities in crisis and the urban environment;
- Leader which aims at rural development;
- Equal, financed by the European Social Fund (ESF), which is focusing on transnational cooperation for combating discrimination and inequalities in the labour markets;
- the development of innovative strategies to support regional competitiveness (*innovative actions*).

The Community has also decided that in the period 2000–6 the indicative allocation of the total resources of the Cohesion Fund among the beneficiary member states would be: Spain: 61–63.5 per cent of the total; Greece: 16–18 per cent; Portugal: 16–18 per cent; and Ireland: 2–6 per cent.

The forthcoming enlargement will bring into the EU countries from CEE with average GDP per head around one-third of the EU-15 average (see Chapter 9). As we have seen (in Chapter 4), the Commission took into account the possibility of accession from 2002 and added to the budget an additional item of expenditure, *available for accession*. However, the impact of enlargement on the structural funds is not yet certain. It will depend on which countries join the Community first and on their ability to absorb EU financial aid, which is subject to *co-financing*, without disturbing their economies.

10.5 EMU and regional divergence

As we have mentioned, conventional neoclassical theory predicts that regional disparities within a country should disappear in the long run by trade and factor mobility. Therefore, in an extension of this argument to inter-country regional disparities, economic integration, which increases trade and factor mobility, should lead to improved allocative efficiency and hence to a narrower gap between poor and rich regions. In contrast to the regional convergence theory, the 'new economic geography' theory argues just the opposite – that economic integration exacerbates regional divergence. The reason for this is that economic integration creates new opportunities for economies of scale and specialization which tend to encourage greater spatial agglomeration and localization in regional activity (Krugman, 1991). Some versions of this theory predict that this process favours the already prosperous and competitive regions, reinforcing increasing returns and cumulative growth in the already prosperous regions, thus contributing to regional inequality. Other versions of the theory argue that the localization of an industry bestows on it important competitive advantages in international markets. These bring benefits to the region in which the industry is located as well as to other regions by diffusion.

These theoretical propositions are relevant to the discussion about the effects of EMU. If EMU is a further step towards market integration and, as is predicted, it does induce economic growth in Europe, what will be its effect on the regions? According to the first version, which is based on the US experience (Krugman, 1993), EMU-fostered growth will lead to regional specialization and deeper interregional divergence. According to the alternative version, EMU will increase regional specialization which would narrow the regional inequalities of Europe (Brauerhjelm et al., 2000). The conclusions are twofold: first, there is yet no clear or definitive answer to these questions; second, economic integration is not the panacea that will solve regional problems. Therefore, regional economic policy will continue to play an important role even under EMU.

10.6 Conclusions

Despite the coordinated efforts of national and EU regional policies and the generous assistance from the ERDF there are still many regions in the Community which lag behind the average regional level of development and growth. Although convergence through integration has occurred and the gap between the rich and the poor regions has narrowed, the ranking of the EU regions in terms of GDP per head has changed little: eight of the regions in the list of the 10 poorest and 10 richest have remained in the same position for more than two decades. This shows that regional disparities are deep-rooted and cannot easily be changed by the existing policies. The forthcoming EU enlargement to CEE countries means that EU regional policies have to be reviewed with two alternatives in mind: (i) either the funds available for regional development have to expand by a drastic revision of the general budget; (ii) or the existing funds will remain unaltered but, as they will have to be shared by more countries, this will be inadequate for the satisfaction of all the member states: accession will beget winners and losers.

Questions

1. (a) What is the objective of EU regional policy?
   (b) Why should regional policy be undertaken in common and not at the national level of the member states?
   (c) Would Economic and Monetary Union (EMU) ease the regional problems of the member states?

2. Discuss the argument that since market economies rely on self-interest to produce efficient allocations of resources, regional problems would best be solved by firms and workers making their own locational decisions without government or EU intervention.

3. Evaluate the following statement: 'One of the consequences of economic integration is to cause regional disparities in living standards to widen, while constraining the ability of member states to pursue their own regional development policies.'

4. Discuss the following statement: 'In spite of the rhetoric about "the market", the European economy neither conforms to the assumptions of the neoclassical model, nor it is likely to be attractive or desirable to seek to make it do so. Therefore, regional policy at the level of the Community is necessary.'

Further reading

For a general introduction to EU regional policies see Bache (1998) and Martin (1998). Eurostat (2000) presents the latest EU regional statistics.

Web guide

The EU site is available at www.europa.eu.int/comm/regional_policy and for current developments in regional policy see www.inforegio.cec.eu.int/dg16en.htm

Social policy

11

The main aim of the Community is to involve all citizens as social partners in the development and implementation of EU policies on the basis of a fair distribution of the costs and benefits of integration. For this, the Community has set up the European Social Policy, which is supplementary to national social policies, and aims at minimum harmonization for advancing its 'social dimension' during economic integration. Within the vast field of social policy, this chapter focuses on the most innovative EU initiatives: the European Social Fund, the Social Charter and the Social Action Programmes, and their implications on national and Community policies, outcomes and social groups.

11.1 Integration and social policy

Introduction

The common social policy is part of a coordinated Community approach which also includes economic, industrial and regional policies for strengthening the European economy and building up 'the social consensus'. Since the member states have their own national social policies, the basic question was whether the Community needed a common social policy at all. The Community's social dimension is an element of the integration process. Collectively, the EU countries spend considerably more on social security than other developed economies (such Japan and the USA). But since the different EU member states for ideological, political, economic and institutional reasons had set different priorities about who should be covered by social policy, to what extent and by how much, the differences among them were (and still remain) significant. Figure 11.1 shows that among the EU countries Sweden and the Netherlands spend the most, and

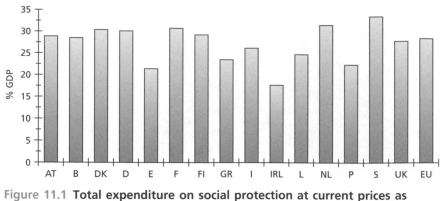

Figure 11.1 **Total expenditure on social protection at current prices as percentage of GDP, 1997**

Source: Data from Eurostat (2001b).

Ireland and Spain spend the least on social protection. But the question is: do the differences in social regimes, institutions and policies of the member states cause such sharp externalities that they need to be internalized by harmonization or even integration? Two answers, leading to different solutions, have been given to this problem:

1. Harmonization is unnecessary because convergence will happen of its own accord through market competition. This approach accepts that different social security systems reflect different preferences in different societies which cannot be reconciled without endangering other policy objectives. Therefore, it favours convergence by market-oriented solutions.
2. The differences in social provisions between the member states will converge by the process of integration, but in a downward direction. Therefore, only *ex ante* harmonization can safeguard the social rights won by workers in the Community's economically more advanced members. Alternatively, countries with low social standards would gain 'unfair' competitive advantages.

The EU started hesitantly with minimal coordination of some social issues relating to the employment of labour and 'living and working conditions' but through time, it has moved more towards the foundations of a European Social Policy. It is worth noticing, however, that EU social policy does not include any interstate income redistribution, which is a fundamental feature of federal regimes.

Treaty provisions

The Treaty of Rome contained few articles specifically addressing social policy issues. They were rather matters of law, essentially dealing with the free movement of labour (TEEC, 39–42) and the freedom of establishment in the context of the common market (TEEC 43–8). Later, the Community coverage of social policy widened by legislation and policy action, but it remained much narrower than the social policy of member states which, given their diversity of economic and social conditions, political traditions and institutional arrangements, retained the main task of dealing with their social problems themselves. However, the completion of the internal market exposed deep differences in social provisions across the member states and confirmed the urgent need for a wider coverage of social issues by a common social policy.

European Social Policy is above and beyond the social policy of the member states. But as European integration advances, the member states have bestowed on the Community social problems which require a common approach for their resolution. Accordingly, in 1987 the Single European Act (SEA) assigned the task of actively promoting social cohesion to the Community. This was followed by the Maastricht Treaty which set 'the raising of the standard of living and quality of life, and economic and social cohesion and solidarity among its Member States' (TEEC, II, 2) as an explicit objective of the Community, and adopted the *Community Charter of the Fundamental Rights of Workers* as an annexed protocol on social policy. The Treaty of Amsterdam (1997) reaffirmed that social policy is a competence which the EU shares with the member states, and consolidated the existing provisions. It also expanded the provisions on *non-discrimination* (TEEC, 13) and renewed the pledge on raising *employment* as a 'matter of common concern' (TEEC, 2). Moreover, it incorporated the *Protocol on Social Policy* into the EU Treaty (TEEC, 136–45) and added *equality between men and women* to the list of Community objectives (TEEC, 2–3). In the light of the radical transformation of Europe's economy and society and the expansion of globalization, in 2001 the EU also proposed an ambitious *Social Policy Agenda* aiming to ensure that economic, employment and social policies work together in a mutually reinforcing way.

11.2 The European Social Fund

The European Social Fund (ESF), which is the longest established Structural Fund, was set up by the Treaty of Rome.[1] New guidelines for managing

---

[1] The Council, acting by qualified majority, introduced a series of reforms to adapt the ESF to changes in economic and social conditions (e.g. in 1971, 1978 and 1984).

the ESF were adopted in 1985 and 1989. By 1995, 80 per cent of the ESF funds were directed to the unemployed 'to improve employment opportunities for workers in the internal market and to contribute thereby to raising the standard of living' (TEEC, 146). The ESF shares the aims of the other Structural Funds (objectives 1, 2, 3: see the ERDF in Chapter 10), with the particular target 'to support measures preventing and combating unemployment and developing human resources in order to promote a high level of employment, equality between men and women, sustainable development and economic and social cohesion.' (EC 2000). To accomplish these tasks, the ESF concentrates its activities in five main areas of action:

- developing active policies to combat unemployment, preventing long-term unemployment and providing support for those entering or re-entering the job market;
- promoting social inclusion and equal opportunities for all;
- developing education and training as part of a policy for lifelong learning;
- promoting a skilled and adaptable workforce, fostering innovation in work organization, supporting entrepreneurship and job creation, and boosting human potential in research, science and technology;
- improving the participation of women in the labour market.

The ESF is administered by the Commission which, by agreement with the member states, directs the majority of the available funds to areas of greatest hardship, objectively chosen according to criteria based on labour market conditions and economic development needs. During a new seven-year period, which started in 2000, the Community and the member states will put into practice with ESF assistance the *European Employment Strategy* which aims to prepare people for work, and to create a better climate for jobs by the application of a series of specially designed programmes. The ESF pays a proportion of a project's costs (usually 45 per cent) and the remaining *match funding* is supplied by private and public sources in the recipient country.

11.3 The Social Charter

Origins

With the move towards the single European market, a sharp discussion began about its social consequences. The debate was started by trade union representatives who expressed the fear that competition in the single market would bring about a downward convergence in social standards. This was based on the argument that the single market would lead to 'social dumping': that the free movement of capital after 1992 would induce labour-intensive industries to migrate from countries of high standards of worker protection to countries where pay and working conditions are poor. Therefore, countries with relatively high social standards would be forced to lower them to attract companies back. These actions could fuel a downward spiral of social provisions, eventually leading to the lowest common denominator of social welfare. It was proposed, therefore, that to avert such an eventuality, the Community should be given more powers to enable it to harmonize the multitude of national regulations on employment and social security in ways that would safeguard workers' hard-won rights. Opponents of this proposal argued that as national differences in social standards are reflected in labour costs, they cannot be eliminated without parallel improvements in labour productivity and adjustment in exchange rates. In other words: (i) the social wage is only one factor in investment decisions; (ii) firms will not invest in countries with low social wages if labour productivity is low; (iii) social dumping will not occur; (iv) therefore, harmonizing social provisions for protection of the 'high-standard countries' is unnecessary. As a compromise between the opposing views and under pressure from the European Parliament and the governments of member states and labour unions, the Commission proposed a *'Community Charter of the Fundamental Social Rights of Workers'*, or the Social Charter,[2] setting out the guidelines on which the European pattern of labour law and concept of society, and the place of labour in that society, should be based. The Social Charter was adopted at Strasbourg in December 1989 and the European Council attached it in the Maastricht Treaty (1992) as an annexed social protocol concerning 14 of the member states, with the UK opting out. The Treaty of Amsterdam (1997) reaffirmed the Social Charter which was finally signed by all the EU member states, including the UK, resulting in the 'reunification of the 15'.

The Social Charter proclaims the major principles underlying rights and responsibilities in the course of integration with regard to the following issues:

1. *Improvement of living and working conditions* by upward approximation within the single market of the organization and flexibility of working hours (working week, duration of employment, part-time work, temporary work, night shifts, etc.).

---

[2] The Social Charter should not be confused with the *Charter on Fundamental Rights* which was drawn up by the Nice Conference (2000) but it is not yet legally binding, nor with the closely related *European Convention on Human Rights* (ECHR) which originated with the Council of Europe and since 1961 has been signed by 22 countries.

2. *Right to freedom of movement* of every citizen who is permitted to exercise any trade or occupation within the Community on the same terms as those applied to nationals of the host country.

3. *Employment and remuneration* on fair terms for all employees (full-time, part-time, permanent, temporary, etc.). A fair wage should ensure workers have the means necessary for their own subsistence and that of their families.

4. *Right to social protection* subject to the proper arrangements of each member state. This may imply the necessity to establish a minimum wage and appropriate social assistance for those excluded from the labour markets (the elderly, the unemployed, those unable to be employed, etc.).

5. *Right to freedom and collective bargaining* for every employer and every worker in the EU, who has the right to belong freely to the professional and trade union organization of his or her choice and to any legally constituted association.

6. *Right to vocational training* of every worker in the EU throughout their working life. A machinery for continuing and permanent training must be set up to that end, enabling every citizen to undergo training, in particular through granting leave for training purposes.

7. *Right of men and women to equal treatment* and equal opportunities, guaranteed and developed by all countries.

8. *Right to information, consultation and worker participation*, which must be developed along appropriate lines and in such a way as to take account of legal provisions, contractual agreements and practices in force in the EU countries. This applies especially to companies or undertakings located in several member states.

9. *Right to health protection and safety at the workplace* by the introduction of appropriate measures and upward harmonization.

10. *Protection of children and adolescents*. All young people over 16 who are in gainful employment must be protected by labour rules arranged in their favour and must receive fair remuneration.

11. *Elderly persons* who are citizens of the Community, receiving a pension, must have sufficient resources to enable them to maintain a decent standard of living. Those elderly persons who are not entitled to a pension and who have no other adequate resources should receive a minimum income and social and medical assistance adapted to their needs.

12. *Disabled people* must be protected by measures which would achieve their integration into working life.

The integration of the Social Agreement

The Treaty of Amsterdam included the provisions of the Social Charter in the Social Agreement which is incorporated into the provisions of

Title XI of the TEEC. This expanded the area of competence of the European Community which can now act in the following fields of social policy:

- improvement of the working environment to protect workers' health and safety;
- working conditions;
- information and consultation of workers;
- integration of persons excluded from the labour market;
- equality between men and women.

To this list, the Treaty of Amsterdam added the possibility that the Council might adopt initiatives specifically designed to combat social exclusion (TEEC, 6), after taking account of the conditions and rules that apply in each member state. Under the co-decision procedure, the Council and the European Parliament might issue appropriate directives, after consulting the Economic and Social Committee (ESC) and the Committee of the Regions (CR).

In the following areas, the Council acts unanimously on a proposal from the Commission, after consulting the European Parliament and the Economic and Social Committee:

- social security and social protection of workers;
- protection of workers when their employment contract is terminated;
- representation and collective defence of the interests of workers and employers;
- employment conditions for third-country nationals legally resident in Community territory;
- financial contributions for the promotion of employment and job creation.

Measures adopted at Community level do not prevent member states from introducing more stringent national social protection measures, provided they are compatible with Community law. In the following sections we review the basics of the Community's social programme and the attempts to coordinate action in some areas of social policy (Commission, 1999).

11.4 The Social Action Programmes

The Commission started the Social Action Programmes (SAP) in 1973 in response to the Paris Summit declaration (1972) that the European Council 'attached as much importance to vigorous action in the social field as to the achievement of the economic and monetary union'. The form of the first programme adopted in 1974 included three main objectives: (a) attainment of full and better employment; (b) improvement and upward harmonization of living and working conditions; and (c) greater involvement of employer and employee organizations in the economic and social decisions of the Community, and of workers in the life of their firms. Although the economic and social conditions within and outside the Community have changed significantly since 1974, the SAP has continued to provide a reference point for several social policy measures implemented by the Community. The major features of these programmes include the following:

- more effective use of the Social Fund to promote employment;
- promotion of general and vocational training;
- measures to facilitate free movement within the Union;
- introduction of a minimum requirement framework in all fields of social policy;
- regulations on compatibility between working and family life and on part-time work;
- application of the equal opportunities principle in all areas of social policy;
- assistance for the poor, the disabled and the elderly;
- joint action to combat racism and xenophobia in society;
- development of the social dialogue.

Under the influence of the Social Charter, the Second Action Programme, covering the period 1998–2000, extended Community action in the field of European employment strategy as stated in the Treaty of Amsterdam. Some of the social policy measures adopted by the Community are described in the following sections.

Unemployment

Following the first oil crisis of 1973 the rate of unemployment in the Community started to rise. The ascent continued through the 1970s, 1980s and 1990s with some countries and regions within countries exceptionally hard hit (Spain, Ireland and Finland). In the EU, the rate of unemployment rose from 5.8 per cent in 1980 to 11.1 per cent in 1995, remaining at 9.2 per cent in 1999 (see Figure 6.2). Two particular developments may have had an influence on the rise of unemployment: (i) technological advancements which required new skills and vocational qualifications, and (ii) globalization which relocated many industries to low-cost foreign countries. Two groups of persons have fared significantly worse than any other population category: (a) the young (aged 15–24), who are twice as likely to be unemployed as older people; and (b) women, who in most countries display higher unemployment rates

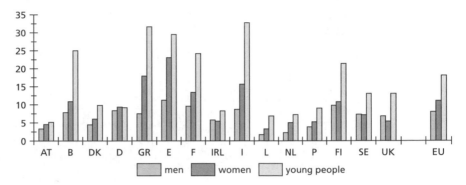

Figure 11.2 Unemployment in the EU countries 1999 (% on total per group)
Source: Data from Eurostat (2001a).

than men. The 1999 EU unemployment rates per group were 7.9 per cent for men, 10.9 per cent for women and 17.9 per cent for the young. Figure 11.2 testifies to the severity of these incidences across member states.

The adverse unemployment statistics did not reflect a lack of concern on behalf of the Community to combat the problem of unemployment. They testify instead to the confined role which was assigned to the common policy for unemployment which was limited to coordinating the work of various national employment agencies, rather than solving centrally the problems of unemployment. Since Maastricht (1992), the member states had decided to implement concerted economic measures, tailored to national requirements, to boost confidence and promote economic recovery. These measures, which were 'consistent with a medium-term framework founded on the principles of convergence', were targeted towards improving the prospects of growth and creating lasting jobs. In addition to advocating new investment, the Commission insisted on 'labour market flexibility', calling for tax reforms that would reduce non-wage labour costs, thus increasing 'growth, competitiveness and employment'. A Confidence Pact for employment was approved at the Florence European Council (June 1996). This pact, however, was no more than a statement of general principles on the need for coordination of macroeconomic policy and redirection of the Structural Funds towards job creation. The Treaty of Amsterdam amended and expanded the previous treaties on matters of social policy, affirming that among the main EU targets of economic and social progress there was the new target of reaching a 'high level of employment' (TEEC, I, 2) without undermining competitiveness. To achieve this objective, the Union was vested with new powers, supplementary to those of the member states, to enable it to apply a 'coordinated strategy' for employment (TEEC, new Title VIII, 125–30). Henceforth, in adopting and implementing Community policy,

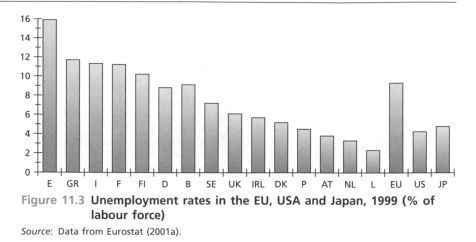

Figure 11.3 **Unemployment rates in the EU, USA and Japan, 1999 (% of labour force)**

Source: Data from Eurostat (2001a).

the repercussions on employment must be taken into account in consultation with the Economic and Social Committee (TEEC, 128–9). The Council and the Parliament, under the co-decision procedure, may also adopt measures promoting employment, advancing investment in vocational training and improving the effectiveness of labour market policy. These measures and a general improvement in economic conditions meant that unemployment fell from the 9.2 per cent EU average in 1999 – which was more than double the rates observed in USA and Japan, see Figure 11.3 – to around 7.7 per cent in 2001. The Employment Guidelines 2000 (adopted at the Helsinki summit, 1999) aim at more flexibility in the labour markets for improving competitiveness and productivity as a further inducement to job creation. Furthermore, the European Employment Strategy (EES) and the member states' National Action Plans for Employment (NAPs) draw up plans which serve as the overall framework for measures to support employment policies under the Structural Funds, and in particular the European Social Fund.

The candidates for accession to the EU also display high levels of unemployment (see Figure 9.3). The EU hopes that before accession most of these countries will have reduced substantially their unemployment problem, mostly by reforming their labour markets and increasing their flexibility.

Equal treatment of men and women

Besides the ethical issues raised by the unequal remuneration and conditions of employment between the sexes in the different member states of the Community, prices and trade may also be distorted if employed women are paid less than men for the same job. In this case, reform requires common action at the level of the Community. The equal treatment of men and women in matters of employment (TEEC,

141) was the subject of several directives during the first stage of customs union (1976–8). The member states were required to:

- repeal all laws, regulations and administrative provisions incompatible with the principle of equal pay for work of equal value;
- abolish all statutory provisions and terms of collective agreements hostile to employing women and fulfil the principle of equal treatment for men and women as regards access to employment, vocational training, promotion and working conditions;
- extend progressively the principle of equal treatment for men and women in matters of social security, the obligation to pay contributions, and the calculation of benefits and allowances.

The integration of all these directives into national legislation was monitored by the Commission. If a member failed to act, the Commission could bring infringement proceedings before the European Court of Justice (ECJ). Private individuals can also claim their rights by bringing action before their national courts, and as a last resort before the ECJ. Agreements and court decisions do not prevent member states from making it easier for women to pursue a vocational activity, or abolish disadvantages in their professional careers.

Since 1982 the Council has adopted a series of Community Action Programmes to promote equal opportunities for women. The fourth programme (1996–2000) was adopted in 1995. Under these programmes, the Community took action on job creation and recruitment of women, vocational training, improvement in market opportunities, information campaigns and adopting measures to promote equal opportunities. However, in practice *direct* sex discrimination (formally and expressly treating equally situated men and women differently) and *indirect* sex discrimination (practice generating different outcomes for men and women) have persisted, occasionally becoming more acute during economic recessions. The Commission's code of practice on equal pay for women and men for work of equal value was adopted in 1996. It also set as a target equality in the participation rate of both sexes. But by 1999, the EU average employment rate for both sexes was 62 per cent, with 72 per cent for men and barely 53 per cent for women, with only the Scandinavian member states (DK, FI, SE) tending towards equality between the sexes – see Figure 11.4. The Treaty of Amsterdam has added the promotion of equality between men and women to the list of Community objectives (TEEC, II, 2–3).

Educational and vocational training

The Community has paid particular attention to the problems of the unemployment of the young, who are caught in a vicious circle: because

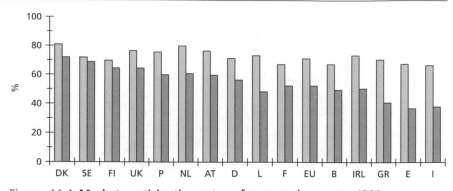

Figure 11.4 **Market participation rates of men and women, 1999**

Note: EU target rate 62 per cent for both sexes. First bar men, second women.

Source: Data from Eurostat (2001a).

they have no vocational training they cannot find a job, and because they have no job they cannot get in-job vocational training. The longer they stay outside the labour market, the worse their opportunities for employment become. One factor contributing to this situation is the fast advance of modern technology (such as information technology, telecommunications, etc.) which bypasses the unemployed and the unskilled. Under the SAP, the Council adopted a Commission proposal to set aside funds for financing the training of young people to help them enter the labour market. It also set up the *European Centre for the Development of Vocational Training* in Berlin, which is delegated to promote vocational education and to plan the harmonization of national standards and training qualifications. Since 1983, the Community has supported vocational training policies at member state and Community levels to reinforce the development of a skilled and adaptable workforce. In 1988, the Council set up the Youth Exchange Scheme for Europe (YES) programme for the promotion of youth exchanges in the Community.

The principles for a common training policy were formalized by the Treaty on European Union. The Community undertakes to contribute to the development of quality education by encouraging cooperation between member states and, if necessary, by supporting and supplementing their action. Community action will aim at developing the European dimension in education and encouraging the mobility of students and teachers, youth exchanges, and exchanges of information (TEEC, 149). The Community will also implement a vocational training policy with the aim of facilitating adaptation to industrial changes and to improving initial and continuing vocational training in order to promote vocational integration into the labour markets (TEEC, 150). To facilitate freedom of movement, the Community aims also at mutual recognition of vocational qualifications, national diplomas and degrees among the member states.

From 1987 the Erasmus programme facilitated the mobility and exchange of university students between higher education establishments of the member states, together with the Lingua programme which included a range of measures designed to improve the linguistic knowledge of students and teachers in the Community. These two programmes were later replaced by Socrates which is targeted towards higher education. In the field of vocational training, a Council resolution has invited member states to improve the integration of continuing vocational training into economic and social development schemes, and has called for training measures inside and outside firms with access for workers and the unemployed, particularly in the fields of information and communication technologies. The Leonardo programme was set up with the aim of implementing a comprehensive Community vocational training policy.

Working time and equitable wages

With unemployment rising, the Paris European Council in 1979 requested the Commission to consider the social and economic implications of a concerted reorganization of working time (entailing a cut in weekly working hours, longer annual holidays, more training leave, and less overtime and shift work). The Commission's proposals led to the 'resolution on the adaptation of working time' which was adopted by Council in December 1979. This was followed by several Commission initiatives which aimed at job creation by a coordinated reduction and reorganization of the current working time, and by limiting systematic paid overtime. In 1982, the Council adopted a recommendation on the principles of flexible retirement, which included a reduction in total working life with entitlement to a retirement pension. The Council also adopted an amended version of the Commission's directive on part-time and temporary work designed to protect and provide minimal guarantees for people engaged in this type of employment.

In 1975, the Council set up by regulation the *European Foundation for the Improvement of Living and Working Conditions* which opened the following year in Dublin. Its objective is to conduct research on shift work and working time, the impact of technological change on work management, and the psychological effects of work conditions. Its programme expanded in 1988 to include employer/worker relations, restructuring the work environment, promotion of health and safety, raising living standards and evaluation of future technology.

In 1993, the EU set a 48-hour limit on the working week, subject to exceptions for certain professions. In 1998, the average working week was 41.3 hours (39.0 for female workers) within a range of 45.7 hours in the UK and 39.1 in Belgium.

A report from the Commission also revealed major differences in the approach of EU member states to the question of minimum or equitable wages. However, there is no firm proposal for a common minimum wage rate across the EU. Member states with a national minimum wage set by law include: B, E, F, GR, L, NL, P, UK. All other member states have minimum wages set through collective agreements.

Disabled people

One of the priority tasks of the SAP was to help disabled people to integrate into the life and work of the Community. To this effect, the ESF made finance available for pilot projects aimed at the rehabilitation of disabled people and in 1981 the Commission prepared an action programme for their employment in a free economy. The programme covered the following:

1. setting up a Community-wide network of *demonstration projects* aimed at improving the quality of vocational rehabilitation facilities currently in operation;
2. improving the exchange of *information and experience* between rehabilitation and training bodies;
3. studies and conferences aimed at drawing up *Community guidelines* for longer-term projects and policies;
4. more financial assistance for the existing Community network of *rehabilitation centres*;
5. further development of the Community's scheme of *pilot housing* schemes for the disabled.

A Community network of model projects was set up, and later the early phase of a computerized Community database on the disabled was launched. A second series of Community action programmes, *Helios*, was adopted with two aims: to ease occupational rehabilitation and economic integration, and to promote social integration and independent living for the disabled. A resolution was also adopted by Council in 1990 promoting full integration of the disabled into the ordinary educational system. Another Community programme, *Horizon*, endeavours to ease the integration of disabled people through the provision of correctly adapted training. The Treaty of Amsterdam added a new article (TEEC, II, 13) which provides for measures to combat discrimination based on disability.

Poverty

Most national social policies include measures aimed at maintaining the income of people living in poverty: the unemployed, one-parent families,

Box 11.1 ▪ Working conditions 2000

1. The EU directive on working time entitles workers to:
  1. a limit of an average of 48 hours worked per week, over a reference period;
  2. a limit of 8 hours worked in every 24-hour period for night work;
  3. a weekly rest period of 24 hours every week;
  4. an entitlement to 11 hours' consecutive rest per day;
  5. an entitlement to a minimum 20-minute rest break where the working day is longer than 6 hours.

  Subject to agreement between representatives of employers and employees, certain derogations may be applied to ensure that the directive continues to afford protection to workers, whilst amending the provisions so that it is appropriately applied to typical working patterns with minimum disruption.

2. In 1998, the average working week in the EU was 41.3 hours. However, an EU-sponsored survey found that 20 per cent of workers work for more than 45 hours per week, and 16 per cent work for under 30 hours a week. A great disparity also exists between employed workers (36.7 hours) and the self-employed (46.6 hours).

3. A 1999 EU-wide survey by Eurostat found that in the EU, on average, women earned a quarter less than men. The figures pertain to full-time employees in all branches of the economy, with the exception of agriculture, education, health, personal services and administration. In terms of gross hourly pay, Germany's new Länder (the ex-East Germany) were closest to parity, female pay being 89.9 per cent of that of their male counterparts. Next came Denmark (88.1 per cent), Sweden (87.0 per cent), Luxembourg (83.9 per cent) and Belgium (83.2 per cent). At the other end of the scale was Greece (68.0 per cent), the Netherlands (70.6 per cent), and Portugal (71.7 per cent). The EU average is 76.3 per cent. However, this must be interpreted with caution, because no account is taken of the different situations of men and women on the EU labour market. First, women and men have different jobs. Second, working women are on average younger: 44 per cent are under 30 as compared with 32 per cent of men. If one applies the male employment pattern to women, the salary gap is narrowed but remains at approximately 15 per cent. Third, there is a difference in educational level: 51 per cent of working women have no more than primary or general secondary education.

Source of information: http://europa.eu.int/en/comm/eurostat/compres

those with low education, those in retirement, families with many children, the sick or disabled, and the homeless and vagrants. The main measure of poverty used in the EU at present is the Eurostat definition: the percentage of people with an income of 60 per cent or less of the median income in the country in which they live.[3] Although this means

---

[3] There are various definitions of poverty. The UN millennium summit, for example, defined an absolute measure of poverty as a state in which someone has less than $1 a day to live on (see Gordon and Townsend, 2001).

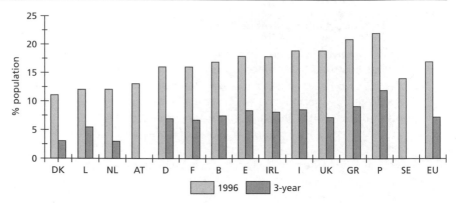

Figure 11.5 Population with income below the poverty line, 1996

Note: Percentage of population below threshold in 1996, and for three consecutive years, 1992–5. AT, SE: no data for three-year period; FI: no data.

Source: Data from Eurostat (2001a).

that the poverty line, in terms of absolute values, differs between countries, it is indicative of relative deprivation in the country concerned. Using this measure, 18 per cent of people in the EU, or more than one in six, had an income below the poverty level in 1996 (see Figure 11.5).

While most EU countries display a rate of poverty below the Community mean (DK, L, NL, A, D, F, B, and probably FI and SE), Spain and Ireland are just at the mean and four other countries (I, UK, GR and P) are above the mean. The case of P, GR, E (and probably IRL) understates the severity of the problem since these are the countries with the lowest median income in the EU. A more statistically reliable index of poverty than the single-year observation is the *persistence* of poverty over several years. Taking a three-year mean score for 1994–6, the population in persistent poverty in the EU is 7 per cent, less than half the figure for a single year. In DK and NL persistent poverty affected only 3 per cent of the population, confirming that poverty in these two countries is not only low but is also a temporary affair. Conversely, in P and GR around a tenth of the population are permanently below the poverty line.

The EU countries' policies for poverty alleviation are based either on a system of non-contributory supplementary benefits (social transfers) – general (in the UK and Ireland) or means-tested (in Denmark and the Netherlands); or on a contributory insurance system, which may leave out those who have not contributed to the system. The problem with transfers is that they tend to cure the symptoms rather than the underlying causes of poverty. It is not surprising therefore that international studies based on standardized data have shown that even in developed countries, despite the existence of extensive welfare programmes, a large section of the population continues to live in dire poverty.

The Community's first anti-poverty programme consisted of 29 pilot schemes and projects in various member states, and two cross-national studies on the general issue of poverty. Based on these studies, the Commission prepared an assessment report which confirmed that, despite the unprecedented growth in national incomes and the expansion of the welfare state since the mid-1950s, poverty had not declined and the gap between the standard of living and opportunities enjoyed by the average citizen and the poor remained wide. The Commission's conclusion was that action against poverty needed to be given high priority and that a major strategy for combating poverty was to reduce unemployment by creating new jobs and sharing existing jobs. Economic convergence and EMU are expected to raise the rate of growth in the Community. However, it remains uncertain whether poverty will also be reduced after these developments. As the Commission has noted, 'unless the Community takes appropriate action and mobilizes its resources more effectively, poverty will continue to exist'.

Social dialogue and industrial democracy

Developing the social dialogue between management and labour at European level, 'which could, if the two sides consider it desirable, lead to relations based on agreement' (TEEC, 139), has preoccupied the Community from early on. In most members of the Community, industrial democracy, which is identified with employee participation in the management of companies, is limited to consultation on matters concerning personnel, working conditions and safety at work. But the Community has felt that industrial democracy has to expand. Moreover, the Agreement on Social Policy formally constrains the Commission to consult the social partners (= management and workers) in advance on initiatives affecting social policy. Furthermore, the new Title on employment gives the social partners a significant role in the coordinated strategy for employment.

Implementation of the TEEC started in 1970 when the Council set up a *Standing Committee on Employment* responsible for securing the ongoing dialogue between the Council, Commission and social partners in order to facilitate the coordination of employment policies. This was followed in 1985 by the *Val-Duchesse* meeting between the President and several members of the Commission and representatives of the European Trade Union Confederation (ETUC), the Union of Industries of the European Community (UNICE) and the European Centre of Public Enterprises (CEEP). They agreed to set up working parties to examine the problems posed by the implementation of a European strategy for cooperation on growth and employment, and by the introduction of new technologies. In 1990, a steering group and the Commission reached agreement on a joint consultation procedure between management and labour, promoted by the Commission, which undertook to take all relevant measures to facilitate its success. Two Commission proposals have been issued to this effect. The first concerned companies set up under the proposed European company law which would be governed by EU law and have a dualistic board structure, comprising a management and a supervisory board with one-third of the members being workers' representatives. However, the European Company Statute has not advanced far (see Chapter 13).

The origin of the second proposal was the *Vredeling directive* (1980) which advocated consultation between management and employees on all major decisions (closures, dismissals, restructuring and so on), and disclosure of comprehensive information about company operations, in particular transnational undertakings. But this proposal attracted strong opposition from both the European Trades Union Confederation (ETUC) and the European employers' organization (UNICE). Eventually, in 1994 the EU ministers for social affairs formally adopted a directive which provides for the creation of works councils for transnational companies with 1000 or more employees in Europe and at least 150 in two member states.

The social dialogue has enabled a certain degree of progress to be made in the social field, e.g. approval of directives on parental leave (1996), part-time work (1997), and fixed-term contracts (1999). Since 1998, enlargement considerations have become a priority at both industry and sectoral levels. The Commission and representatives of management and labour from the EU and the applicant countries met at a conference in 1999 to examine the implications of enlargement in the light of both the social provisions of the treaty and the employment strategy. But no further progress has emerged on the issue of industrial democracy.

Migrant workers

The numbers of migrants and asylum seekers in the Community have risen sharply in recent years. In 1998, there were 19 million non-nationals in the EU-15 (6 million from within the EU and 13 million from non-EU countries), 5 per cent of total population, compared with 4 per cent in 1990. Most of these immigrants are found in Germany (7.3 million), France (3.6 million) and the UK (2.1 million). The Community also receives illegal migrants and refugees, for whom no reliable estimates exist. In the past, most migrants were unskilled workers who took up rough, poorly paid jobs which local workers refused to do. But this situation has been complicated further in recent years by the increasing immigration of better-qualified people. Besides poor housing and inadequate training and education facilities, the migrants face specific problems, such as

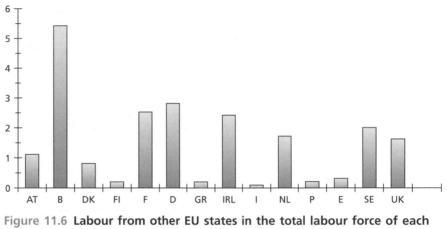

Figure 11.6 **Labour from other EU states in the total labour force of each member state, %, 1998**

Notes: Luxembourg's high share of 36.2 per cent (not shown) is about five times higher than the next highest, that of Belgium.

Source: Data from Eurostat (2002b).

linguistic and religious differences, which adversely affect their social integration in the community.

Community policies have been directed towards improving the social conditions of migrant workers and their families as part of the overall social policy programme. The basic policy rules were outlined in Regulation 1408/71 on *Social security for migrant workers*, the sole purpose of which is to coordinate (and not to harmonize) the member states' social security legislation. Under the Community system of free movement of labour, workers and the self-employed who are nationals of one member state and work in another have total access to social security in the state of their work on the same basis as the nationals of that member state, and they can accumulate employment insurance and pension rights in one state and export them to another. But in general the internal migrants' numbers across the EU remain small – see Figure 11.6. The forthcoming EU enlargement to CEE is expected to increase internal migration to the west, not only of unskilled labour but also of highly skilled and educated personnel in search of employment or better-paid jobs. Migrant workers and their families are provided with specific measures on language teaching, vocational training, social security, housing, social services, schooling, and economic, political and trade union rights, all of which aim at the obliteration of discrimination.

The Treaty on European Union (1992) created the third pillar on Justice and Home Affairs (JHA) with one of its tasks being the study of issues relating to asylum, visas and migration. Over the years the JHA has agreed only on a common definition of a refugee; otherwise the formal harmonization of policy remains limited. The *Schengen Agreement* (1985, updated in 1990) intended to abolish internal border controls for all people and to adopt common measures to strengthen external border controls. These included a common visa policy, asylum application processing policy, and judicial cooperation and information exchanges. The Schengen Agreement was incorporated into the Treaty of Amsterdam, confirming the EU as the proper high authority on matters of immigration and asylum. But this has not been accepted by all member states.

Health protection

The supply of healthcare services and the regulations governing healthcare markets differ across the EU member states in both quantity and quality. There is nothing in the treaties about aiming at a common market in healthcare. However, with advancing integration certain allocation disadvantages arising from different national regulations could become more prominent. It is possible that in the course of EU integration the interstate migration of labour may be influenced not only by purely economic reasons but also by healthcare provisions. Similarly, interstate patient flows may intensify by the 'cross-border shopping' of medical treatment to countries supplying better healthcare at lower charges, if any. Such eventualities confirm that national healthcare policy has economic and social spillovers which give rise to positive and negative externalities beyond the confines of a member state.

The primary aim of health policy is to improve citizens' health. The TEEC accepted that health and safety at work is a proper subject for Community initiative and in its social policy it refers to 'the need to promote improved working conditions and an improved standard of living of workers'. Hence the Advisory Committee on Safety, Hygiene and Health Protection was established in 1974 and European Action Programmes on safety and health at work were adopted by the Council in 1978, 1984 and 1988. The SEA (1986) extended the legal provisions for Community action, adding that 'the member states should pay particular attention to encouraging improvements . . . in the working environment, as regards the health and safety of workers.' Consequently, the Community's task was limited to encouraging cooperation, but not the direct harmonization or unification of healthcare provisions. But as the date for completing the internal market (1992) was approaching, it became clear that the consequent liberalization of factor mobility within the Community could increase the immigration of people to countries with relatively high social provisions, including healthcare. It was postulated, therefore, that an explicit common approach to public health policy might be necessary. Thus, a 'Public Health' Title was included in the treaties (TEEC, XIII) affirming explicitly that 'the activities of the Community include . . . a contribution to the attainment of a high level of health protection' but 'excluding any harmonization of the laws and regulations of the Member States' (TEEC, XIII, 152). The Community's activities were restricted to coordinating the activities of the member states but also fostering cooperation with third countries and competent international organizations in the sphere of public health, such as the World Health Organization (WHO). Since 1993, the Commission has identified the following areas for action relating to public health: 'Health promotion, education and training; Health data and indicators, and monitoring and surveillance of disease; Cancer; Drugs; AIDS and other communicable diseases; Intentional and unintentional accidents and injuries; Pollution-related diseases; Rare diseases'. Emphasis was also placed on the dissemination of information and evaluation of policies and their effectiveness. Subsequently, Community activity in the field of public health has taken three forms: (i) promoting health and safety in the workplace; (ii) improving living and working conditions, e.g. by increasing controls over environmental pollution; and (iii) coordinating medical and health research and funding public awareness campaigns (such as 'Europe against AIDs' and 'Europe against Cancer').

Although the Commission's recognition of the importance of EU health policy was welcome, its disease-by-disease approach to policy targeting and implementation has been criticized as limited, and calls have been made for a horizontal, interdisciplinary approach. This was realized much earlier than anticipated, when the European Parliament called for the development of 'common health policy definitions, objectives and priorities'. It also urged the Commission to draw up a report on the state of health in the EU, analysing trends and assessing the effects of public health policies and 'setting minimum levels of health care that each member state must provide for its citizens'. Under the influence of these developments and the shortcomings of the previous arrangements, the Treaty of Amsterdam (1997) radically changed the health provisions. In contrast to earlier provisions, the Community can now adopt measures aimed at ensuring (rather than contributing to) 'a high level of human health protection' not only by 'the prevention of disease' but also by 'improving public health'. Consequently, among the areas of cooperation between member states the new article 152 lists not only diseases and major health scourges but also all causes of danger to human health, as well as the general objectives of improving health. The new treaty has also adopted the integration principle, that health protection should be taken into account when drawing up and implementing all other policies. Acknowledging the principle of subsidiarity, the provisions of the treaty explicitly respect national competencies in healthcare. Nevertheless, the treaty approves of Community involvement in this field, provided that national responsibilities are taken into account, if an action by a member state causes transboundary externalities or it is subject to economies of scale and results can 'be better achieved by the Community'. All these actions refer explicitly to *public* health policy which in countries progressing towards economic integration is considered as one of the sectors that require coordination. Otherwise, harmonization was specifically excluded and national healthcare in the member states remains the concern of the countries themselves. But changes may be expected even in this field. National healthcare systems, while very different in design, delivery and funding, are confronted with similar core challenges both now and for the future:

- People are living longer and traditional family structures are changing.
- Care technologies are developing fast and cost money.
- EU citizens have new demands of health and care systems as consumers of care.

Across the EU national healthcare systems face identical problems: how to achieve and maintain universal access to healthcare and care for the elderly, a high quality of care and financial viability of care systems in the long run.[4] The free mobility principle of the single market may help a common solution to the integration process to emerge (see Box 11.2).

Consumer protection

The common market is for the benefit of both consumers and producers but initially the TEEC contained no formal legal basis for consumer protection. However, programmes and directives dealing with consumer protection have existed since 1975. Consumer policy became more active after the advent of the SEA and the move towards the single market. Since 1986, several Council resolutions have emphasized the need for a high level of protection for consumers' basic rights to health and safety, economic justice, redress for damages, information and education, and consultation to enable them to take advantage of the Community market. All these were enshrined in the Treaty on European Union under a specific title on consumer protection (TEEC, XIV). The treaty declared

---

[4] Since 1970, EU citizens' life expectancy at birth has risen by 5.5 years for women and almost five years for men. The share of the total European population older than 65 is set to increase from 16.1 per cent in 2000 to 27.5 per cent by 2050, while those over 80 years old are expected to account for 10 per cent of population by 2050, compared with 3.6 per cent in 2000. Therefore, public expenditure on healthcare is expected to rise during 2000–50 by between 0.7 and 2.3 GDP points.

Box 11.2 ■ A common health policy?

The Treaty of Amsterdam (1997) radically changed public health provisions by stating explicitly:

1. A high level of human health shall be ensured in the definition and implementation of all Community policies and activities. Community action, which shall complement national policies, shall be directed towards improving public health, preventing human illness and diseases, and obviating sources of danger to human health. Such action shall cover the fight against the major health scourges, by promotional research into their causes, their transmission and their prevention, as well as health information and education. . . .

5. Community action in the field of public health shall fully respect the responsibilities of the Member States for the organization and delivery of health services and medical care.

(TEEC, XIII, 152)

Following this treaty, the Community decided to develop public health policy on the basis of the following actions:

■ improving information for the development of public policy;
■ developing a rapid reaction capability to respond rapidly to threats to public health;
■ combating lifestyle-related diseases by joint efforts in health promotion and prevention.

Two EU-level advisory groups were set up within the Directorate General V (Employment and Social Affairs) to coordinate the national and Community responsibilities on health matters: the *High Level Committee on Health*, which consists of officials from the member states and whose function is to advise the Commission on policy developments; and the *Interservice Group on Health*, which includes among its tasks the promotion of awareness of the impact on health and the integration of health protection in other Community policies.

Article 152 of the TEEC provides the EU with limited competence in health promotion but explicitly rules out the extension of this competence to healthcare organization and delivery (Hitiris, 1997). However, in April 1998 the European Court of Justice (ECJ) made two rulings regarding cross-border health delivery which may have immense implications for the future provision of national healthcare in the member states. The rulings pertained to two cases of Luxembourg citizens, one of whom obtained orthodontic treatment in Germany while the other purchased spectacles in Belgium, without the prior authorization of the Luxembourg healthcare system, and were refused reimbursement by the Luxembourg insurance fund. The ECJ upheld the claimants' cases under existing treaty provisions governing the free movement of goods and services, and it thus extended the single market principles to the delivery of health services to patients (Mountford, 2000). Is this the beginning of EU's 'medicine without frontiers'?

that the Community would contribute to a high level of consumer protection through measures adopted in the single market. The Council, acting on qualified majority voting (under TEEC, 252), would adopt specific measures, supporting the policies of the member states, to protect the health, safety and economic interests of consumers. As a result, several directives have been published which deal with relevant issues such as misleading advertising, product liability and guarantees, access to justice, distance selling, and cross-border bank services. In April 1995 the autonomous Consumer Policy Service became a full Directorate-General (DG XXIV) to safeguard consumer interests in all stages of the decision-making process.

11.5 Evaluation

The EU countries' different levels of economic development, unequal growth potential and diverse social regimes have resulted in different social policy provisions which do not contribute to 'cohesion' and can cause adverse externalities across countries. Since social policy standardization by market forces is necessarily slow, the Community has established institutions and introduced mechanisms to help the convergence of social provisions and policies in the member states, if possible in an upward direction. This is attempted primarily by the coordination and harmonization of existing national social policies, but also to some extent by initiating common social provisions and policies for the development of a fairer society, in the case of the EU strictly based on non-interstate income redistribution. The three most important developments in this respect are the establishment of the European Social Fund with its general aim the 'improvement of the living and working conditions' in the EU, the Social Charter, which advanced the foundation of the Community's 'social dimension', and the implementation of Community policy by the Social Action Programmes. These developments became necessary after the completion of the internal market and the move towards EMU which were expected to raise the rate of economic growth and, at the same time, exacerbate the existing problems of social divergence. To prevent this from happening, the member states and the Community were required to continue the policies already pursued (with regard to unemployment, low pay, working conditions, vocational training, migrant workers, industrial democracy, and so on) and to undertake new ones. Furthermore, with the rise in unemployment, technological advances and globalization it was felt that the Community could co-ordinate centrally the search for solutions to social problems, which may differ in extent but are otherwise common in all countries, by guiding the member states towards harmonization of social provisions and by showing the direction that social policy in the member states should take. Although the social divide is still deep, the Community's social policy is a step in the right direction.

Questions

1. What is the ESF and how does it attempt to reach its objectives?

2. Discuss the argument that the Social Charter and active policies to promote convergence are necessary because economic integration may itself lead to widening disparities and inequalities both within and between the member states.

3. Discuss the view that the social dimension of the internal market programme may exacerbate the problem of regional disparities by putting up obstacles to interregional labour mobility in Europe while increasing the labour costs of the poorer regions.

4. 'The fact that social policy has benefits as well as costs means that the validity of arguments about "social dumping" – that countries gain a competitive advantage through having lower social standards – is doubtful.' Discuss.

5. Consider the following argument and explain why the Community has introduced the Social Charter: 'Comprehensive harmonization of wages, labour costs, and social security systems are neither necessary nor useful as a precondition for a common market. Abolishing all regulations that distort the market will suffice.'

6. Discuss the following statement: 'The disparities in social policy (and therefore in its cost) are not an obstacle to the functioning of the single market. These disparities effectively translate into differences in the distribution of national income, and as long as the majority of a country's population prefers a distribution of national income different from that of the other countries, disparities between them pose no problems.'

Further reading

For a review of the problems and achievements of European Social Policy see EC (2000), Commission (2000a), and Eurostat (1998b and 2001a). Special topics on EU social issues are published in the *Journal of European Social Policy*.

Web guide

Information about the ESF is available at www.europa.eu.int/comm/employment_social and for general issues in social policy at www.europa.eu.int/scadplus

Transport

12

Transport is a key sector with links in every other sector of the economy. For this reason the EU treaties have dedicated a separate Title to the foundation of a Common Transport Policy (CTP). But despite treaty provisions the EU was unable, or the partners were unwilling, to implement such a radical policy. After completing the internal market, the EU moved decidedly towards transport integration by opening up the national markets and introducing Trans-European Networks, which made it possible to come up with plans for the establishment of a European transport infrastructure binding all member states together with the help of Community funding. Over the last ten years, the main objectives of the CTP have generally been achieved, resulting in increased competition, better-quality services and lower prices.

12.1 The problem

Besides trade, the Treaty of Rome contained separate Titles for only two economic sectors, agriculture and transport, the latter being the more important. Today the agricultural sector contributes less than 2 per cent of the EU-GDP and employs just 5 per cent of the workforce. The transport sector accounts for 4 per cent of the EU-GDP and employs 4.2 per cent of the total working population, or 9 per cent if we add those employed in the transport equipment industry and in transport-related businesses. About 1 per cent of the EU-GDP is invested each year in the transport infrastructure, and households spend 14 per cent of their annual income on transport. Transport is a service sector with many cross-links with other sectors. Many industries (motor, aircraft, shipyards, road building, steel production, etc.) depend on transport. Transport accounts for 31 per cent of total energy consumption and nearly 45 per cent of the consumption of petrol, 85 per cent of that by road transport alone.

Regulation

Two of the most important problems of the sector are investment and resource allocation. Both of these problems are connected with the issue of 'regulation', that is government intervention in transport. In general, regulation is advised as a remedy for market failures causing misallocation of resources and welfare loss. Economic theory recognizes three broad reasons why unregulated markets may fail to allocate resources efficiently. These reasons and an additional fourth also apply to transport:

1. There is market power that allows firms to enjoy excessive rents by sustaining prices higher and volume of output lower than competitive levels. In this case competitive solutions are desirable and feasible but are not achieved because of actions by incumbents.

   Market power has detrimental effects on static and dynamic economic efficiency. In transport this problem is often the cause (and effect) of economies of scale: in certain cases, carriers need to be large (railways, air-traffic control, airports and ports), and this creates barriers to entry. The means to realize the benefits of economies of scale is to accept the monopoly and to regulate its behaviour. This is the case of natural monopoly: an industry in which technical factors preclude the efficient existence of more than one producer. Therefore:
   (a) competitive solutions are not feasible; and
   (b) regulation is preferable to perfect competition.

2. There are externalities that prevent private marginal costs and benefits from reaching equality with social marginal cost and benefits.

   This occurs when the welfare of one economic agent (person, firm) is directly affected by the actions of another: for example, when there is no explicit charge for the use of road space and one road user imposes congestion costs on others. The external costs more often mentioned with reference to transport are divided into three categories. The first are primarily experienced by other transport users, but not taken into account by transport users in deciding their level of activity, for example road users' accidents and congestion. The second category includes environmental effects, such as noise and atmospheric pollution, with costs falling on the community at large rather than on the users or the builders of the transport system. The third category concerns transport's impact on land use and value and the location of economic activity (housing, production, employment).

3. There is asymmetric information about product quality between the contracting parties (sellers/buyers) that prevents them from reaching optimum exchange.

   In this case competitive solutions are feasible but undesirable. Technical specifications, frequency and rigour of servicing, qualifications of carriers and similar issues associated with risk and safety (for example in air transport) are typical examples of this problem and are usually subject to regulation.

4. There is 'excessive' competition that allegedly would destroy all except one or two firms, which would then set non-competitive prices, for example by forming a cartel.

Price and entry regulations of airlines, trucking, shipping, etc., are often justified by this line of argument.

Government intervention in transport comprises market organization (*structural regulation*) and behaviour (*conduct regulation*). In general two kinds of broad attitudes about regulation in transport exist which have resulted in two approaches, the 'commercial' and the 'social', each with different policy implications. The 'commercial' approach tends to regard transport as a service. The objective of government transport policy is to facilitate the market forces to operate efficiently. Government intervention aims at improvement of the structure and organization of the market, so that supply matches the market demand in both quality and quantity, and at the lowest possible cost. The 'social' approach holds that transport not only serves the existing centres of social and economic activity, but also affects trade and industrial development and the distribution of employment, population and land use, as well as the quality of life of the community. So under the second approach transport policy is an instrument for pursuing wider economic and social goals, such as growth, location of production, energy conservation, quality of life, the environment and so on. Therefore government intervention is more widespread and active under the 'social' than under the 'commercial' approach to transport policy. Clashes between advocates of the two different views occur often, whenever a major transport project comes under discussion – for example, when building new motorways or airports, closing rail lines, bus services, and so on.

Intervention

Whatever the approach, 'commercial' or 'social', an important characteristic of the sector is the pervasive presence of intervention. The government is omnipresent in transport, first as investor in the infrastructure and next as provider of services directly to the public or indirectly by subsidizing other carriers, as the recipient of transport taxes, and as the legislator of numerous regulations about the operations of the industry. In general, governments attempt to control the quality, quantity, organization and resource allocation of the sector. The first three of these objectives are usually pursued by regulation and appropriate legislation, the last one by economic management. Quality controls are mostly regulations dealing with safety aspects (speed limits, minimum standards, working conditions, qualifications of operators, pollution, congestion, etc.). Quantity controls attempt to match the (usually public) supply with the requirements of the market. The organization of the sector is concerned with the ownership of the industry, which in many countries is partly public enterprise, and the structure of the market (monopoly, oligopoly). Economic management for the objective of resource allocation aims at improved efficiency.

Transport is characterized by high *indivisibilities*, i.e. technical externalities that impinge on both pricing and investment. Many investments in the sector are large, display considerable economies of scale, have a long life-span and are infrequently made. Thus investment is usually undertaken monopolistically by the public sector, for example by provision of the infrastructure. Therefore, problems arise with the financing of transport projects and the allocation of the costs. A far more complex problem is pricing the output of the sector, and the relationship between the prices of public and private transport services. In its turn, pricing directly affects the resource allocation and the efficiency of the sector. Efficiency is here taken to mean the benefit to the community derived from the goods and services that transport produces. Optimality implies deriving the maximum benefit from transport at the least possible cost.

Modality

Further complications arise from the multiplicity of forms of transport or *modes* that contribute to the total output of the sector, complementing each other or competing with each other. Production by different forms entails a manifold infrastructure (rail tracks, roads, ports, airports) and a multifarious sectoral output. The latter are usually heterogeneous and cannot be easily aggregated, evaluated and compared between different modes. Economies of scale may favour one mode more than another and in the longer run technological change may offer advantages to a particular mode. Therefore, it is also difficult to devise and implement comprehensive transport policies that would encourage fair competition between the different modes of transport.

12.2 Common Transport Policy

Complexities

The reason economic unions require a common transport policy is that transport is an important production input and thus transport costs constitute a major component of output price. It is estimated that on average 25 per cent of final costs are accounted for by transport costs. Therefore, transport directly affects the degree of competition in the market. So a determined country can alter its comparative advantage and its trade flows by policy-induced changes (subsidies, taxation) of transport costs. Therefore, within a common market, trade liberalization and a common transport policy should be implemented simultaneously.

However, the cross-links between transport and other sectors of the economy mean that the act of introducing common transport policies has repercussions on many other economic sectors. This characteristic, combined with the fact that a large section of the sector is not directly involved with interstate trading and thus is exclusively in the domain of a state's domestic policy, suggests that agreement on common transport policies cannot easily be reached. On the other hand, if a common transport policy is ever devised, it would be a major advance towards integrating a large section of the members' economies.

As a major component of market price, transport cost affects relative prices and trade. Since a prime objective of the European Community was to liberalize and promote interstate trade, transport would play an important role. It was therefore essential to harmonize national transport policies to bring forward a coordinated and efficient Community transport system, able to stimulate competition, help reduce costs, and assist the development of interstate trade based on comparative advantage. So the Commission aspired from the start to introduce a common transport policy in step with trade liberalization. But the six original members of the Community had diverse interests and priorities in their national transport sectors which diverged for reasons of geography and of distinctly different national attitudes to state intervention, regulation, conservation, land use and the environment. What all of them had in common was that for both economic and social reasons they exerted a huge number of state controls on the quality and quantity of transport in the form of rates, quotas and licensing. For these reasons, the field where the common policies were to be applied was uneven and the policies had varying implications on the prices of traded goods and different social effects on the community at large. This made the search for a common transport policy a difficult and lengthy enterprise. However, the importance of transport as a complement to market integration was recognized from early on. Transport was one of the three sectors specifically mentioned in the Treaty of Rome among the principal sectors (external trade and agriculture are the other two) for which the Community intended to develop common policies (TEEC, II, 3). These policies were to serve a dual objective: first, to set up an integrated and efficient transport sector able to assist market integration, regional development and economic growth; and, second, given the involvement of transport in every other economic sector, to use transport as an instrument designed to further the general aims of the Treaty.

Treaty provisions

The specific framework of Community transport policy is presented in a separate Title (TEEC, V, 70–80) which outlines the basic principles for developing a more detailed set of policies. The actual design and implementation of the common transport policy were left, however, to the discretion of the Council and other Community institutions. In articles 70–1 the contracting parties agree to pursue the objectives of the treaty on transport by a common transport policy which 'shall be pursued by the Member States' and by a specified institutional procedure. Article 80 states that the common policy would apply to transport by rail, road and inland waterways, but also to shipping and aviation, provided this extension is decided by the Council acting by a qualified majority, which was duly done. Among other general policy guidelines, article 71 defines the objectives of the common transport policy as: '(a) common rules applicable to international transport; (b) the conditions under which non-resident carriers may operate transport services within a Member State; (c) measures to improve transport safety; (d) any other appropriate provisions' (TEEC, 71). Agreement on these issues formed a fundamental prerequisite for achieving the short-term objective of establishing the customs union. The remaining articles of the Title contain particular rules for removing the unfair practices of member states against carriers of other member states, for relating charges levied at frontier crossings to real costs, and for regulating state financial aid at the Community level. Article 79 sets up an advisory committee of experts, usually drawn from the transport ministries of the member states, to advise the Commission (on technical, financial, legal and related matters) on how to frame the common transport policy.

Principles

Setting up a common transport policy proved to be a difficult and slow process for three main reasons: (a) differences of opinion regarding the interpretation of the treaty; (b) different attitudes towards intervention in transport; and (c) conflicts of interest which divided the member states. A two-stage process of formulating a Community transport policy can be distinguished: deciding what the common policy should be about and attempting to apply the policy.

The main objective of the common transport policy was assumed to be the gradual replacement of national transport policies by the progressive implementation of free competition throughout the Community market subject to consistent rules in line with social and economic needs. Transport in the Community was expected to be competitive and operator-oriented. Therefore, the central aim of the common transport policy was *deregulation*: to set the transport operators free from restrictive controls, to remove discrimination and to coordinate investment, especially on 'trunk routes of Community importance'. Therefore, more emphasis was placed on the 'commercial' than on the 'social' approach to policy orientation.

The transport market was to be organized under the general principles of the market economy: free competition; free choice of means of transport by users; equality of tax treatment, social charges and subsidies for modes of transport and for carriers; financial and commercial independence for the operators; and coordination of transport infrastructures. Public intervention was not excluded ad hoc, but the understanding was that, whenever it would occur, it was expected to be minimal and discreet, having as its main function the supervision of the transport market for attaining operational efficiency. Since the beginning, deregulation has been the cornerstone of Community transport policy. The main objective of the CTP is still 'to allow free competition and only to create Community rules where the proper functioning of the transport market makes them absolutely necessary'.

First setback

In the general spirit of these principles the Commission issued an ambitious Action Programme for the common transport policy which included the following:

1. liberalization of national markets based on commercial criteria as a precondition for integrating the members' transport sectors;
2. organization of the transport market based on competition;
3. harmonization of state intervention in the fields of fiscal, technical and operational measures as a step towards removing discrepancies between transport sectors.

However, these liberalization proposals, which were not confined to interstate transport but extended over the national transport systems within the member countries, had a hostile reception. The implementation of the CTP started with a regulation prohibiting discrimination in transport on grounds of nationality (under TEEC, 75). With some degree of justification, the member states considered this regulation and the Action Programme as an attempt to abolish national sovereignty in transport in the hope of establishing a competitive common market. Therefore, progress was slow. Finally, under pressure from the governments of the member states, which repeatedly displayed their unwillingness to introduce changes in the status quo of their transport sectors, the Action Programme was abandoned as unrealistic. Instead of an all-embracing and general transport programme, a series of ad hoc policy measures was introduced (normalization of railways accounts, Community quotas for road haulage, common rules for granting subsidies, etc.), known collectively as the 'mini-programmes', focusing on one major objective: getting rid of the formalities at borders between member states of the Community.

Second setback

With enlargement of the Community to nine member states in 1973 the need for a new approach became clear. It was realized that a common transport policy could not begin before the intervention policies of the member states were harmonized, starting from the core. Thus the emphasis shifted from an attempt to regulate transport operations and pricing to developing a common infrastructural policy. Hence, the Commission presented a new version of the CTP based on the following basic elements:

1. gradual implementation of the principles of market economy with free competition in the transport market and approximation of the starting conditions between states;
2. coordination of the national taxation of commercial vehicles;
3. the approximation of national provisions governing relations between the railways and the state;
4. harmonization of social legislation, improvement of working conditions, transport safety regulations, etc.;
5. coordination for developing a common transport infrastructure.

The Council took note of the latest proposals but agreed to act on them when the conditions would permit it. But nothing came about for a long time. Therefore, in September 1982, the Parliament decided to bring proceedings against the Council to the Court of Justice for failing to carry out its obligations under the treaty (TEEC, I, 3 and 70). The Court held that the Council had indeed infringed the treaty by 'failing to ensure freedom to provide services in the sphere of international transport and to lay down the conditions under which non-resident carriers may operate transport services in a member state'. However, since the treaty does not define exactly what the CTP should consist of, the Court could only recommend to the Council to work continuously towards drawing up such a policy. Meanwhile, EU enlargement to 12 members introduced new difficulties by widening the heterogeneity of the already diverse transport sector of the Community. Thus the introduction and implementation of common policies were again postponed until another day.

12.3 CTP in the single market

All these setbacks did not mean that nothing happened to advance a common transport policy. By 1985, the Community had adopted some 200 pieces of transport legislation. Moreover, many member states, with aid from the EIB and the ERDF, undertook major national investment projects in transport infrastructure. But all these projects made only a minor contribution towards setting up a Community transport policy. Everything changed with the Single European Act and the prospect of completing a common market, not only in commodities but also in services, and transport services in particular. Because it was so very fragmented, the transport sector was given pride of place in the internal market programme and as a result more progress was made in the five years before 1992 than in the previous thirty.

The Common Transport Policy (CTP) in the internal market aimed at integration of the transport sectors and the introduction of measures to ensure optimization by 'sustainable mobility' based on elimination of distortions of competition between modes and simplification of frontier crossings. The Community transport programme was divided into three main areas:

1. development of the infrastructural network;
2. liberalization of markets;
3. standardization of safety and working regulations.

Infrastructure

Investment in interstate infrastructures is not subject to national cost–benefit assessment, because it does not provide benefits only to the country in which the investment is undertaken. The need for interstate infrastructures thus becomes a supranational issue with benefits and costs ensuing to the Community as a whole. However, Community action is not a substitute for the action of the member states which will continue to be responsible for developing and maintaining the transport infrastructure within their frontiers. Therefore, in this function the Community principally performs as the coordinator, guiding the national authorities in such a way that the national transport networks combine to meet the Community's present and future needs. Infrastructure projects of importance to the Community as a whole receive Community financial support. In particular, the Community provides aid for projects aiming specifically at (a) the elimination of notorious bottlenecks within the Community or straddling its external frontiers; (b) the improvement of major traffic links between member states; and (c) the integration of peripheral areas into the Community network. Infrastructural investment is also financed by the ERDF as one of the means for reducing interregional inequalities.

Market liberalization

The internal market programme has opened up national markets to competition. Therefore, road hauliers can now do business throughout the Community, airlines and shipping companies are free to carry people and goods from one Union country to another, including between destinations within a member state which is not their own (this is known as *cabotage*), and rail transport and inland waterway transport are opening up to competition, though more slowly.

Harmonization is also pursued with the aim of creating a level playing field for everyone. But this has required the removal of different and conflicting national rules and standards. Europe's transport sectors had standards which were often incompatible, in areas such as air-traffic control, the weights and dimensions of heavy goods vehicles, train signalling systems, etc. Harmonization was also needed in social, environmental and safety matters which without common rules contained the risk of causing distorting competition. A transport undertaking which is governed at home by very strict rules on safety, social legislation or pollution standards, pays more for its equipment and workforce than one which is bound by less stringent rules. As a result it may lose out in free competition. For this reason a body of standards and regulations currently operates in the EU to iron out these disparities and enable transport undertakings to compete fairly with one another. This process of harmonization is still incomplete, but in progress.

Environment

Economic growth and increasing use of transport cause negative externalities. In the EU the proportion of total CO_2 emissions generated by transport rose from 19 per cent in 1985 to 26 per cent in 1995, and it is estimated that, if nothing is done to reverse the trend between now and 2010, that figure may well reach 40 per cent. This will be extremely serious, because CO_2 accounts for 80 per cent of the greenhouse gases that may cause global warming (according to the Kyoto protocol, see Chapter 14). Road transport and urban traffic generate half of all CO_2 emissions, with private cars responsible for 50 per cent of the total and road haulage for 35 per cent. Road transport is rising faster than the rate of economic growth and thus the level of all CO_2 emissions from transport is accelerating. Air traffic produces about 12 per cent of transport-related CO_2 emissions, which is not much but it rises by 6 per cent a year. The rise in transport also causes traffic jams, congested airspace, and accidents. The other modes of transport (railways, inland and sea waterways) are less energy-intensive and therefore less important polluters of the environment.

The European Commission has proposed measures which would enable all CO_2 emissions from transport to be halved between 1998 and 2010. The proposal covers four broad fields: measures for possible fuel savings by private cars; progress towards fair and efficient pricing in transport; completion of the internal rail transport market; and measures aimed at better integration of the various modes in intermodal transport systems for both passengers and freight.

Intermodality and sustainable mobility

The completion of the single market and economic growth gave a boost to the rate of growth of transport. But the pattern of this growth has been uneven, favouring some modes of transport over others. The volume of freight moved by road, for example, increased by about 3.5 per cent a year between 1980 and 1996. The growth in air passenger traffic was even more impressive: 7.8 per cent between 1980 and 1990 and 6.1 per cent between 1990 and 1996. Freight movements by rail, on the other hand, have steadily declined: down 1.1 per cent between 1980 and 1990, and down 2.6 per cent between 1990 and 1996, whilst carriage by inland waterway and traffic through the Union's principal sea ports have remained static. The growth in transport is expected to continue after EMU and EU enlargement. Between 1992 and 2010 road transport is expected to rise by 42 per cent, rail transport by 33 per cent and air transport by 74 per cent.

Reviewing all these developments, the European Commission arrived at the conclusion that most problems had arisen because the different modes of transport have each evolved in an isolated, non-complementary fashion, competing with each other and causing transport market *compartmentalization*. The Commission, therefore, proposed to correct these imbalances in the CTP by redirecting it to aim at seven objectives:

1. the establishment of Trans-European Networks, which will enable citizens to travel and businesses to deliver their goods without hindrance or risk from one end of the Union to the other;
2. the integration of transport systems by linking up networks, enabling transport flow to switch from the roads to less-polluting or underused modes: rail, inland waterways or short sea shipping, thus reducing external costs generated by pollution, noise, congestion and accidents;

3. protecting the environment by the strictest standards of pollution control, possible tax measures to influence behaviour, research work and better use of public transport;
4. improving safety by training, the harmonization of construction standards, the introduction of EU-wide technical inspections and better infrastructure;
5. adopting social safeguards in the form of regulated admission to the occupation of transport operator and training requirements;
6. strengthening the internal market by liberalization and harmonization;
7. reinforcing the dimension of the single market by doing away with the EU's internal borders in transport and by replacing bilateral transport agreements between each of the member states and non-EU countries by European agreements and procedures reflecting the reality of the single market.

The proper application of these principles will enable the EU to realize the ultimate objective of its common transport policy: sustainable mobility.

12.4 Recent developments

The successful opening up of the transport market over the last ten years has led to unequal growth in the different modes of transport. Road now represents 44 per cent of the goods transport market compared with 44 per cent for short sea shipping, 8 per cent for rail and 4 per cent for inland waterways. In passenger transport, road represents 79 per cent of the market, air 5 per cent and railways 6 per cent. Although these developments were expected as the result of lifting the EU's internal frontiers, their external costs of congestion and environmental pollution have also increased. In the following, we examine recent developments in the EU's different modes of transport.

Air transport

The air transport industry is growing at rates well above the average growth of the EU economy. Traffic in terms of passengers per kilometre has risen by an average of 7.4 per cent a year since 1980. The number of scheduled carriers in the EU has risen steadily since 1993, from 132 to 164 in 1998. Every year since 1993 more than 20 new carriers have been set up in the EU (although many also leave the market). Employee numbers in civil aviation rose from 435 000 in 1988 to 490 000 in 1996. The number of airline staff rose from 325 000 to 350 000 over the same period. But the boom in air transport has meant that, in addition to increased pollution, the problems of airport overcrowding and overloaded air-traffic control systems are becoming more acute. Europe's airport infrastructure is coming closer to the limits of its capacity and more investment is being undertaken or planned in nearly all the member countries.

Liberalization of air transport in the EU was completed in three successive stages. The first 'package' of measures, adopted in 1987, brought a first relaxation of the rules. In 1990, a second 'package' continued this opening up of the market, with greater flexibility in pricing and the allocation of seat capacity. These measures, applicable in the first instance to passengers who benefited from lower fares, were extended to freight in 1990. The third 'package' in the liberalization of air transport started in 1993. This gradually freed the provision of services within the EU, culminating in 1997 in the liberalization of cabotage. The measures that brought market liberalization included:

- a *Community licence* to all EU carriers for unrestricted access to all domestic markets;
- a *level playing field* for competition;
- the *allocation of slots* to enable new carriers to enter the liberalized market, despite the congestion problems;
- *ground handling* services to be gradually opened up to competition and to achieve full liberalization by December 2003;
- competition in *computerized reservation systems* which handle 70 per cent of all bookings, and are owned by the major airlines: a regulation (1989, amended 1999) prohibits these airlines from giving themselves an exclusive advantage;
- *airport charges* to be regulated so that the deterrent effect they might have on new operators will be reduced;
- strict rules on *state aid* to airlines to ensure that it is given only for purposes of restructuring without distorting market competition: under these rules, the EU has authorized state aid to seven airlines since 1987 (Sabena, Iberia, Aer Lingus, TAP, Air France, Olympic Airways and Alitalia);
- the adoption by the Commission on 27 September 2000 of a proposal for a European Parliament and Council regulation, which would put in place a Community system of *air safety* and environmental regulation and would set up an aviation safety agency;
- a policy of integration of *environmental concerns* into sectoral policies, called for by the Treaty of Amsterdam.

The growth of the aviation industry was halted, however, in the autumn of 2001 by terrorist attacks in New York which plunged the air industry into a crisis, while the world economy descended into recession. Many airlines, which were already under severe pressure from falling demand and ill-judged investment, announced massive job cuts and reduced flight schedules, while some major ones filed for bankruptcy (such as Sabena). Although state aid has been authorized for some of them, it has become clear that the European air transport industry contains far too many small and medium-sized firms which cannot reach optimum capacity size to benefit from economies of scale. It seems possible, therefore, that a new reconstruction and consolidation of the aviation industry will soon come about with many bigger European airlines.

Maritime transport

By virtue of the Community's geography and importance as the world's biggest trading area, merchant shipping and maritime policy are key elements of the CTP. In 1999, 41 per cent of the EU's external trade in value terms (imports and exports) was conducted by sea, 21 per cent by road, 25 per cent by air, 2 per cent by rail, 0.5 per cent by waterways, and 11.5 per cent by other means (pipeline, etc.). But 71 per cent of the total weight of external trade is carried by sea. Maritime companies controlled by EU nationals command 35 per cent of the world fleet, and some 40 per cent of EU trade is carried on vessels owned or controlled by EU interests. The maritime transport sector – including shipbuilding, ports and related industries and services – employs around 2.5 million people in the EU.

As in other areas of transport, the principle governing EU maritime policy is that of free competition, combined with safety and environmental protection. The process of liberalization and opening up national markets to competition within the EU is almost complete. With the exception of the southern member states, which have been allowed a gradual opening of their markets until 2004, maritime cabotage has been liberalized since 1999. There is thus virtually total freedom to provide services within the EU. However, a side effect of the process of liberalization has been that a large part of the EU fleet has registered under 'flags of convenience', i.e. in countries which charge lower taxation and care less about social legislation and safety or environmental standards. Hence by 1998, just 11 per cent of the world's shipping sailed under a member state flag, compared with 32 per cent in 1970, at the cost of public revenue and job losses for EU nationals. The EU has attempted to remedy this situation by a new strategy consisting of:

■ positive measures to help operators facing international competition, such as aid to preserve EU employment;
■ promotion of sea shipping as an environmentally friendlier alternative to road transport;

- improving the qualifications of crews by developing and assisting suitable training programmes;
- improving safety;
- supporting research and technological development.

Inland waterways make up another long-standing but less important mode of transport in Europe, handling about 12 per cent by weight of the external trade of the Community at comparatively low infrastructure cost. The CTP has aimed at the harmonization of national and international measures, improvement in competitive conditions and long-term balance of supply and demand. Cabotage became possible from 1 January 1993.

Railways

Rail transport in Europe has experienced a worrying decline for nearly 30 years, especially in the area of freight. In 1970 the railways carried 32 per cent of all freight in the 15 countries of the present EU. By 1996 the figure was just 14 per cent. Over the same period, the proportion of freight going by road rose from 49 per cent to 73.7 per cent. Railway passenger traffic also declined from 10 per cent in 1970, to 6 per cent in 1999.

The main reason for this state of affairs is that railway transport is less competitive and less trustworthy than road haulage. Road, unlike rail, provides a door-to-door service. Since railways are a safe and environmentally clean mode of transport, revitalizing them is a top priority of the EU's Common Transport Policy.

In recent years many EU countries have privatized the previously public railway companies, in some cases resulting in the fragmentation of the railway system and diseconomies of scale. An objective of the CTP is the increase of railways' efficiency and competitiveness within the EU's integrated transport system, but privatization is not (Article 222). In 1996 the Commission published a White Paper advocating a greater role for market forces, which would encourage operators to cut their costs, improve the quality of service and innovate. It also suggested the creation of rail-freight freeways across Europe prompting the railways to concentrate more on competitiveness and sound financial management. This required the separation of railways' management from the state for achieving greater transparency in the use of public funds. Most of the member states have followed these general principles by setting up in recent years bodies which manage the railway infrastructure but are separate from the railways. An EU directive requires member states to appoint a body to oversee the fair and non-discriminatory allocation of the railway infrastructure which may only be used by railway undertakings which hold an approved operating licence. The directive does not, however, cover railway undertakings whose activity is confined to urban, suburban and regional transport or the road vehicle shuttle service through the Channel Tunnel.

The establishment of international freight freeways began on 1 January 1998. The main idea behind this innovation is to improve the quality of rail freight services by eliminating some of the obstacles which deter railway undertakings from bidding for international services. There are four freeways in service at present:

- North–South, linking ports in northern Europe with those of the south;
- Scanways, linking Denmark, Finland, Norway and Sweden;
- Belifret, linking Belgium, Luxembourg, France, Italy and Spain;
- UK-Sopron, which is still under discussion, which would provide an east–west route from the UK to Hungary, with onward connections to other central and eastern European countries.

A common condition for all freeways is that they are available for cabotage, allowing a consignment to be loaded and delivered at any point along the route, whatever the country concerned, with freight terminals made available to railway, road and inland waterway operators on terms which are fair and non-discriminatory. However, the freeways are not yet an altogether unqualified success due to their high charges (mostly because of the level of fees charged for using the infrastructure) relative to those of other modes of transport.

Three new directives, known as the 'Rail Infrastructure Package', were adopted by the Council in 2001, and must be implemented by the member states by March 2003. These directives aim at the development of a Trans-European Rail Freight Network (TERFN), which would start with a length of approximately 50 000 km, but by 2008 would be extended to the entire European rail network. In practical terms, this means that any licensed railway operator can run freight services across member states over the entire rail network in Europe.

Road transport

The volume of road freight haulage grew by 3.5 per cent a year between 1980 and 1996, and by 7 per cent in the case of cross-border freight. The roads now take about 75 per cent of freight traffic within the EU, compared with less than 50 per cent in 1970. As regards passenger road transport, the key mode is the private car and the spectacular growth in car use. The number of cars has tripled in the last 30 years, at an increase of 3 million cars each year. In 1975 there were 232 cars per 1000 people; now there are 444.

As of 1 January 1993 any road operator wishing to carry goods or passengers between at least two member states must hold a Community

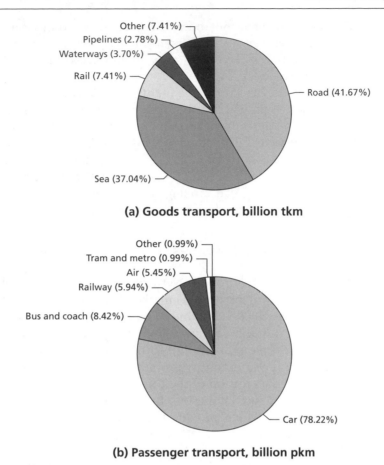

(a) Goods transport, billion tkm

(b) Passenger transport, billion pkm

Figure 12.1 **Goods and passenger transport shares in the EU, 1999**

driving licence issued by the member state in which he or she resides. This document gives unlimited access to the whole of the single market. To obtain it a number of conditions set by the member states themselves *plus* one which is binding on all 15 states must be met: the issuing country must enforce the requirements of the EU directive on admission to the occupation of a road haulage operator or a road passenger transport operator, which imposes rigorous criteria as regards the good reputation, professional competence and financial standing of road transport firms.

To stop competition from intensifying at the expense of safety, the EU has introduced legislation on the technical inspection of vehicles, driver qualifications and mandatory rest periods, and the carriage of dangerous goods. Since 1985, all heavy goods vehicles in the EU have been fitted with a tachograph – a monitoring device which records the vehicle's activity and enables the authorities to check that statutory driving times have not been exceeded. The Community law, in force since January 1994, also stipulates that speed limiters must be fitted to heavy goods vehicles set to a maximum speed of 90 kph (lorries) and 105 kph (coaches).

In 1997 the EU launched a highly ambitious campaign for road safety. In addition to annual checks, random roadside inspections and pollutant emissions analyses have been mandatory since 1998. Private cars must also be inspected at least every two years. To promote environmentally friendlier road transport, the Community has introduced stricter emission standards and a road tax system which favours 'clean' vehicles. Since 1 July 1998, road cabotage in the movement of freight throughout the single market has become fully liberalized.

Trans-European Networks in Transport (TENs-Transport)

The idea of Trans-European Networks emerged in the 1980s in conjunction with the proposed single market. It made little sense to talk of a big market, with freedom of movement within it for goods, people and services, unless the various regions and national networks making up that market were properly linked by a modern and efficient infrastructure. Hence the Community promoted the development of TENs as a key element for the creation of the internal market and the reinforcement of economic and social cohesion. In this, the Community had the backing of the treaties which provide the legal basis for the TENs (TEEC, XII, 154–6), which are set to promote 'the interconnection and interoperability of national networks as well as access to such networks'. The construction of TENs (in transport, energy and telecommunications) was also an important element in the 1993 strategy on growth and employment.

The Community guidelines for the development of the Trans-European Transport Network (1996) set out the objectives and priorities of the TENs-Transport. All links – roads, railways, airports – meeting these objectives and priorities, whether already in place or yet to be built, form part of the TEN and as such are deemed to be 'of common interest'. Each section of a route comprising the TEN automatically qualifies for financial aid from the EU, in accordance with specified rules. Qualifying projects may entail the building of a new section or upgrading an existing network of road or railway, building combined rail/road transport terminals, airports, etc. In principle, the EU will fund not more than 50 per cent of the cost of preliminary studies (feasibility studies), and 10 per cent of the cost of the work. The balance must be met out of public or private sector funds. Each project must:

- offer guaranteed financial viability;
- be judged on its merits;

Box 12.1 ■ Trans-European Networks

The EU's hotly contested plans for liberalising rail freight were finally agreed with the European Parliament late on Wednesday, after a process of conciliation in which the Commission brokered a compromise between the Parliament and the EU Council of Ministers . . . [But] opening up the rail sector faced considerable difficulties. The infrastructure in many countries is completely different, with signalling varying across the EU, four different axle widths, four train heights and five electrical systems. Trains are often held up for as much as an hour at borders because of different technical specifications . . . The plans, which will affect 90 per cent of EU cross-border rail freight, involve separating the infrastructure from the operating companies. The latter will then be able to apply for licences to carry cross-border freight as long as they also obtain a safety certificate from each country through which their services pass . . . The freight plan aims to reinvigorate the sector where the average speed of trains has fallen to 16 km an hour. The decline in rail's share of the freight market has dropped from 32 per cent in 1970 to just 13 per cent . . . Businesses in the member states have urged a more open rail network as an important part of improving the EU's competitiveness.

The plan, which faced strong opposition in many countries, particularly France, will come into effect in 2003 and will initially cover the trans-European network of main cross-border routes. In 2008 the liberalisation will apply to the whole rail network. It will provide guaranteed access for companies that want to use the network in any country . . . Proposals to open up the passenger sector are likely to follow a similar pattern, but a Commission spokesman said: 'It is a bit more complicated, including the need to convince member states there is a real need for it.'

The Financial Times, 24 November 2000

- be consistent with the Union's other policies, notably as regards competition, the rules on the award of public contracts, and the environment. Therefore, an environmental impact assessment must have been made for each project.

A large number of projects of common interest have already benefited from financial support from the Community budget through the TEN budget line as well as the Structural Funds and the Cohesion Fund, the latter for TENs in the 'cohesion countries' only (E, GR, P, IRL). The European Investment Bank (EIB) has also greatly contributed to the financing of these projects through loans. The Community decided from the beginning to allocate at least 55 per cent of funds for TENs-Transport to railway projects and not more than 25 per cent to roads. Almost two-thirds of railway investment has gone to high-speed routes, new and upgraded. More than 54 per cent of projects on the road network involved work to improve existing roads rather than build new ones.

12.5 Conclusions

After many false starts, the liberalization and market integration of the transport sector of the Community is taking off. The reason for this delay is to be found in the complexity of the sector but also in the habitual intransigence of member states towards establishing a common policy which would open their transport sectors to competition by firms of other member countries, and thus restrain the power of national authorities to interfere in their transport sectors. The search for a common transport policy reached a decisive point with the completion of the single market. Abolishing frontier controls meant market integration which required the creation of a transport sector able to serve this large market. Against this background the Community decided to adopt an overall approach to transport, combining improvements to infrastructure and means of transport and their rational use, enhancing the safety of users, and achieving more equitable working conditions and better environment protection. To facilitate the move towards integration of the market for transport, the Community has undertaken to support the development of Trans-European Networks which will establish links across member states' transport networks.

Questions

1. (a) Why do countries regulate their transport sectors?
   (b) What are the reasons for harmonizing transport policies and finally integrating the market for transport services in an economic union?
   (c) Has the EU achieved transport policy harmonization?

2. (a) Discuss the following argument: 'The only general requirement for a common market in transport is the freedom of access to the transport infrastructure at non-discriminatory terms for each potential supplier of transport services.'
   (b) Who will pay for the provision of a transport infrastructure in this case, and how?

Further reading

The Commission's White Paper on transport (2001b) is a good source of information on recent and current issues.

Web guide

Information on transport is available at <u>www.europa.eu.int/en/comm/</u> <u>transport</u> and statistics are available at <u>www.europa.eu.int/en/comm/</u> <u>energy_transport/etif/</u>

Industrial policy

13

Industrial policy is largely a national responsibility of the member states. The Community's role is to ensure that the single market operates in accordance with the rules of an open and competitive system. The Community's industrial strategy consists of policies aimed at improving the business environment and the legal framework necessary for speeding up the structural adjustment and the competitiveness of European industry under free international trade conditions.

13.1 Introduction

Industrial policy

In almost every country industry is a high-priority sector of the economy for production, employment and growth, among other reasons, because of the positive externalities which industry is supposed to exercise on other sectors of the economy, and thus on technological progress and economic growth. Preference for industry invariably implies some degree of government industrial policy, direct or indirect.

The focus of arguments for government involvement in industrial policy is, first, the issue of market failure and, second, the competition between different sectors within a country and between similar sectors between countries. Economic analysis distinguishes between market failures which are caused by (i) externalities in production or consumption, (ii) market power by producers or consumers, and (iii) asymmetric information between buyers and sellers. These distortions usually cause a divergence between private and social costs or benefits resulting in inefficiencies and misallocation of resources. Therefore, there is an a priori case for intervention.

In general, there are two types of government industrial policy: (a) *regulatory*, in which the state acts to remove market imperfections; and (b) *developmental*, in which the state intervenes to change the market outcome. Since governments in different countries have differing preferences for industry over other sectors, or for particular types of industry (capital-intensive, advanced technology, etc.), and differing views as to market failures, which markets they ought to regulate and so on, industrial policies across countries are multifarious and heterogeneous. By their implications for different sections of a country's population, regions and pressure groups (employers and employees, producers and consumers, government and voters, etc.), industrial policies always have both economic and political dimensions. Moreover, industrial policy is intermingled with trade policy. The issues of market power, rate of return, innovation and technological change are the subject of both domestic industrial policy and foreign trade policy. Similarly, aid to industry, protection from foreign competition, and taxes and subsidies on production are policies that affect both industry and trade.

For strategic policy

The advocates of activist government policy argue that, besides the issue of market failures and the general preference for industry, market forces provide inadequate incentives to invest in sectors essential for economic growth, such as high-risk new-technology industries. High-tech industries, which are often characterized by economies of scale and imperfect competition, are engaged in activities which require a large expenditure on research and development (R&D) for pioneering and improving technology. The problem is that while firms in these industries can appropriate some of the benefits of their innovations, they cannot do so fully. In other words, these firms generate external economies by benefiting parties external to the firm, but they are not adequately rewarded for this service. The proponents of this line of argument claim therefore that if the state does not assist these firms to invest and innovate in high technology, the country may end up with the wrong industrial mix. Hence the role of active industrial policy is to identify and promote the growth of those industries that generate substantial spillover benefits to other industries or individuals. It is suggested, therefore, that the equalization of social and private costs and benefits requires the subsidization and protection from foreign competition of those sectors which are *strategic* for the future progress and growth of the country.

Against strategic policy

The problem with the strategic industrial and trade policy is that it does not only justify interventionism but it also involves international confrontation by countries following similar policies. Of greater danger is the possibility that on the pretext of strategic trade policy some countries might attempt to revive 'old-fashioned protectionist policies' (Krugman, 1994). Accordingly, in contrast to the proponents of the strategic arguments for protection, the advocates of no intervention hold that governments only need to remove all impediments to the smooth working of markets and that any attempt to designate as strategic particular sectors of the economy is misguided and unwarranted. Under conditions of perfect competition between firms within and between countries, absence of externalities and free entry and exit in industry, the market would allocate resources optimally by equalizing factor returns across sectors and by specialization of production and trade between countries in accordance with comparative advantage.

Transnational power

Yet another school of thought maintains that developmental industrial policy in the form of 'coherent national economic planning' and 'strategic decision making in industry' (Cowling, 1990) are necessary for reasons pertaining to three central tendencies in modern market economies:

- the power of large transnational corporations to influence to their advantage the economic policy of any country by switching their investment and production, or threatening to do so, to another country;
- the narrow economic horizon of the market and, in particular, of the financial institutions which adopt a short-term perspective about investment, thus retarding industrial development and deterring research and innovation;
- the biased allocation of industrial production and, in general, economic and cultural activity in favour of the developed centre and against the regions (i.e. centripetalism).

Compromise policy

In reality, competition within and between countries is not always perfect, nor are private returns to factors of production always equal to social returns. Therefore, in principle there is scope for government policy designed to improve industrial performance in the domestic market. Moreover, if the industries concerned generate substantial positive externalities or display increasing returns to scale, an industrial-cum-trade policy in their support may bring additional benefits to the country by shifting the terms of international competition to domestic firms' advantage. The gains to one country are clearly achieved at the expense of other countries. In general, if assistance to certain industries is to be provided, it should be general and non-discriminatory, aimed at market improvement and taking forms other than protection by tariffs or quotas which discriminate between home and foreign sales. However, the gains from intervention are limited by uncertainty about the appropriate policies, by entry that dissipates gains, and by the general equilibrium effect that when one sector is promoted, resources are diverted to it from other sectors. In general, industrial policy describes the attempt by governments to encourage resources to move into particular sectors that the government designates as important for future economic growth. While in less-developed economies this may bring new resources into production, in developed countries it transfers resources from one activity to another in the same or different regions. Therefore, in developed countries industrial policy promotes one activity at the expense of others.

13.2 EU industry

Perspective

With manufacturing output of €4000 billion in 1999, the European Union is the world's leading industrial producer. Its share in the triad EU–Japan–USA was 40 per cent against Japan's 23 per cent and the USA's 37 per cent. But Europe does less well in the value added by the sector: the USA is the leader of the triad with a 47 per cent share. The four largest industrial member countries (D, F, I, UK) accounted for more than 73 per cent of the total EU industrial production during 1994–7, with Germany the clear leader with about a 30 per cent share in the total (Figure 13.1). In 1999, the three largest industries in the EU, based on their shares of total value added, were:

- electrical and optical equipment (14 per cent)
- transport equipment (12 per cent)
- basic metal products (12 per cent).

Between them, these three industries also accounted for 36 per cent of the total employment in EU industry (Figure 13.2).

Total EU manufacturing employed 23.3 million persons in 1999, 2.5 million fewer than in 1985. But the structures of manufacturing

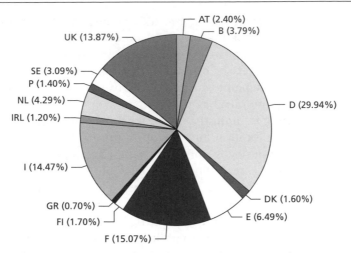

Figure 13.1 **EU manufacturing: member states' shares, 1994–7**

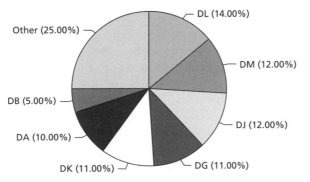

Figure 13.2a **Share of EU industries in value added, %, 1999**

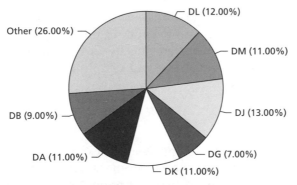

DL = electrical and optical equipment, DM = transport equipment,
DJ = basic metals and products, DG = chemicals, DK = machinery equipment,
DA = food and beverages, DB = textiles and leather

Figure 13.2b **Share of EU industries in employment, %, 1999**

employment and production differ considerably between EU countries. Where sectors of the industry are concerned, the disparities between different countries are even greater. These divergences are a consequence of unequal levels of economic development, degrees of specialization, and other geographic, historical and economic factors. Market integration in the Community has provided new opportunities and challenges for restructuring EU industry, taking advantage of the large market, economies of scale, reallocation and the opportunities for specialization. However, while EU industry is undertaking rapid changes, it also faces increasing international competition from old competitors and newly industrializing countries (NICs), and from recent trends towards globalization of the world economy. As a way forward, merger activity has increased on an international scale and many firms have lost their European identity by joining transnational corporations, exploiting new technologies and production processes, and competing in the world market.

Before the EU

We remarked earlier that countries in general intervene in their industrial sectors for a variety of social, economic and political reasons. In the countries making up the EU, different attitudes towards the free market led in the past to different forms and degrees of government intervention, with the implication that the industrial policies at the national level of the member states had been diverse. Many decentralized market economies, such as those of EU countries, had followed mixed industrial policies, actively promoting structural change in some sectors and simultaneously submitting other sectors to free-market forces. In the past, many countries protected their industries from foreign competition and also made heavy use of industrial subsidies. The latter took a variety of forms, such as tax and interest rate preferences, financial assistance for investment, research and development (R&D) grants, and labour employment subsidies at the national and regional levels. In countries in which the government participated directly in industrial production through public enterprises, assistance had occasionally been provided to cover operating deficits.

Joining the EU

Membership in a common market implies acceptance of the consequences of reallocation of production. This means that many industries which in the past were cushioned by interventionist policies will be exposed to increasing competition in the enlarged market, and in the process some of them will perish. Under these circumstances it is likely that governments may attempt to protect threatened industries and jobs and to enlarge their country's share of high-return industries. Therefore, integration may itself induce a tendency for more intervention by national industrial policy which operates against integration and could even lead to trade war between member states. This danger calls for coordination and harmonization of industrial policy during the process of market integration.

In addition to all these reasons, in the EU a common industrial policy is also needed if Community industry is to take advantage of the opportunities for rationalization, specialization and growth offered by the enlarged market. Improvements in the allocation of resources and reorganization of industry on an EU-wide scale are expected to raise economic welfare by increasing the rate of growth of production, employment and income. This could take place at the same time as certain member states suffer adverse industrial shifts through market liberalization and competition.[1]

Under free-market and competition-oriented principles there is no case for intervention in industry by a common industrial policy. Nevertheless, the Community has to create the legal environment in which competitive industry will operate. Consequently, the Treaty of Rome entrusted the Commission with powers, independently of the Council of Ministers (but under the supervision of the Court of Justice), to dismantle restrictive practices by companies or governments which inhibit free trade between the member states and act against the interest of the consumers. While these issues were under discussion in the 1970s, two events took place that radically changed the context and orientation of industrial policy:

- two dramatic increases in the price of oil which raised the rate of inflation;
- increased competition from newly industrializing countries (NICs).

Most of the developed and the less-developed economies found themselves unprepared for these events and unable to adapt promptly to the changing economic conditions. Rigidities in the allocation of resources and the falling volume of demand and production led to increasing unemployment. As in some countries the old and uneconomic industries became increasingly uncompetitive, a strong tendency developed towards contraction of the manufacturing sector and a decrease in output and employment: that is, *deindustrialization*.

Against a background of halting economic growth, increasing international competition and rapid changes forced by technological progress,

---

[1] The possibility of significant reallocation of industrial production adds another reason for the necessity for adjustment assistance by redistribution among the member states through the EU budget.

many countries altered their approach towards industrial policy by becoming more interventionist and by resorting to increasing protectionism, mostly by non-tariff barriers to international trade. A marked change in favour of an interventionist industrial policy was also observed among members of the Community.

In the following sections we examine how the Community attempted to develop a common industrial base and to formulate a coherent common industrial policy, while still aiming at enlargement, liberalization and integration of the internal market.

13.3 For a common industrial policy

First attempts

The economic conditions of the 1950s and 1960s favoured the non-interventionist approach to industrial policy. Therefore it is not surprising that in the Treaty of Rome there is no specific reference to a common industrial policy. The treaty dealt only with the rules of competition and certain aspects of implicit industrial policy, such as the freedom of capital and labour movements, the right of establishment and the creation of a single market. This was not the case with the two other Communities, the European Coal and Steel Community (ECSC) and Euratom (EAEC), which by the nature of their interests and objectives were empowered to use interventionist policies. The ECSC aimed at a common strategy for the modernization of the coal and steel industry, which suffered from overmanning, low productivity, excess supply and uncompetitiveness in the world market. Euratom's objectives were to promote atomic energy and to facilitate nuclear research in the member states.

Implicitly, industrial policy within the Community-wide market included more than implementation and supervision of the rules of competition. The existing diverse national industrial policies, which ensued from different ideologies and power structures between the government, labour unions and employers in each member state, had to be harmonized so that they would eventually converge to form the common industrial policy of a single market. Direct and indirect subsidies to industry had to be coordinated for some sectors and eliminated from others. Similarly, the Community had to ensure that the existing structure of industry was open to adaptation and change so that it could take advantage of the opportunities presented by the enlarged market to achieve maximum economies of scale. Research and development at the scale of the common market also had to be centrally coordinated and facilitated in order to provide the necessary momentum for industrial development and adaptation. The first steps towards performing these tasks were taken after the merger of the three Communities in 1967 and the establishment of a Directorate-General for Industrial Affairs to coordinate the work of the Commission in the areas of the internal market, regional policy, industrial policy, competition, transport and energy.

The first major task of the Commission was to draw up a profile of the Community's industrial structure and to put forward proposals for setting up a Community industrial policy. However, with different members advocating different economic approaches and pursuing different national industrial policies, there was no consensus about what the objectives of the common industrial policy should include. In 1972 the Paris summit committed the forthcoming enlarged EU-9 Community to adopting a programme of action setting up 'a single industrial base for the Community as a whole' to enable it to compete effectively with the fast-growing industries of the USA and Japan. The Commission followed by submitting a programme for the harmonization of national regulations, company law and capital markets for the benefit of EU industry which 'is, and will continue to be, based largely on free enterprise, on agreements freely concluded between workers' and employers' organizations, and on programmes carried out by regional public authorities'. Although the Council adopted this programme, its practical implications were minimal, once again because of the lack of a consensus among the Community partners regarding the necessity and the content of a common industrial policy.

But while the Community remained undecided, the economic recession, which began after the increase in oil prices, led to massive unemployment and falling output. At the same time, with increasing low-cost export supplies from Japan and the NICs, the Community was experiencing loss of competitiveness in both internal and world markets. Lacking a common policy, the member states reacted individually to these events by resorting to inward-looking economic policies which gave priority to the short-term protection of industries, jobs and the standards of living within their own frontiers. These short-sighted policies intensified the fragmentation of the Community market and thus integration reached a stalemate and convergence suffered a setback. This situation compelled a reappraisal of both the objectives and the policies which would be required for a new drive towards European unity. The ensuing discussions showed clearly that for a solution to these problems three interdependent objectives must be pursued simultaneously: unification of the internal market, common industrial policy and improved competitiveness in international markets. Next the Community moved forward to complete the internal market.

The European Company Statute (ECS)

The Single European Act provided for research and technological development to strengthen the competitive position of the Community at international level. It also inaugurated an action programme for small and medium-sized enterprises[2] (SMEs) to simplify administrative, financial and legal constraints and to encourage cooperation and partnership between firms from different regions of the Community. Later on, the 1987 European summit in Brussels also declared that the Community's 'common economic area' called for 'swift progress with regard to the company law adjustments required for the creation of a European company'.

Proposals for a European Company Statute (ECS) in the form of a European public limited liability company were first submitted and rejected in 1970. The objective of the ECS was to provide the legal framework for the formation of a type of company (a '*European Company*' or '*Societas Europaea, SE*') which could operate on a Europe-wide basis and be governed by a single Community law directly applicable in all member states. The ECS would therefore offer companies established in more than one member state a means of restructuring their business in a way which best reflected the commercial realities of the integrated market, and of reducing their operating costs by avoiding the need for a complex network of subsidiaries governed by different national company laws. Later on, the ECS was also identified as the most appropriate legal instrument for attracting private capital for the establishment of large Trans-European Networks (TENs). The ECS proposal has, however, been blocked in the Council for many years, largely as a result of differences of opinion among member states over the issue of worker involvement (see Chapter 11). Instead of the ECS, EU firms have had at their disposal since 1989 a new legal tool for transnational cooperation enabling them to collaborate in joint activities, such as research and development, purchases, production and sales. This is provided by the European Economic Interest Grouping (EEIG) status which is governed by Community law and helps firms across borders to become more competitive by spreading risks or using joint services with partners in other member states. A directive requiring transnational companies to inform and consult their workforce on cross-border business decisions was adopted in 1994.

With the approach of 1992, the market reacted swiftly. Many industrial and financial corporations entered into transnational alliances or joint ventures within the EU to pursue a clear post-1992 strategy. Cross-border mergers and acquisitions, which started to reach record levels in

---

[2] SMEs are independent businesses with fewer than 250 employees. They make up 90 per cent of the Community industry.

1989, along with many joint ventures, were spurred by the notion that market power and profitability requires a large share in the single market. At the same time, mergers provide instant access to foreign suppliers, factories, sales and marketing networks and often cheaper labour. Likewise, many medium and small-scale companies realized that the only way to survive the competition was to team up with larger companies. At last, the prospect of the single market started to change the shape and structure of European industry and, in turn, to influence the countries' attitude towards the need for a Community industrial policy.

13.4 New directions

Treaty provisions

The situation changed radically with the TEU (1992) which for the first time gave the EU explicit competence in industrial policy. The Community's industrial policy does not replace that of the member states which 'shall consult each other in liaison with the Commission and, where necessary, shall coordinate action' (TEEC, 157). But 'strengthening of the competitiveness of Community industry' and 'promotion of research and technological development' are among the 'activities' which the Community will undertake in the course of pursuing its objectives (TEEC, I, 2–3). The Commission may take initiatives to promote the competitiveness of European countries whenever it is threatened. The common industrial policy will be market-oriented and pro-competition and

> shall be aimed at:
>
> - speeding up the adjustment of industry to structural changes;
> - encouraging an environment favourable to initiative and development of undertakings throughout the Community, particularly small and medium sized undertakings;
> - encouraging an environment favourable to cooperation between undertakings;
> - fostering better exploitation of the industrial potential of policies of innovation, research and technological development. (TEEC, 157)

The Commission's task is to contribute to the achievement of these objectives through the policies and activities it pursues under other provisions of the treaty. The Council, acting *unanimously* on a proposal from the Commission, could decide on specific measures to support the action of the member states.

But the meddling of the Community in industrial affairs was criticized by the non-interventionists who argued that by legitimizing 'industrial policy' the Community failed to live up to its fundamental resolution in favour of an economic constitution geared to free markets and undistorted competition. It is clear, however, that the treaty empowered the Commission as *coordinator* rather than as *regulator*, and primarily set the legal and administrative framework within which the industry, research and technology would operate more efficiently. Otherwise, the Community industrial policy continued to consist of 'guidance and advice, pilot projects and limited funding'. Thus the more recent initiatives include benchmarking, seminars, conferences, peer reviews, research and analysis that help provide a clear picture of the business environment and the existing problems. Enterprise policy is financed by the Innovation Programme. Other sources of finance, more directly targeted to enterprises, include the Structural Funds and the European Investment Bank (EIB), which supports projects and provides loans through financial intermediaries working at national, regional and local level. The schemes funded include training programmes, promoting access to new markets, improving quality, protecting the environment, fostering cooperation, etc.

In conjunction with the drive towards lowering unemployment, the Community adopted measures of financial assistance for job-creating initiatives, in particular small and medium-sized enterprises (SMEs). This assistance is administered by the European Investment Fund (EIF) and consists of three complementary facilities: a 'risk capital window' for the start-up phase; a system of guarantees based on risk-sharing arrangements to increase the availability and volume of loans; and a system of financial contributions for the setting up of new transnational joint ventures.

Enterprise Europe

At the beginning of 2000, the Community changed the structure and the institutions of its industrial policy by replacing the Directorate-General (DG) for Industry and SMEs and the DG for Information Society by a new DG for Enterprise Policy which set its programme for 2000–5 according to the following sections:

■ Action plans to promote entrepreneurship, competitiveness, and enterprise policy in a knowledge-based economy. The aim of these initiatives is to make the EU 'the most competitive and dynamic knowledge-based economy in the world, capable of sustainable economic growth with more and better jobs and greater social cohesion' (Lisbon European Council, 2000).
■ Multi-annual programmes for enterprises, in particular SMEs. In December 2000, the Council adopted the new programme over several years which provides for action in more than 30 countries in the EU,

the European Economic Area and the applicant countries for accession to the EU.

- An Action Plan for Innovation which aims at three main objectives: (i) to promote an innovation culture, both in society and in the economy; (ii) to establish a good business environment in terms of legal, regulatory and financial provisions to promote innovation; (iii) to promote more effective links between research, innovation and business.
- Improved industrial competitiveness of European industry.
- Technical harmonization.
- Strategy for integrating the environment into industrial policy by implementing environmental management and audit systems, new strategies and objectives, and measures aimed at sustainable development.

The Commission also declared its intention of developing a programme based on 'benchmarking'. This involves the regular comparison of industrial activities in the Community with best practices in other companies and sectors within the EU or worldwide. Some of the areas targeted for benchmarking are price, quality of service, and innovation in information technology, transport, telecommunications and financial services.

After the success of the European Strategic Programme for Research and Development in Information Technology (ESPRIT, introduced in 1983), which brought together firms and research centres across Europe, the EU formally set as one of its objectives the strengthening of the scientific and technological bases of Community industry, encouraging it to become more collaborative and more competitive at international level (TEEC, 163–73). The Community supports businesses, research centres and universities in their research and technological development activities, especially by opening up national public contracts, defining common standards and removing the legal and fiscal barriers. It also supports their efforts to cooperate with one another and takes the initiative to coordinate R&D activities between the Community and member states, aiming to help business to exploit the potential of the internal market to the full.

13.5 Problem industries

In addition to across-the-board measures concerning industry in general, the members of the Community have been taking specific measures to cope with particular problem industries. Further to action taken at the national level and approved by the Commission, the Community operated in the past an ad hoc industrial policy by intervening selectively in industrial sectors to reduce excess capacity, coordinate national subsidies or control competing imports. For the modernization and restructuring of industry with specific regional or social objectives, Community financial assistance has been provided by the ERDF and the ESF. The ECSC provides loans, financed by borrowing, exclusively to coal and steel industries. However, the Commission has control over aids granted to industries by member states (TEEC, 87–9). The EIB also makes available loans to small and medium-sized enterprises (SMEs) specifically for investment projects which, through the dissemination of new technology and innovation, may advance the competitiveness of Community industry.

For certain key industries, the 'crisis sectors', which for a long time have been under threat from international competition or are facing over-capacity problems or are in need of modernization, the Community has become directly involved in the coordination of the policies of the member states. The more important of these industries are now discussed.

Steel

The steel industry was once one of the most important manufacturing industries of the Community. But since 1974 it has been contracting in both output and employment. Since the steel industry is traditionally concentrated in a few areas, the effects of its decline have created devastating regional problems.

The problems of the steel industry are not new: concern about steel and coal was the reason for establishing the European Coal and Steel Community (ECSC) in 1951. But while in the 1950s and 1960s the problem of the steel industry was how to respond quickly to rapidly expanding demand, since the 1970s it has been how to contract under the pressure of declining demand and rising foreign competition. The difficulties of the industry stem from the sudden change in demand after a long period of growth (6.6 per cent per year during 1960–74) to a rapid collapse. The reasons for this change were, first, the generalized economic slowdown after the first oil price shock in 1974; second, the technological change in both prcoduction and utilization techniques and the increased competition from plastics and other substitutes; and, third, the emergence of energetic competition from non-traditional producers, such as Japan, China, Brazil, Russia and other newly industrializing countries (NICs).

As 75 per cent of steel consumption is accounted for by construction/ civil engineering and automobiles, the industry is highly dependent on the economic situation in these two sectors. Economic growth resulted in a steady expansion of demand in the 1960s, which induced major capacity-increasing investment programmes. This activity continued even after the first economic crisis of 1974, under the assumption that the difficulties of the industry were cyclical and temporary. High fixed costs and entry and exit barriers combined to bring about chronic market failure – the inability of the sector to make timely adaptations to changes in demand and competition. Thus, when the recession started to bite, it led the European steel industry to massive underutilization of capacity (62 per cent in 1980), substantial staff reductions (by 50 per cent between 1974 and 1986) and a slump in prices. Accumulating financial losses had adverse effects on new investment for modernization. Thus, the industry became dated, with low productivity, and unable to compete effectively with technologically advanced new foreign producers. Consequently, between 1974 and 1976 steel imports to the Community rose by 133 per cent, while exports fell by 32 per cent. Meanwhile, the extra production capacity, which was laid down before the crisis, came into line causing an upsurge in the competition for orders among the EU producers, with further downward pressure on prices which fell on average by 50 per cent within two years.

At the recommendation of several study groups, the Community implemented a series of plans (e.g. the Simonet Plan and the Davignon Plan) aimed at the reconstruction of the steel industry by modernization at the expense of reduction in capacity and employment. Although these measures had a degree of success, the second massive rise in oil prices in 1979 intensified the predicament to the extent that in 1980 the Community was forced to declare the steel industry in 'manifest crisis'. Accordingly, in 1981 the Commission enacted the 'steel aids codes' decisions which introduced mandatory production quotas on firms and imposed further restrictions on imports. Simultaneously, the efforts for restructuring the industry continued with the objectives of reducing excess capacity and increasing efficiency and productivity. As the steel industry has heavy fixed costs, entry barriers are high so that the industry is mostly oligopolistic. Increased competition from cheaper imports induced merger activity which exacerbated the oligopolistic structure of the sector. Thus, in 1990, almost half of the Community's production of crude steel was produced by five companies, and 73 per cent of the total output by the biggest 15 companies.

The crisis continued well into the 1990s with employment cut down by another 65 per cent between 1989 and 1999 (see Figure 13.3). The trend continued in 2000: demand for steel fell by 3 per cent, and while imports increased by 27 per cent, exports rose only by 16 per cent, confirming that the EU's steel deficit was spreading, mostly due to the uncompetitive level of domestic prices. The worldwide downturn in economic activity in 2001 meant falling demand and further stress on the steel industry from large increases in stocks which were exerting downward pressures on prices. Therefore, the need to improve competitiveness continued while technological developments and globalization showed

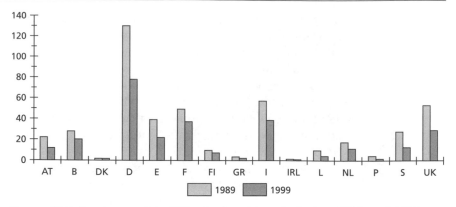

Figure 13.3 **Employment in EU's steel and iron industry, 1989 and 1999 (000)**

Source: Data from Eurostat (2001c).

that the Community steel industry should move towards specialization and the manufacture of quality products with higher value added. Net job losses in the Community steel industry arising from such restructuring were estimated at 5000 in 2001, with the UK expected to remain by far the worst affected country in the Union.

Textile and clothing industry

Foreign competition and slow growth in demand have meant that the Community's textile and cloth (T/C) industry is in long-term decline. The trend for globalization has increased competition, especially from the large Asian textile nations, such as India, Indonesia, Pakistan and – above all – China. In the past, the intensification of competition had led to protection, but this problem was mitigated by the Multi-Fibre Arrangement (MFA) which came into force as a 'temporary' departure from normal GATT rules in 1974. The MFA's initial intention was to help third-world exporters in the short term, without greatly diverting from the longer-term GATT objective of bringing the T/C sector under the trade liberalization rules. Under the MFA, exports of textiles from LDCs to the EU increased significantly, e.g. by 54 per cent in 1986–7. After the Uruguay Round of trade liberalization, a new agreement on textiles and clothing was signed which specified that the T/C sector would be fully incorporated into the World Trade Organization's (WTO) framework of trade liberalization within 10 years, i.e. by the end of 2006.

As a result of the incessant competitive pressure of foreign producers, the share of imports in the EU's consumption has been increasing, e.g. for textiles from 12 per cent to 24 per cent, and for clothing from 30 per cent to nearly 50 per cent between 1990 and 2000. The sinking of the EU industry is mainly caused by the labour-cost differentials between developing countries and Europe. The EU industry has responded to this challenge by substantial restructuring and modernizing, and by improving its cost structure through *outsourcing* labour-intensive operations – transferring their production to low labour-cost countries. The EU industry is thus concentrating on the production of high-quality output, attempting to maintain its competitive advantage by focusing on design, fashion, innovation, and higher productivity. All these developments have resulted in a sharp decline in employment, by 47 per cent in textiles and by 40 per cent in clothing between 1980 and 1995. In contrast, employment in Europe's Far Eastern competitors increased by 50 per cent in textiles and 100 per cent in clothing during the same period. The European industry now consists of a large number of mainly small and medium-sized enterprises (SMEs) which employ about two million people (mostly in the countries of large production: I, D, UK, F and E). With expectations of a moderate rise in domestic demand and the removal of all quantitative import restrictions in 2005, the future of the industry does not appear promising.

Shipbuilding

Since shipowners operate worldwide and are not in any way constrained to buy from domestic sources of production, shipbuilding is pre-eminently a world industry. The problems of this industry started in the 1960s as a result of price competition. Japan, South Korea and other developing countries new to shipbuilding, expanded their shipyards (mostly built with Japanese capital and maintained by extensive production subsidies) and dominated world production. In an attempt to offset the comparative disadvantage, other shipbuilding states supplied their industry with subsidies. Although at the time the high rate of growth of world trade sustained a rising demand for more shipbuilding, the subsidies to the industry at worldwide scale led to excess capacity. When the increase in the price of oil caused recession and a slump in international trade, the market for shipping collapsed and declining freight rates led to a world shipping surplus, and hence to shipping overcapacity and a fall in orders for new ships. The shipbuilding industry thus ended up with a vast structural imbalance between world capacity and world demand.

In countries with a tradition in shipbuilding, this situation resulted in more state intervention in the form of aid to shipyards, which were facing particular difficulties because many were old and therefore technically uncompetitive. These problems were particularly severe in EU countries where most shipyards could neither operate on a large scale nor compete with the modern shipyards of Japan and South Korea. Consequently, the EU's share in total world production declined sharply, from about 31 per cent in 1976 to 19 per cent in 1987. Thus, despite cuts in production and workforce (by 50 per cent and 40 per cent respectively between 1976 and 1980), the Commission estimated that further reductions in capacity and manpower were inevitable.

In an attempt to correct distortions in competition, the Community issued a series of directives for the harmonization of members' state aid, by fixing a ceiling and limiting the eligibility for financial assistance to investments that improved productivity and competitiveness. Initially, the intention of the Community was to phase out state aid to the industry and liberalize the market. But it soon became clear that 'the continuation of the crisis has serious consequences for the Community shipbuilding industry which makes the immediate abolition of such aid impossible' (Commission 1981). Hence, the phasing out of state aid was postponed indefinitely and the aid ceiling was raised. Between 1981 and 1986 direct subsidies in the form of *crisis aid* to the shipbuilding industry of 25 to 50 per cent of value added were common in the EU countries. The EU's long-term objective was to restructure the industry by adjusting its capacity and activities to the Community's market and to the volume of maritime traffic and social and strategic interests. Hence the Commission launched the programme *Renaval* to assist declining shipbuilding regions by redirecting them to activities which would generate new jobs. Negotiations launched in 1989 under the auspices of the OECD between the main shipbuilding countries (the EU, Japan, South Korea and Norway) led in July 1994 to agreement on the elimination of all obstacles to market competition starting from 1996. But after the 1997 Asian economic crisis and the fall in the Korean currency, Korea gained more competitiveness and its global market share in new orders showed a sharp increase, from 29 per cent to 40 per cent in 2000. This expansion in Korea's market share has mainly been at the expense of Japan (its share falling from 38 per cent to 25 per cent), though the EU's share also fell (from 18 per cent to 15 per cent) (see Figure 13.4). But the rest of world's share (representing mostly China, Taiwan and Poland) has risen (from 15 per cent to 25 per cent). Despite these changes, demand remained low, prices fell, and the surplus capacity of world production now stands at 25 per cent.

The automotive industry

The automotive industry (passenger cars, vans, trucks and buses) is multinational in ownership and transnational in the location of production. After governments started withdrawing from ownership in the 1980s, the producers became private firms which through mergers, acquisitions and global consolidation radically changed the structure of the industry on a worldwide scale. As a result, the automotive industry has become a highly concentrated global industry. In the EU the industry is characterized

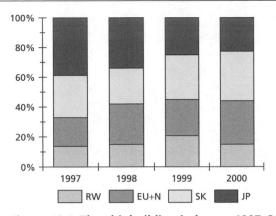

Figure 13.4 **The shipbuilding industry, 1997–2000, %**

Notes: RW = Rest of world; EU + N = EU *plus* Norway; SK = South Korea; JP = Japan

Source: Data from Lloyd's *Register of Shipping*.

by a small number of high-volume manufacturers selling their output to consumers primarily through 'authorized' dealers, each having a monopoly over a geographical area. In 2000, the big producers in the EU car industry included DaimlerChrysler, Volkswagen (VW), BMW, Ford, General Motors (GM), Renault-Nissan, PSA (Peugeot-Citroën), Fiat (now 20 per cent owned by GM) and Porsche. Several Japanese car makers have plants in the EU: Nissan, Toyota, Suzuki, Honda, and Mitsubishi (now controlled by DaimlerChrysler). Two Korean-based companies, Hyundai and Daewoo, export significant numbers of cars to the EU. Figures 13.5 and 13.6 show that Volkswagen is the clear sales leader in the EU market. The EU truck, bus and coach sector includes Volvo-Renault, Scania (partly acquired by VW), Iveco, DaimlerChrysler, MAN and Daf.

Vehicle manufacturers must remain at the cutting edge to survive. Despite the consolidation, there is an overcapacity in production for cars worldwide as well as in Europe. Therefore, further rationalization of the industry with more mergers and acquisitions is likely to end with only six global car-making groups, together with a small number of independent niche players.

The European automotive industry is influenced by both member states' policies and EU common policies. The latter mainly deal with regulations pertaining to vehicle construction, safety and environmental protection, and the automotive market structure and competition. The prevalence of 'exclusive dealerships', the Community's 'block exception' from the rules of competition for motor vehicle distribution (until September 2002, see Chapter 3), and the oligopolistic structure of production have meant that prices in the single market vary between countries by as much as 30 per cent.

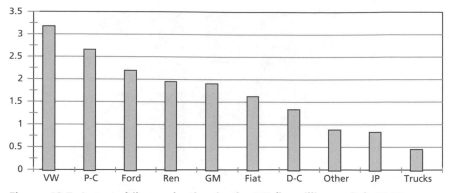

Figure 13.5 Automobile production in the EU (in million units), 2000

Note: cars = passenger cars + light commercial vehicles; VW = Volkswagen AG; P-C = PSA
Peugeot Citroën; Ford = Ford Europe Inc (including Volvo cars); Ren = Renault SA;
GM = GM Europe; Fiat = Fiat-Iveco; D-C = DaimlerChrysler AG; Other = BMW AG, MG
Rover, Porsche; JP = Japanese manufacturers; Trucks = trucks + buses and coaches by
MAN Nutzfahrzeuge AG, Volvo trucks VT, Scania AB, DAF Trucks NV, Other European

Source: Data available at www.acca.be

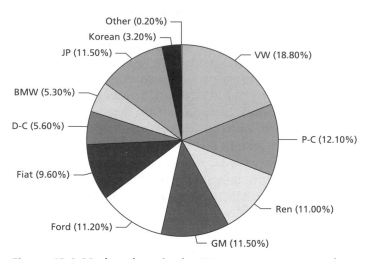

Figure 13.6 Market share in the EU's passenger-car market, 1999
Source: Data available at www.acca.be

The European car market, which collapsed in 1993 (–17 per cent vs.
1992), has shown in recent years an average rate of growth of around
4 per cent annually for each category of vehicle (registering passenger
car sales of 14.6 million in 1999). Moreover, the EU runs a significant
positive trade balance on motor vehicles and components, but with a
deficit in the case of Japan and Korea. Overall, the industry shows
increasing profitability, which is closely associated with market shares.

For this reason, the major producers tend to expand their global market by investing in third countries, exploiting new methods of sales (e.g. via the Internet), and adopting new technology emanating from advances in the electronics industry. But the increase in vehicle sales is not an unqualified welfare-increasing success: between 1991 and 1999 in the EU, passenger cars in use increased by 17 per cent (to 172 million) and commercial vehicles by 25 per cent (to 22 million), with all the consequences of congestion and pollution.

Advanced technology industries

Electronics, biology and genetic engineering, aerospace, nuclear energy, etc. are key industries which are expected to play an important part in the functioning and development of the economy now and in the future. A reason for promoting these industries is their positive externalities which propagate knowledge and innovation that other firms can also use without being charged, i.e. an example of positive externalities and *market failure*. Where the private costs are high while the benefits can accrue to parties other than the firm that produces them, then there is a prime case for subsidizing the industry.

In general, government intervention in the form of technology policies is considered necessary because of market failure in the process of technological change which is characterized by externalities and spillovers, uncertainty in the face of incomplete information and unfair international competition for gaining strategic advantages. At the level of economic unions, a common technology policy also aims at the pooling of scarce resources and elimination of wasteful duplication of research. Therefore, on the basis of these arguments, it is suggested that collaboration in research, promotion and, if necessary, investment should be a constituent part of the common policy for the development of Community advanced technology industries. To this effect the Commission has made a number of proposals and has taken initiatives for the formulation of policy, as for example in the sector of information technology.

The market for information technology (computers, electronic components, databanks, modern telecommunications, etc.) is expanding rapidly worldwide. In the Community, domestic industry is lagging behind its principal American and Japanese competitors, both in development and in market shares. To remedy this state of affairs, the Community has taken several measures aimed at the coordination of the research efforts of the member states with additional funding from the Community budget. In an attempt to create a European Research Area (ERA), as agreed by the Amsterdam Treaty, the Community launched a new 'framework programme for Research and Technological Development 2002–2006' to support cooperative research, promote mobility and coordination and invest in mobilizing research in support of EU policies. However, compared with the USA, Japan and some of the newly industrializing countries, the EU commits a small proportion of its resources to R&D. From 1980 to 1996, the EU consistently lagged behind the developed Asian economies (including Japan), NAFTA, and EFTA with less than 2 per cent of GDP invested in research. In 1993, the dynamic Asian economies (Korea, Singapore, Taiwan) passed the EU for the first time to reach 2.2 per cent of GDP, compared with the EU's 1.8 per cent, the USA's 2.5 per cent, and Japan's 2.8 per cent. But, as Figure 13.7 shows, some EU member states are leading investors in R&D. For example, since 1986 Sweden has led the world in overall R&D intensity (3.9 per cent in 1997). Of the EU-15, Finland, France, Germany and the Netherlands spend more than 2 per cent of their GDP on R&D. In 1998, four member states (D, F, I, UK) together accounted for almost 75 per cent of the total R&D expenditure in the European Union.

The EU's trade performance in high-tech products is generally improving, but is still weak compared with the US and Japan. The EU's exports of high-tech products amounted to 12 per cent of its total exports of manufactured goods to non-EU countries, compared with 24 per cent for the USA and 25 per cent for Japan. But there are exceptions: as a result of Ireland's strong specialization in new technology during recent years, high-tech products now account for 37.6 per cent of its total exports. In second place among the member states comes the UK, with 22 per cent of its total export trade in high-tech products, followed by France (16.2 per cent), the Netherlands (16 per cent), Sweden (15 per cent), Denmark (12.2 per cent), Finland (11.7 per cent) and Germany (11.4 per cent). The other member states are relatively non-specialized in exports of high-tech products.

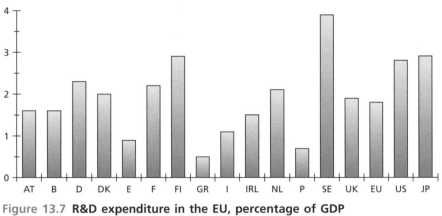

Figure 13.7 **R&D expenditure in the EU, percentage of GDP**

Note: Data for F, IRL, GR, SE, UK 1997. All others for 1998.

Source: Data from Commission (2000d) and OECD (2000).

13.6 Conclusions

The EU economies are following a long-established trend of restructuring away from the primary and secondary sectors and towards services and high value-added products. But manufacturing is still an important economic sector of the Community for production, trade and employment. In recent years the industry has operated against a background of slow growth of demand, rising unemployment, increasing international competition and rapid changes brought about by technological progress. Although these are problems which to some extent are shared by all members of the Community, industrial policy still remains largely a national responsibility. The Community has taken steps to ensure that, in accordance with a system of open and competitive markets, the conditions and the legal framework necessary for speeding up the structural adjustment and competitiveness of European industry will develop.

The Community's industrial strategy consists of policies aimed at improving the business environment, by working towards integrating the European market, promoting the necessary changes in industry's structure, and coordinating the activities of the member states. The single market has given a welcome boost to cross-border mergers, acquisitions and joint ventures which are shaping a new structure of production and distribution. The Community has also launched several integrated programmes of research to help the EU to catch up with its rivals in the application of modern technology. In general, R&D expenditure and the rates of industrial production and productivity achieved by most EU member states are persistently below those of its main competitors, such as the USA and Japan. An implication of these differences in performance is that in external markets the Community is rapidly losing ground in high-technology innovation and trade. Market integration and coordination of industrial policies and research are expected to have a favourable impact on the competitiveness and performance of EU industry without the need to resort to any form of aggressive and confrontational strategic trade policy. This will contribute to the efforts to reduce unemployment and increase growth and welfare.

Questions

1. (a) What is the reason for government regulation in the market?
   (b) Does the lack of perfect competition justify government intervention in the form of strategic industrial targeting and trade policy?
   (c) Is there any need for an interventionist common industrial policy in Europe?

2. Compare and evaluate the following statements:
   (a) 'The role of government should be restricted to regulation to remedy various kinds of market failure. Industrial policy on a European level should confine its role to coordinating the national policy measures for liberalization of the market and making sure that the game is played in accordance with the rules.'
   (b) 'The present significance of the economic might of Japan and the USA, and the power of multinational corporations provide strong grounds for active intervention in strategic decision-making in industry and trade at both national and European levels.'

Further reading

Eurostat (2001c), *Panorama of European Business*, presents a comprehensive picture of EU industry.

Web guide

Information is available at www.europa.eu.int/comm/enterprise and www.europa.eu.int/comm/research

Energy and the environment

14

Diverging energy and environmental policies between the members of an economic union can distort competition. Moreover, the negative externalities of energy production and consumption on the Union, and the world environment and different national standards of environmental protection, mean that international cooperation is indispensable. In this chapter, we examine the EU's attempts to coordinate the energy policies of the member states. With regard to the environment, the Community is coordinating policy in the single market and, in cooperation with third countries and competent international organizations, is promoting measures for the abatement of regional and worldwide environmental problems.

14.1 Energy policy

Introduction

Energy conditions the whole of economic and social life. In the total consumption of energy of the Community the household sector takes the largest share: industry (27.6 per cent), transport (32 per cent), and the household and tertiary sectors (40.4 per cent). As an input in production, energy has no close substitutes and can often account for 20–50 per cent of input costs. Therefore, a low pricing policy, for example by subsidizing domestic supply and imports, would reduce producer costs and distort trade prices and competition. Moreover, domestic energy shortages and dependence on imported energy expose a country to risks, and may also cause price fluctuations with repercussions on production and supply, economic crises and even recession. Therefore, in most countries, the energy sector has attracted state policy intervention because of concern about security of supplies in a volatile world market.

Two of the three Communities making up the EU are concerned exclusively with energy. Thus from the beginning energy policy in the EU was divided between the European Coal and Steel Community (ECSC) for coal, the European Atomic Energy Community (EAEC) for nuclear power and the European Community (EC) which was allocated responsibility for oil, gas and electricity. The Community is not self-sufficient in energy production and therefore is highly dependent on the whims of foreign suppliers. Although the proportion varies depending on the source of energy from country to country and from region to region, today the Community depends on imports for almost 50 per cent of its fuel consumption. When in the 1950s and 1960s the imported energy sources were becoming cheaper, the pressing problem was how to avoid becoming dangerously dependent on foreign supplies, mostly oil, and how to preserve and develop domestic sources of energy, mostly coal. But as international prices continued to fall, while the economies of the EU member states were growing rapidly, the problem of limited domestic energy sources and increasing reliance on imports became more acute, precipitating unemployment. The quintupling of oil prices in the next few years deepened the crisis, causing inflation and more unemployment. At the time, the EU member states reacted to these events with a lack of coordination, preferring to use their own national energy policy rather than commit themselves to a Community policy.

Early attempts at a common policy

The Treaty of Rome did not mention energy as a field of explicit EU competence. However, the first steps for a common policy were taken in 1964 when the ECSC adopted a protocol on energy which set as Community objectives fair competition between the different sources of energy, security of supply, low-priced supply and freedom of choice for consumers. It also called for a coordinated system of state aid for coal production and consumption by the steel industry based on national subsidies. Otherwise no common policy was reached, mainly because of plentiful cheap sources of supply from abroad and the different needs of the member states, some of which depended heavily on imports.

Another attempt to set up a common energy policy was taken in 1968 when the Commission proposed in a memorandum the objectives and procedures for establishing a common market in energy leading to lower energy prices. This would have meant removing the state monopolies which many member states operated, harmonizing energy taxes and proceeding with the planned Common Transport Policy. But although the Council approved the basic outlines of the proposal, no measures of practical importance were introduced.

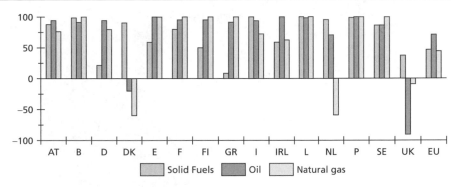

Figure 14.1 European Union: net imports of fuels, 1998

Note: Negative numbers indicate that the country is a net exporter.

Source: Data available at www.europa.eu.int/comm/energy_transport/etif
     energy_general_overview

The conditions changed radically when the Organization of Petro-leum Exporting Countries (OPEC), operating as a cartel, raised prices by more than 475 per cent after the first oil shock in 1973, and by another 134 per cent after the second oil shock in 1979. The oil-importing coun-tries have since started to adopt energy-saving measures and to search for and develop alternative sources of energy supply, such as nuclear and hydroelectric power, natural gas and, wherever possible, domestic extrac-tion of oil. In 1974 the Commission decided to set targets designed to reduce the EU's import dependence by diversification and conservation policies from about 63 per cent in total energy consumption (97 per cent of which was imported chiefly from the Middle East and North Africa) to less than 50 per cent. This meant developing domestic energy sources and reducing consumption by the rational use of energy. This initiative led to some success, mostly in changing the energy balances rather than the structure of the energy market, which in the case of the EU is com-posed of countries which display widely varying reliance on imports for their fuels requirements (as shown in Figure 14.1). This explains in part the Community's inability to agree on a common approach and to make its weight felt in the world energy market. The heterogeneity of the energy sources and needs across the member states and the continuous promotion of national interests prompted the Commission to redirect its stand from a common energy policy to the coordination and harmoniza-tion of national policies by setting collective targets for rationalization of production, consumption and imports of energy. These targets are coupled with measures to encourage energy saving, which receive Com-munity assistance, and marginal cost pricing. The Community budget has also made large grants towards demonstration projects of energy saving and research for developing renewable energy resources including atomic fusion (such as the Joint European Torus, JET).

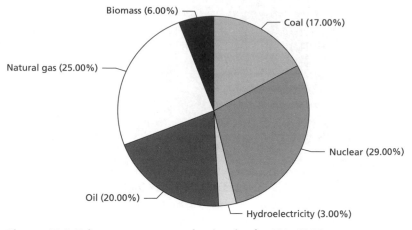

Figure 14.2 Primary energy production in the EU, 1996
Source: Data from Eurostat (2001e).

The continual volatility of energy prices and supplies have at last persuaded the EU states to cooperate on the issue of energy. Many member states have striven to rationalize and diversify their production of energy which increased by about 9 per cent between 1990 and 1996. Figure 14.2 shows that Europe's main energy sources are nuclear energy, accounting for 28 per cent of total production (largest producer F), natural gas (25 per cent, largest producers DK and NL) and oil (20 per cent, largest producer the UK). Despite the efforts at diversification, OPEC countries still supply 62 per cent of the Community's oil imports, but this is down from 86 per cent in 1980 to 40 per cent of the EU's total energy imports. Currently, the EU accounts for 17.8 per cent of world oil consumption (against 25.7 per cent for the USA and 7.7 per cent of Japan).

The contribution of the energy sector to overall employment in the Community is relatively small, about 7 per cent of total industrial employment. However, energy is an important user of investment resources, taking up around 25 per cent of total industrial gross fixed capital formation. The energy sectors of the EU member states are large and diverse in terms of ownership, which in many countries displays a high but diminishing state presence, and of concentration in few resources: electricity, gas, oil, coal and nuclear energy.

The Common Energy Policy

The common policies were formalized by the Treaty on European Union (1992) which confirmed that the Community would undertake 'measures in the sphere of energy' (TEEC, II, 3) and would contribute 'to the establishment and development of trans-European networks in . . . energy infrastructures' (TEU, 154). The Community's decision to establish the single market comprised also a common market for energy which would be subject to liberalization and integration by joint investment in infrastructure and supply networks across internal frontiers. At the same time, the close links between energy and the environment highlighted the importance of energy's environmental dimension and the role of sustainable development in Community energy policy.

The objective of the Common Energy Policy is to bring together Community actions on energy with regard to the following main issues:

- *security of supply* by managing the growing external dependence of the Union on imports;
- *competitiveness* of the European energy industry in the world, without in any way neglecting the safety, quality and durability of energy equipment, or public service objectives;
- *protection of the environment* by implementing an energy policy compatible with sustainable development objectives, particularly through more rational use of energy and the development of renewable sources;
- *common research* and technological development in the energy sector.

Since 1998, the Community has adopted framework programmes over several years to pursue its energy policy activities and strategies. With regard to security of supply, the Community has undertaken actions aimed at:

- diversifying energy sources, through the development of relations with supplier countries and research on alternative energy sources;
- promoting the rational use of energy;
- providing support for energy investment financed by the Structural Funds or through the trans-European networks, and initiating technical assistance programmes and research and development, both in the areas of nuclear and non-nuclear energy.

Regarding the integration of energy markets, the Community issued directives aimed at transparency of prices to final consumers and progressive liberalization of the electricity and gas markets, facilitating the transit of gas and electricity between the Community's major grids. On the promotion of sustainable development, the policy aims to ensure the compatibility of energy-related and environmental objectives, the rational and efficient use of energy resources, the promotion of new and renewable energy sources and consistency between the different programmes.

The following are among the projects initiated by the Community:

- SYNERGIE, for strengthening international cooperation in the energy sector;

■ ALTENER, which is part of the Community's strategy to limit carbon dioxide emissions, to improve energy efficiency and to promote renewable energy sources, such as solar energy which has no carbon emissions;

■ SAVE, for the encouragement of the rational and efficient use of energy resources.

The Commission has also put forward two proposals on the taxation of energy products. The first, presented in 1992, is designed to impose taxes on carbon dioxide and on energy with the intention of limiting the emissions of greenhouse gases. The second, presented in 1997, would establish an overall tax system for the taxation of energy products. But in 2001 the two proposals were still at the negotiation stage for lack of political agreement among the member states.

Trans-European Networks in Energy (TENs-Energy)

On 13 March 2001 the Commission adopted a set of measures to open the gas and electricity markets up fully by 2005 for the benefit of European consumers. These measures will reinforce the conditions which encourage real and fair competition, and introduce a genuine single market by the operation of Trans-European Networks in Energy (TENs-Energy). The objective of TENs-Energy is to facilitate the establishment of networks for the transmission of electricity or natural gas. These networks involve:

(1) in the electricity sector:
■ connection of isolated electricity networks
■ development of interconnections between the member states
■ development of interconnections with third countries
(2) in the natural gas sector:
■ introduction of natural gas into new regions
■ connection of isolated gas networks
■ increased reception and storage capacities
■ increase in transport capacities (supply gas pipelines).

The introduction of TENs-Energy would also have an impact on relations with third countries. Interconnections have been made with certain Mediterranean countries, the countries of central and eastern Europe and Norway. At the instigation of the Community, the European Energy Charter was first signed in 1991 by 38 countries. A revised agreement was signed in 1994 by more than 50 countries, including the United States, Japan, Canada and the countries of central and eastern Europe. The Charter is an attempt to secure energy supplies for the growing needs of the industry of the Community while at the same time providing oil- and gas-producing states with finance for the modernization of their energy sources and a secure outlet for their output. In the Community, the Charter gives the legal commitment of the member states to international cooperation over energy and covers protection for investment in energy, trading in energy and environmental aspects of energy.

14.2 The environment

The problem

There are many definitions of what constitutes the environment and therefore what is environmental damage. For the purposes of Community policy, the European Commission defined the environment as 'the combination of elements whose complex interrelationship make up the settings, the surroundings and the conditions of life of the individual and of society, as they are or as they are felt'. Whatever its definition, the environment is used primarily in three ways: as a consumption good, a supplier of resources and a receptacle of wastes. Every industrial process and human activity affects the environment through the depletion of finite natural resources, pollution and destruction of the countryside. In recent years, as global warming, acid rain, ozone depletion and other environmental hazards have multiplied, environmental issues have played an increasing role in domestic policy-making and international trade negotiations.

Economic activities of private agents, such as production or consumption, often have spillover effects that generate benefits or inflict costs on others and are not properly reflected in market prices: the *negative* or *positive* externalities. As we have seen (for example, in Chapters 12 and 13), externalities cause a divergence between the private costs and benefits, which determine the individual activities, and the collective or social costs and benefits. In such situations, public policy can play a positive role by correcting the divergence between social and private costs or benefits. Pollution is a negative externality, the byproduct of production or consumption causing a cost which is not reflected in a market price, clearly a 'market failure'. Thus, a byproduct of production, such as smoke polluting the environment, is not taken into account in the producer's private cost on which the output price is based and, therefore, the producer's cost is lower than the social cost.

Many of the problems that are faced in the area of environmental economics arise from the lack of clearly defined 'property rights' over natural resources, that is titles of ownership of resources such as air or water which the polluter uses and abuses freely. If nothing is done about it, finite resources will be depleted, the environment will be damaged by effluents and toxic wastes and public health will be harmed. Presumably, the externality may be removed by assigning property rights on the resources. Theory has shown that under perfect competition, when property rights are clearly defined and there are precisely identified polluters and polluted, completely free trade of all property rights will lead to economic efficiency. Furthermore, the efficient outcome is independent of how the property rights are assigned (Coase, 1960). It is suggested, therefore, that a solution to the problem of externalities is the allocation of property rights. This clearly means that there is no necessity for the government regulation of pollution problems. Critics counter, however, that this conclusion is based on perfect competition which might be a convenient fiction for constructing elegant theoretical economic models, but does not adequately describe the real world (Pearce and Turner, 1989). Moreover, many aspects of the environment are public goods, such as air, and thus can only be subject to government regulation. For this, the government has first to determine the public's demand for environmental quality before deciding the efficient level of pollution. As a rule, the optimal outcome is where the marginal cost of pollution reduction equals the marginal benefit of pollution abatement. In practice, it is usually difficult to measure accurately both the costs of pollution and the benefits of abatement.

Principles

Policies for the elimination of the externality attempt to remove the divergence between private and social costs by direct regulation, such as a tax on the polluting activity, or by the use of *standards*. Figure 14.3 illustrates the case of a negative production externality causing welfare effects to three economic groups: the producers of the good, the consumers of the good, and the government. We assume that the pollution is 'bad' for the society, which consists of these three economic groups.

In Figure 14.3, we assume that pollution is increasing in proportion to the quantity of output, and affects exclusively the country of production. The costs of the pollution are borne by the society as *external* cost of production. Therefore, the private marginal cost of production, PMC, which is the competitive supply curve, is below the social marginal cost, SMC, at every level of production. In the absence of an environmental policy, producers set the quantity of production according to the private supply curve PMC, and the competitive market reaches equilibrium at price P_0 and production Q_0. However, at equilibrium price P_0 the social marginal cost is Q_0B per unit of output, giving SMC > PMC. Social optimality can be obtained by *internalizing the externality*, equating the market price with the social marginal cost. At quantity Q_1, this occurs by

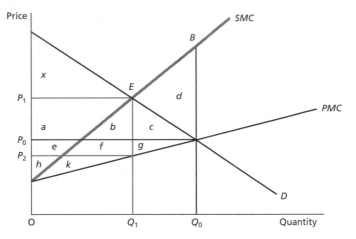

The vertical axis measures the production costs and output price of an activity that causes pollution as a side effect. The horizontal axis measures the quantity of output. D = demand, PMC = private marginal cost, SMC = social marginal cost. The divergence between SMC and PMC, which is rising proportionally as the production of output increases, is caused by production pollution. Under: (1) *No policy*: Equilibrium at price P_0 and output Q_0. Welfare effect: consumers = $x + a + b + c$; producers = $h + k + e + f + g$; pollution= $-(k + f + b + g + c + d)$; net effect = $(x + a + e + h) - d$. (2) *Anti-pollution policy by optimal tax*: Equilibrium at price P_1 and output Q_1. Welfare effect: consumers = x; producers = h; government = $a + b + e + f$; pollution = $-(k + f + b)$; net effect = $(x + a + e + h) - k$. (3) *Anti-pollution policy by supply regulation*: Equilibrium at price P_1 and output Q_1. Welfare effect: consumers = x; producers = $h + e + a + b$; pollution = $-(k + f + b)$; net effect = $(x + a + e + h) - k$. Under both policies the overall effect is identical and 'better' than under no policy, but the distributional effects of the two policies between consumers, producers and government are different.

Figure 14.3 **Optimal pollution policies**

the price rising to P_1 which can be reached by levying a tax on the polluter equal to the external cost of the pollution, the so-called *Pigovian tax*. Thus, in Figure 14.3, levying the marginal tax $P_1 - P_2$ will make the firm pay the full social marginal cost of its production, and thus eliminate the externality, PMC + $(P_1 - P_2)$ = SMC. The welfare effects of the tax policy show that the society gains from the reduction in production and hence pollution, but with a different impact for each social group. The alternative policy is to restrict directly the production of the good causing pollution at the optimal level Q_1. This will also raise the market price from P_0 to P_1 and society's net gain will be exactly the same as under the previous policy. But in the absence of tax revenue for the government, the allocation of costs/benefits between producers and consumers is different.

Another form of anti-pollution policy is for the regulator not only to restrict the production of the good but also to specify how the reduction in pollution should be achieved: a regulatory command policy. From a welfare point of view, 'market-based' policies and instruments for the control of pollution, such as taxes, emission charges, subsidies and tradable permits are in general 'better' than regulatory command policies. The advantage of using the market mechanism is that it gives the polluter more choice of the means to reduce pollution and, obviously, among equally effective policies, the polluter will choose the cheapest. It is claimed, therefore, that the market approach may provide the industry with incentives to develop new and more cost-effective technologies for reducing pollution.

International aspects of pollution

Pollution and environmental policy have an international dimension because: (a) pollutants may be mobile across national boundaries (e.g. acid rain) or cause global common problems (e.g. ozone depletion); and (b) even if pollution is a purely domestic event, policies to correct it by one country could raise production costs which might affect its international competitiveness or induce pollution-intensive industries to relocate to countries with laxer environmental policies. Environmentalist groups often argue that trade liberalization and economic integration, which expand production, threaten the environment through increased pollution and depletion of natural resources. However, this argument is in general false because it is production, not trade, that causes the problem. Using an environmental policy to deal with the pollution problem directly and following with trade liberalization will be the best (= welfare increasing) policy. This result is obtained by identifying the source of the problem (production pollution) and using a policy targeted to deal with its cause (anti-pollution). Using other policies which have an indirect effect on the problem (e.g. a trade policy) introduces further distortions which might make the situation worse: a clear example of second best analysis. Therefore, the optimal solution to this problem is to intervene directly at the production stage and not indirectly through the trade sector. Unfortunately, in the absence of international cooperation, sometimes there may be no other alternative than to punish the offending party by trade policies.

In international economic relations, and therefore also in economic unions, problems may arise from different approaches to environmental questions, some countries choosing to improve their environmental quality, thus increasing production costs by internalizing the externalities of pollution, while others may care less about their environment and do less or nothing to improve it. Complications may arise even if all countries do apply policies to optimize their pollution levels because of differences in *assimilative capacity*, that is the ability of the environment to reduce pollutants by natural processes. Since assimilative capacity can differ across regions and countries, even similar production processes causing similar levels of pollution may affect production costs and prices dissimilarly, and hence competitiveness and the international allocation of production and trade. Similar problems arise from different consumer preferences and income levels across countries, which may cause divergence between countries in the demand for environmental quality and in the response of policies for the environment. These issues bring forward the issue of the international transmission of pollution and the need for international environmental policy coordination.

In the case of trans-frontier pollution, such as global warming, water contamination and acid rain, an efficient pollution tax would include the social costs imposed on other countries. However, policies such as the 'polluter pays' principle (PPP) are difficult to implement because polluting countries have little incentive to raise their prices and reduce their competitiveness by internalizing the social costs they impose on others. When the pollution problems are global, international cooperation is indispensable for both sharing the costs and eliminating the 'free-rider problem'[1] of the pollution abatement policies. If the pollution is contained within national borders and some countries apply controls to contain it while others do not, trade distortions may arise which may call for corrective measures. Since countries and regions differ in their preferences for environmental quality, income level and assimilative capacity, attempting to impose one country's environmental standards on another, for example by using trade restrictions, e.g. tariffs, can cause more harm than good by adding to the distortions of pollution the production and consumption inefficiencies of tariffs. Moreover, discrimination against imports because of their production methods is illegal under international trade agreements (see Box 14.1).

The policies of world trade liberalization have raised the possibility that countries may adopt laxer environmental regulations than their competitors for fear that this may put their industry at a competitive disadvantage or even cause the relocation of industrial plants to countries operating as 'pollution havens'. Environmentalists argue that this reasoning may lead all governments to relax their pollution controls in order to protect their domestic economies, thus undermining attempts to solve global environmental problems. These arguments lead to the conclusion that, since enforcement of global standards through trade restrictions is a non-starter, only harmonization of environmental rules

---

[1] The free-rider problem arises (most usually with 'public goods') when no individual is willing to contribute towards the cost of something and when they hope that someone else will bear the cost instead.

Box 14.1 ■ International trade agreements and the environment

GATT article XX provided that governments should take measures to protect the health and safety of their citizens, and some governments attempted to apply the terms of the article for environmental reasons. However, GATT did not permit member states to exclude imports of products merely because of the way they are made. The reason given was that domestic health and safety regulations should not be applied unilaterally on foreign countries because this could open the gate to all kinds of protectionist mischief. The same principle applies under the WTO. Thus a WTO panel found that an EU import ban of US beef produced with growth-promoting hormones violated the WTO agreements because the EU had not definitively demonstrated that such beef would harm consumers. The EU argued that according to the opinion of independent scientific advisors there is risk associated with meat produced in this way and it did not lift the ban. Instead, it put forward a proposal to make the ban WTO-compatible.

Under the WTO, the member states agreed that 'their relations in the field of trade and economic endeavour should be conducted with a view to . . . expanding the production of and trade in goods and services, while allowing for the optimal use of the world's resources in accordance with the objective of sustainable development, seeking both to protect and preserve the environment' (Preamble, WTO, 1994). Consequently, the WTO recognizes that member countries may exclude imports manufactured or harvested in ways that violate international agreements if both the restricting and the offending countries are signatories, such as the Montreal Protocol for the protection of the ozone layer and the Convention on International Trade in Endangered Species. Environmentalists maintain, however, that by being in favour of free trade which induces more demand, more production and thus more pollution, the WTO does not really care about nature and the environment. It is this reasoning that led to the wrecking of the Seattle WTO Conference by anti-trade demonstrators on 30 November 1999.

Source: www.wtowatch.org/faq and http://www.wto/org

across countries would prevent governments from acting unilaterally by adopting trade restrictions on imports from countries with lower environmental standards. Not surprisingly, such import-restricting policies frequently find favour with import-competing domestic industries. However, empirical studies have shown that in competitive markets, when some countries impose more stringent environmental policies than others, the resulting losses of competitiveness are rather small, one of the reasons being that such policies may induce innovation of cost-effective 'green technologies'. Therefore, in practical terms, environmental concerns about internationally traded goods are often no more than covert protectionism.

In the case of economic unions, adopting a common environmental policy implies neither equalization of the members' environmental policies nor optimization at the level of the union. It only means endorsing some minimum 'harmonized' standard to reduce pollution in and between the member states, and often in the world, with the objective of improving environmental quality while preserving fair competition and free trade. A common policy also intends to discourage factor migration to regions of lower environmental standards to take advantage of lower production costs. Other things being equal, common environmental standards would benefit regions and states of the union with higher assimilative capacity and lower abatement cost.

14.3 The EU and the environment

Foundations of the common policy

One of the principal objectives of the countries comprising the EU is 'the constant improvement of the living and working conditions of their people' (TEEC, Preamble). This objective entrusts the Community with a clear responsibility to ensure high standards of environmental quality and is the chief reason for inaugurating a Community environmental policy. A second reason is that differences in national environmental legislation could affect the operation of the common market by creating distortions in competition and technical barriers to trade. Therefore, countries with high environmental standards (such as Denmark and Germany) have tended to argue for harmonization at a high level, while other member states urge a more flexible form of harmonization. The third reason is that often pollution is not constrained within the borders of a country, but is an international problem that requires international solutions.

In deciding to frame a European environmental policy, the Community was also responding to increased public awareness of the problem and concern about the state of the natural and man-made environment. Protection of the environment was not a specific power of the Community although the Treaty of Rome expressly specified that 'health, safety, environmental protection' shall be based on 'a high level of protection' (TEEC, 95). But when by the early 1970s environmental concerns started spreading worldwide, the European Council declared in 1972 that environmental issues were on the policy agenda of the Community. The Single European Act (1986) clarified this issue by declaring that 'a policy in the sphere of the environment' (TEEC, II, 3) is among the Community's tasks for establishing the common market. Consequently, under a new Title assigned to the environment, the treaty elevated action on the environment to the status of 'Community policy' with the following specific objectives:

- 'preserving, protecting and improving the quality of the environment;
- protecting human health;
- prudent and rational utilization of natural resources;
- promoting measures at international level to deal with regional or worldwide environmental problems' (TEEC, XIX, 174).

Community policy is based on the following principles:

- *the preventive principle;*
- *the polluter pays principle;*
- *the source principle* (i.e. environmental damage should be rectified at source);
- *the precautionary principle* (i.e. that policy will be undertaken even if the evidence on cause and effect is not scientifically established, subject to the 'potential benefits and costs of action or lack of action');
- *the integration principle.* The Treaty on European Union clarified that the goal of the Community is 'sustainable growth respecting the environment'. Accordingly, subject to the subsidiarity principle, the Community's task is to coordinate the policy of the member states in the interest of avoiding competition distortions in the single market.

Subsequently, the Treaty of Amsterdam enshrined *sustainable development* as one of the Union's integration principles (TEEC, I, 6), requiring all proposals by the Commission to be based on an appraisal of their environmental impact. Accordingly, after a Community harmonization measure has been adopted, member states must protect the environment by either existing or new national provisions.

The Treaty has also established a more efficient decision-making procedure for environment policy, replacing unanimity in the Council by qualified majority voting as the general rule. The Community monitors the implementation of the common environmental law (in accordance with TEEC, 211). In exercising its duty, the Commission may issue infringement warnings to offending parties and, as a last resort, refer cases to the European Court of Justice (see Box 14.2).

Environment Action Programmes

Environmental matters have preoccupied the Community at least since the early 1970s. In 1972, the first United Nations Conference on the Environment took place and was soon followed in the same year by an agreement among the EC-6 to lay down the common principles for future Community action on the environment. This was followed by the First Environment Action Programme (EAP, 1973–7) which, along with

Box 14.2 ■ Environment law infringement

The European Court of Justice yesterday for the first time fined a European Union member state for failing to comply with one of its earlier judgments. In the historic ruling, Greece was ordered to pay a penalty of €20,000 ($19,000) a day from yesterday for failing to halt the discharge of toxic and dangerous waste into the River Kouroupitos in the Chania region of Crete. The fines will continue until the Commission is satisfied Greece complies with two directives protecting the environment from such uncontrolled dumping. The move was immediately hailed by the European Commission, which brought the case, as 'an important signal to member states that they must fulfil all their obligations under EU law'.

Yesterday's Kouroupitos River case was the first time the court used powers to fine a member state, introduced in 1993 under EU's Maastricht Treaty. The case itself began in 1987 when the Commission received a complaint about uncontrolled dumping of industrial, military and hospital waste in a ravine near the river's mouth. In its judgment, the court said that the Commission's suggestion was a 'useful point of reference' for the penalty it fixed. In determining the fine, the court took into account the 'particularly serious' nature of the infringement, its 'considerable' duration and Greece's ability to pay. The funds will be paid into the 'own resources' account of the EU budget. The Greek government said that it would pay the fine.

Financial Times, 5 July 2000

similar programmes that succeeded it, set up the framework for Community environment policy and led to the adoption of a series of directives on the protection of natural resources (air, water), noise abatement, conservation and waste management. These programmes confirmed that the Community objective of economic growth was linked with protection of the environment and conservation of natural resources, not only within the EU but internationally by Community involvement in multilateral environmental conventions aimed at global and regional collaboration. In 1987 the Community established in Copenhagen the European Environmental Agency (EEA) to monitor the environmental performance of EU member states and to act as a think-tank in the field of environmental legislation, providing the Commission and national authorities with technical, scientific and economic information necessary for adopting measures to protect the environment.

The Fifth EAP (1993–7) concentrated on 'sustainable development' and dealt with the form that growth must take to safeguard the environment. The programme also provided for specific financial aid mechanisms, such as the Cohesion Fund and the financial instrument for the environment, LIFE, which were designed to support priority measures for implementation of Community environmental policy and technical assistance to non-member countries. The Sixth EAP (2001–10) identified four priority action areas:

- climate change
- nature and biodiversity
- environment and health
- natural resources and waste.

Since previous experience has proved that the problem the EU is facing is not lack of environmental policies but the implementation of these policies, the new EAP focuses on the active involvement and accountability of all sections of society, including the polluters and the polluted.

Policy and outcomes

Even before the action programmes, the EU member states had adopted their own national measures to protect the environment. However, different preferences, assimilative capacity, levels of pollution, patterns of ownership and utilization of natural resources meant that the degree of environmental protection differed significantly between countries. Even under the Common Environmental Policy the member states will differ in the action they take and in the outcome they achieve. The diverging levels of pollution and attitudes to anti-pollution policy have meant that the Community environmental policy is the result of a compromise based on the lowest common denominator. Member states that expect higher levels of environmental protection, and can afford it, are free to apply it. Two examples may suffice to support this observation. Figure 14.4 shows the differing extent of air pollution, arising from three types of emissions per head of population across the EU states. L, GR and I hold the record of the highest incidence per head, while AT, D, and NL have the lowest. Figure 14.5 shows the share of each member state's contribution to the emissions of carbon dioxide (CO_2) in the Community total. Since the largest sources of carbon dioxide emissions are heat and electricity generation and transport, as shown in Figure 14.6, the four biggest, more urbanized and industrialized member states (D, UK, I, F) make the largest contribution to the EU level of CO_2, nearly 70 per cent of the total. In recent years Community environmental policy has grown significantly so that the EU is currently playing an important role in the global fight for pollution control. The Community policy deals with all sources of environmental deterioration, such as waste management; noise, air and water pollution; discharges; nature and biodiversity; industrial risks; and civic protection from technological hazards. In the following we examine some aspects of the common environmental policy at sectoral level.

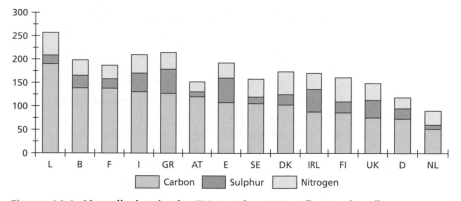

Figure 14.4 Air pollution in the EU member states (kg per head)

Notes: Carbon monoxide + Sulphur dioxide + Nitrogen oxide
Different years of period 1995–9.

Source: Data from OECD (1999).

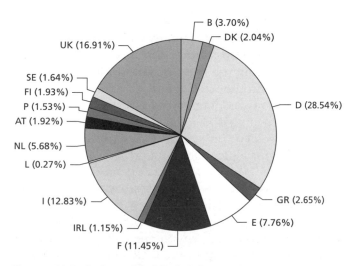

Figure 14.5 Carbon dioxide (CO_2) emissions in the EU, 2000
Source: Data from Eurostat (2001d, 2001c).

Agriculture and the environment

The natural environment is partly a public good and a natural resource for utilization and enjoyment by the public at large. The intensification of agricultural practices has substantial externalities that have detrimental effects on the environment, affecting the landscape, damaging wildlife and polluting the water. Therefore, agricultural policy, which influences farmers' decisions, and environmental policy need to be coordinated. In many countries environmental protection is an explicit agricultural policy objective. Policies that can affect farmers' land use and production decisions include: (a) voluntary measures such as education and training, moral persuasion, and technical assistance; (b) regulatory measures such as performance standards (maximum discharge rates or maximum pollutant levels) and direct controls on outputs, inputs and technology; and (c) incentive-based measures such as taxes, subsidies and transferable discharge permits.

Until the 1980s, the Community had separate sets of policies for agriculture and the environment. The CAP support policies have had negative spillover effects on the environment by raising farm output and land prices which:

- encourage intensive cultivation and construction in rural areas
- induce over-exploitation of land causing soil erosion
- encourage high livestock density
- stimulate heavier use of chemical fertilizers and pesticides that increase pollution.

From the mid-1980s, agriculture, which occupied 57 per cent of the EU's total area, has been subject to the common environmental protection policy applied by the national authorities and the Community. At the EU level, environmental policy is based on 'sustainable development' which directs the Community to deal with the root causes of environmental problems rather than responding to damages after they occur. But the agreement on agricultural reform has placed an environmental prerequisite for agricultural support. Since 1992, 'codes of good agricultural practices' have been mandatory and subsidies are offered to farmers who reduce livestock density, decrease fertilizer and pesticide use, or switch to organic farming. The Amsterdam Treaty set out the basic principles of balanced and sustainable development and a high level of environmental protection. Accordingly, environmental considerations form an important element in the reforms of the CAP and structural policy. Rural development policy is also designed to support farmers while protecting the environment and preserving nature. As a result, agricultural production and fertilizer use have started to decline after more than two decades of sharp growth.

The Community law and policies concerning the environment are included among the criteria for membership which the applicant countries of central and eastern Europe have to meet in order to avoid an 'environmental gap' between them and the EU member states. The applicant countries have to transpose all existing Community environmental law into their national legislation and to integrate the environmental dimension into all their policies.

Transport and the environment

Transport is causing externalities leading to market failure. The external costs of transport can be divided into three categories: (a) those experienced by other transport users, such as congestion and accidents; (b) those causing pollution in the environment affecting both current and future generations of the whole population, such as CO_2 and noise; and (c) those affecting other sectors, such as land use. The economic problem is how best to move to equality between marginal social benefits of transport and its marginal social costs. Besides the general reasons for Community involvement with the environment, exhaust emission curbs on motor vehicles that are tighter in one member country than in another would mean restricting interstate transport, while different national standards, for example concerning passenger cars, form impediments to free factor mobility and free trade. In transport, the Community has concentrated its efforts to curb pollution within its borders and at international level as a signatory to several international conventions to protect the environment. But increased awareness of the environmental implications of policies and mounting problems of congestion have convinced many observers that what the Community needs is not deregulation, but increased regulation in transport.

The transport sector is closely associated with natural resources both as a consumer of energy derived from fossil fuels (oil, coal, etc.) and as a user of land. But it is also one of the main causes of air and noise pollution. As Figure 14.6 shows, transport is the second most important man-made source of CO_2 emissions, with passenger car traffic alone generating about 12 per cent of the EU total. To reverse this trend, the

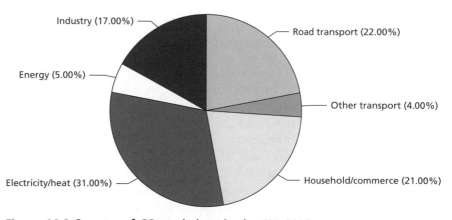

Figure 14.6 Sources of CO_2 emissions in the EU, 2000
Source: Data from Eurostat (2001c).

Community has adopted a strategy to cut vehicle emissions by improving the fuel economy of vehicles and by using differential taxation as the means for purchasing 'cleaner cars'. Increased use of public transport and the railways are major challenges for the Common Transport Policy. Transport is also a major consumer of materials, such as steel, plastics and rubber, the production of which is often implicated in environmental damage. Transport infrastructures – airports, seaports, roads and railway lines – are considered intrusive on the natural environment. The Community has issued directives dealing with a wide variety of environmental problems emanating from transport: for example, the maximum permitted noise levels and emissions of pollutants by different modes of transport; pollution at sea; land-use planning for road transport; air and noise pollution by heavy goods vehicles; and town traffic. The Community aims at standardization, which includes control of gas emissions and maintenance of air quality, limits on the weight and speed of heavy vehicles, and special procedures for the carriage of dangerous goods. Pollution-charging measures aim at a better account of the external costs of transport.

Another issue which has preoccupied the Community's environmental policy is sea transport accidents causing pollution, such as oil spills, affecting people's livelihood, local wildlife and the environment. The Community has proposed an action programme to improve safety and pollution prevention measures at international and Community level, including (a) the harmonized implementation of existing international rules throughout the Community; (b) measures to ensure tighter ship inspections by port states; (c) the coherent and harmonized development of navigational aid and traffic surveillance facilities; (d) support for international cooperation for drawing up international safety regulations.

International cooperation

The TEEC, article 174 specifies that the Community 'shall co-operate with third countries and with competent international organizations' to promote measures at international level dealing with worldwide environmental problems with regional implications. Hence, the Community is a party to more than 30 conventions and agreements on the environment and takes an active part in the negotiations leading to the adoption of regional and global environmental policies. Among the global agreements are included: the Vienna Convention for the Protection of the Ozone Layer (1988), the Montreal protocol on substances which deplete the ozone layer (1988), and the UN Conventions on Biological Diversity and Climate Change (1994). One of the latest is the Kyoto protocol (1997) on global warming which requires the signatory states to reduce their greenhouse gas emissions by at least 5 per cent of their 1990 levels during the period 2008–12. To achieve this commitment, the EU has to take action in the economic sectors which produce polluting gases, chiefly transport, energy, agriculture and industry.[2]

14.4 Summary

We have examined two issues in this chapter: energy and the environment. In the field of energy the European Community objective is to loosen its dependence on foreign imports by:

- developing its own resources of energy
- developing alternative and environmentally friendly sources of energy
- saving energy.

The EU has recognized that integration and development cannot be based on the depletion of natural resources and the deterioration of the environment. Therefore, the Community is attempting to develop a sustainable energy policy, taking full account of the environmental impact of energy production, transmission and consumption. In the field of environmental policy the Community has developed a strategy based on the basic principles of sustainable development:

- integration of environmental policy in other Community policies;
- the polluter pays;
- taking precautionary measures before there is a problem;
- benefit/cost analysis of action or lack of action;
- harmonization, monitoring of compliance, and the punishment of offenders.

Although the Community has achieved quite a lot in both energy and the environment, much remains that requires action by both individual member states and the Community at large.

Questions

1. (a) Does environmental protection distort trade?
   (b) Are free trade and environmental policies mutually exclusive?

---

[2] However, the Kyoto protocol was derailed by the refusal of the US government to ratify the agreement.

2. (a) Does the European Union need an environmental policy?
   (b) What should it consist of?
   (c) Would a European environmental policy weaken the EU's competitive position in world trade?
   (d) Should the European Union impose restrictions on imports from countries of low environmental standards?

3. (a) Why would countries choose different levels of environmental quality?
   (b) If the demand for environmental quality differs between the member states, why should there be a common environmental policy in the Community?

4. Should the EU demand that firms polluting the environment should be closed down?

Further reading

On EU environmental policy see Barnes and Barnes (1999) and McCormick (2001). On the problems of no compliance/implementation of EU directives see Knill and Lenschow (2000). A summary of information on the Sixth EU Environment Action Programme is in Commission (2001c).

Web guide

- Information on energy is available at www.europa.eu.int/energy and for statistics at www.europa.eu.int/en/comm/energy_transport/etif/
- Information on environment is available at www.europa.eu.int/environment and on energy and environment at www.europa.eu.int/scadplus/en
- The European Environment Agency's site is at www.eea.eu.int/
- The OECD gives details on national pollution taxes for its member states at www.oecd.org/env/policies/taxes/index.htm

Europe in the twenty-first century

15

We are used to thinking that major changes in the traditional relations between countries take place violently, through conquest or revolution. We are so accustomed to this that we find it hard to appreciate those that are taking place peacefully in Europe ... European unity is the most important event in the West since the war, not because it is a new great power, but because the new institutional method it introduces is permanently modifying relations between nations and men.

(Monnet, 1962)

After five decades on the road to integration, the European Union is judged a success story. The single market for goods, people, services and capital, and a single currency is completed. But now, in a fast-changing and globalized world, the Union faces new challenges by expansion to more than ten new member states, and this has brought forward the long-overdue need to reform its institutions and to bring them closer to its citizens. A successful programme of reforms and their implementation will benefit both the European Union and the world at large.

15.1 Introduction

European integration started after Word War II for four principal reasons:

1. to prevent a recurrence of the calamity of war, which devastated Europe twice in the twentieth century, by forming new institutions to cement the economies of the member states into an interdependent coalition;
2. to establish a voice and a place of dignity for Europe in the postwar world which was dominated by two superpowers, the USA and the Soviet Union;

3. to raise the economic and social standard of living in the member states;
4. to encourage political unification by economic coordination and harmonization of national policies.

Although the political and economic conditions in Europe and the world have changed over the last 50 years, the original motives for European integration remain valid today.

The European Community started as a customs union and remained on the road to further economic integration for more than three decades before attempting to form a common market. During these years its membership more than doubled from six founding states to the current 15, and the divergence between the members on economic and social matters increased. Therefore, convergence, which had been an ambition since the start of European integration (Treaty of Rome, Preamble), became a priority. At the dawn of the new challenge of EU enlargement, which will almost double its member states, it is time to examine what Europe has achieved so far and where it is heading in the future.

15.2 European integration, 1958–2001

The American experience demonstrates clearly the economic case for integration and the advantages of a large integrated economy in exploiting to the full the benefits of economies of scale, specialization and comparative advantage. However, many considerations, some of them primarily political, have to be overcome before contemplating economic integration between sovereign countries. Integration of free and independent nation states by peaceful means is uncommon in the history of mankind.

Despite the economic heterogeneity and the divergence of opinion about its immediate and future objectives that successive expansions brought, the Community pursued its two principal ambitions: in the medium term, to improve the living and working conditions of the citizens of the member states; and, in the long term, to unite Europe. Both of these objectives required the members to reconcile their national policies and targets by abandoning their purely nationalistic activities and objectives in such a way that they could work together to build the economic union. This proved to be a difficult task. The pattern of relationships between the states comprising the European Union has roots in history both for and against European integration and cannot change easily from one day to the next. 'The Europeans had to overcome the mistrust born of centuries of feuds and wars' (Monnet, 1962). The common elements in the cultural and political heritage of Europe were mingled with nationalism, conflict of interest, old enmities and often new friction. It took the European nations a very long time to learn 'to halt the decline which has been Europe's penalty for the follies of two world wars' (Monnet, 1962).

The procedure and the timetable for completing the first phase of integration, the customs union, had been defined in the Treaty of Rome, and were completed ahead of schedule. The subsequent steps of the process of integration were only lightly sketched in the treaty. Inadequate treaty provisions about both aims and timetable, and the volatile international economic environment of the 1970s and 1980s, meant that common policies for establishing the common market were introduced piecemeal after protracted negotiations and over long intervals of inactivity. The requirement for unanimity in decisions of major importance for the participating states was another factor which impeded the progress to integration. The single market project took seven years from conception to implementation. Ratification of the Treaty on European Union, which was based on compromise often at the expense of clarity, was only possible after granting opt-outs to some members, two referenda in Denmark and protracted parliamentary debates in the United Kingdom. These events led to crises, loss of economic and social credibility, slowing down the drive towards integration.

We can criticize the Community for using suboptimal policies and indirect ways to reach its objectives, for being slow and ineffective and for achieving too little in a very long time. But it would be unrealistic to subject the process of decision-making in the Community to optimality criteria. Decisions are reached by bargaining and compromise between (6, 9, 12 or 15) independent states which, having regard for their national interests, relinquish one aspect of national sovereignty after another, every time a decision for more integration is taken. Given that political ideologies and the commitment to integration differ between governments and that in democratic countries governments are not monolithic and change quite often, it should not be surprising that Commission proposals take one form after another before they are finally approved and become policies. Despite all these problems, after the success of the single market project, the 'Community Method' scored another success by erecting the second major component of the European Union: EMU in 2002.

Box 15.1 ■ Jean Monnet and the birth of the European Community

Jean Monnet (1888–1979) was born in Cognac, France. During the First World War he worked in London in the office of economic cooperation amongst the Allies. In 1920–3 he worked as Deputy Secretary-General of the newly established League of Nations. For the next 15 years he was active in international finance and worked in his family's cognac business. In 1943, during the Second World War, Monnet declared:

There will be no peace in Europe, if the states are reconstituted on the basis of national sovereignty . . . The countries of Europe are too small to guarantee their peoples the necessary prosperity and social development. The European states must constitute themselves into a federation.

After the Second World War, Monnet was put in charge of the Commissariat du Plan responsible for the economic recovery of France. In 1949, Monnet realized that the friction between Germany and France for control of the Ruhr, the important coal and steel region, was rising to dangerous levels, presaging a possible return to hostilities as had happened after the First World War. Monnet, together with a few collaborators, drafted a revolutionary proposal: to pool, under the control of a European government, Franco-German coal and steel resources. The Monnet Memorandum to foreign secretary Schuman states:

By pooling basic production and the establishment of a new High Authority, whose decisions will be binding on France, Germany and the countries that join them, this proposal will lay the first concrete foundations of a European federation, which is indispensable to the maintenance of peace.

The proposal was accepted and one year later, by the Treaty of Paris (1951), six countries (France, Germany, Italy, Belgium, Holland and Luxembourg) founded the European Coal and Steel Community (ECSC).

Monnet had another great plan, the European Defence Community, but it came to nothing. In 1954 Monnet resigned from the High Authority and in 1955 founded an Action Committee for a United States of Europe through which, until his death, he tirelessly called on the European political class not to abandon the path of European unity. In 1976 at a European Council in Luxembourg, it was decided to confer the title 'Honorary Citizen of Europe' on Jean Monnet for his work as a founder of the European Community.

The strategy chosen by Monnet for constructing European unity by economic means was the gradualist, or functionalist, method, starting with the creation of the ECSC. Initially Altiero Spinelli* and the federalists criticized Monnet's functionalist approach, because it allowed confederal features of European politics, by which the governments retained a power of veto, to exist alongside supranational bodies. Instead they proposed the constituent method as the only democratic way to build a Europe of the people with the involvement of the people themselves. The history of the European Community shows that, while Monnet's gradualist method made it possible to start the process of European unification, Spinelli's constituent method is indispensable in order to bring it to completion.

Further reading: Brinkley and Hackett (1991), Duchêne (1994), Pinder (2001).

* Altiero Spinelli (1907–86) started his campaign for a United Europe in 1943. After World War II he continued to support the fast-track federalist approach for a United States of Europe, in contrast to the then dominant slow-moving Community approach advocated by Monnet. As a European Commissioner responsible for industrial policy (1970–6), and later as a member of the European Parliament (1976–86), Spinelli was the force behind the constitutional campaign that led to the directly elected European Parliament and the treaty establishing the European Union.

15.3 European integration after 2002

> European union will not prove equal to the new challenges unless it grows into a union founded on federal structures with limited but real powers and fully developed democratic institutions, based on a constitution to be ratified by national parliaments.
>
> *(Bulletin of the European Community, 1–2, 1993)*

Until 2002, the EU essentially developed by 'negative integration', pulling down obstacles to the creation of a single market. EMU was the first major construction project for the evolution of Europe. But EMU and the operations of the European Central Bank (ECB) have raised questions about 'legitimacy', 'accountability', 'transparency' and 'democratic deficit'. There is still one essential component missing from the policy arsenal of the Union: a Common Fiscal Policy (CFP). But the institution of a CFP cannot be addressed before a reconsideration of the 'governance of Europe'. The argument is that the creation of effective economic institutions for Europe will depend on effective institutions for governing Europe. Moreover, eastern and Mediterranean enlargement would lead to growing differentiation, complexity and internal heterogeneities which cannot be resolved effectively except by restructuring the Community's governance system and the power of its central government.

It is now recognized that the EU cannot go further if it sticks to the piecemeal 'Community Method' of economic integration. Therefore, steps towards political integration must come next, before proceeding with further economic integration. The question of the governance of Europe is already under discussion. The European Council's Laeken Declaration (15 December 2001) adopted a broad mandate for a forthcoming constitutional convention. The aim of the convention will be to reform and simplify EU institutions and make them more democratic, transparent and accessible to the people of Europe, able to pursue the political, economic and social integration of the enlarged Union. Starting with its inaugural meeting on 1 March 2002, the convention is meeting to propose solutions to issues such as:

- the role of the European Union in a fast-changing globalized world;
- the role of national parliaments and the European Parliament in making the EU more democratic, more transparent and more efficient;
- the role of national parliaments in the governance of Europe and a better division and definition of competence in the Union;
- whether to rewrite the core of the existing EU treaties as a formal 'constitution for European citizens'.

It is, therefore, already clear that from 2002 onwards European integration will increasingly be focused on issues of politics, defence, justice, security and home affairs.

Integration is a dynamic process which involves the division and reallocation of both economic and political power between the member states and the Union. Economic decisions at the level of the Community have political implications. Indeed, for some observers, economic integration is only the means for achieving the ultimate objective, that of political integration. Conversely, political aspects, both domestic ones and interstate ones, trespass on economic policy-making at the level of the Community. Membership in the Community widens the horizon of politics and lessens the degrees of freedom available to a member state government to design and carry out domestic economic policies. Community policies may be opposed by member countries under pressure from interested parties, by Community-wide pressure groups or even by Community institutions such as the Commission or the European Parliament. For the Community, a policy that conforms with its objectives, increases the cohesion between the members and contributes to the process of economic and political integration, is a good policy. For each member state's government, Community policies are acceptable if they do not harm that government's standing in domestic politics and can be presented to their electorates as beneficial for the country or for specific influential groups of the population of the country (farmers, producers, consumers, and so on). In general, there are limits to the extent governments can retreat from the status quo by changing their current domestic politics and economics in search of common policies in the Community. Given these constraints, we should consider the progress the Community has made so far as a qualified success.

Since the mid-1980s the European Community has made more progress towards integration than in any comparable period before. The EU's steady progress towards integration at a time of historic transformations in geopolitical, economic and military structures has also changed the attitudes and the behaviour of outsiders towards it. Integration makes the world smaller. As the main international trade power, the EU and the policies it follows are affecting the economic, political and security policies of all the countries in Europe and the world. Thus the success of European integration is important not only for Europe but for the future of international economic, social and political relations. While the postwar European order is breaking down, the members of the European Community have signed a treaty that lays the foundations for an economic and political superpower, in effect the United States of Europe. What is hoped for is that: 'The natural attitude of a European Community based on the exercise by nations of common responsibilities will be to make these nations also aware of their responsibilities, as a Community, to the world' (Monnet, 1962).

Further reading

See Armstrong and Bulmer (1998) and Commission (2000b).

Web guide

Information is available at www.europa.eu.int/comm/laeken_council/index_en.htm

References

Abe, A. (1999), *Japan and the European Union*, Athlone Press, London.

Ackrill, R. A. (2000), 'CAP reform 1999: a crisis in the making', *Journal of Common Market Studies*, 38, 343–53.

Armstrong, K. and Bulmer, S. (1998), *The Governance of the Single European Market*, Manchester University Press, Manchester.

Artis, M. J. (1988), 'The EMS in the face of new challenges', in P. Arestis (ed.), *Contemporary Issues in Money and Banking*, Macmillan, London.

Artis, M., Krolzig, H.-M. and Toro, J. (1999), *The European Business Cycle*, Discussion Paper Series, No. 2242, Centre for Economic Policy Research, London.

Bache, I. (1998), *The Politics of European Union Regional Policy*, Sheffield Academic Press, Sheffield.

Baldwin, R. E. (1989), 'The growth effects of 1992', *Economic Policy*, 4 (9), 247–82.

Baldwin, R. E. (1992), 'Measurable dynamic gains from trade', *Journal of Political Economy*, 100, 162–74.

Baldwin, R. E., François, J. F. and Portes, R. (1997), 'The cost and benefit of eastern enlargement', *Economic Policy*, April.

Barnes, P. and Barnes, I. (1999), *Environmental Policy in the European Union*, Edward Elgar, Cheltenham.

Begg, I. and Grimwade, N. (1998), *Paying for Europe*, Sheffield Academic Press, Sheffield.

Brauerhjelm, P., Fiani, R., Norman, V., Ruaner, F. and Seabright, P. (2000), 'Integration and the regions of Europe: how the right policies can prevent polarization', *Monitoring European Integration*, 10, Centre for Economic Performance, London.

Brinkley, D. and Hackett, C. (eds) (1991), *Jean Monnet: The Path to European Unity*, Macmillan, Basingstoke.

Bryson, B. (1994), *Made in America*, Secker and Warburg, London.

Camps, M. (1965), *What Kind of Europe?*, Chatham House Essays, London.

Cecchini, P. (1988), *The European Challenge: 1992: The Benefit of a Single Market*, Wildwood House, Aldershot.

Cini, M. and McGovan, L. (1998), *Competition Policy in the European Union*, Macmillan, London.

Cnossen, S. (1990), 'The case for tax diversity in the EC', *European Economic Review*, 34, 471–9.

Cnossen, S. (1996), 'Company taxes in the European Union', *Fiscal Studies*, 17, 67–97.

Coase, R. H. (1960), 'The problem of social cost', *Journal of Law and Economics*, 3, 1–44.

Commission (1963), *Report of the Fiscal and Financial Committee* (the Neumark Report), Brussels.

Commission (1981), *General Report on Activities of the European Communities*, Luxembourg.

Commission (1984), *Agriculture in the United States and the European Community: a Comparison*, Agricultural Information Service of the Directorate-General of Information, no. 200.

Commission (1985), *Completing the Internal Market*, White Paper from the Commission to the European Council, Luxembourg.

Commission (1987), 'The Single Act: a new frontier', *Bulletin EC*, Supplement.

Commission (1988a), 'The economics of 1992', *European Economy*, no. 35, Luxembourg.

Commission (1988b), *Studies on the Economics of Integration*, vols. 1–3, Research on the 'Cost of Non-Europe': Basic findings, Luxembourg.

Commission (1989), *Report on Economic and Monetary Union in the European Community*, Committee for the Study of Economic and Monetary Union, Luxembourg.

Commission (1991), *The Regions in the 1990s*, Fourth Periodic Report on the Social and Economic Situation and Development of the Regions of the Community, Office for Official Publications of the European Communities, Luxembourg.

Commission (1996a), *A Common System of VAT*, XXI/1156/96, Brussels.

Commission (1996b), 'Economic evaluation of the Internal Market', *European Economy*, no. 4.

Commission (1997), 'Agenda 2000', *Bulletin of the European Union*, Supplement 5/97.

Commission (1998), *Financing the European Union*, report on the operation of the Own Resources system (COMM, 560).

Commission (1999), *The Amsterdam Treaty – A Comprehensive Guide*, Luxembourg.

Commission (2000a), *Social Protection in the EU Member States and the European Economic Area*.

Commission (2000b), *White Paper on European Governance, Brussels*, Brussels SEC(2000) 1547/7 final.

Commission (2000c), The EU Economy: 2000 Review, *European Economy*, No. 71.

Commission (2000d), *Policies for Promoting Research and Development*.

Commission (2001a), 'The EU and the threat of US safeguards against steel imports', Background memo, Brussels, 6 June.

Commission (2001b), *European Transport Policy for 2010: Time to Decide*, White Paper.

Commission (2001c), *Environment 2010: Our Future, Our Choice*, Luxembourg.

Commission (2001d), *VAT Rates Applied in the Member States of the European Community*, Document DOC/2905/2001 – EN, Brussels.

Commission (2001e), *Eurobarometer*, 55.

Commission (2001f), *European Economy*, No. 72.

Commission (2001g), *The European Union and the World*. Office for Official Publications of the European Communities, Luxembourg.

Commission (2002), *General Budget of the European Union for the Financial Year 2002*.

Corden, W. M. (1972), 'Economies of scale and customs union theory', *Journal of Political Economy*, 80, 465–75.

Council of the EC (1992), *Treaty on European Union* (the Maastricht Treaty), Office for Official Publications of the European Communities, Luxembourg.

Cowling, K. (1990), 'New directions for industrial policy', in K. Cowling and H. Tomann (eds), *Industrial Policy after 1992*, Anglo-German Foundation, London.

Crafts, N. F. R. (1996), 'Post-neoclassical endogenous growth theory: what are its policy implications?', *Oxford Review of Economic Policy*, 12/2, 30–47.

Cram, L., Dinan, D. and Nugent, N. (1999), *Developments in the European Union*, Basingstoke, Macmillan.

Davies, N. (1996) *Europe, A History*, Oxford University Press, Oxford.

Devereux, M. (1992), 'The Ruding Committee Report: an economic assessment', *Fiscal Studies*, 13, 96–107.

Duchêne, F. (1994), *Jean Monnet: The First Statesman of Interdependence*, Norton, London and New York.

EC (1977), *Report of the Study on the Role of Public Finance in European Integration* (the MacDougall Report), Brussels.

EC (1981), 'Guidelines for European agriculture', *Bulletin EC*, Supplement 4.

EC (1997a), 'The European Union as a World Trade Partner', *European Economy*, No. 3.

EC (1997b), 'Towards a Common Agricultural and Rural Policy for Europe', *European Economy*, No. 5, p. 9.

EC (1999a), *The Amsterdam Treaty: A Comprehensive Guide*, Luxembourg.

EC (1999b), *Bulletin EU*, 3, 18–19.

EC (2000), *Employment and Social Affairs: Current Status 15 October 1999*, Luxembourg.

EC (2002), *General Budget of the European Union for the Financial Year 2002*.

ECB (1999a), 'The stability-oriented monetary policy strategy of the Eurosystem', *ECB Monthly Bulletin*, January, 39–50.

ECB (1999b), 'The operational framework of the Eurosystem: description and first assessment', *ECB Monthly Bulletin*, May, 29–43.

The Economist (1998), 'The merits of one currency', 24 October, 135–6.

Eichengreen, B. (1993), 'European monetary unification', *Journal of Economic Literature*, 31, 1321–57.

Eijffinger, S. C. W. and De Haan, J. (2000), *European Monetary and Fiscal Policy*, Oxford University Press, Oxford.

Emerson, M., Aujean, M., Catinat, M., Goybet, P. and Jacquemin, A. (1988), *The Economics of 1992: The EC Commission's Assessment of the Economic Effects of Completing the Internal Market*, Oxford University Press, Oxford.

Euroconfidentiel (1999), *The Rome, Maastricht and Amsterdam Treaties – Comparative Texts*, Euroconfidentiel, Belgium.

Euroconfidentiel (2000), *The Guide to EU Information Sources on the Internet*, Euroconfidentiel, Belgium.

European Bank For Reconstruction and Development (2000), *Transition Report*, EBRD, London.

European Parliament (1998), *Fact Sheets on the European Union*, Office for Official Publications of the European Communities, Luxembourg.

Eurostat (1998a), *Globalisation Through Trade and Foreign Direct Investment: A Comparative Study of the European Union, the United States of America and Japan*, Office for Official Publications of the European Communities, Luxembourg.

Eurostat (1998b), *Social Portrait of Europe*.

Eurostat (1999), *Agricultural Statistical Yearbook*.

Eurostat (2000), *European Communities 2000*.

Eurostat (2001a), *The Social Situation in the European Union 2001*.

Eurostat (2001b), *The Statistical Guide to Europe 2001*.

Eurostat (2001c), *Panorama of European Business*.

Eurostat (2001d), *Yearbook 2001*.

Eurostat (2001e), *Europe in Figures 2000*, fifth edition.

Eurostat (2002a), *Regional Gross Domestic Product in the European Union 1999*, No. 1.

Eurostat (2002b), *Eurostatistics*, Monthly, various issues.

Frankel, J. A. and Rose, A. K. (1998), 'The endogeneity of the optimum currency area criteria', *Economic Journal*, 108, 1009–25.

Gordon, D. and Townsend, P. (2001), *Breadline Europe: The Measurement of Poverty*, The Policy Press, Bristol.

Gylfason, T. (1995), *The Macroeconomics of European Agriculture*, Princeton Studies in International Finance, no. 78, Princeton, NJ.

Haas, E. B. (1971), 'The study of regional integration', in Lindberg, L. and Scheingild, S. (eds), *Regional Integration*, Harvard University Press, Cambridge, MA.

Hine, R. C. (1994), 'International Economic Integration', in Greenaway, D. and Winters, A. L., *Surveys in International Trade*, Blackwell, Oxford, 234–72.

Hitiris, T. (1988), *European Community Economics*, Harvester-Wheatsheaf, London.

Hitiris, T. (1997), 'Health care expenditure and integration in the countries of the European Union', *Applied Economics*, 29, 1–6.

Hitiris, T. (2001), 'The UK and the European Union', in Sawyer, M. (ed.), *The UK Economy*, 15th edition, Oxford University Press, Oxford.

Hufbauer, G. C. (1990), *Europe 1992: An American Perspective*, Brookings Institution, Washington, DC.

Ingersent, K. A., Rayner, A. J. and Hine, R. C. (eds) (1998), *The Reform of the Common Agricultural Policy*, Basingstoke, Macmillan.

Issing, O., Gaspar, V., Angeloni, I. and Tristani, O. (2001), *Monetary Policy in the Euro Area: Strategy and Decision-Making at the European Central Bank*, Cambridge University Press, Cambridge.

Keen, M. and Smith, S. (1996), 'The future of value added tax in the European Union', *Economic Policy*, October, 375–420.

Kenen, P. B. (1969), 'The theory of optimum currency areas: an eclectic view', in R. A. Mundell and A. K. Swoboda (eds), *Monetary Problems of the International Economy*, Chicago University Press, Chicago.

Knill, C. and Lenschow, A. (eds) (2000), *Implementing EU Environmental Policy: New Directions and Old Problems*, Manchester University Press, Manchester.

Krugman, P. (1990), 'Policy problems of a monetary union', in P. De Grauwe and L. Papademos (eds), *The European Monetary System in the 1990s*, Longman, London.

Krugman, P. (1991), *Geography and Trade*, MIT Press, Cambridge, MA.

Krugman, P. (1993), 'Lessons of Massachusets for EMU', in Torres, F. and Giavazzi, F. (eds), *Adjustment and Growth in the European Monetary Union*, Cambridge University Press, Cambridge, 241–69.

Krugman, P. (1994), *Peddling Prosperity*, W. W. Norton and Co., New York and London.

Laffan, B. (1997), *The Finances of the European Union*, Macmillan, Basingstoke.

Lavigne, M. (1999), *The Economics of Transition: From Socialist Economy to Market Economy*, Macmillan, London.

Levin, J. H. (2002), *A Guide to the Euro*, Houghton Miffin Company, New York.

Lockwood, B., de Meza, D. and Myles, G. (1995), 'On the European VAT proposals: the superiority of the origin over destination taxation', *Fiscal Studies*, 16, 1–17.

MacDonald, R. and Taylor, M. P. (1991), 'Exchange rates, policy convergence, and European Monetary System', *Review of Economics and Statistics*, 73, 553–8.

Martin, R. (1998), *Regional Policy in the European Union*, Centre for European Policy Studies, Brussels.

McCallum, J. (1995), 'National borders matter: Canada–US regional trade patterns', *American Economic Review*, 85, 615–23.

McCormick, J. (2001), *Environmental Policy in the European Union*, Palgrave, Basingstoke.

Monnet, J. (1962), 'A ferment of change', *Journal of Common Market Studies*, 1, 203–11.

Mountford, L. (2000), *Health Care Without Frontiers?*, Office of Health Economics, London.

Mundell, R. A. (1961), 'A theory of optimum currency areas', *American Economic Review*, 51, 657–65.

Munk, K. J. (1989), 'Price support to the EC agricultural sector: an optimal policy?', *Oxford Review of Economic Policy*, 5(2), 76–88.

Musgrave, R. (1983), 'Who should tax, where, and what?', in C. McLure (ed.), *Tax Assignment in Federal Countries*, Australian National University Press, Canberra, 2–19.

Neven, D. J. (1990), 'Gains and losses from 1992', *Economic Policy*, 10, 14–62.

Oates, W. E. (1972), *Fiscal Federalism*, Harcourt Brace Jovanovitch, New York.

Oates, W. E. (1991), 'Fiscal federalism: an overview', in R. Prud'homme (ed.), *Public Finance with Several Levels of Government*, Proceedings of the 46th Congress of the International Institute of Public Finance, The Hague/Koenigstein.

OECD (1990), *Modelling the Effects of Agricultural Policies*, OECD, Economic Studies, Paris.

OECD (1999), *Environmental Data*, OECD, Paris.

OECD (2000), *Main Science and Technology Indicators*, OECD, Paris.

Panagariya, A. (2000), 'Preferential trade liberalization: The traditional theory and new developments', *Journal of Economic Literature*, 38, 287–331.

Pearce, D. W. and Turner, R. K. (1989), *Economics of Natural Resources and the Environment*, Harvester, London.

Peck, M. J. (1989), 'Industrial organization and the gains from Europe 1992', *Brookings Papers on Economic Activity*, part 2, 277–99.

Pentland, C. (1973), *International Theory and European Integration*, Faber, London.

Pinder, J. (2001), *The European Union – A Very Short Introduction*, Oxford Paperbacks, Oxford.

Pomfret, R. (1997), *The Economics of Regional Trading Arrangements*, Clarendon Press, Oxford.

Rose, A. (2000), 'One money, one market: The effect of common currencies on trade', *Economic Policy*, 30, 9–45.

Ruding Report (1992), *Report of the Committee of Independent Experts on Company Taxation*, CEC, Brussels.

Sala-i-Martin, X. and Sachs, J. (1992), 'Fiscal federalism and optimum currency areas: evidence for Europe from the United States', in M. B. Canzoneri, V. Grilli, and P. R. Masson (eds), *Establishing a Central Bank: Issues in Europe and Lessons from the United States*, Cambridge University Press, Cambridge, 195–219.

Song, Y.-H. (1995), 'The EC's Common Fisheries Policy in the 1990s', *Ocean Development and International Law*, 26, 31–55.

Tavlas, G. (1993), 'The "New" Theory of Optimum Currency Areas', *The World Economy*, 16, 663–85.

Thirwall, T. (2000), 'European unity could flounder on regional neglect', *The Guardian (Society)*, 31 January, 23.

Werner Report (1970), 'Report to the Council and the Commission on the realization by stages of Economic and Monetary Union in the Community', *Bulletin EC*, 11, Supplement.

Wildasin, D. E. (1990), 'Budgetary pressures in the EEC: a fiscal federalism perspective', *American Economic Review*, 80, Papers and Proceedings, 69–74.

World Bank (2000), *World Development Indicators*, World Bank, Washington, DC.

World Bank (2001a), *World Development Report*, World Bank, Washington, DC.

World Bank (2001b), *World Development Indicators*, World Bank, Washington, DC.

Index

Guildford College
Learning Resource Centre

Please return on or before the last date shown
This item may be renewed by telephone unless overdue

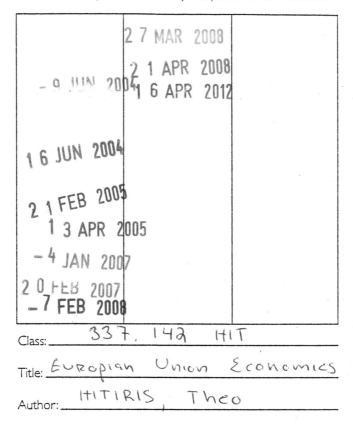
Class: _337. 142   HIT_

Title: _Europian Union Economics_

Author: _HITIRIS, Theo_